Wordsworth's Fun

Wordsworth's Fun

MATTHEW BEVIS

The University of Chicago Press
Chicago and London

The University of Chicago Press, Chicago 60637
The University of Chicago Press, Ltd., London

Published 2019
Printed in the United States of America

28 27 26 25 24 23 22 21 20 19 1 2 3 4 5

ISBN-13: 978-0-226-65205-4 (cloth)
ISBN-13: 978-0-226-65219-1 (paper)
ISBN-13: 978-0-226-65222-1 (e-book)
DOI: https://doi.org/10.7208/chicago/9780226652221.001.0001

Library of Congress Cataloging-in-Publication Data

Names: Bevis, Matthew, author.
Title: Wordsworth's fun / Matthew Bevis.
Description: Chicago ; London : The University of Chicago Press, 2019. | Includes bibliographical references and index.
Identifiers: LCCN 2019002936 | ISBN 9780226652054 (cloth : alk. paper) | ISBN 9780226652191 (pbk. : alk. paper) | ISBN 9780226652221 (e-book)
Subjects: LCSH: Wordsworth, William, 1770–1850—Criticism and interpretation. | Wordsworth, William, 1770–1850—Themes, motives. | Comic, The, in literature.
Classification: LCC PR5892.C6 B48 2019 | DDC 821/.7—dc23
LC record available at https://lccn.loc.gov/2019002936

♾ This paper meets the requirements of ANSI/NISO Z39.48-1992 (Permanence of Paper).

For Rebecca, Noah, and Rosa

Is a smile like life,
A way things look for a while,
A temporary arrangement of the matter?

I feel like the first men who read Wordsworth.
It's so simple I can't understand it.

RANDALL JARRELL, "The One Who Was Different"

Contents

Facing Him

> I marvel how Nature could ever find space
> For the weight and the levity seen in his face:
> There's thought and no thought, and there's paleness and bloom,
> And bustle and sluggishness, pleasure and gloom.
> "A CHARACTER; IN THE ANTITHETICAL MANNER"[1]

"You could tell fra the man's face his potry would niver have no laugh in it."[2] One of Wordsworth's neighbors in Westmoreland may have been judging a book by its cover, but he wasn't the first or last to draw attention to something deeply unfunny. A few years after Wordsworth's death, Walter Bagehot composed an obituary of sorts when discussing the "power of making fun": "no human being more entirely destitute of humour is perhaps discoverable anywhere in literature, or possibly even in society."[3] Whether offering censure or praise, several have concurred with this vision of comic destitution, which is why William Hazlitt's first impressions of the man still come as a shock:

> The next day Wordsworth arrived from Bristol at Coleridge's cottage. I think I see him now. He answered in some degree to his friend's description of him, but was more quaint and Don Quixote-like. He was quaintly dressed (according the costume of that unconstrained period) in a brown fustian jacket and striped pantaloons. There was something of a roll, a lounge in his gait, not unlike his own Peter Bell. There was a severe, worn pressure of thought about his temples, a fire in his eye (as if he saw something in objects more than the outward appearance), an intense, high, narrow forehead, a Roman nose, cheeks furrowed by strong purpose and feeling, and a convulsive inclination to laughter about the mouth, a good deal at variance with the solemn, stately expression of the rest of his face.[4]

Hazlitt is picking up on something that isn't central to Wordsworth's style, but it's not peripheral to it either. It's hard to describe the trait without exaggerating; it might provisionally be characterized as a feeling for comedy rather than comedy itself. Yet that way of putting it underplays the resonance of Hazlitt's phrase "convulsive inclination," its fusion of energy and stealth, presence and absence. This book argues that Wordsworth's quixotic creativity owes much to this mixture, one that is vitally related to his hopes for his writing and to his sense of the risks and embarrassments that such hopes entail. An inclination to laughter, I want to suggest, is not a sideshow to some mirthless main event, but a formative influence on his work. It's also part of a larger story about the shaping of modern poetic experiment.

An encounter with Wordsworth involves the sense of an intimacy both ventured and withheld. Hazlitt noted elsewhere that he was "grave, saturnine, with a slight indication of sly humour, kept under by the manners of the age or by the pretensions of the person,"[5] and a few years later Thomas Carlyle said that Wordsworth reminded him of "a dim old lichened crag on the wayside, the private meaning of which, in contrast with any public meaning it had, you recognised with a kind of not wholly melancholy grin."[6] Kind of. Not wholly. It's not clear what the private meaning is. One word for it might be *fun*. But what *is* fun? For the word's etymology, the *OED* can only (aptly) say "Origin uncertain." The activity is more than a little unhinged or off guard: "The sighs which Mathew heav'd were sighs / Of one tir'd out with fun and madness."[7] It could also be less than virtuous; the *OED*'s first instance of the word in the modern, familiar sense of diversion or amusement comes from Wordsworth's beloved Swift: "Tho' he talk'd much of virtue, his head always run / Upon something or other she found better fun." In 1755, Samuel Johnson's *Dictionary* stigmatized *fun* as "a low cant word." The following year witnessed the birth of *funny*, meaning "mirth-producing, comical," and by the turn of the century the word also encompassed the "curious, queer, odd, strange." Funny ha ha and funny peculiar had become not so much options but partners, and Wordsworth, as we shall see, is fascinated by this partnership. In addition, the older meaning of *fun* with which he was conversant is "A cheat or trick; a hoax, a practical joke." Fun is a compound of amusement and bemusement, pleasure and inscrutability, and when people are indulging in it, they become hard to read.

Wordsworth was writing at a time when new meanings of pleasure were being disclosed and navigated. *Fun*, *funny*, and associated phrases took on fresh life: "for the fun of the thing" (*OED*'s first instance: 1750), "to have fun" (1760), "what fun!" (1776), "fun-loving" (1776), "bit of fun" (1797), "funster" (1788), "the funny" (1821), "funny-looking" (1824), "funny bone" (1826), "funniness" (1836), "funny business" (1838), "funny man" (1839), "funnyism" (1839). The poet's own avatar of fun, "The Tinker," "can't go wrong go where he will: / Tricks he has twenty / And pastimes in plenty,"[8] and he speaks for those who want to go wrong in order to go right. Wordsworth trusts to the tinker precisely because of an uncertainty about whether he's trustworthy:

The Tinker shakes his head,
Laughing, laughing, laughing,
As if he would laugh himself dead.
And thus, with work or none,
The Tinker lives in fun[9]

The man is a figure for the creative instinct, an instinct that involves a kind of absorption (he lives "in fun," not simply for it). He embodies a commitment to waywardness within vocation, a craving that may be a threat as well as a resource, and his laughter brings an as-if-ness that resists simple parsing. Fun may not be good for him (or us), may be a pathological abandonment that will have to remain fugitive, but it is coveted nonetheless. Wordsworth is both perplexed by and fiercely protective of his fun, and part of the pleasure lies in the thrill of shaping the lines themselves (note that little pause after "And thus," or the rhythmic dallying of "with work or none"—both building to the nothing-that-may-be-something of the final line). In the following chapters I'll keep returning to what that something might mean; for, as Henry James observed of the relation between reader and writer, "It all comes back to that, to my and your 'fun'—if we but allow the term its full extension; to the production of which no humblest question involved, even to that of the shade of a cadence or the position of a comma, is not richly pertinent."[10]

So: *Wordsworth's Fun.* The words point in different directions—toward a study of the strange ways in which this poet takes his pleasures or toward a claim about how he may contribute to ours. I want to explore how these two possibilities play out in an oscillating drama, a debate staged between Wordsworth's sense of his writing as a commitment to the privacy and oddity of self-experiencing and as a call to an audience that might somehow echo or vouch for that experience. His poetry is driven by a need to *have* pleasure as well as by a wish to make sense of it, and that pleasure is often felt as paradoxical, riddling, solitary. His first poem in *Lyrical Ballads* speaks of a loner's "morbid pleasure"; the opening lyric in *Poems, in Two Volumes* begins with a recollection of times when he went "in discontent / Of pleasure high and turbulent, / Most pleas'd when most uneasy"; and the first reference to the feeling in *The Prelude* tells of "an act of stealth / And troubled pleasure."[11] In his quest to become more intimate with his pleasures and in his refusal to become the saboteur of them, Wordsworth frequently sought to disregard what others wanted for him—and from him. A vital part of his achievement is founded on that disregard, but while he wasn't all that concerned about whether his pleasures were permissible, he was drawn to wondering whether they could be transmissible.

The advertisement for *Lyrical Ballads* is dreaming of a public when it speaks of "that most dreadful enemy to our pleasures, our own pre-established codes of decision," and the closing sentence of the advertisement for *Poems, in Two Volumes* explains that the poems "were composed with much pleasure to my own mind, and I build upon that remembrance a hope that they may afford profitable pleasure to many readers."[12] Often in Wordsworth there is a hope that gratifications will become relational and communal, but everywhere in him there is an insistence that whatever else they are, our pleasures must be our own.[13] The autonomy of his amusement is in fact his bequest, for that autonomy is conceived as the best sponsor and encourager of amusement in others. The green linnet is delightful on account of its being "sole in thy employment," "Scattering thy gladness without care, / Too bless'd with any one to pair, / Thyself thy own enjoyment."[14] Elsewhere, he watches a group dancing ("They dance not for me, / Yet mine is their glee!"), and this intuition that fun is most catching when least caring is ubiquitous in the poetry: "*Thus pleasure is spread through the earth / In stray gifts to be claim'd by whoever shall find.*"[15] True pleasure, Wordsworth seems to say, is always a little chancy or unpredictable. And to have fun with him, we need to stray.

*

A host of other activities and words (*laughter, play, fooling, humor*) orbit around fun, and in the four main sections of this book I aim to stay true to the turbulence surrounding the phenomenon by avoiding strict demarcations between these terms. For now, following Hazlitt's lead, I want to approach Wordsworthian fun by staying on the surface, especially that oddest of surfaces; Wordsworth's face, Hazlitt noted, was "not unlike" that of Peter Bell, which implies a surreptitious link between creator and creation. But what is a face? James Elkins suggests that it's something like a blank sheet that cries out for a design, or a work in progress that, as we look at it, prompts in us a desire to *complete* it: "To read a face, to get a message from it, to see it *as a face*, we need to posit that it exists with a whole mind. . . . It happens exactly the same way when we look at a work of art. . . . We need to assume that a face or artwork is the product of a single imagination or a single mind."[16] To attempt to complete the face, then, is to imbue it (and the person behind it) with coherence, to shape it into something that makes sense to us. Still, as budding physiognomists we run the risk of making things too coherent, of turning our very "need to assume," our desire to *see*, into a refusal to look.

When looking at Wordsworth—and looking *for* him—Hazlitt provided an object lesson in how we might yet face him. The day after their first meeting, "Wordsworth read us the story of *Peter Bell* in the open air; and the comment upon it by his face and voice was very different from that of some later critics! Whatever might be thought of the poem, his face was as a book where 'men might read strange matters.'"[17] As Hazlitt no doubt recalled, Peter Bell's face is itself a strange matter:

> His face was keen as is the wind
> That cuts along the hawthorn fence;
> Of courage you saw little there
> But in its stead a medley air
> Of cunning and of impudence.
>
> He had a dark and sidelong walk,
> And long and slouching was his gait;
> Beneath his looks so bare and bold
> You might perceive his spirit cold
> Was playing with some inward bait.[18]

You "might" perceive that, or you might not: to read past the face too quickly could be to take the bait. Peter's medley air intimates not a sense of humor, exactly, but a sensing of humor. This "sensing" is one of the main subjects of this book.

One feels that the sidelong nature of Peter's walk is somehow related to the obliquity of Wordsworth's lines. When Shelley paid Wordsworth the conflicted compliment of *Peter Bell the Third*, he thought of readers asking "is he joking? / What does the rascal mean or hope?" And then he imagined the poet (after "a grave look collecting") issuing a question of his own:

> "Is it my genius, like the moon,
> Sets those who stand her face inspecting,
> That face within their brain reflecting,
> Like a crazed bell-chime, out of tune?"[19]

That Wordsworth had to "collect" his look might suggest he's not wholly in earnest. Yet he's not quite *not* in earnest either. He's shaping ways of being and writing that make spectators feel somehow confused—or compromised. For all their inwardness, his poems are intent on facing you; they stare and reflect back, as when the narrator of "The Thorn" turns to you with a suggestion:

> Some say, if to the pond you go,
> And fix on it a steady view,
> The shadow of a babe you trace,
> A baby and a baby's face,
> And that it looks at you;
> Whene'er you look on it, 'tis plain
> The baby looks at you again.[20]

The lines are characteristic of Wordsworth—or of one face of Wordsworth—in that they make you wonder whether it would be obtuse or ingenious to attempt to read something (anything) into them. And yet, the writing's very spareness feels surreptitious, its emphasis on the "plain" anything but plain. "Babe" is the sort of word that keeps the thing at arm's length so that the reader can pry in comfort. But the shift to "baby"—and then to "a baby's face" (a body part, not a person)—is riveting. Although we were invited to look on it ("on" hints at the safety of spectatorship), it looks *at* us, seems to ask what we think we're doing here.

When conceiving one possible audience for *Peter Bell* from inside the poem itself, Wordsworth again asks gentle readers to look into a pool of water to see what they can see:

> Is it some party in a parlour,
> Crammed just as they on earth were cramm'd—
> Some sipping punch, some sipping tea,
> But as you by their faces see
> All silent, and all damn'd?[21]

To face lines like these is to face a couple of questions. Is this funny? And, if so, why isn't it funnier? Wordsworth could not be described as being comfortable with humor, but then such comfort—so cozy, so collusive—is what makes some humor unbearable. Perhaps a calculated ungainliness may be ventured at this early stage via a Wordsworthian negative: this poet is not unfunny.[22] His work flourishes and sometimes flounders in the difficulty of our knowing how to take it, and Shelley's uncertainty—"is he joking?"—can be revisited by recalling another moment from *Peter Bell.* It marks the only occasion that Wordsworth allows the word *joke* into his published work. The potter's ass turns his head toward Peter's face and grins:

> And though, no doubt, a sight like this
> To others might have come amiss,
> It suited Peter to a hair.
>
> And Peter, grinning with a joke,
> His teeth in approbation shewed,
> When, cruel blow to Peter's mirth,
> He heard a murmur in the earth,
> In the dead earth beneath the road.[23]

We are never let in on the joke, but we can at least surmise that the mirth feels menacing (as a show of teeth, a grin has bite), that not everyone would have sensed humor in the same situation, and that the fun can't last. An especially rich piece of comic writing is likely to be funnier—and less funny—than its reader thinks it is. And while the life of a good joke is often in league with the unabashed, the perilous, the tendentious, it may also prompt its audience to ask whether solemnity is sometimes an act of bad faith or an avoidance of true seriousness. If, as Schopenhauer suggested, humor is "the seriousness concealed behind a joke,"[24] then Wordsworth is interested in humor—and in what the sharing, getting, and not-getting of jokes may say about us.

There is such a thing, his poetry insists, as a failure to be confused. In *The Prelude*, he recalls that the face of every person whom he met was "as a volume to me,"[25] but looking at (or into) faces and books is rarely a straightforward matter. One of his most perceptive early readers—Thomas De Quincey—noted that "whosoever looks searchingly into the characteristic genius of Wordsworth will see that he does not willingly deal with a passion in its direct aspect, or presenting an unmodified contour, but in forms more complex and oblique, and when passing under the shadow of some secondary passion."[26] De Quincey countenances the comic in an analogous way: "It is *not* two-headed, but a one-headed Janus with two faces:—the pathetic and the humorous are but different phases of the same orb; they assist each other, melt indiscernibly into each other, and often shine each through each like layers of coloured chrystals placed one behind another."[27] Wordsworth likes to rhyme *guile* with *smile*, for a smile, he says, is "double-dealing,"[28] and versions of this double-dealing appear wherever he looks. He observes "A pale face, that seem'd undoubtedly / As if a *blooming* face it *ought* to be,"[29] and elsewhere, having watched the matron of Jedborough in "the prime of glee," he watches her some more:

> I look'd, I scann'd her o'er and o'er;
> The more I look'd I wonder'd more:
> When suddenly I seem'd to espy
> A trouble in her strong black eye;
> A remnant of uneasy light,
> A flash of something over-bright![30]

Such moments are invitations to us to scan the poems themselves with a mixture of affection and hesitancy (Wordsworth's exclamation mark is itself a little over-bright). It's not so much depth as opposed to surface that holds the key to meaning (he only *seemed* to espy); it's the play between them that encourages meaning to proliferate.

Faces present the problem of other minds, but Wordsworth is also caught up in the difficulty of reading his own mind as he comes face to face with himself via the oddity of his relations with others. In unpublished draft lines for one of his Matthew elegies, he can't decide whether he should "sigh" or "smile" in response to his loss (he tries out both words in manuscript), and adds,

> I think of thee in silent love
> And feel, just like a wavering leaf,
> Along my face the muscles move,
> Nor know if 'tis with joy or grief.[31]

The simile sounds merely poetical until you realize that the leaf is being compared not with the "I" but with the facial muscles; one's body breeds self-estrangement. Wordsworth is interested in the kind of experience that makes people unsure of how they are—or should be—reacting. During the 1830s he can be found enjoying a book titled *Thoughts on Laughter* in which Addison is quoted as saying, "In order to look into any person's temper, I generally make my first observation upon his laugh. . . . People are never so much unguarded as when they are pleased. . . . It is then, if ever, we may believe the faces."[32] "If ever" is a nice touch; even laughing faces can make you unsure about what you should believe.

When facing Wordsworth, we need to allow him to be something other than predictable or dependable.[33] Benjamin Haydon's comments are telling in this respect: "Wordsworth's face always puts me in mind when he laughs as if he was an old satyr who had suddenly been transformed into a Lake Poet," he explained; "there is something so lecherous, animal & devouring lurking in those wrinkles & straggling decayed teeth—depend on it he is an old beast, cloaked in piety and verse."[34] This stresses the noncerebral, creaturely element of laughter on which Wordsworth had seized in his younger days (talk of satyrs recalls Peter's getting in touch with his ass via a grin). Haydon may affect to have cornered his quarry here, but a few years later he recorded in his diary,

> "Pray," said I to Wordsworth, "what did you mean, many years ago, when I took you accidentally into Christie's (Pall Mall at that time) and we saw Cupid & Psyche kissing—what did you mean, after looking some time, by inwardly saying, '*the Devils.*'" He laughed heartily & replied, "*I can't tell.*"[35]

How are we to read this face, this laughter, this reply? Wordsworth might be confessing reticence or bewilderment or both. The following chapters tease out the implications of this ambiguity while arguing for versions of the laughable in Wordsworth that can withstand—and augment—what he refers to in *The Prelude* as "the test of thought."[36] When he wrote a sonnet in praise of one of Haydon's portraits, he spoke of "the unapparent face" and of "those signs / Of thought, that give the true poetic thrill; / That unencumbered whole of blank and still."[37] A similar blend of concentration and occlusion, delirium and vacancy, lies close to the heart of this most Dionysian of poets.

*

Humor abhors a vacuum, and any argument for Wordsworth as a peculiarly humorous creature needs to situate itself in relation to broader questions about influence and reception. Despite praise in some quarters, many of Wordsworth's early readers thought he was ludicrous—if inadvertently so, the more fool him; if willfully so, the more fool him. "It may be considered as characteristic of our poet's writings," observed Hazlitt in *The Spirit of The Age*, "that they either make no impression on the mind at all, seem mere nonsense-verses, or that they leave a mark behind them that never wears out. . . . To one class of reader he appears sublime, to another (and we fear the larger) ridiculous."[38] In this book I wonder again why, as Sara Coleridge put it, "The Lyrical Ballads are laughed at and disliked by all with very few excepted,"[39] but I do so with the feeling that Wordsworth's detractors were picking up on something in the poetry that later supporters have tended to downplay, or excuse, or deny. Two hundred years later, Wordsworth has left his mark and Hazlitt's smaller class of reader has won out; a disparity has emerged between our vision of him as serious, earnest, severe, and so on, and the unwillingness of his first readers to see his work as fulfilling the requirements for what they expected "serious" poetry to be. This disparity can be put down to a revolution in literary taste, a revolution that owes much to Wordsworth himself, but I want to keep another option in play. This poet is drawn to a fervency of perception and experience that resists clear-cut distinctions between seriousness and levity and that puts us in seriocomic quandaries when we try to talk about him. I'm interested, then, in those moments when Wordsworth's modern-day admirers admit to feeling uncertain about how to judge the poetry, or when they don't quite know whether—or what—they are admiring, as when David Ferry offers an interpretation of "The Idiot Boy" but feels the need to add that "One hesitates to push such a reading very far because one hesitates to be ridiculous";[40] or when Donald Davie hears the rhythm of the last couple of lines of "A slumber did my spirit seal" as "gleeful" and then admits that "If we hear it in this way, we can hardly believe what the verses say."[41] Such comments come closer to what it feels like to read Wordsworth than those which offer austere praise. One has to be willing to be ridiculous, or inappropriately gleeful, to get at just how odd he can be.

For the majority, though, a comic Wordsworth is still a bad joke. "The attempts to find that Wordsworth has a sense of humour never work," Christopher Ricks has recently observed; "Every now and then, people fabricate some account of 'The Idiot Boy' by which they found it humorous, or so on. . . . Never, the arguments never work."[42] A sense of humor is being treated here as a sensus communis, as though the funny were a matter of universal assent. But there have been testimonies (if not always "arguments") that tell another story.[43] Reading him with university students, Basil Bunting noted that "The class are astonished to find that Wordsworth was not a humourless old woman. They even laughed often and long at 'The Idiot Boy'. I've hopes of them."[44] The question of what the class was laughing at can remain open for now, but there's no necessity to read Bunting's hopes as misplaced—or to see his students' responses as "fabricated." When M. H. Abrams insists that "Wordsworth is an accomplished comic poet" or when I. A. Richards takes critics to task for missing Wordsworth's "deep self-critical humour," they sound no less certain than Ricks that those *other* readers of Wordsworth had got him wrong.[45] For this poet, true humor, like true poetry, is a kind of gamble—with himself as well as with others. Not the least of his qualities is his ability to provoke division by writing poems that make it hard for us to remain balanced.

Such divisions have a long heritage, and the first reader to have found himself knocked off balance was Coleridge. Avoiding the philosophical poem that Coleridge felt to be his calling, Wordsworth became intent on writing "small Poems" (his friend lamented that he had "deserted his former mountain Track to wander in Lanes & allies"),[46] and even *The Prelude* was to become a resistance, not an overture, to the tortuous dream of *The Recluse.* Having loitered in book 7 of *The Prelude* to take in the pantomimes, the comic theaters, and the faces he really loved—"the laugh, the grin, grimace / And all the antics and buffoonery, / The least of them not lost"[47]—Wordsworth pauses:

> More lofty Themes,
> Such as at least do wear a prouder face,
> Might here be spoken of; but when I think
> Of these, I feel the imaginative Power
> Languish within me[48]

"At least" readies us for the provocation of "wear" (even those prouder faces are a cover story for something other than the lofty). Such talk of "Themes" is one of Wordsworth's many resistances to the idea that importance is important, a droll testament to a feeling that his pleasures, like his imaginative powers, lie elsewhere. A moment later, he will be immersing himself in the horrifying yet absorbing experience of Bartholomew Fair ("buffoons against buffoons / Grimacing, writhing, screaming"[49]), wondering what he's doing back here again but sensing nevertheless that this is the place to be.

Coleridge's reservations about what Wordsworth was making of his gift are indicative of larger debates about what poetry is meant to stand for—now as well as then. When he later complained that his friend sometimes wrote "in a sort of bravado"[50] and that his "mode of composition does not satisfy a cultivated taste,"[51] he was opting for a word that Wordsworth had often been asked to swallow (and one he'd tended to spit out: "We live in a timid age of taste," he'd said many years earlier).[52] The first appearance of the adjective *Wordsworthian* raises the question of taste as well; in 1815, the writer for the *Sporting Magazine* was proud to declare that "I am enough of a Wordsworthian not to confine my tastes to the received elegancies of society."[53] So the stereotype comes into being to tell of a singular resistance, and the most celebrated early attacks on the poet came from someone who made it his business always and only to have good taste. Wordsworth's poetry, Francis Jeffrey explained, exemplified "false taste," "perverted taste," "bad taste."[54] Taste is an assurance that there are some forms of fun about which one needn't feel confused or conflicted, and Wordsworth's vulgarity (another of Jeffrey's favorite words) serves as a reminder that one can always tell poets from poetasters.[55]

Wordsworth himself warmed to less settled pronouncements. In the early writings of Edmund Burke, taste is not regulative but desirous; it signals a curiosity about the strange and an appetite for recklessness that may or may not turn out to be a form of replenishment.[56] Such an appetite is, in Burke's words, "antecedent to any reasoning, by an instinct that works us to its own purposes, without our concurrence."[57] A disreputable courting of ridicule—and an attraction to the laughable—is one manifestation of this appetite, and Wordsworth began his dubious experiments in taste when the very notion of the humorous was becoming linked to the category of the aesthetic. In 1791, he singled out *The Spectator* as one of the few things he'd read in modern literature. Addison's essays were the first sustained attempts to resist a moralized, hierarchical sense of laughter as a sign of mere scorn, and the first to suggest that one's response to the comic is analogous to one's response to the beautiful.[58] Alexander Gerard's *Essay on Taste* (1759) then accorded the humorous the status of a distinct object of taste, and a few years later, when the *Gentleman's Magazine* observed that "what is humour is as much a question of taste, as what is beauty,"[59] it was acknowledging that the two realms were being conceptualized as part of a discourse dealing with potentially detached responses to objects. Commentators increasingly set themselves against earlier Hobbesian accounts of laughter as a form of satirical delight in superiority (as Coleridge remarked, "To resolve Laughter into an expression of Contempt is contrary to fact, and laughable enough")[60] and began to read the laugh as a sign of pleasure in incongruity or as an entertainment of different perspectives in one form. At the end of the century, in his *Critique of Judgement* Kant put forward an analogy between jokes and works of art, figuring laughter as a minor version of the disinterested play of understanding.

Laughter itself was becoming aestheticized, yet some versions of this alliance render humor—and poetry—a little too cool for Wordsworthian tastes. (On occasion, it is as hard to believe in aesthetic disinterestedness as it is to believe someone when they claim they are "*only* joking.") Even so, at a time when debates about humor shadowed discussions about the privilege and predicament of art, the question of how a poem could be laughable was posed with new urgency. A couple of years before *Lyrical Ballads* was published, Friedrich Schiller's touchstone essay "On Naïve and Sentimental Poetry" included sustained discussion of laughter, of the figure of the Fool, of "play," of humorous poetry, and of the purpose of comedy as "the highest after which man has to struggle."[61] Such high purpose was not a philosophical position for Wordsworth, but it was related both to his struggle to become a poet and to his faith in writing as a form of psychological and moral exploration. That faith was complicated as well as enriched by his own strange humors, and he was not averse to a certain dry comedy when speculating on what ethics can and cannot do for us. In an early notebook, situated between the first fragments of *The Prelude* and a record of his conversations with Klopstock, one finds his fragmentary "Essay on Morals," the opening sentence of which reads "I think publications in which we formally & systematically lay down rules for the actions of Men cannot be too long delayed."[62]

*

I hope to prolong the delay by staying true to an instinct Wordsworth once described as a "devious mood": "A local spirit of its own, at war / With general tendency."[63] My main focus is on Wordsworth's writing from the 1790s up until the publication of *Poems, in Two Volumes*, but I'm not much concerned with his "development" (or lack of it) and so provide local essayings into various aspects of his work. I proceed episodically, not chronologically. This introduction and the following twelve chapters are offered as a nonepic baker's dozen and as a circuitous journey toward the subject of the final chapters: the thirteen-book *Prelude* of 1805. I spend a lot of time reading particular poems very closely, mindful throughout of Wordsworth's claim that "words themselves / Move us with conscious pleasure,"[64] and of his insistence that "the composition of verse is infinitely more of an art than Men are prepared to believe, and absolute success in it depends upon innumerable minutiae."[65] Elsewhere, in more unbuttoned fashion, he admitted that "Little matters in Composition hang about and teaze me awkwardly, and at improper times."[66] These awkward "Little matters" are what interest me most. As Wordsworth wrote in the advertisement to *Lyrical Ballads*, those who read him "will perhaps frequently have to struggle with feelings of strangeness and aukwardness."[67] The struggle is an echo of his own mood during composition: "in struggling with words," he observed, one is "led to give birth to and dwell on thoughts."[68] Attendance to innumerable minutiae is the making—not the mere dressing—of thought, and thought is always steeped in strange feeling for him. Style itself is an approach to life, a way of inhabiting experience, and the intensity of Wordsworth's engagement with words is an ethical quest as much as it is an aesthetic one.

Close readings of humor—and finicky approaches to fun—can be as turgid as explanations of jokes. As Max Eastman rightly observed, "the correct explanation of a joke not only does not sound funny, but it does not sound like a correct explanation."[69] A joke is like Kant's idea of an aesthetic experience, one that is always in search of a concept and never quite finding it, and to write about humor is always to risk tactlessness—to show too little tact, indeed, by attempting to be too thorough. The risk is compounded when one decides to inflict a penchant for detailism on an apparently nonfunny poet (even a sympathetic reader might ask: "*Wordsworth's Fun*? It's worth a speculative essay—but a book?"). I'm aware that the following chapters are imperiled by a certain relentlessness and by a laboring of the apparently simple. Yet Wordsworth often sought to bring home the strangeness of the seemingly obvious. He anticipated that "the *nimia simplicitas* of my diction will frequently be complained of,"[70] and Richard Mant—the author of an early parody, *The Simpliciad*—was one of many who obliged. (Years later, on finding himself at dinner with Mant, Wordsworth noted, "I was somewhat drolly placed in such company."[71]) This book seeks to keep him there and to find a language for discussing his radically droll mixture of simplicity and duplicity, one to which later writers were beholden. When Elizabeth Barrett spoke of "a simplicity startling to the blasé critical ear as inventiveness," and when Robert Frost recognized in Wordsworth "that lovely banality and the lovely penetration that goes with it,"[72] they were paying their respects to an intuition he had held dear from the start: the simple is the essence—not the opposite—of the complex.

All this is not to deny that some of Wordsworth's attempts at lightness can be very heavy handed. (It's hard to keep a straight face on learning that the *OED*'s first instance of the phrase "laughter-stirring" comes from *The Excursion.*) In later life, the sage of Rydal Mount was in no mood for comedy, as his son-in-law Edward Quillinan recalled:

> Mr W. said to night that there was no *immortality in laughter*—in reference to the effect produced on mankind by authors.—That there was not a jest nor a stroke of humour from beginning to end in the sacred writings.—That Aristophanes & the other Greek & Roman writers of comedy were not really popular & that even Shakespeare's comedies *did not lay hold of us.* That Don Quixote was admirable but rather melancholy than laughter-moving.—That the most pathetic of all authors were to be found in the Scriptures & in the Greek Tragedians, and in Shakespeare.—He thought the French writers of light dramas the most effective in laughter moving—but no wit, founded on manners or fashions, could endure, however good.[73]

This outburst feels almost like an act of vengeance on humorous writings and a renunciation of a previous self—or a present one he can't quite accept.[74] Two days later, as if in atonement, he is drawn to speak of his own experiments in comedy: of "The Idiot Boy," "Mr W. says that he never wrote anything more currently than this poem, nor when he was in a happier & more poetical state of feeling. It is a great favourite with him" (the following day he championed *Benjamin the Waggoner* and *Peter Bell*).[75] The link between writing *currently* and feeling poetical is the crucial one; it doesn't exactly refute the claim that there is no immortality in laughter, but it does serve as a reminder that, when things were going well, the young poet couldn't have cared less about immortality.

Recalling his foundational experiences of reading, Wordsworth celebrated a particular kind of writing. His school days, he noted, "were very happy ones, chiefly because I was left at liberty, then and in the vacations, to read whatever books I liked. For example, I read all Fielding's works, Don Quixote, Gil Blas, and any part of Swift that I liked; Gulliver's Travels, and the Tale of the Tub, being both much to my taste."[76] Add to this Wordsworth's translations of Chaucer and Ariosto, along with the three writers who are his most treasured modern poetical exemplars—Burns, Cowper, and Thomas Percy—and it's striking that all these writers' greatest achievements were in seriocomic modes. In the following chapters I explore Wordsworth's engagement with these figures, along with his debt to the comic forms of Shakespeare, Pope, and others (the work and play of allusion in his poetry is a central part of the story I want to tell). In 1791 he can be found boasting (disingenuously, but revealingly) to William Mathews that the only modern novel he's read is *Tristram Shandy* ("I rather think that my gaiety encreases with my ignorance"), comparing one of his friends to Yorick, and urging his respondent to read *Rape of the Lock* as a cure for his melancholy.[77] For a man who was apparently distrustful of wit, his library shelves make for suggestive reading: among his copies of Lucian, Aristophanes, Molière, Rabelais, and Erasmus, one finds titles like *Wit's Commonwealth* (1604) and *Wit's Recreations, augmented, with ingenious conceites for the wittie and merry medecines for the melancholie* (1641).[78]

A sense of wit's recreative commonwealth can be gleaned from an astonishing passage copied into Wordsworth's commonplace book in 1800. The text was also a favorite of Coleridge's—"an old friend of mine," he called it: "Beyond any other passage in any Language it carries along a regular Admiration with a still increasing Surprize, till the mind rests at length in pure *Wonder*."[79] It comes from Isaac Barrow's reflections on the various lives of wit, and that Wordsworth should chose to copy it out at such length is itself revealing:

> Sometimes wit lieth in pat allusion to a known story, or in seasonable application of a trivial saying, or in forging an apposite tale: sometimes it playeth in words and phrases, taking advantage from the ambiguity of their sense, or the affinity of their sound: sometimes it is wrapped in a dress of humorous expression; sometimes it lurketh under an odd similitude; sometimes it is lodged in a sly question, in a smart answer, in a quirkish reason, in a shrewd intimation, in cunningly diverting, or cleverly retorting an objection: sometimes it is couched in a bold scheme of speech, in a tart irony, in a lusty hyperbole, in a startling metaphor, in a plausible reconciling of contradictions, or in acute nonsense: sometimes a scenical representation of persons or things, a counterfeit speech, a mimical look or gesture passeth for it: sometimes an affected simplicity, sometimes a presumptuous bluntness giveth it being; sometimes it riseth from a lucky hitting upon what is strange, sometimes from a crafty wresting obvious matter to the purpose: often it consisteth in one knows not what, and springeth up one can hardly tell how. Its ways are unaccountable and inexplicable, being answerable to the numberless rovings of fancy and windings of language. It is in short, a manner of speaking out of the simple and plain way (such as reason teacheth and proveth things by), which by a pretty surprising uncouthness in conceit or expression doth affect and amuse the fancy, stirring in it some wonder, and breeding some delight thereto. It raiseth admiration, as signifying a nimble sagacity of apprehension, a special felicity of invention, a vivacity of spirit, and reach of wit more than vulgar; it seeming to argue a rare quickness of parts, that one can fetch in remote conceits applicable; a notable skill, that he can dexterously accommodate them to the purpose before him [;] together with a lively briskness of humor, not apt to damp those sportful flashes of imagination. (Whence in Aristotle such

> persons are termed . . . dexterous men, and . . . men of facile or versatile manners, who can easily turn themselves to all things, or turn all things to themselves.) It also procureth delight, by gratifying curiosity with its rareness or semblance of difficulty: (as monsters, not for their beauty, but their rarity; as juggling tricks, not for their use, but their abstruseness, are beheld with pleasure:) by diverting the mind from its road of serious thoughts; by instilling gaiety & airiness of spirit; by provoking to such dispositions of spirit in way of emulation or complaisance; and by seasoning matters, otherwise distasteful or insipid, with an unusual, & thence grateful tang.[80]

Throughout this book, I aim to treat fun in the broad, beguiling way that Barrow treats wit here. By looking more for hints, tones, repertoires, and applications than for a stringent definition, I ask readers to allow a considerable degree of latitude to the range of things fun might mean, but my hope is that this will provide a fresh angle on a poet we are in danger of knowing too well. To put the matter slightly differently, my claim is not simply that Wordsworth is more fun than he appears but that fun is more Wordsworthian than we think. Like wit, fun consists in one knows not what and springs up one can hardly tell how, because the funny-witty person, by being answerable to the numberless rovings of fancy and windings of language, is not fully in control of his or her power. Wit is a way with words, but it is also the process through which words have their way with you.

*

"Wordsworth often says some very silly things, or things which will continue to sound silly until one has read a great deal of literary criticism."[81] A great deal of criticism has been published in the half century since Robert Pinsky made that remark. The priorities and allegiances of Geoffrey Hartman's monumental book helped to set an agenda: a poem like *Peter Bell* didn't even merit discussion, and while Hartman felt that "The Thorn" was Wordsworth's most experimental poem (alongside "Simon Lee" and "The Idiot Boy"), he was quick to add, "this does not mean that the experiments are not failures."[82] Since then, more attention has been given to Wordsworth's "failures"; David Bromwich, for example, has written finely on *Peter Bell*'s "great daring, and incorrigible genius," on the fully achieved nature of "The Thorn" and "The Idiot Boy" ("there is nothing else like them in literature"), and he chose to lead off his essays in *Moral Imagination* by taking "The Idiot Boy" very seriously indeed.[83] Nonetheless, a need to guard against Wordsworthian silliness endures. As Maureen McLane has recently observed, however much he has been historicized, psychoanalyzed, deconstructed, queered, ecocriticized, eulogized, interred, and revived, "Wordsworth in many ways remains

'Wordsworth'—the elaborately consolidated figure . . . the gigantic yet (or therefore) satirizable figure."[84] A laughable Wordsworth is still only a diminished one, and he continues to be conceived in terms of the "two voices" that J. K. Stephen heard so long ago, voices that are not in conversation with each other: "one is of the deep," and speaks with "the storm-cloud's thunderous melody"; the other is of "an old half-witted sheep / Which bleats articulate monotony."[85]

The following chapters find more continuities than differences between the allegedly sublime and silly versions of Wordsworth. So while I study some poems for the seriousness of their comedy, I'm also interested in how an elegy, or an ode, or an epic like *The Prelude* can be read for the comedy of its seriousness. I am not attempting to save Wordsworth from himself but rather seeking to resist certain compartmentalizations and to present ways of experiencing him as a little less like "Wordsworth." It has rightly been said many times, in different ways, that his subjectivism makes him the father of modern poetry.[86] But his place in literary tradition can be reoriented if we also consider him as alert to the possible absurdities of introspection and read him, say, in the light of Nietzsche's claim that "everything very personal is essentially *comical*"[87] or of Luigi Pirandello's feeling that "by the rebellion of precisely the subjective elements of the spirit, which characterizes the Romantic movement, humor asserted itself freely."[88] When Wordsworthian perception is serious, Wordsworthian apperception is often humorous—and vice versa. If this double act isn't always permitted to assert itself "freely" in his work, it is discernable more often than might be expected, and it is linked to his craving for modes of rebellion that are both private and public. Some years ago, when acknowledging the revitalizing effect that deconstructionist and historicist approaches were having on studies of the poet, John Bayley paused to wonder whether something was being missed: a sense of him as "a comically familial human being."[89] I keep that person in mind in the chapters that follow. The tragicomedy of Wordsworth's family romance is considered at various points—stories of parenting and orphaning, marriages and non-marriages, commitments and truancies—but some aspects of this plotline take time to emerge, so a brief excursus here via a neglected poem will help to foreshadow the trajectory of my approach.

Benjamin the Waggoner is usually seen as uncharacteristic or unworthy of "Wordsworth." Yet the poem meant a great deal to him; "The 'Waggoner' was written con amore," he observed, "as the Epilogue states almost in my own despite."[90] It's suggestive that he should jokingly imagine a confession of his love as somehow working against him; here, as elsewhere, his humor relies on the gravity of what it makes into fun. The story begins on a hot night in June.

A sultry breeze comes "With a haunting and a panting / Like the stifling of disease."[91] Benjamin is walking with his horse and wagon past Wordsworth's house: "where the Dove and Olive-bough / Once hung, a Poet harbours now—."[92] The wagoner thinks of the old times when he used to drink there (he drank a lot), and then he thinks of the "honest folks" who now inhabit the place: "It is a doubt with Benjamin / Whether they be alive or dead."[93] While Benjamin attempts to stay on the straight and narrow, one senses that he longs for trouble. Trouble duly arrives, but via an unlikely circumstance. Coming across a lady and her baby in a storm, he offers to help. Then, when a shady, roguish sailor figure emerges from the dark (the lady's husband, as it turns out), Benjamin shelters mother and child in his wagon while the husband follows behind as they continue on their journey. They reach an inn, the two men go inside, temptation beckons. As wagoner and sailor are drawn in to "their own delight and fun," Benjamin gets thirsty.[94] In a scene that crosses Hogarth with Sterne with something wholly unfamiliar, the hero's faithful dog growls in warning, but Benjamin, "triumphant Soul! . . . in opposition quaff'd / A deep, determin'd, desperate draft."[95] The fun increases when the sailor suddenly wheels out his party piece, a scale model of *The Vanguard*, one of Nelson's flagships. In good set mock-heroic terms, he rehearses the battle against the French on the floor of the inn while the punters look on. "You may smirk and smile," says the sailor to the skeptical onlookers, but he insists, "if you look near / You'll find you've much in little here!"[96]

One thing leads to another, and little turns into much once again when Benjamin's boss, learning of his adventuring the next morning, decides to fire him. So the wagoner's attraction to the sailor—his willingness to tolerate or humor him—contributes to his own undoing. The poem closes with an epilogue in which Wordsworth addresses the reader much as the sailor had addressed those who had smirked:

> A sad Catastophe, say you—
> Adventure never worth a song?
> Be free to think so, for I too
> Have thought so many times and long.
> But what I have and what I miss
> I sing of these, it makes my bliss.
> Nor is it I who play the part,
> But a shy spirit in my heart
> That comes and goes, will sometimes leap
> From hiding-places ten years deep.
> Sometimes, as in the present case,
> Will shew a more familiar face,

Returning like a Ghost unlaid
Until the debt I owe be paid.[97]

The writing initially flirts with ineptness or inaptness before the rhythms steady themselves and something inexorable starts to make itself felt. It's as though the whimsical suddenly finds itself bound up with the irrepressible, as though Wordsworth's recourse to the comic strain is apprehended as a kind of reparation or compulsion. He has been hedging his seriousness to serious effect; humor is linked to the "shy," to an impulse that seeks expression but that doesn't want to express itself too clearly. ("Ten years deep" is noteworthy in this regard: exactly ten years before he started writing the poem, Wordsworth was preparing to leave France—and a pregnant Annette Vallon.[98]) The only other time he refers to "hiding-places" is in *The Prelude* ("the hiding-places of my power / Seem open; I approach, and then they close; / I see by glimpses now"),[99] and his lighter flights of fancy are no less concerned to see into the sources of this power.

As Benjamin and the sailor are about to enter the inn, the narrator observes,

The Sailor Man, by nature gay,
Has no resolves to throw away;
And he has now forgot his Wife,
Hath quite forgotten her, or may be
Knows what is the truth, I wis—
That she is better where she is,
    Under cover,
    Terror over,
Sleeping by her sleeping Baby.[100]

Although the Terror was over when the poet wrote these lines, memories of mother, baby, and the war with France lingered on. At the beginning of the poem, Benjamin is overheard saying to himself, "I've been a sinner, I avow, / But better times are coming now."[101] Yet Wordsworth's writing stays in touch with past demons, and it seeks to couch itself as fun—or "*in* fun"—in order to do so. The comings and goings of the shy spirit in his heart are related to his singing of "What I have and what I miss," and if he doesn't quite want to take responsibility for what has been written or for the seriousness of the game playing as it has unfolded here, this only confirms fun's explorative, revelatory power for him. In a note to the published version, Wordsworth gave some additional suppressed verses "as a gratification of private feeling, which the well-disposed reader will find no difficulty in excusing."[102] Such gratifications may or may not be excused, but the need for—the *demand* for—a well-disposed reader speaks volumes. He wants us to read his attempts at comedy in a similar spirit as we might read his private life.

In a manuscript note Wordsworth observed that "this Poem was at first ~~writ~~ thrown off ~~from~~ under a lively impulse of feeling."[103] The shift from the "writ" to the "thrown off" implies not so much that he wrote the poem but that the poem wrote him. It's similar to a jotting he made on a scrap of paper in an early notebook: "I was surprized to find what / I had written."[104] The poems are often self-surprising in this way. He wrote *Benjamin the Waggoner*, I think, to get rid of something, or to get something off his back, and one thrown-off word—it's hard to know whether it's an errant slip of the tongue or a commitment to errancy—comes at the very moment that Benjamin drinks deep: "triumphant Soul! . . . in opposition quaff'd / A deep, determin'd, desperate draft." As far as I'm aware, nowhere else in his work does Wordsworth spell *draft* like this (he always opts for the common spelling *draught*). The poem was dedicated to Charles Lamb, so indulging in a pun while Benjamin indulges in a tipple would be fitting in more than one way. Whether or not the poet is being waggish alongside his wagoner, the draft tells of the desperately deep determination of poetry—a story written as a draft, a work in progress, a testament to Wordsworth's inability to have the last word on what his past means to him.

To face Wordsworth is to face an oddity—a queerness, a funniness, a temperament that entertains glimmers of humor in order to get to other places it needs to be, or that runs to humor in order to process things it can't wholly escape. Those who simply read this as poor comedy, or failed fun, might quote lines from *The Borderers* in support, when Rivers turns and says to Mortimer of the old man he wants dead: "'Tis his own fault if he hath got a face / Which doth play tricks with them that look upon it."[105] Wordsworth has that kind of face, yet so does everyone else when looked at in a certain way. Some time ago, when thinking about Buster Keaton's face, Hugh Kenner observed, "If we are haunted by analogies with Wordsworth, we shall find no apposite quotation."[106] The analogy—delightfully implausible, uncannily possible—is returned to a few pages later: "Wordsworth is the last eminent imitator, the last until Buster Keaton, of that eighteenth-century paladin, The Man of Sense, who moved through his world beset by the unsleeping perils of the ridiculous."[107] To consider this movement and posture as a form of deadpan is a good way to approach Wordsworth. We are accustomed to reading him as kin to the bird at the opening of "Resolution and Independence"—"Over his own sweet voice the stock-dove broods"[108]—yet when Wordsworth broods on the dove's voice in another poem, he picks up on something unexpected. He first says of the bird that "Somewhat pensively he woo'd," but listening more intently, he hears the tune as a medley—and as another of those pleasurable, stray gifts to be claimed by whoever shall find them: "He sang . . . Of serious faith, and inward glee; / That was the Song, the Song for me!"[109] To listen out for this strange fusion of seriousness and levity in Wordsworth's own song is to ask how—or whether—that song could also be ours.

LAUGHING

Evading and then relaxing and then stipulating and then hearing that there is a protection is not the whole way to have it said that there has been laughing.

GERTRUDE STEIN

Echoes

> My own voice chear'd me, and, far more, the mind's
> Internal echo of the imperfect sound
>
> *THE PRELUDE*[1]

I begin where the poetry often begins—not with straightforward incitements to laughter but with oddly charged depictions of it. Wordsworth was surrounded by people who knew when to laugh. In the eighteenth century's most widely read treatise on the subject, James Beattie explained that "A man of breeding will be careful not to laugh much longer, or much oftener, than others; nor to laugh at all, except where it is probable, that the jest may be equally relished by the company."[2] Wordsworth was not careful in this way. *The Prelude* is withering about such well-bred, confirmatory echoings—and about the refined literary type who is always ready "With apt and graceful laughter" ("Arch are his notices, and nice his sense / Of the ridiculous").[3] From the start, the poet was attracted to less readable outbursts: in a draft of *Descriptive Sketches* he describes how, "Not undelightfully," a woman "laugh'd as if she knew not why," and in a later lyric he growls at those who "must laugh / By precept only," comparing them unfavorably with meadow flowers that take more liberties.[4]

Can flowers laugh in a way that challenges precept? Apparently so:

> I wandered lonely as a Cloud
> That floats on high o'er Vales and Hills,
> When all at once I saw a crowd
> A host of dancing Daffodils;
> Along the Lake, beneath the trees,
> Ten thousand dancing in the breeze.
>
> The waves beside them danced, but they
> Outdid the sparkling waves in glee:—
> A Poet could not but be gay

In such a laughing company:
I gaz'd—and gaz'd—but little thought
What wealth the shew to me had brought:

For oft when on my couch I lie
In vacant or in pensive mood,
They flash upon that inward eye
Which is the bliss of solitude,
And then my heart with pleasure fills,
And dances with the Daffodils.[5]

Lucy Aikin felt that Wordsworth's decision to use the word *laughing* was typical of his gaucherie (a "capricious and entirely arbitrary" association, she said).[6] Not entirely arbitrary, for *laughing* accentuates the bobbing movement of the flowers, and Wordsworth may have been aware of the root of the Greek word for laughter (*gel-*), which connects it to ideas of brightness or gleaming light.[7] The daffodils are, after all, outdoing the sparkling waves (elsewhere, Wordsworth speaks of the "Bright Star! with laughter on her banners" and of a face "bright with laughter").[8] Still, the review bothered him. He lost his nerve and changed *laughing* to *jocund* in the next version while vowing to restore his original choice in a later edition.[9]

Other lines flirt with the laughable too. The opening words carry a glint of self-relish inside their gloom (as Stevie Smith once noted, "And then, of course, if one's lonely, one often feels rather superior too. One *is* different from other people, is one not?").[10] The poem's music also houses a kind of whimsicality; only four words go beyond a disyllable, but they all arrive as clinching sounds of rhyming pairs in order to stress the oddity of the tune ("Hills/Daffodils"; "glee/company"; "mood/solitude"; "fills/Daffodils"). Walter Pater discerned in Wordsworth "a sort of half-playful mysticism" hinted at by "a certain quaint gaiety of metre,"[11] and both quaintness and gaiety are played up by what the rhythm does to the rhymes in the middle stanza. First there's that late pause in the opening line ("but they"—as if to say, "the waves were good, but the flowers . . . ah, now, they were *really* impressive"); then "glee" coaxes a new sound out of "compan*y*"; and then comes the accenting of the speaker's surprise as the rhyme resurfaces in "to *me*." Writing like this asks to be lightly indulged even as it invites a second look. "I gaz'd—and gaz'd" feels blankly lacking in thought as well as a possible catalyst for it. The speaker might be looking back and laughing at his own silliness—or at yours for not taking him seriously.

When recalling the day that inspired the poem, Dorothy Wordsworth noted in her journal that the daffodils "danced & seemed as if they verily laughed," but something else she remembered about that day is interesting. After they reached an inn, Wordsworth sat down to read a volume of William Congreve's comedies and "a volume of Enfield's Speaker."[12] One piece in Enfield's anthology—Samuel Johnson on "Good Humour"—may have stayed with him. "Good humour," Johnson suggested, is "a state between gaiety and unconcern . . . when the first transports of new felicity have subsided":

> It is imagined by many, that whenever they aspire to please, they are required to be merry, and to shew the gladness of their souls by flights of pleasantry, and bursts of laughter. But though these men may be for a time heard with applause and admiration, they seldom delight us long. We enjoy them a little, and then retire to easiness and good humour, as the eye gazes awhile on eminences glittering with the sun, but soon turns away to verdure and to flowers.[13]

This shares Wordsworth's reservations about laughter as a social grace (in *The Idler* Johnson had poked fun at himself for "diligent imitation of the best models . . . from laughing only to shew that I was pleased, I now began to laugh when I wished to please.")[14] The passage also echoes Johnson's mixed feelings in *Lives of the English Poets* about Congreve's "quick and sparkling" comic dialogue, where he observes the dramatist's early zenith (the period he was able to "shine in eminence") before noting that his plays were not "dictated by nature": "we are rather amused with noise . . . than entertained with any true delineation of natural characters."[15] Yet Johnson's dichotomy between the gay abandon of public felicity on which the eye gazes for a while and the calmer pleasures of contemplative humor is not faithfully echoed by Wordsworth. To turn to flowers here—even when gazed at through that inward eye that is the bliss of solitude—is to turn back to laughing, sparkling, sun-drenched scenery. The "shew" about which Johnson raises concerns is now celebrated; "What wealth the shew to me had brought" points less toward the idea of a show as "a feigned or misleading appearance" and more toward other senses given in the *OED*: a revelation born of a chance encounter (*show* as "An appearance or 'promise' *of* or *for* something that is to come"), or a "spectacle elaborately prepared" and put on for one's entertainment.

If the world of Congreve's drama is playing somewhere in the background—and Wordsworth spoke of Johnson's comments on Congreve elsewhere—then this may bear on why the daffodils are described as a laughing "company" ("a party of players, a theatrical corps" [*OED*]).[16] The flowers' laughter is cherished, I think, because it is felt to lie somewhere between an intention and an instinct: it may be their performative, theatrical way of calling to the poet, hoping to shake him out of his mood by getting him to join the club, or a sign of their being unselfconsciously in tune with their own natures. Certainly, the bright blandishments of Restoration comedy are some distance from Romantic lyricism, yet Wordsworthian humor is not so much the avoidance as the internalization of wit (something akin to Isaac Barrow's cherished sense of the witty as "quirkish" and as involved in "sportful flashes of imagination").[17] The poet's rumination is fed by a memory of repartee, and the poetry includes a yearning for gaiety and sociality, a sociality that is in fact constituted by a sense of separation: Wordsworth is "In" the daffodils' company most truly when he's recalling it, and the ecstatic stress on the togetherness of "with" in the lyric's final line comes only when distance lends enchantment to the view. This is a comedy of mind, not manners, but it includes a desire for *shared* pleasures—a vision of consensus without coercion.

Wordsworth's first readers, however, tended to read the drama as laughably inconversable. Anna Seward thought the whole performance ridiculous: "Surely if his worst foe had chosen to caricature this egotistic manufacturer of metaphysic importance upon trivial themes, he could not have done it more effectually!"[18] Talk of "caricature" isn't entirely misplaced, yet the poem doesn't explore what the mind manufactures, exactly, but rather what happens *to* the mind (Wordsworth had "little thought" of its significance back then). He notes elsewhere that "One enjoys objects while they are present but they are never truly endeared till they have been lodged some time in the memory."[19] Our past is often more vivid than our present, and there's a rueful comedy in the fact that we keep missing out on our experiences while we're having them. Even when the past event is later recalled, it doesn't return because it has been deliberately summoned; the daffodils sportfully flash into view when nothing could be farther from his thoughts (the movement is a mirror image of one in *Lyrical Ballads*: "in a grove I sate reclined / In that sweet mood when pleasant thoughts / Bring sad thoughts to the mind").[20] He can't even bring himself to write "For now when on my couch I lie," for it merely happens "oft," not always. The poem registers the incongruity of the self to itself; lonesomeness, vacancy, pensiveness, pleasure, and bliss are entangled. Everything tells of the integrity of incoherence.

The inconstancy of the lyric's subject is felt most strongly in the quality to which Coleridge would take objection: "the inconstancy of the style . . . he sinks too often and too abruptly."[21] The shift from radiant recognition to the bathos of the final couplet is his prime example: "And then my heart with pleasure fills, / And dances with the *daffodils*" (Coleridge's italics). The inverted syntax and the final metrical gambit play up the decision not just to reiterate *that* word but to end the poem by rhyming on it. *Daffodil* has a history linking it to "*daffing . . . frolicking, merriment*,"[22] and the *OED* conjectures that *daft* and *daff* may be etymologically related (a *daff*, in Northern dialect, still signified "a simpleton, a fool" in the nineteenth century; *daffy* as noun was colloquial for *daffodil* from 1777). Wordsworth's ending invites accusations of daftness, yet it also braves them. Although the alliterative bounce of the last line lowers the tone, it does so to catch the sound of a quickening heartbeat (there's also a shock of insight in "And *then* my heart"). The poem is strengthened by how it surprises itself, by how it discovers (and keeps rediscovering) that remembered rapture is confusing, embarrassing even, but also a source of sustenance. To be open to ridicule is to be open to possibility.

Molesworth is adamant that "Weedy people say la and fie and swoon when they see a bunch of daffodils,"[23] but who, the poem insinuates, is the nonweedy person? For all the whimsy of their self-involvement, the three stanzas chart a movement from the "I" as merely lonely to the "I" as the declared representative of a type ("A Poet") to the sense that this type includes everyone: the flowers do not flash upon "my inward eye" but upon "*that* inward eye"—a psychological fact, not a personal predilection. The bliss includes a sense of the self's unruly, potentially ridiculous life as it exists in company with other lives; the poet's heart is "weedy" (to draw out Molesworth's pun), for it *fills* with pleasure in a way similar to those laughing daffodils that suck up water from the nearby lake. Yet his ludic, ludicrous fantasy of return to the flowers' noncerebral, biological core of being—and of himself as replenished by that being—is itself couched in a figure that has to humanize the flowers. To the joyous hilarity that may blossom from the roots of unthinkingness must be added the caprice and the confusion of a thinking being who sometimes needs his sense of humor in order to help him ease the very burden of his thoughtfulness. Wordsworth was wealthy indeed when he but little thought what wealth the show to him had brought, but he was not wealthy enough—or, rather, he was in need of other kinds of wealth too—because only through the revisiting of experience could he become laughable in all the ways he wanted to be. Something here is deeply yet obscurely funny, funny enough to be serious.

*

The figure of echo has remained fairly well hidden up to now—too well hidden, perhaps. "I wandered lonely as a Cloud" contains echoes of another story, and Wordsworth's deft variation on that story hints at key aspects of his own creation and reception myths. The poet's inward "I" is sometimes lying in pensive mood, sometimes in love with solitude, and he appears to be hoping for a union with a flower at the water's edge, one whose Latin name is telling. Ovid's Narcissus was also given to "wandering through the lonely countryside"; "As he lay upon the bank he gazed . . . with fixed gaze" until he finally faded away into a flower. He often returned to the image he adored, but "his tears disturbed the water, so that the pool rippled, and the image grew dim"; "Where are you fleeing?" he implored the shadow.[24] When George Beaumont told Wordsworth that a friend had criticized the lyric about the "Daffodils *reflected in the water*," he replied, "My Language is precise. . . . Let me ask your Friend how it is possible for flowers to be *reflected* in water where there are *waves*. . . . The very object of my poem is the trouble or agitation both of the flowers and the Water."[25] In the *Metamorphoses*, Narcissus shunned not only the wood nymph Echo "but many other spirits of the waters,"[26] so it's fitting that part of his punishment will be effected by ripples in the water's surface. Such agitation lives on in Wordsworth's lyric.

Ovid was one of Wordsworth's first loves, and his fascination with this particular episode can be discerned elsewhere.[27] Leonard Barkan suggests that the primary effect of the encounter between Narcissus and Echo is comic, but it's more seriocomic—serious because nothing would appear to be more important than desire; comic because nothing is less amenable to control.[28] Ovid's version conceives desire as in some sense always unrequited (Echo's passion is unanswered too as she pines away for love of Narcissus), and while Wordsworth ends with a dance amid the bliss of solitude, Christopher Ricks offers pause: "'of' is so adept . . . 'the bliss of solitude' may rather mean the bliss that is the blissful part of solitude. As we may speak of 'the rewards of the academic life,' acknowledging that there are those other things."[29] It is possible, Wordsworth once noted, to have "all the poverty of solitude, nothing of its elevation,"[30] and those other things were glanced at with humorous sadness in Dorothy's original journal entry: she noticed mossy stones on which some of the flowers "rested their heads . . . as on a pillow for weariness."[31] They are like the speaker who lies on his couch, or like Ovid's protagonist who "laid down his weary head on the green grass."[32]

Wordsworth had a pronounced interest in figuring laughter itself as echo. Rivers tells Mortimer in *The Borderers*,

> Some scoffed at him with hellish mockery,
> And laugh'd so loud it seem'd that the smooth sea
> Did from some distant region echo us.[33]

The sea may be supporting or resisting the crew's mockery; echo could endorse the fearful natural order of things or scoff at man's inhumanity to man. *The Prelude* recalls a walk home from an all-night party on a morning in which "The Sea was laughing at a distance."[34] *At a* distance, not *in the* distance: the sea doesn't simply echo Wordsworth's mood; it is also somehow laughingly beyond him. De Quincey would later suggest that laughter thrown off from "the fields of ocean" is something "that hides, or that seems to evade mustering tumult . . . mimicries of earth-born flowers that for the eye raise phantoms of gaiety, as oftentimes for the ear they raise echoes of fugitive laughter."[35] The fugitive, phantasmal nature of laughter apprehended as echo or as trace bears on the question of why Wordsworth's first readers were put out by his laughing daffodils. Laughter projected onto objects has a reputable classical pedigree, after all, so such objections initially seem odd. Elsewhere, he imagines birds, vales, rills, stars, and sky as laughing, but in "I wandered lonely as a Cloud," the laughter is not simply a pathetic fallacy. It flashes into the writing as a mysterious force, like Elizabeth Bishop's sense that "all the trees laughed at some joke," or John Ashbery's feeling that "laughter danced in the dim fields beyond the schoolhouse: / It was existence again in all its tautness."[36] In Wordsworth's River Duddon sonnets, when the rill "undaunted . . . laughing dares the Adventurer,"[37] the critic for *Monthly Review* thought that "undaunted" was "an allowable and ancient liberty" but that "laughing" extended "a liberty into a licentious usage."[38] Licentious, perhaps, because of a doubt regarding whether the laugh answers back to or takes its bearings from the human. Laughter in Wordsworth rarely signals a reiteration of what is already consciously known. For those readers who demand that poetry accede to their knowingness, that it give them "usages" for which they can account, the echoic sound may well be discomforting.

Like laughter, Echo herself is an elusive figure. Condemned to repeat snatches of other voices, after the nymph dissolves into nature in Ovid she becomes even more equivocal, for the act of returning only part of an utterance may serve to lyricize, augment, and sponsor it or to diminish and ridicule it. John Hollander observes that "whenever possible, Echo's fragmentary response frequently involves a pun or other alteration of sense,"[39] and this feeling for a sound that goes both ways—toward either assent or mockery—resonates with the rhythms of both parody and laughter. In 1802, Coleridge spoke of how he and others called out names in a sheepfold, listening to their voices rebounding from the surroundings: "Echo came upon Echo and then Hartley & Derwent & then I laughed & shouted. . . . It leaves all the Echoes I ever heard far far behind, in number, distinctness & *humanness* of Voice."[40] Collective humanness is reiterated and reinstated here, but a few months later Dorothy heard something less safe:

> [The echo] shouted the names of our fireside friends in the very tone in which Wm. and C. spoke; but it seemed to make a joke of me, and I could not help laughing at my own voice; it was so shrill and pert, exactly as if some one had

> been mimicking it very successfully, with an intention of making me ridiculous. . . . The echo is an excellent laugher[41]

The marvel of this echo is like the vision of the world afforded by prosopopoeia, with the landscape again giving back an intimation of the human. But instead of turning laugh into voice, Dorothy is compelled to laugh *at* her voice. Nature seems to be parodying her, yet her response feels at once nervous and accepting. Some of Wordsworth's early parodists were less willing to entertain such mixed feelings, so had fun at his expense with the figure of echoic laughter; in "A Lyrical Ballad" (1804), Robert Rose observed that "No sooner did they laugh, te, he! / Than Dock-street echoed back the sound; / And Second-street replied haw! haw! /And so it went around."[42]

Coleridge, Dorothy, and Rose were all harking back to one particular poem from *Lyrical Ballads* singled out by Wordsworth as containing "the greatest genious of any poems in the 2[d] Vol."[43] The poem casts further light on the peculiarity of Wordsworthian humor as a means of defending and dissolving boundaries, and it contains the longest laugh he ever set himself to describe. Some parts of it might even be read as self-parody, but only if that mode is understood as a form of self-exploration.[44] "To Joanna" is another of his shrouded reworkings of the Narcissus and Echo story, a story that, as James Williams has observed, is "a *locus classicus* of speaking and not-speaking, half-articulation, eloquent absence . . . the kind of myth which, presented *in* poetry, becomes almost irresistibly a myth *of* poetry . . . a way of conceptualizing the complex business of reflection and self-reflection which seems characteristic of the 'modern' poetic subject."[45] For Wordsworth, such reflective acts are bound up with a funny feeling that would continue to haunt him, a feeling for the laughable object's potential to tap the cryptic energies of the laughing subject.

The poem begins with an opposition. Joanna, the poet claims, looks askance on those like him who "look upon the hills with tenderness, / And make dear friendships with the streams and groves."[46] He is a "transgressor," "Dwelling retired," while she is strongly devoted to love of "living Beings." So he is Narcissus-like and she is Echo-like. Recalling the time Joanna last visited, he remembers her watching him while he marveled at how different aspects of the natural scenery seemed to blend into "one impression, by connecting force":

> —When I had gaz'd perhaps two minutes' space,
> Joanna, looking in my eyes, beheld
> That ravishment of mine, and laugh'd aloud.
> The rock, like something starting from a sleep,

Took up the Lady's voice, and laugh'd again:
That ancient Woman seated on Helm-crag
Was ready with her cavern; Hammar-Scar,
And the tall Steep of Silver-How sent forth
A noise of laughter; southern Loughrigg heard,
And Fairfield answer'd with a mountain tone:
Helvellyn far into the clear blue sky
Carried the Lady's voice;—old Skiddaw blew
His speaking trumpet;—back out of the clouds
Of Glaramara southward came the voice;
And Kirkstone toss'd it from his misty head.

Charles Lamb pronounced this one of his favorite passages in *Lyrical Ballads*,[47] while Coleridge saw it as exemplifying a style "peculiarly Wordsworth's own."[48] It's certainly peculiar—and it's hard to know whether to take it as apocalyptic or absurd. In classical epic reechoing rocks tend to signal great forces of nature in tune with some manly or heroic deed, while for those writers indulging in mock-epic accents, the same figure is played for laughs.[49] Wordsworth's rendition is pitched somewhere between these poles, glimmering with cosmic significance even as he appears to be offering an account of local landmarks. Personification flirts with the ridiculous ("misty head" sounds like a mountain with a hangover), but a phrase like "something starting from a sleep" has an eerie resonance, one that lasts longer than any readerly smile it might provoke.

In a note Wordsworth explained that on Helm-Crag there is "a Rock which from most points of view bears a striking resemblance to an Old Woman cowering. Close by this rock is one of those Fissures or Caverns."[50] Given that echoes of uncertain portent are in the air, it's suggestive that the poem is set in Echo's canonical domain: "rocky caves (*solis ex illo vivit in antris*). . . . Within such hollow spaces she withers away."[51] (Denise Riley has the maiden pointedly say "My body goes rocky when I hang round Narcissus.")[52] As Echo, Joanna is an ambiguous supplement to the poet-Narcissus and his rapt enthusiasm, although it should be noted that this Narcissus is not so wrapped up in the landscape that he fails to notice what Echo is doing:

there was a loud uproar in the hills.
And, while we both were listening, to my side
The fair Joanna drew, as if she wish'd
To shelter from some object of her fear.[53]

Note the momentary glint of mischief at the line-end ("as if she wish'd . . ."; as if she wished *what*, precisely?). When Wordsworth satirizes the literary connoisseur in *The Prelude* for his apt and graceful laughter, he notes that "fear itself . . . Touches him not."[54] True laughter—inapposite, unbidden—touches fear, draws a person toward buried sources of desire. And while Joanna appears removed from Wordsworth's ravishment (does her laugh register fond recognition, or embarrassment, or incomprehension?), her response brings the two people unnervingly closer. The very echo her laugh provokes is also a rejoinder to it, an acoustic reminder that her life is itself a "connecting force"—heard, taken up, and answered by the world around her. This is I think why the laugh is redescribed as a "voice" three times in ten lines; the word edges the sound toward the threshold of language, as though the poem wants to keep faith with the idea of a conversable universe.

Even so, the nature of the conversation is tricky to decipher. Although Wordsworth's language seeks to embody Echo ("she laughed *aloud* . . . there was *a loud*," "the clear *blue* sky . . . old Skiddaw *blew*"), laughter appears to unhinge and untune; it is "noise" and "uproar," not simply "tone" and "speaking." Henri Bergson observed that "Laughter appears to stand in need of an echo . . . would fain be prolonged by reverberating from one to another . . . to continue in successive rumblings, like thunder in a mountain."[55] He adopts the figure in order to defend his claim that laughter is the marker and forger of social consensus; people laugh at what is odd in order to return it to normality ("Our laughter is always the laughter of a group").[56] But Wordsworth very rarely depicts more than one person laughing, and the poem doesn't suggest that Joanna's laughter means either to chastise or to reform. As a sound that echoes itself and that invites other echoes, laughter can be a search for forms of community, but it is frequently shadowed by risk—a stolen pleasure that betokens a loss of bearings. In this poem, "the Lady's voice" is initially given a confirmatory echo ("Took up the Lady's voice . . . Carried the Lady's voice") before becoming simply "*the* voice," unmoored from any definite sense of agency and ownership. We know where the laughter is, but we don't where we are with laughter.

*

In "To Joanna," the question of whether laughter is an appropriate response *in* the poem appears to be bound up with a question about whether laughter would be an appropriate response *to* it. But if Wordsworth is indeed offering an allegory of self-conception and reception, one in which a poet stages a relationship with an audience that laughs at him before finding that their laughter rebounds and echoes back on them, then the allegory is complicated by an awkward detail. Just before the laugh and its aftereffects are paraded for the reader's attention, the speaker makes a confession: his account is apparently a strange kind of joke—a smoke screen, riposte, and provocation to a local priest he'd encountered who'd bothered him with various questions about Joanna. "Now, by those dear immunities of heart / Engender'd betwixt malice and true love, / I was not loth to be so catechiz'd," he says, so he invents the tall story about the laugh. Wordsworth's later gloss on "To Joanna" is even weirder and suggests that the resonances of laughter and the inner workings of both his desire and his imagination are somehow coimplicated. He explains that he begins the story "in a certain degree to divert or partly play upon the Vicar" (*in certain degree . . . partly*) but that, having begun, "my mind partly forgets its purpose . . . I am caught in the Trap of my own imagination. I entirely lose sight of my first purpose," taking fire in "some fit of imagination."[57] What started out as a bit of fun turns into something else entirely; in telling the tale, he becomes unclear about whether he's telling the truth or not.

It's as though Wordsworth gets lost inside his need for this laugh and what it might say about him. In which case, he is the confused, desirous double of Joanna, not her foil, as little privy to what his fit of imagination commits him to as she is to what her fit of laughter portends. (In the poem itself, the speaker admits that the exact significance of what happened "Is not for me to tell.") For many of Wordsworth's contemporaries, laughing at an object or a person (a Lake poet, say) or trying to laugh it off by making a joke about it is a way of claiming that it is beneath you. For Wordsworth himself, it's more like an admission that you don't know how to react to something—or a confession of a suppressed reciprocity. In this sense, laughter becomes a surreptitiously strong indicator of what is important; it suggests a crisis in confidence that provides a route to unplumbed depths of feeling. The imaginative, like the laughable, is both a refuge and a "Trap," and to submit to the force of either is to commit to a process of unknowing one's boundaries. "To Joanna" becomes the story of a poet laughing at a vicar, a woman laughing at a poet, and a landscape laughing at a woman, and the cumulative effect is to make everyone unsure of who gets the last laugh.[58]

Not surprisingly, Wordsworth's tale leaves the vicar speechless: "our cordial Friend . . . in the hey day of astonishment / Smil'd in my face." "Our cordial Friend" is a droll, almost goading phrase; the vicar is being tendered as the gentle reader's surrogate. (I'm reminded of a story by Clarice Lispector in which an explorer faces the prolonged laughter of a woman and finds that he can only smile back "without knowing exactly to what abyss his smile responded."[59]) We may wish to distance ourselves from our cordial friend, but we share some of his astonishment and are even a little anxious about whether we've got the joke. Adam Phillips has suggested that "when we talk of getting it—the joke, the point, the work of art—we need to be aware of the anxieties that collusion apparently spares us."[60] "To Joanna" trusts to Wordsworth's intuition that both laughs and poems are forms of unconsummated meaning, and to his feeling that not knowing how to take them isn't necessarily a sign that you've misunderstood them. What he does know is that—as part of his idealized sense of his own identity and reception—he needs Joanna's echoing laugh to inform the life of his writing. His poetry must channel the delectable yet disorienting energy of the laughter, and the impropriety of "wild-hearted Maid," into its own way of being. Somewhere inside the poem is a fantasy of Narcissus and Echo (poet and audience) as partners in transgression; if they are not permitted to touch, they may at least conspire.

The feeling that Wordsworth wants to be unmanned or extended by laughter, that Joanna is his alter ego and not merely his antagonist, would have been strengthened for the poem's first readers when they encountered it shortly after reading something else in *Lyrical Ballads*: the first passage from *The Prelude* to appear in print, a passage that would later head up "Poems of the Imagination" in Wordsworth's collected *Poems* of 1815. The fragment about the boy of Winander recalls him offering mimic hootings to the owls in the hope that they might answer him:

> And long halloos, and screams, and echoes loud
> Redoubled and redoubled, a wild scene
> Of mirth and jocund din. And, when it chanced
> That pauses of deep silence mock'd his skill,
> Then, sometimes, in that silence, while he hung
> Listening, a gentle shock of mild surprise
> Has carried far into his heart the voice
> Of mountain torrents, or the visible scene
> Would enter unawares into his mind
> With all its solemn imagery, its rocks,
> Its woods, and that uncertain heaven, receiv'd
> Into the bosom of the steady lake.[61]

You could say that he puts himself in Joanna's position, becomes a reader of himself by listening to—and wondering at—the laughable mirth he's helped to create. Echoing calls, mockery, "din": the first few lines recall and revise Milton's account of the building of the tower of Babel, along with the laughter it inspired:

> each to other calls
> Not understood, till hoarse, and all in rage,
> As mocked they storm; great laughter was in heaven

And looking down, to see the hubbub strange
And hear the din[62]

Wordsworth had deemed the laughter worthy of remark in his copy of *Paradise Lost*, writing in the margin that "This picture is not consonant to what might be expected from superior beings spectators of such a scene."[63] Making himself the superior yet tender spectator here, he looks down and back at his own mortal folly. And yet, as sky is received into the bosom of the lake, and as both are received into his mind, the rendezvous with water brings Narcissus into view once more. (At the end of his tale Ovid notes that "Even then, when he was received into the abode of the dead, he kept looking at himself in the waters of the Styx."[64]) We are told that the boy of Winander is dead, but the alluring shift of tense ("Has carried," not "Had carried") implies that some part of this lost, echoic life refuses to be laid low.

Deepened subjectivity is registered as a shocked, perplexing rebirth, and for Wordsworth it often stems from a sense of difference amid company, from an awareness of enigmatic, laughing audiences—daffodils, mountains, owls, imagined readers—who nonetheless vouch for his existence. He sinks into the landscape of his mind only as ever-desired Echo partially resists or mocks his skill, and although he sees the steady lake and perhaps sees himself in it, the unbecalmed voice of "torrents" is still present (recall his later comment on those other narcissi: "the very object of my poem is the trouble or agitation both of the flowers and the Water"). Wordsworth is always falling for himself in both senses of that term. He seeks a place that will embody and welcome the self, and he duly arrives at it. But he is never quite himself when he gets there.

Fits

The promises of Poets are like the Perjuries of Lovers, things at which Jove laughs.

LETTER TO LORD LONSDALE[1]

When thinking about what poetry might be and do, Wordsworth is often drawn to reading laughter as a premonition, not merely a response. And if laughable echoes offer him a spur to self-exploration and also a means to emblematize his own demands for poetry in relation to those of his audience, then fits are the vehicles for a more provocative, more visceral testing of boundaries. It's appropriate that he should provide the *OED*'s first instance of the word *fitfully* in the language—in *Descriptive Sketches*, "Fitfully, and in flashes, through his soul, / Like sun-lit tempests, troubled transports roll"—for he is in many ways the poet of troubled transports. *Fit* and associated words lead a double life in his writing. In *The Tuft of Primroses*, the man

in the fitful hours
Of his tranquillity, had not ceas'd to touch
The harp or viol which himself had framed
And fitted to their tasks with perfect skill.[2]

Tranquility is more than simply tranquil ("had not ceas'd to touch" isn't quite frantic, but it does hint at compulsion). The music's fitness is within touching distance of its fitfulness. Elsewhere, Wordsworth delights in how "As in a fit of Thespian jollity, / Beneath her vine-leaf crown the green Earth reels."[3] Dionysian revels peep through that crown, for mother nature is reeling drunk. Anne Carson has spoken of something that "may lie at the heart of Dionysianism for those who worship the god as he wishes to be worshipped: the shock of a possible, entirely other self within you at any moment, a self begun but never performed."[4] In Wordsworth's writing, this self is apprehended as tragicomic thrill, laughable turmoil, unrenounceable possibility.

The second half of this chapter will look closely at one of his strangest fits of passion, but I want first to consider some other conceptions of laughter with which he would have been familiar. Both Wordsworth and Coleridge were drawn to depicting the fitful mood of the laugh as a kind of malfunction of the reasonable. The pilot's boy in *The Rime of the Ancient Mariner* "Who now doth crazy go / Laugh'd loud and long."[5] Elsewhere, when Coleridge recalls how "on entering the public House I fell down in an hysterical Fit with long & loud weeping to my own great metaphysical amusement,"[6] it's hard to say whether the physical or the metaphysical takes precedence. In Wordsworth's early fragments one encounters "half-clad Madness . . . laughing from a blasted tree"[7] or Night laughing "Like a chain'd madman."[8] In "The Three Graves," a ballad he cowrote with Coleridge, a young Edward seeks marriage to Ellen. Her mother Mary, after initially giving her consent, suddenly confesses her own passion for the suitor, and Wordsworth's narrator reports,

> Then Edward started from his seat,
> And he laughed loud and long:
> In truth, good mother, you are mad
> Or drunk with liquor strong[9]

Coleridge commented:

> The Lover's eyes were now opened: and thus taken by surprize, whether from the effect of the horror which he felt, acting as it were hysterically on his nervous system, or that at the first moment he lost the sense of the guilt of the proposal in the feeling of its strangeness and absurdity, he flung her from him and burst into a fit of Laughter.[10]

The laugh may be knee-jerk reaction or dawning realization, physical onset or cognitive recovery. That said, Edward laughed loud *and long*, so the time taken may allow for both options, marking the journey from somatic response to cerebral processing. Whatever the exact reason for the laugh (it's noteworthy that Edward might, in laughing, have lost a "sense of guilt"), Mary isn't the only one here who appears mad or intoxicated. The laugher echoes the laughee.

In the Aristotelian tradition, *Homo ridens* is distinguished from the animals by the fact that he can laugh. As the first edition of the *Encyclopedia Britannica* noted in 1771, laughter is "an affection peculiar to mankind". Yet the second edition of 1780 spoke of "animal-laughter . . . from the gentle impulse excited in a child by moderate joy, to that terrifying and even mortal convulsion which has been known to accompany a change of fortune." As affection, the laugh tells of human achievement and agency; as convulsion, it recalls us to our predicaments or afflictions. And, as the *Encyclopedia* suggests, the laugh may signal health or danger. Wordsworth had read in David Hartley's *Observations on Man* that laughing "nervous persons" verge on madness (or, at least, indulge in an activity that "greatly disqualifies their understandings for the search after truth"). Yet laughter could also have positive effects; besides offering relaxation, Hartley notes, it "has a tendency to remove many prejudices from custom and education."[11] Other lines of inquiry were pursued in Kant's discussion of laughter, a translation of which Wordsworth read in the *Monthly Magazine* in 1796.[12] Laughter here is "merely corporeal, although it is aroused by ideas of the mind":

> In everything that is to provoke a lively, uproarious laughter, there must be something nonsensical (in which, therefore, the understanding in itself can take no satisfaction). . . . [Laughter is] a movement that is conducive to health, which alone, and not what goes on in the mind, is the real cause of gratification in a thought that at bottom represents nothing.

Laughter, he concludes, is therefore "*animal.*"[13] Yet can a pleasure be "merely" corporeal when it is aroused by ideas, and do laughable thoughts themselves represent "nothing"? For Wordsworth and for others in his circle, these questions were not yet settled.

The poet's early depiction of laughter in *Descriptive Sketches* had alluded to Erasmus Darwin's *The Loves of the Plants*, and the translator of Kant's discussion in the *Monthly* was Thomas Beddoes.[14] Early in 1798, Wordsworth wrote to his publisher asking for a copy of Darwin's *Zoonomia* "*by the first carrier,*" citing "very particular reasons" for doing so.[15] In that book, Darwin reads laughter as a series of "reiterated screams":

> Every combination of ideas, which we attend to, occasions pain or pleasure . . . unmixed pleasure, if it be great, becomes painful, like all other animal motions from stimuli of every kind; and if no other exertions are occasioned at the same time, we use the exertion of laughter to relieve this pain. . . .
>
> The pleasurable sensations, which occasion laughter, are perpetually passing into the bounds of pain; for pleasure and pain are often produced by different degrees of the same stimulus; as warmth, light, aromatic or volatile odours, become painful by their excess. . . . When the pleasurable ideas, which excite us to laugh, pass into pain, we use some exertion, such as a scream, to relieve the pain, but soon stop it again, as we are unwilling to lose the pleasure; and thus we repeatedly begin to scream, and stop again alternately. So that in laughter there are three stages, first of pleasure, then pain, then an exertion to relieve that pain.[16]

This is almost as dizzying and agonizing as a good laugh. The experience is first envisaged as a safety valve, but things are then complicated by a sense that laughter is an accompaniment to pleasure, not simply a regulation of it. So the laugh is a rhythmic hybrid of pleasure and pain, a composite of passionate irruption and controlling mechanism.

These ideas became subject to testing. Coleridge reported: "Both I & Mrs Coleridge have carefully watched our little one and noted down all the circumstances . . . under which he laughed for the first six times—nor have we remitted our attention—but I have not been able to derive the least confirmation of Hartley's or Darwin's Theory."[17] One can imagine a disgruntled Darwin calling for a larger data set (Coleridge would in fact come to support the thesis),[18] but the theory was important to Wordsworth less for what it definitively confirmed than for what it allowed him to see and say about the life of his poetry. Here is a celebrated passage from the Preface to *Lyrical Ballads* (the section in square brackets was added in 1802):

> The end of Poetry is to produce excitement in coexistence with an overbalance of pleasure. Now, by the supposition, excitement is an unusual and irregular state of the mind; ideas and feelings do not in that state succeed each other in accustomed order. But if the words by which this excitement is produced are in themselves powerful, or the images and feelings have an undue proportion of pain connected with them, there is some danger that the excitement may be carried beyond its proper bounds. Now the co-presence of something regular, something to which the mind has been accustomed when in an unexcited or a less excited state, cannot but have great efficacy in tempering and restraining the passion by an intertexture of ordinary feeling, [and of feeling not strictly and necessarily connected with the passion. This is unquestionably true; and hence, though the opinion will at first appear paradoxical, from the tendency of metre to divest language, in a certain degree, of its reality, and thus to throw a sort of half-consciousness of unsubstantial existence over the whole composition, there can be little doubt but that more pathetic situations and sentiments, that is, those which have a greater proportion of pain connected with them, may be endured in metrical composition, especially in rhyme, than in prose.][19]

Darwin figured laughter as both release and restraint, a means of indulging in pleasure as well as of curbing it. Wordsworth sees metrical form as an analogous force: it assists and heightens passion (he says later that meter may "greatly contribute to impart passion to the words"), but it can also act to temper it.[20] For the scientist, "unmixed pleasure, if it be great, becomes painful," so "we use the exertion of laughter to relieve this pain"; for the poet, an overbalance of pleasure may lead to an excitement that could include "an undue proportion of pain." Meter is called in to steady the ship.

Laughing fits and poetic fits, then, enable people to bear their feelings, yet both types of fit are themselves painful pleasures. Darwin noted that people had expired from laughter while also claiming that others had "died instantaneously from the painful excess of joy, which probably might have been prevented by the exertions of laughter."[21] To laugh or not to laugh? Subsequent work at the Pneumatic Institute, informed by Brunonian medical theory and by Darwin's monistic account of the mind and body as a continuum, led Beddoes and Humphry Davy to experiment with nitrous oxide as a stimulant that would bring patients into "healthy" equilibrium. Beddoes reported that subjects who inhaled the gas were "compelled to laugh, not by any ludicrous idea, but by an impulse unconnected with thought, and similar to that which is felt by children full of health and spirits."[22] Yet as both Beddoes and Davy conceded, the gas wasn't always therapeutic (one subject cried and laughed alternately before relapsing into a hysterical fit).[23] There was doubt about whether the apparently thoughtless laughing body should be left to its own devices—and something similar could be said of poetic bodies of thought.

Coleridge would argue in *Biographia Literaria* that the effects of meter were like that of "a medicated atmosphere," but he also noted that meter should betoken presence of mind as well as body: "There must be not only a partnership, but a union; an interpenetration of passion and of will, of *spontaneous* impulse and of *voluntary* purpose."[24] Wordsworth's comments on meter are shadowed by related concerns. When claiming that the chief cause of pleasure to be obtained from metrical language is "the perception of similitude in dissimilitude," he observes that the principle is "the great spring of the activity of our minds and their chief feeder," but he adds that "From this principle the direction of the sexual appetite, and all the passions connected with it take their origin."[25] Sometimes he reads meter as a sign of artifice and order, as creator and corollary of reflective thought, and at other times as the embodiment of the spontaneous, the organic—an expression of the natural language of instinctive feeling.[26] In his later Preface to *Poems* (1815), he observes,

> Poems . . . cannot read themselves; the law of long syllable and short must not be so inflexible,—the letter of metre must not be so impassive to the spirit of versification,—as to deprive the Reader of a voluntary power to modulate, in subordination to the sense, the music of the poem;—in the same manner as his mind is left at liberty, and even summoned, to act upon its thoughts and images.[27]

The letter of metrical law is to the spirit of versification as body is to mind: the former exerts pressure on the latter while not necessarily circumscribing, complementing, or controlling its operations. Modulated versification is, in effect, the action of the mind on sense impression. Yet the question arises as to whether either a poem or a body is entirely at the behest of voluntary power. For a mind to be left at liberty is not the same thing as its being *summoned* to act. Summoned by whom? Or, more pointedly, by what?

This theorizing is complicated by poems that depict (and, as we shall later see, those that may arouse) laughable experiences. To return briefly to "The Three Graves,"

> Then Edward started from his seat,
> And he laughed loud and long:[28]

"Laughed" is officially unstressed; obeying the letter of metrical law, we hear, "And **he** laughed **loud** and **long**." Yet *laugh* nearly always appears in a stressed position in Wordsworth's poetry, and the weight of the word, along with the accompanying alliterative pattern, prompts us to modulate the sound: "And he **laughed loud** and **long**." To go with the former option is to stress the volition of the act by stressing the pronoun (Edward is just that little bit more in control of himself); to go with the latter is to accentuate the sense that his laughter is instinctual. To feel the pull of both options is to feel the tussle between a mind-body at liberty to act and a body-mind that has been summoned to act. Edward laughed as he "started" from his seat; the verb's primary sense is "to rise suddenly . . . to stand up," but the *OED*'s other definition is pertinent: "to undergo a sudden *involuntary* movement of the body, resulting from surprise, fright, sudden pain, etc." So he started as he laughed: the movement was made *by* him, but it also happens *to* him. The fits and starts of agency are being apprehended through the tissue of physiology.

If prosody is one means of exploring relations between poetical and corporeal fits, other aspects of Beddoes's and Davy's experiments suggest broader analogies. After trying nitrous oxide in Bristol in the Autumn of 1799, Coleridge left to visit Wordsworth in the Lakes. He stayed in contact with Davy, and his comments on the effects of the gas were printed in Davy's study, *Researches, Chemical and Philosophical, Chiefly Concerning Nitrous Oxide*, published in the summer of 1800. Coleridge acted as an enthusiastic agent for the book, and during the period he was advising Wordsworth on the composition of the Preface, he wrote to the chemist offering further reflections.[29] Wordsworth read Davy's book, and during the second half of 1800 Davy became the main proofreader for the second edition of *Lyrical*

Ballads.[30] Alongside the testimony of others who had tried nitrous oxide, the chemist detailed his own sensation: initial laughter was followed by a state in which "voluntary power was altogether destroyed. . . . I existed in a world of newly connected and newly modified ideas."[31] Many described an experience in which volition was suspended even as they received an invigorated feeling of "vital power"; subjects were not able to say *why* they laughed but instead how they felt *as* they laughed. Searching for a suitable analogy, one said that "I felt like the sound of a harp"; another claimed that his feelings "resembled those produced . . . by reading a sublime passage in poetry."[32]

One person's sublime is another's ridiculous, and sceptics took to poetry itself in order to mock the apparent nonsense spoken by those under the influence: "thy living beverage whilst I quaff, / I laugh—ha, ha—yet know not why I laugh."[33] Davy acknowledged that many who tried nitrous oxide "appeared ludicrous to those around,"[34] but he also pointed out that the current state of the language of feeling was a constraining factor on the public reception of his experiments. "When pleasure and pains are new or connected with new ideas," he explained, "they can never be intelligibly detailed unless associated during their existence with terms standing for analogous feelings."[35] Laughing gas, by helping individuals to push against the limits of the sayable, created fresh opportunities for apprehending new patterns of feeling—or new relations between old ones. When Davy read in Wordsworth's Preface of poetic "experiments," of the poet's expectation that some readers would experience "a more than common pleasure," and of the main purpose of the volume ("to illustrate the manner in which our feelings and ideas are associated in a state of excitement"), he would have noted parallels with his own research.[36] Like Davy, Wordsworth conceded the risky nature of the associative outbursts that such experiments entailed: "I have no doubt that in some instances feelings even of the ludicrous may be given to my Readers by expressions which appeared to me tender and pathetic."[37] The effects of a lyrical ballad, like those of laughing gas, could make you feel giddy.

*

Imagine an exquisitely beautiful night, bathed in moonshine. A man travels alone in a pleasurable trance, feeling for a moment a sensation "so intense and pure as to absorb existence," which then modulates into a state between "sleeping and waking." He feels a little ridiculous (at one point he tries to explain to a bystander what he's experienced), but, well, there it is—the thing happened. That is a compressed account of Davy's night walk under the influence of nitrous oxide.[38] And now imagine another scene:

Strange fits of passion I have known,
And I will dare to tell,
But in the lover's ear alone,
What once to me befel.

When she I lov'd, was strong and gay
And like a rose in June,
I to her cottage bent my way,
Beneath the evening moon.

Upon the moon I fix'd my eye,
All over the wide lea;
My horse trudg'd on, and we drew nigh
Those paths so dear to me.

And now we reach'd the orchard-plot,
And, as we climb'd the hill,
Towards the roof of Lucy's cot
The moon descended still.

In one of those sweet dreams I slept,
Kind Nature's gentlest boon!
And, all the while, my eyes I kept
On the descending moon.

My horse mov'd on; hoof after hoof
He rais'd and never stopp'd:
When down behind the cottage roof
At once the planet dropp'd.

What fond and wayward thoughts will slide
Into a Lover's head—
"O mercy!" to myself I cried,
"If Lucy should be dead!"[39]

Even before the scandalous reveal (or nonreveal) of last two lines, the behavior of the language is odd. The transition from dreamy talk of "the evening moon . . . the descending moon" to the anatomical coolness of "planet" makes the moon more alien, heavier somehow, turns it from balladic-Romantic backdrop into something with a life of its own. And then there's the shift from the abruptness of "At once the planet dropp'd" to the insinuating drift of "will slide." For a moony, moonstruck lover, the speed with which a guiding light disappears could well spark thoughts about what else might suddenly vanish, but "slide" slows down the mental event, makes the idea seep into the lover's headspace in an unusually visceral way. It's not simply the thought itself that is strange but the manner in which it is felt to arrive.

"And there the poem ends!" exclaimed Francis Jeffrey. For him, as for others, the ending was typical of the "grotesque masquerade habit" of Wordsworth's speakers and of their creator's "wilful aberrations from ordinary nature."[40] Willful, no doubt, but aberrations occur *within* the ordinary (the shock of something suddenly imagined can be just as physically awful—sometimes more so—as the reaction to its really happening). In any case, one suspects that Jeffrey's real gripe is with Wordsworth's refusal to round his poem off, his unwillingness to provide guidance on how we are meant to take it, as though it were a joke without a punchline. Yet Wordsworth didn't think his poems precluded laughter; he was in fact quite certain that they could inspire it. An early version of the poem that he sent to Coleridge contained a final stanza after the speaker's pronouncement:

> I told her this; her laughter light
> Is ringing in my ears;
> And when I think upon that night
> My eyes are dim with tears.[41]

This casts eerie light on the published version. In *Paradise Lost*, Milton had spoken of those "That laugh, as if transported with some fit / Of passion,"[42] and a *fit* may be "a violent access or outburst of laughter" as well as "a part or section of a poem," "paroxysm of lunacy," or "capricious impulse" (*OED*). Wordsworth composed the first draft of the poem in Germany a week or two after he had purchased *Reliques of Ancient English Poetry*, in which Percy had included a long note on *fit*: "a FIT of mirth" was provided by the old minstrels, and the word at one time "peculiarly signified the pause, or breathing-time, between the several parts" of poems; it meant not only "a sense of ridicule or sarcasm" but "a poetic strain."[43] With these meanings and with the ending of the first version in mind, Lucy's laughter itself becomes one of the strange fits of passion the speaker has known. Indeed, the speaker has *known* it, not simply *felt* it.

Superiority theorists of laughter would no doubt claim that Lucy is laughing it off, or laughing at the narrator: it's a mark of her cool assurance that she can take his odd pronouncements so lightly. Incongruity theorists might feel that she's laughing at the unexpectedness of it: did her lover tell her his fears immediately upon arrival rather than opening with a more conventional gambit by saying how much he's missed her? But when heard alongside the inquiries of Darwin, Beddoes, and Davy, Lucy's laugh resonates more strangely. She handles the lover's confession with a response that betokens both pleasure and pain; if her laugh could speak, it might whisper "You say the sweetest things," and also "How could you even think such a thing?" Her fit of passion—like his fond, wayward thought—signals both the strength and the fragility of their partnership. His thought is in fact a prelude to the rhythms of her laughter, because his excess of pleasure in loving her is the very thing that disrupts that pleasure.

I think Wordsworth's decision to cut these lines was his way of trusting to the implicit provocations of his poetic form and to the incongruous, laughable feelings they could encourage. Some of these feelings can be sensed before the end of the poem is reached, partly through the way in which fits of meter play with our expectations as they go about embodying and exploring the nature of passion. Paul Fry has offered a sensitive reading of the metronomic aspect of meter in Wordsworth—its "hoof-after-hoof"-ness—as a mark of a blessed return to the nonhuman inside the human, a return to a thinghood we have in common with all being. Wordsworth, he suggests, "invests the unreflecting time-keeping of consciousness in the regular movement of hoofed animals," and meter assists and embodies a "hypnosis that cancels difference."[44] Certainly, the onward trudging of the horse in "Strange fits of passion" appears to be tied to the speaker's trance, to the side of him that's in touch with automatism, yet the meter isn't ever wholly metronomic or mechanical; it contains hints of other ways of hearing—and being.

Percy's sense of the fit as "the pause, or breathing-time, between the several parts" finds echoes elsewhere in Wordsworth (he speaks of "fits of silence / Impelled to livelier pace,"[45] and of how "Many a stop and stay he makes, / Many a breathing fit he takes"[46]). In this poem, the life of the fit as caesura both threatens and enlivens meter:

> And now we reach'd the orchard-plot,
> <u>And,</u> as we climb'd the hill
> . . . .
> <u>And,</u> all the while, my eyes I kept
> On the descending moon.

The commas after *And* were not present in the original manuscript, but Wordsworth added them for the first published version. They half disrupt the iambic tread, tempt us to stress *And*, yet the sound of raised expectations is not fulfilled, acting rather as a premonition of the blend of climax and bathos at the poem's close. A dialogue between narrator and reader might be imagined:

> "***And***, as we climbed the hill . . ."
> "Yes, yes, *and what*?"

"Oh, the moon descended still."

. . . .

"***And***, all the while . . ."
"Ah, yes—go on, go on."
"Oh, just what I've already said; I kept looking at the moon."

Even if we follow the meter to the letter of the law, we are not simply sucked into a trance but into the fits and starts of trance itself: "And, all the while, my eyes I kept / On **the** descending moon." To preserve the meter, *the*—long e, not short—is required, but this feels a little laughable. (Invoking Henri Bergson's theory of laughter, we could say that too stringent an adherence to meter is sometimes the herald of the comic because we sense that meter has been encrusted onto voice as "something mechanical is encrusted onto the living."[47]) The line sounds hypnotized, sunken into a sort of rapt distractedness, initially as far from the desirous as one might wish. But given that in this lunatic lover's head the shining moon is associated with Lucy (her name, from *luce*, means light), what is intimated is the way in which the sex drive can be read as the mark of the mechanical from within the human; the movement of the horse and the sight of the moon are driving the speaker to distraction in both senses of that phrase. One may prolong anticipation, make delay itself an element of one's desiring, and comedy frequently takes notice of the fact that—unlike most animals—humans enjoy their appetites not simply as necessities but as luxuries. Man's desire makes him creaturely, but his willingness to play with desire makes him something else entirely.

Sex is comedy. The prime mover of this poem—the figure on horseback—is part of a long, frequently comic tradition of knight-errantry and errancy (from Cervantes and Sterne to Burns and Burger and beyond) in which the horse signifies the beast within and the horseman the control of that beast. As Cowley observed in a discussion of voluptuous men and "all the *et caetera* of their passions": "If I want skill or force to restrain the Beast that I ride upon . . . I am at that time rather his Man, than he my Horse."[48] When subject to strange fits of passion, Wordsworth sometimes thought of such things and found them tangled up in dreams of how lovers might feel when apart. Take this letter to his wife:

> Last night I *suffered*; and this morning I tremble with sensations that almost overpower me . . . and Thou most probably art thinking of me and losing all sense of the motion of the horse that bears thee, in the tenderness and strength of thy conceptions and wishes, and remembrances. . . . find the evidence of what is passing within me in *thy* heart, in thy mind, in thy steps . . . in thy limbs as they are stretched upon the soft earth; in thy own involuntary sighs

> and ejaculations, in the trembling of thy hands, in the tottering of thy knees, in the blessings which thy lips pronounce, find it in thy lips themselves, and such kisses as I often give to the empty air, and in the aching of thy bosom, and let a voice speak for me in every thing within thee and without thee. . . . Ah Mary I must turn my pen from this course.[49]

The stretching, sighing, trembling, tottering, and all the *et caetera* of the passions might be laughable for any reader who wasn't in the mood—or who wasn't inclined to get into it. When Mary loses all sense of motion of the horse that bears her, it need not be supposed that she has nothing on her mind—or, rather, that other things aren't brought to mind. The picture is what Wordsworth imagines of and for her as well as what he needs from her (his "most probably" is delicious), and it's also his way of daring to murmur, under cover of projection, in the lover's ear alone ("find the evidence of what is passing within me in *thy* heart"). One is tempted to say more—and wary of saying too much. Perhaps he's relishing the idea of their both alternately taking up the position of horse and rider.

*

"Strange fits of passion," I'm suggesting, is conceived as a serious comedy of desire, a study of the links between the amorous and the absurd as passion gets played out between mind and body, semantics and sound effects, the fitted and the fitful. And the poem becomes blacker, and more bewilderingly laughable, as other stops, stays, and breathing fits are registered. "When she I lov'd, was strong and gay"; "lov'd" (not "love"), accentuated by that strangely placed comma, is suggestive. The speaker could mean that Lucy is in fact dead and buried now, or merely dead to him. Just before composing the poem, Wordsworth read "A lover of Late" in Percy's *Reliques*, and some parts of it—"I sighed and sobbed, and cryed, alas! / For her that laught, and called me ass"—may have prompted the ending of his first version. Percy's narrator ends by bracing himself against such humiliation and even seems to glory in a newfound power: "The asse Ile leave to her disdain; / And now I am myselfe againe."[50] "Strange fits of passion" contains flashes of this feeling, for while the poem appears to relive as well as to recount the fearful thought of losing Lucy, it could also be a laying to rest, and even a kind of boast:

> Strange fits of passion **I** have known,
> And **I** will dare to tell,
> But in the lover's ear alone,
> What once to **me** befel.

At no other point in the poem is *I* placed in a stressed position. Here, the emphatic pronouns set the thing going with a vigorous narratorial swagger ("Me, well . . . *I've* known some things in *my* time; do I dare tell 'em? You bet I dare"). Like laughter, metrical pulse is not simply the mark of possession but the medium of self-possession—or the dream of such control. I can imagine the narrator laughing as he begins and ends his tale (the story needn't be read with the gravity of an Ancient Mariner; it could just as well be read with the twisted gusto of a Long John Silver). There's a gleeful, conspiratorial relishing of power in "What once to me be**fel**," for maybe the narrator is chuckling to himself as he ventures a pun on that last word, a pun to which listeners can't yet be privy, for we have not yet encountered the planet dropping behind the house. And then there's the stress on *once*, as though to say, "It happened *once*, but I conquered it and put it behind me. That's why I love to tell the tale. Now, if you think you can handle it, listen in." "And I will dare to tell" is another way of saying "And now I am myselfe againe."

Hearing the poem like this, something else emerges from its closing confession: "'O mercy!' to myself I cried, / 'If Lucy should be dead!'" *To myself*: this initially sounds like padding, for who else was there to cry to? Maybe his concern about her is blended with, or even engulfed by, his shady attraction to what the thought says about him. A couple of years earlier, Coleridge had written a sonnet beginning "Oft o'er my brain does that strange fancy roll," which depicted something similar:

> O my sweet baby! when I reach my door,
> If heavy looks should tell me thou art dead,
> (As sometimes, through excess of hope, I fear)[51]

A few months after reading "Strange fits of passion," Coleridge wondered whether such feelings told of more than merely an excess of hope. In a letter to Poole, while speaking of his closeness to Wordsworth, he offered a daring disclosure:

> Hartley, my *only* child!—Dear Lamb! I hope, *he* won't be dead, before I get home.—There are moments in which I have such a power of Life within me, such a conceit of it, I mean—that I lay the Blame of my Child's Death to my absence—*not intellectually*; but I have a strange sort of sensation, as if while I was present, none could die whom I intensely loved.[52]

This strange sensation animates Wordsworth's poem. To revel in your own power is to tempt fate, which is no doubt why the lover calls for mercy: the thought makes him feel guilty. But, in addition, if you take exorbitant pleasure in your own power of life, others may feel the same about theirs; will you—or something in you—die when they decide to take their absence from you or when you cease to be intensely loved by them? Like "Strange fits of passion," Coleridge's words register the piercing and enervating power of narcissism. De Quincey observed in another context that "It is delightful to call up what we know to be a mere mimicry of evil, in order to feel its non-reality; to dally with phantoms of pain that do not exist."[53] For Wordsworth's speaker to imagine that Lucy could be dead is to excite himself, to toy with what he can dream up—and to get a kick from what he can face down.

In "Retro," before letting the poem end in laughter, John Ashbery observes,

> It's really quite a thrill
> when the moon rises above the hill
> and you've gotten over someone
> salty and mercurial, the only person you ever loved.[54]

The moon now rises rather than descends, as though the speaker has gone through "Strange fits of passion" and come out the other side. But the rueful humor of Ashbery's lines captures both the delight of getting over someone and the sense that the delight may be a kind of repression, or a kind of loss. It sees Wordsworth's poem through the looking glass, hearing the laughter that originally lay behind it and that lies buried within it, for whether gearing up for or getting over a lover, desire will spring ludicrous surprises. Wordsworth's narrator began by saying that he would speak in the lover's ear alone, so if we use only our ears, not our eyes, if we imagine ourselves back into the founding moment of the balladic (and also the lyrical) and permit ourselves simply to listen to the poem as read aloud, we may be in for another surprise:

> "O mercy to myself" I cried,
> "If Lucy should be dead!"

It could be a mercy to him if she *were* dead; then he'd be free of his enticing but unbearable longing, his sense of dependency. In his translation of Kant's discussion of laughter, Beddoes included Kant's aside that the "animal or bodily" feeling of laughter was itself "not pleasure, but self-esteem, which raises us above the want of pleasure."[55] When heard, Wordsworth's lines allow for a flicker of this feeling—"'O mercy to my**self**' I cried"—by hinting at the self's tragicomic need to get rid of needing. The poem mutters under its breath of the animosity inside strong affection, tells of a fantasy in which one does away with desire by doing away with the object of desire.

Rather than scoffing at the teller of the tale, one early reviewer confessed, "perhaps every mind has, at one time or other, and probably more than once, felt this undefinable and unaccountable suggestion, both sudden and transitory, of a superstitious presentiment of calamity from some such trivial occurrence."[56] The slide from *perhaps* to *probably* (and from "at one time" to "more than once") suggests that the poem is surreptitiously working its magic. To have *known* such strange fits of passion (in the carnal sense, as well as others), to have let this knowledge befall us once more, is to have fulfilled one of Wordsworth's hopes for his writing, which is "to remind men of their knowledge, as it lurks inoperative and unvalued in their own minds."[57] It *lurks* because of our vested interest in seeing the uncomfortable as the unvaluable, and it is lurking, too, in one of Coleridge's notebook entries: "laughter . . . a little convulsive motion to get rid of pleasure rising into pain / —this worthy of further Thought / —Love—*Desire*.'[58] The first comment leans on Darwin, but Wordsworth's poem contains the further thought required to show how "Love—*Desire*" may have a rendezvous to keep with the laughable. If *Love* is the mind's word, *Desire* is the body's, and debates between mind and body about whether the words are closer to being synonyms or antonyms can generate an uneasy comedy. It is these confluences of pleasure and pain that frequently propel Wordsworth's writing: as an attraction toward strange fits of self-fulfillment and self-sabotage (laughs, passions, poems); as a need to experience and to anatomize such fits; and as a wish to pass them on to readers as an unnerving bequest.

The precise nature of that bequest—or, rather, the imprecise nature of it—may be felt by taking one last look at the final stanza of the first version:

> I told her this; her laughter light
> Is ringing in my ears;
> And when I think upon that night
> My eyes are dim with tears.

When wondering what possessed him to tell her this, we may also wonder what that telling did to her. Could he now be regretting his decision? Perhaps her laugh was pathological and fits turned to fitting. As Darwin would have put it, she may have "expired from immoderate laughter"—or, as Wordsworth would have put it, she began "Laughing, laughing, laughing, / As if she would laugh herself dead."[59] The speaker's own fears and desires could have come to fruition through the very recounting of them. From Demeter's laughter at the antics of Baubo, to Sarah's laughter in Genesis and beyond, feminine laughter has long been linked to sexual surges as well as to creative urges.[60] So, among other consummations devoutly or devilishly to be wished, the poem hints at a *petite mort.* Satirists of Davy's experiments implied that his gas led to scenes of hysteria and sexual debauchery, and research into the laughing body's effect on the mind was conducted alongside studies that considered movements in the opposite direction.[61] As Gavin Budge has observed, "the pervasive somatisation of mental processes in Darwin's philosophical medicine only accentuated the imagination's potential to be implicated in bodily disorder and cure,"[62] a potential in which Wordsworth and Coleridge took considerable interest.[63] *Zoonomia* featured case studies of those who had died as a result of being seized by a delusion or an "insane idea," and at the end of "The Three Graves," Edward's hysterical laughter became contagious. The final stanza (written by Coleridge) notes "Then Ellen shrieked, and forthwith burst / Into ungentle laughter." The pause at the line end is grotesquely, laughably brilliant; Ellen simply "burst." The more ungentle the laughter, the less likely you are to survive it. Corpsing indeed.

When poetry is conceived as a Brunonian stimulant and curative medium, what might be said for laughable poetry—writing that depicts, embodies, and inspires wayward fits of passion? Beddoes would come to stress the pathogenic potential of thoughts—particularly imaginative or literary thoughts—by asking

> Who has not found how much the ideas of the mind influence bodily members? . . . Tendency to miscarriage, and even dropsy of the ovarium, may be caught from the furniture of a circulating library. . . . The juvenile library! With submission I must consider it little better than a repository of poisons. What acrimonies will it not engender in the habit? What obstructions in the body?[64]

One can dissent from the assumptions that feed these particular fears ("Women and small children are such delicate, nervous creatures, are they not?") without dismissing the broader point, and both Coleridge and Wordsworth were sympathetic to such arguments (Coleridge is credited by the *OED* for the invention of the word *psychosomatic*).[65] All of which brings an extra turn of the screw: if it can be dangerous to hear—as well as to utter—confessions like those ventured in "Strange fits of passion," then Wordsworth's decision to drop the last stanza and to add a new opening in which the speaker whispers sweet nothings in the reader's ear (rather than in Lucy's) is all the more intriguing. If we continue to listen, a lover is what we are, which raises a question about what is now to happen to us, his latest passion.

According to one cultural historian, Davy's experiments at the Pneumatic Institute "showed that emotion *might have no moral purpose at all.*"[66] Whether they quite *showed* this is debatable. Even so, it's worth recalling the satire in *The Prelude* on the man who always laughs "With apt and graceful laughter"—a man, he drolly adds, of whom it might be said: "briefly, the moral part / Is perfect."[67] Wordsworth is not interested in perfect morals or apt laughs—both things, for him, are monstrosities because they are not creaturely enough. And if we conceive ourselves as stand-ins (or replacements) for the endangered, laughing Lucy, we may entertain the possibility of a poet who warms to the idea that his writing might be bad for us—or bad for the part of us that only wishes to be thought good. "Strange fits of passion" does not quite know where it stands on passion, which is what makes it such a characteristic example of the strangeness, and the peril, of Wordsworthian fun, for it seems to conceive its reader as accomplice and as antagonist, as beloved and as quarry. "We make others real only by imagining them; both the lover and the murderer know this."[68] So does the poet—along with those who read him with a taste for the enlighteningly and darkly laughable. We can persist in imagining for ourselves a safely ennobling Wordsworth if we want, but the man who speaks of "the strong creative power / Of human passion"[69] knows, too, of passion's weaknesses, its all-too-human cravings, its decreative delights. As he confesses in *The Prelude*, "The Poet, gentle creature as he is, / Hath, like the Lover, his unruly times; / His fits when he is neither sick nor well."[70]

Pains

dear delicious pain
"SONNET, on seeing Miss Helen Maria
Williams weep at a Tale of Distress"[1]

"Strange fits of passion" allows the comedy of errors to be shadowed by a comedy of terrors, and its creator values the uncertainty raised in a reader's mind about whether he is sick or well—or some combination of both. When Wordsworth sent the poem to Coleridge, he spoke of it as something "which I hope will amuse you."[2] He declined to spell out the nature of this amusement, but I think it's related to his glee at bending a story about an allegedly perverse passion into a means of exploring the perversity *of* passion. The ballad is characteristic of that side of him that takes pleasure in how what is deemed merely inappropriate can be revealed as uncanny, and this pleasure is taken to new heights (or depths) when he focuses on other losses both imagined and endured. If echoes dally with the laughable, and if fits consort with it, what might pains do? Turning now to Wordsworth's renowned interest in suffering, I want to suggest that even here (*especially* here) he is willing to risk an odd kind of humor—and to have a curious kind of fun.

Sometimes, in fact, he appears almost brazenly casual. "By the bye," he wrote to Walter Scott in 1806, "you will not be displeased to find that you and I have, as I understand, fallen upon the same subject; the melancholy catastrophe of the Man and the Dog in the Coves of Helvellyn. What a happy day we had together there! I often think of it with delight."[3] The story of the man who fell to his death didn't come between Wordsworth and his pleasure that day, nor did it stop him "falling upon" the subject for poetic purposes. His poem "Fidelity" introduces the scene with a flourish:

There, sometimes does a leaping Fish
Send through the Tarn a lonely chear;
The Crags repeat the Raven's croak,
In symphony austere[4]

"To call the noise of a fish leaping 'a lonely chear,' is certainly an absurdity," exclaimed Lucy Aikin, which makes you wonder what she made of the decision to rhyme *chear* with *austere*.[5] It's as though the narrator and the inhabitants of the world he depicts haven't yet decided whether the carnage is to be read as tragedy or comedy. Is the poet a Raven or a Fish? Does he feed on corpses (the remains of the fallen man—"a human skeleton"—appear in the next stanza), or does he leap at the chance to rise above it all? Hazlitt may have been having a little fun with Aikin (and with Wordsworth) when he later wrote that fish

> are the gravest of all animals and the quietest withal. True, they may now and then make a frolic leap out of the water; but then they are like Englishmen at a carnival—they are out of their element. What can be graver that a cod's head and shoulders? What are you laughing at, Monsieur?[6]

A comic Wordsworth may well be a fish out of water, but something about agony brought out the absurdist in him.

A critic for *The Eclectic Review* noted that Wordsworth's "gravity is often so facetious, and his humour is so often grave, that we have been at a loss to know whether to take him as in jest or in earnest."[7] Even if you take him in jest and laugh along, you might still be at a loss. During the eighteenth century, superiority and incongruity theorists alike tended to read laughter as a transitive force—as ridicule aimed at an object, or as amusement at some perceived incongruity within it. But the poets were becoming interested in the phenomenology of laughter and in readings of the laugh itself as an incongruity. From this perspective, the laughing person embodies as well as observes a strange combination. "Excess of sorrow laughs," Blake proclaims, while Shelley senses that "Our sincerest laughter / With some pain is fraught," and Keats notes that "while we are laughing the seed of some trouble is put into the wide arable of events."[8] "*Some* pain" and "*some* trouble" are pained, troubling approximations. Not only does laughter interrupt speech, it also makes it hard for laughers to put their feelings into words once they have recovered their sobriety. "Why did I laugh tonight? No voice will tell," Keats's sonnet begins; "I say, why did I laugh? O mortal pain!"[9] What, he seems to be asking, does laughter want?

Pains do not preclude pleasures. As Kant noted in his reflections on laughter, "a deep pain can still please the one who suffers it."[10] When compiling a selection of poetry for Lady Lowther in 1819, Wordsworth extracted a passage from George Wither's *The Shepherd's Hunting* that imagined "blackest discontents" as "pleasing ornaments," and he also admired Margaret Cavendish's *Mirth and Melancholy*, in which Melancholy is said to delight in croaking frogs, hoarse ravens, shrieking owls, "The tolling bell, which for the dead rings out; / A mill, where rushing waters run about."[11] "Very noticeable," Wordsworth commented, "no person could have hit upon that union of images without being possessed of true poetic feeling."[12] The unexpected brio of those rushing waters (they don't just run, but "run about") makes Melancholy suddenly less stodgy than expected. Wordsworth knew true poetic feeling by its ability to perceive connections between moods ordinarily regarded as distinct, and—as so often—it was Coleridge who provided inspiration.

In the early days of their friendship, when Wordsworth was "very fond of C. laughing at all his jokes & taking all opportunities of shewing him off,"[13] Coleridge tended to show off (and show up) what he referred to as the "fantastic wantonness of woe."[14] If, as Horace Walpole claimed, "this world is a comedy to those that think, a tragedy to those that feel," then Coleridge's poems read like tragicomedies: "Thou bleedest, my poor Heart! and thy distress / Reasoning I ponder with a scornful smile."[15] Elsewhere, he marks a "tear, slow travelling on its way" as it "Fills up the wrinkles of a silent laugh— / In that sweet mood of sad and humorous thought."[16] He writes to remove himself a little (but only a little) from his suffering; a letter in hexameters to Wordsworth and Dorothy in December 1798 asks them to "Read with a nod of the head in a humouring recitativo" as they are treated to a rendition of his ailments: "Every thought is worn *down*,—I am weary, yet cannot be vacant. / Five long hours I have tossed, rheumatic heats, dry and flushing."[17] It sounds like a parody of "Tintern Abbey," for five long hours is hardly the length of five long winters, and "I am weary" isn't quite the heavy and weary weight of all this unintelligible world.[18]

Such humorings of pain help to make Coleridge a delightfully conflicted parodist of the woebegotten. In *Biographia Literaria* he recalls that he was the first to expose (with "*risu honesto*") the sins most likely to beset a young writer; as "Nehemiah Higgenbottom," he composed a sonnet that "had for its object to excite a good-natured laugh at the spirit of *doleful egotism*" ("Oh *my poor heart's* INEXPLICABLE SWELL!" the speaker intones).[19] Thomas Love Peacock had these mergers of the lamentable and the laughable in his sights when he had Mr Flosky explain in *Nightmare Abbey* that "It is the fashion to be unhappy . . . the art of being miserable, for misery's sake, has been brought to great perfection in our days."[20] The fashion had a name—Sensibility—yet the art of genteel sorrow it bred was not unaware of its potential for comedy. The exponents of the sentimental mode were its earliest parodists: when Sterne says of *A Sentimental Journey* that it "shall make you cry as much as ever it made me laugh,"[21] he is pointing up the instability of tone in the book itself, and when the countess in Henry Brooke's *The Fool of Quality* cries "I love to weep! I joy to grieve! It is my happiness, my delight, to have my heart broken in pieces,"[22] readers may wonder whether to indulge or deplore such voluptuous twaddle. Self-parodic knowingness isn't necessarily a defense for this sort of thing, but Coleridge was alert both to the insights and the oversights of the mode. "Poetry—excites us to artificial feelings—makes us callous to real ones," he observed, even as he conceded elsewhere that "poetry without egotism comparatively uninteresting."[23] Wordsworth takes these provocations further. He would later smile at his own early penchant for the "tragic super-tragic,"[24] but parodies of sentiment do not lead him simply to mock artificial feelings. As he explores whether one can always tell artificial and real feelings apart, he is led to consider whether what makes egotism interesting could be related to what makes it laughable.

*

Before looking closely at the best-known elegy in *Lyrical Ballads*, I'll approach it by some less well-trodden ways. "I would not be misunderstood," Wordsworth writes in the preface to *Lyrical Ballads*, "but wherever we sympathise with pain, it will be found that the sympathy is produced and carried on by subtle combinations with pleasure."[25] This insight isn't confined to other people's sufferings, and he is often drawn to other varieties of pleasured pain:

> Sad fancies do we then affect,
> In luxury of disrespect
> To our own prodigal excess
> Of too familiar happiness.[26]

Reading these lines aloud is itself a luxury; the metrical virtuosity, the prodigality of the polysyllables, accords a lovely shapeliness to excess. Elsewhere, small grammatical disruptions quietly signal the moral psychologist at work and play: "I looked and looked along the silent air, / Until it seemed to bring a joy to my despair."[27] "To," not "from," for joy can be located *within* despair. In "The Mad Mother," the protagonist realizes that "I am happy when I sing / Full many a sad and doleful thing,"[28] and in "Ruth," the lady is

> in a prison hous'd,
> And there, exulting in her wrongs,
> Among the music of her songs
> She fearfully carouz'd.[29]

"Among" is pleasurably weird, makes the songs seem less like *her* songs and more like tunes with a life of their own that well up from the depths of her despair ("fearfully" may refer to what it feels like to watch her but also to her own shock at the very strength of her exaltation).

Another poem in *Lyrical Ballads*—"'Tis said, that some have died for love"—rarely gets attention in studies of Wordsworth, but it does helpfully tease out his interest in the anarchic exuberance of grief. The title alludes to Rosalind's response to Orlando in *As You Like It* when he tells her he would die for love: "men have died from time to time and worms have eaten them, but not for love."[30] (That Rosalind is many fathoms deep in love with Orlando should serve as a warning; Wordsworth's title isn't merely sarcastic.) The narrator begins by informing readers that "here and there" graves can be found "Because the wretched man himself had slain, / His love was such a grievous pain."[31] He then settles down to speak of one particular lover: "He loved—The pretty Barbara died, / And thus he makes his moan." The lover makes moan primarily by berating his surroundings: he orders buildings to rethink their position ("Oh! move thou Cottage from behind that oak") and then turns his attentions to the natural scenery: "Roll back, sweet rill! back to thy mountain bounds," he opines; "Be anything, sweet rill, but that which thou art now." The birdsong is especially galling:

> Thou Thrush, that singest loud and loud and free,
> Into yon row of willows flit,
> Upon that alder sit;
> Or sing another song, or chuse another tree!

This is a prime exhibit for what Wordsworth elsewhere describes as "the foolishness of grief."[32] One suspects that if the man has so many angst-ridden words to spare, he's probably in a safe enough place. Yet he doesn't come across as merely affected. Apostrophes to oaks, clouds, waterfalls, and mountains accentuate the littleness of the speaker and his grief, which in turn renders that grief ridiculous and oddly more poignant *because* it is ridiculous. When projected against such a backdrop, his sorrow (*all* sorrow) is both exorbitant and trifling.

Even within his heartache, there glimmers an abiding appetite for life, something akin to what Marianne Moore described as "grief's lustiness."[33] "Thou eglantine," he cries, "to see thee nodding in the air / . . . Disturbs me, till the sight is more than I can bear," but he keeps looking nonetheless, feasting his eyes on the way it arches "(Even like a rainbow spanning half the vale)." The parentheses are a spry touch, as though to say "Woe is me, the eglantine mocks me (oh, but look, how lovely!)." The shift recalls a strange moment in *The Borderers* when a grief-stricken Mortimer says

if this be not enough
To make mankind merry for evermore
Then plain it is as day—that eyes were made
For a wise purpose—verily to weep with! [*Looking round.*]
A pretty prospect this, a master-piece
Of nature—finished with most curious skill[34]

"Did ever any body grieve with so much sang froid?" one critic objected.[35] But grief does not preclude such oscillations, and torment may try to answer back to itself. Barbara's erstwhile lover is similarly soothed by having such beguiling objects against which he can pit his stricken energies, and the energies themselves tell of something self-delighting inside his disturbance.

Once the lover's moan is over, the narrator steps in and ends the poem.

The man who makes this feverish complaint
Is one of giant stature, who could dance
Equipp'd from head to foot in iron mail.—
Ah gentle Love! if ever thought was thine
To store up kindred hours for me, thy face
Turn from me, gentle Love, nor let me walk
Within the sound of Emma's voice, or know
Such happiness as I have known today.—

So the depiction of how far a gigantic, quickstepping knight at arms has fallen was meant, apparently, as a prelude for this tender outpouring. This is the only poem in *Lyrical Ballads* that closes with a dash, as though to accentuate its challenge. From one perspective, the narrator's invocations are as silly as the lover's (Love has as little thought for the former as the house did for the latter when he cried "Oh! move thou Cottage from behind that oak"). Wordsworth is playing on the potentially embarrassing nature of apostrophe in order to suggest that the speakers are posturing or waxing lyrical, but, by exaggerating the laughable oddity of the trope, he also points to the passions that can inform it. Sometimes apostrophe is the language of last resort for those who are desperate for somebody to talk to.

Poems like this bring to mind a passage from Chaucer that Wordsworth translated a couple of years later. In *The Prelude* he would recall how "I laugh'd with Chaucer . . . Heard him . . . tell his tales / Of amorous passion,"[36] and such passion is tragicomic in *Troilus and Criseyde* too, particularly in the passage Wordsworth selected (bk. V, lines 519–656). The hero is bereft ("Lord, this simple Troilus was woe," as Wordsworth drily puts it). Like the lover in "'Tis said, that some have died for love," Troilus apostrophizes buildings, calling out "O Palace desolate . . . / Thou ought'st to fall and I to die;

since she / Is gone who held us both in sovereignty"; and, like the narrator, he calls out to Love for help, adding that things have got so bad that "Men thence a book might make, a history" of his plight. Indeed they might. Troilus aestheticizes his heartache ("And of himself did he imagine oft, / That he was blighted, pale"), casts himself as the object of everyone's contemplation ("All which he of himself conceited wholly / Out of his weakness and his melancholy"), and revels in his own creative responsiveness to distress ("it pleased him in his songs to show / The occasion of his woe").[37] Wordsworth's version preserves Chaucer's smilingly capacious play of perspectives: Troilus's sense of himself as trapped within the role of Courtly Lover, his need for that role as a defense against his suffering, and his pleasure in the role for the opportunities it has given him to be the man that he is.

Such writing explores both the mawkishness and stylishness of amorous agony, the many ways in which one may *practice* suffering. And when, in the poem from *Lyrical Ballads*, Wordsworth's narrator tells gentle Love that, if she has pains in store for him, she shouldn't let him know such happiness as he has known today, the sentiment is delightfully preposterous as well as belated, for the strength of his happiness has the opposite of happiness built into it. Elsewhere, Coleridge imagines being "bereft alike of grief and glee,"[38] and Wordsworth's poetry senses not just the connection between such feelings but also the laughable quality that they may have in common. The self-pleasing imagination, no less than the self-lacerating one, is forever dreaming up ingenious ways to cope with its own excess of emotion. Both the narrator who fears the possibility of losing Emma and the lover who mourned the loss of Barbara are delirious as they while and wail away the time.

*

What scandal might be perpetrated if these figures were seen as relatives of the man who mourns for Lucy? The lyric that follows "Strange fits of passion" in *Lyrical Ballads* (and with which Stoddart claimed it had "a secret connection"[39]) is simply titled "Song":

> She dwelt among th' untrodden ways
>   Beside the springs of Dove,
> A Maid whom there were none to praise
>   And very few to love.
>
> A Violet by a mossy Stone
>   Half-hidden from the Eye!
> —Fair, as a star when only one
>   Is shining in the sky!

She *liv'd* unknown, and few could know
When Lucy ceas'd to be;
But she is in her Grave, and oh!
The difference to me.[40]

Geoffrey Hartman didn't want readers to make a blunder, so he offered a gloss for the star simile: "not, of course, a stingy compliment, but an allusion to Hesper which carries with it the suggestion of brief if intense emergence."[41] Why "of course"? Hartman assures us that the poet has everything under control, and this assurance is I think representative of a critical tendency that has sought to minimize the potential for comedy—whether placed or *mis*-placed—in Wordsworth. Samuel Butler ventured an alternative:

> The superficial reader takes it that he was very sorry she was dead; it is, of course, possible that he may have actually been so, but he has not said this. On the contrary, he has hinted plainly that she was ugly, and generally disliked; she was only like a violet when half-hidden from view, and only fair as a star when there were so few stars out that it was practically impossible to make an invidious comparison. If there were as many as two stars the likeness was felt to be at an end.[42]

There's more where this came from ("if Wordsworth had murdered her, either by cutting her throat or smothering her"), and although Butler's commentary is partly a parody of interpretation, his euphoric tendentiousness takes us closer to Wordsworth's oddity by highlighting just how often the reader has to smooth over—or smooth out—the language of his poems. F. W. Bateson put the problem most starkly: "How can *ways* be *untrodden*?" he asked, "If there were a very few who loved Lucy there cannot have been, literally, *none to praise* her. And if she had really *lived unknown* how could there be even a *few* who knew when she ceased to be?"[43] Poetry's call on readers to make inferences from compacted, shrouded language is hardly unusual, but Wordsworth's poem raises the stakes.[44] To Bateson's last questions, it might be replied that you can adore someone without praising them (one needn't always admire what one loves); and that, given that a maid is a virgin, Lucy lived "unknown" in the carnal sense. It would be odd to allude to such delicate matters in an elegy, but then this may turn out to be the least odd thing the speaker is doing. When Coleridge said that "Wordsworth's words always mean the whole of their possible meaning,"[45] he was drawing attention to their plainest senses as well as their figurative resonances. This poet's words have a disconcerting tendency to mean what they say.

In a discussion of the apparently laughable things we encounter in some poems, Wordsworth begins the second of his *Essays upon Epitaphs* with a joke from Charles Lamb, who, when reading the eulogies on tombstones, often finds himself wondering "Where are all the *bad* People buried?"[46] Wordsworth smiles at the question while taking its implications seriously. Here is his general argument, followed by two of his examples and commentaries (the first by the Marquess of Montrose on Charles I, and the second by an anonymous writer printed on a tombstone in Westmorland):

> The strangeness of the illustrative images, the grotesque spelling, with the equivocal meaning often struck out by it, and the quaint jingle of the rhymes. These have often excited regret in serious minds, and provoked the unwilling to good-humoured laughter. Yet, for my own part, without affecting any superior sanctity, I must say that I have been better satisfied with myself, when in these evidences I have seen a proof how deeply the piety of the rude Forefathers of the hamlet is seated in their natures, I mean how habitual and constitutional it is, and how awful the feeling which they attach to the situation of their departed Friends—a proof of this rather than of their ignorance or of a deadness in their faculties to a sense of the ridiculous. . . .
>
> Great, good, and just, could I but rate
> My griefs, and thy so rigid fate;
> I'd weep the world to such a strain,
> As it should deluge once again.
>
> . . . His soul labours;—the most tremendous event in the history of the Planet, namely, the Deluge, is brought before his imagination by the physical image of tears. . . . Hyperbole in the language of Montrose is a mean instrument made mighty because wielded by an afflicted Soul, and strangeness is here the order of Nature. Montrose stretched after remote things but was at the same time propelled towards them. . . .
>
> In her concenter'd did all graces dwell:
> God pluck'd my rose that he might take a smel.
>
> . . . Can any thing go beyond this in extravagance? Yet . . . I should myself have had no doubt, after recovering from the first shock of surprize and disapprobation, that this man, notwithstanding his extravagant expressions was a sincere mourner. . . . He deems in his simplicity that no hyperbole can transcend the perfections of her whom he has lost . . . in spite of his outrageous expressions, the under current of his thoughts was natural and pure.[47]

The man who wrote these words in 1810 was not quite the same one who wrote the *Lyrical Ballads.* That man would have been less concerned to note his satisfaction at perceiving piety, more wary of the tasteful good manners with which "good-humoured" laughter might conspire, and more on his guard against the implications of relating "disapprobation" to "surprize." For the younger Wordsworth, an "awful" feeling was not necessarily to be contrasted with "a sense of the ridiculous."

This is not to take away from the force of his readings here or from his larger point. On the surface, he appears to be saying "Don't laugh; despite the outrageous silliness of the phrasing in these epitaphs, something important is being said," but beneath this defense lies a more intrepid thought: "Yes, laugh, but note that the outrageous silliness of the phrasing is part of the passion—and part of what makes it moving." Wordsworth's line of inquiry throws light on certain aspects of "Song"—not least on its equivocal meaning, the strangeness of the illustrative images, and the quaint jingle of the rhymes. When, in a letter to Coleridge, he refers to this poem and to "Strange fits of passion" as "little Rhyme poems which I hope will amuse you,"[48] part of the amusement lies in the passionate inanity of grief, its blend of the self-abnegating and the self-involved. If the speaker of "Song" were in a different mood, he might be willing to concede to Bateson, "Well, okay, not '*untrodden* ways,' just not trodden very much," and so on. It's as though he's mindful of a need to rise to the occasion, or as though the poet who stands behind him is willing to hazard a deliberate precariousness in the writing in order to explore this need.

Now, to return to that tricky "star" and to gaze upon it in its setting. In their *Essay on Irish Bulls* (1802), the Edgeworths spoke of some hyperboles as "sanctioned by genius" and observed that "The bounds which separate sublimity from bombast, and absurdity from wit, are as fugitive as the boundaries of taste."[49] A poet hoping to create the taste by which he is to be enjoyed will be willing to break bounds on occasion. Coleridge noted that "poetic Hyperbole . . . often borders very near an Irish Bull" and added that although hyperbole is a form of mental bombast, it is a fault "of which none but a man of genius is capable."[50] In Wordsworth's copy of *Biographia Literaria*, this comment is marked up in the margin: "The *bull* namely consists in the bringing together two incompatible thoughts, with the *sensation*, but without the *sense*, of their connection."[51] Coleridge adds that the psychological condition that leads to this state is the "disproportionate vividness of two distant thoughts, as it extinguishes or obscures the consciousness of the intermediate images or conceptions, or wholly abstracts the attention from them."[52] The extravagant accidence of Wordsworth's genius—or, if one prefers, the strains of the speaker's psychological condition—can be felt in the disproportionate vividness of the middle stanza of "Song." Mary Shelley was the first of many to ask, how can Lucy be both like the half-hidden violet and like the blazingly visible star? ("It always appeared to me rather a contrast than a similitude."[53]) Frances Ferguson claims that the images "attempt to translate the essence of the beloved object into analogies which are hopelessly overparticularised."[54] Maybe so, but the star may cast a glint of light back onto the violet, making the half hidden more palpable to the imagining eye. The awkwardness of the attempt is part of the stanza's power; like the movements toward hyperbole, the speaker's images may be taken not wholly for what they say but for what he wishes they could show.

In his *Instituto Oratoria*—the text from which Wordsworth chose the epigraph to the 1802 *Lyrical Ballads*— Quintilian observed that hyperbole "very often raises a laugh" (sometimes "on the side of the speaker,"' and sometimes against him). After noting the dangers of the rhetorical figure, he added, "It is better to go too far than not to go far enough."[55] Throughout "Song," it could be said of the speaker that "he stretched after remote things but was at the same time propelled toward them" and that this propulsion includes a kind of pleasure, a reveling in one's own power to handle grief, as though figuration could answer back to loss. Elsewhere, in *Essays upon Epitaphs* Wordsworth observes,

> how fond our Ancestors were of a play upon the Name of the deceased when it admitted of a double sense. . . . It brings home a general truth to the individual by the medium of a Pun, which will be readily pardoned, for the sake of the image suggested by it, for the happy mood of mind in which the Epitaph was composed.[56]

Wordsworth often succumbs to punning in apparently grave contexts—not least when he's handling the word *grave* itself—and where there's a pun, there's something more than pain.[57] Perhaps the etymology of Lucy's light-bearing name suggests the "shining" radiating from the center of the poem. We can't say (yet) that "Song" is happy, but it's not only *un*happy.

What we can say is that whatever else it is, hyperbole is a gamble. In his essay "On Laughter and Ludicrous Composition," James Beattie wrote,

> Every body knows, that hyperbole is a source of the sublime; and it is equally true, that amplification is a source of humour. But as that which is intrinsically mean cannot be made great, so neither can real excellence be rendered laughable, by mere amplification. A coxcomb, by exaggerating the charms of a beautiful woman, may make himself ridiculous, but will hardly make them so.[58]

Beattie's wish to guard the boundaries between the sublime and ridiculous relies on presuppositions that Wordsworth both courts and resists, for one of the central features of lyric utterance as he conceives it is a skepticism about the category of the "intrinsically" mean. In some kinds of writing, the overstatement or understatement of a case allows writer and reader to agree on value; a norm is established through an exploration of what lies on either side of it. But Wordsworth's fun is centrally related to the pleasure he takes in making it difficult to agree on that norm, for who is to say when "the charms of a beautiful woman" like Lucy are exaggerated? If beauty is in the eye of the beholder (this is part of the force of "the difference to me"), her charms rely solely on whether one is able—or willing—to feel charmed. Because it is at once easy and hard to hyperbolize the object of one's affections (in a sense, there is no object, only the affections), the feelings themselves are always both sublime and ridiculous.

Henry Crabb Robinson's admiration of "Song" led him to note in his diary that "the opposition between the apparent strength of the passion and the insignificance of the object is delightfully conceived."[59] The opposition hints at a humor that the poem countenances but does not exactly confirm, for Robinson's phrasing—"the *apparent* strength of the passion"—intimates that the speaker may be working up his own feeling rather than simply feeling it. Desire is sharpened—and even constituted—by lack. Perhaps the speaker undervalued Lucy when he knew her, registers the "difference" more strongly now that she's gone, and so overcompensates (his hyperboles being a form of atonement or self-punishment for his neglect—or an unwitting confession of his mixed feelings). A flair for masochism is one of the prerogatives of the grief stricken; masochism, like poetic composition, can be a means of gleaning pleasure from pain—and control from dependency. "*There is a pleasure in poetic pains / Which only Poets know*"; Wordsworth liked Cowper's lines so much that he started one of his own poems with them.[60] It might be added that, in certain moods, everybody is a poet.

*

With these pleasurable pains in mind, the ending of "Song" can be heard as different from itself—or different from what readers generally expect (and demand) from Wordsworthian elegy:

> She *liv'd* unknown, and few could know
>   When Lucy ceas'd to be;
> But she is in her Grave, and oh!
>   The difference to me.

This is I think the only time in his writing that Wordsworth hazards a rhyme on the word *oh* at the line end, and here it lends the poetry a half-inappropriate, almost lilting quality. And then "diffe**rence**" gets an odd lift from the metrical pattern (in a late manuscript, Wordsworth underlined the first *e* to indicate that the reader should pronounce all three syllables).[61] It's hard to decide whether "The **difference** to **me**" sounds more like someone choking up or whether it edges perilously close to a sort of sing-along at a crucial moment. All this might prompt a second glance at the poem's title, which initially appears to be a generic placeholder, yet this is the only poem Wordsworth ever chose to title simply "Song." The first line—"She dwelt among *th' un*trodden ways"—contains another rarity, for he hardly ever signals this elision in so direct a manner.[62]

These features imply that "Song" is to be sounded *as song*, with readers making elisions or extensions where necessary (one in each stanza: "th' un"; "violet"; "difference"). Sounding the poem this way, we accord it a quality that Wordsworth once recommended to a budding poet, having just read works in which he felt the man's grief was as yet "too keen to allow of your treating the Subject in that mitigated tone that *Poetry* requires."[63] And Wordsworth has an ear for how the mitigated may drift into the pleasurable, into the sound or swing of "A happy man, and therefore bold to look / On painful things" (the poet's description of himself in *The Prelude*).[64] As Chesterton put it in another context, "When a young man can elect deliberately to walk alone in winter . . . when he takes pleasure in storms and stricken peaks, and the lawless melancholy of the older earth, we may deduce with the certainty of logic that he is very young and very happy."[65] This hyperbole is as acutely, uncannily logical as Wordsworth's recourse to "therefore" in the lines from *The Prelude*. Who, he asks in *Descriptive Sketches*, "Can guess the high resolve, the cherish'd pain / Of him whom passion rivets to the plain?"[66] Cherished pain is another of those strange fits of passion that includes a guilty, baffling, yet riveting sense of one's own vitality as one dwells on death.

Wordsworth's careful, enraptured reading of the ballad tradition—particularly of Percy's *Reliques*—has a bearing on these delicate matters. At one point, Percy speaks of a madrigal that "contains so complete an example of Bathos, that I cannot forbear presenting it to the reader." The song includes a refrain in which, having spoken in awe of the wonders of nature, the poet says "These things seem wondrous, yet more wondrous I, / Whose heart with fear doth freeze, with love doth fry."[67] Percy later singles out a sonnet that "concludes with the finest anti-climax I remember to have seen"; this speaker, having lamented how the earth "Refuses food to fowl, to bird, and beast . . . And surfeits cattle with a starving feast," ends by proclaiming: "Curs'd be that love and mought continue short, / Which kills all creatures, and doth spoil our sport."[68] In both cases, the fineness of the anticlimax is generated by the shift from the world to the self, and the feeling is close to the one Wordsworth later anatomized in Montrose's poem: "the most tremendous event in the history of the Planet, namely, the Deluge, is brought before his imagination by the physical image of tears." The speaker centers his eye on a terror or tragedy as a prelude to having everything center on him.

"The difference to me" houses a similar feeling. Bateson claimed that the "symbolic aggrandizement of Lucy and the sublimity it confers upon her react upon the poem's conclusion, and it is their combination that converts the near-bathos of the last line into 'the most perfect pathos', as Keats called it."[69] I'm not sure there's a complete conversion; near-bathos exists alongside pathos, helps to make it and to threaten it. (What, in fact, is a most perfect pathos? A feeling from which a person might refuse to recover, or one that countenances something other than its own poignancy?) The aggrandizement of Lucy confers sublimity, but it is the conferral—not simply the sublimity—that the poem registers because she is both a feeder of and a pretext for the abasing yet all-important "me." Certainly, the pathos is enhanced by the beauty of the understatement after the previous flirtations with hyperbole (words fail the speaker, or maybe he can't bring himself to go into more detail). Yet, given the emphasis in the penultimate line—"But **she** is in her Grave" (the only time *she* takes a stress)—rhythm and sense subtly conspire so as to invite us to hear "The **diff**erence **to me**." Lucy's lost opportunities and lost potential (the difference it made to her) and the speaker's own feelings of loss needn't be mutually exclusive, yet might not "But she is in her Grave"—*her* grave, not *the* grave—also carry a tinge of envy and even a kind of reproach?

I have a friend whose father said to him one New Year's Eve, "It's been an awful year, what with your brother's divorce, your aunt's cancer, and now your mother's problems at work. Why do these things always happen to me?" A comparison between this man and the poem's speaker might, as Wordsworth put it in *Essays upon Epitaphs*, "excite regret in serious minds," and that regret may not be lessened by the rejoinder Wordsworth offered elsewhere: "Minds that have nothing to confer / Find little to perceive."[70] Yet, as he noted at the beginning of *The Prelude*, there are moments in which "Humility and modest awe themselves / Betray me, serving often for a cloak / To a more subtle selfishness."[71] *Often*, not always, which is what makes humility and modest awe such tricky feelings to handle. In "Song," as in other poems he wrote in Goslar, Wordsworth allows the elegiac to be ghosted by the absurd by allowing for the possibility of similar betrayals.

Those who are willing to allow for puns in elegies—as Wordsworth himself was—could say that the implications of "Song" are half hidden from the "I." His words are spoken by him and for him but also against him and through him. "No doubt, from the first day, we have spoken only to obtain what isn't given to us," Jean-Bertrand Pontalis observed, "for if it often comes to mind that we are forever separated from language, that is because language is separation and tells only of separation. . . . It is the distant, insistent echo of all our losses; it makes us go through them again, in every direction."[72] The speaker of "Song" knows this—or his language knows this for him. To go through losses in this manner isn't in any simple sense to get through them, but the very singing of loss tells strangely, pleasurably, of the many ways in which pain may be conjured with. The lyric testifies to Wordsworth's fascination with how, at moments of high pressure, a speaker's language falls short of or exceeds his intentions and as a result does tragicomic justice to the full complexity of his feeling. The last stanza of "Song" is in league with the boldness of one of this poet's less celebrated preoccupations: the incongruity of grief—its self-watchful abandon, its felt melodrama, even its latent sense of its own ridiculousness.

Life does not cease to be funny when people die any more than it ceases to be serious when people laugh.[73] When Hazlitt observed of the poems in *Lyrical Ballads* that "Fools have laughed at, wise men scarcely understand them,"[74] he cannily left it undecided as to whether the two groups were synonyms or opposites. It could be as foolish not to laugh at the poems as it could be to assume that, if you *do* laugh, you are sure that you understand them. Looking back on the *Lyrical Ballads* in 1815, Charles Elton offered an acute commentary on their reception:

> As, perhaps, no publication ever produced so great a stirring of the general feeling, such a bristling up of alarmed prejudices, and such a perplexed consciousness of inexplicable delight, none, perhaps, ever made in so short a period so deep and affecting an impression. But the alleged infantilities of style and subject were insisted upon with such perserving acrimony, as to frighten effectually away the timid and self-wondering approbation of a portion of the public. They who had been secretly affected with pleasure grew ashamed of their feelings, and were eager to recant their applause, and to join the safe side of the laughers.[75]

Elton is diagnosing what Stevie Smith would later refer to as "that brittle laughter that covers so much *fear* of not being on the right bus."[76] The unsafe side of the laughers is the side the poems are on, and, for Wordsworth, laughter is itself most truly "self-wondering" when experienced as "a perplexed consciousness of inexplicable delight." His hopes for his poetry included the belief that it might make pains less acute by rendering them less vague; and also that by bringing secret pleasures into public view, it could encourage readers to be surprised by their feelings without becoming ashamed of them. By pushing at the limits of the acceptable and the sayable through a refusal to censor the presence of the laughable, his writing contains what the narrator of *The Ruined Cottage* describes as "a strange, / Amusing but uneasy novelty."[77] We might say of the writing's laughable echoes, fits, and pains what Wordsworth said of Montrose: "strangeness is here the order of Nature." And when Wordsworth was writing strangely, writing well, he didn't quite know whether he was laughing or not.

PLAYING

At the table where they were playing dice, a tall, thin woman sat knitting. I asked her what could be won at this game, and she answered: *Nothing!* When I asked her whether anything could be lost, she said: *No!* This game struck me as very important.

GEORG CHRISTOPH LICHTENBERG

Children

the boy
Shouted & shouted at the plant to see
The playful life it led

DRAFT MS FRAGMENT FOR *Michael*[1]

How might one lead—or be led by—a "playful life"? Up to this point, *Lyrical Ballads* has taken center stage, but for other inflections of fun we need to look elsewhere. The next three chapters focus mainly on poems outside *Lyrical Ballads*, taking on an unholy trinity—the child, the reprobate, and the idler—and asking why so much seems to be at stake when these figures loom into view. John Taylor Coleridge's initial assessment two hundred years ago would appear to have stood the test of time and serves as a warning to any commentator who wishes to embark on a fool's errand: "Playfulness is not Wordsworth's forte," he insisted in 1819. But perhaps playfulness is more interesting than a forte; it could be his weakness, or his secret. A few months later, Coleridge detected in the poems "a subdued under-tone of humour, a playful hint," or at least he thought he did: "those playful hints (they are in general so slight, that we can call them by no other name)."[2] He is wondering how something so negligible can carry such resonance, which is exactly how Wordsworth felt about the activity of play itself. Although the poet tends to relate play to Fancy (as opposed to the august operations of the Imagination), the energy with which he writes about it hints at a strong allegiance:

> The law under which the processes of Fancy are carried on is as capricious as the accidents of things, and the effects are surprising, playful, ludicrous, amusing, tender, or pathetic, as the objects happen to be appositely produced or fortunately combined.[3]

Often, in the poetry, the capricious turns fortunate, and the accidental is no less relished than the apposite. As Crabb Robinson noted, "I have heard Wordsworth speak of his poems of fancy as if he deemed them not inferior to his poems of imagination."[4]

This chapter gravitates toward the primal scene of fanciful play: childhood. But I should say at the outset that children as such move in and out of the spotlight; I'm interested in how other concerns—growth, change, self-making and self-defense, the continuities and discontinuities of personhood—orbit around images of the child. A good place to begin is with the lyric that heralded a new beginning for Wordsworth after *Lyrical Ballads.* Early in 1802, he found himself writing a different kind of poem, one that would lead Coleridge to suspect the emergence of "a *radical* Difference" between them:[5]

TO A BUTTERFLY

Stay near me—do not take thy flight!
A little longer stay in sight!
Much converse do I find in Thee,
Historian of my Infancy!
Float near me; do not yet depart!
Dead times revive in thee:
Thou bring'st, gay Creature as thou art!
A solemn image to my heart,
My Father's Family!

Oh! pleasant, pleasant were the days,
The time, when in our childish plays
My Sister Emmeline and I
Together chaced the Butterfly!
A very hunter did I rush
Upon the prey:—with leaps and springs
I follow'd on from brake to bush;
But She, God love her! feared to brush
The dust from off its wings.[6]

Despite—or because of—the deluge of exclamation marks, one senses that a fresh yet fragile poetic life is struggling to be born. Whimsy modulates nostalgia, but disquiet shadows whimsy. "A very hunter did I rush" strikes a mock-heroic note, relishing the older-and-wiser perspective that makes writing like this possible. Past experience is being humored, not merely longed for. Yet half-hidden anxieties make themselves felt: "Dead times revive in thee" doesn't simply mean that the present revivifies the past but that it brings back times when death was around. Wordsworth later commented on the lyric that "My Sister and I were parted immediately after the death of our Mother who died in 1778, both being very young,"[7] which sheds light on that oddly estranged line "My Father's Family!" (as though the family were no longer quite the speaker's own once death had arrived). Dorothy noted in her journal,

> we were talking about the pleasure we both always feel at the sight of a Butterfly. I told him that I used to chase them a little but that I was afraid of brushing the dust off their wings, & did not catch them—He told me how they used to kill all the white ones when he went to school because they were Frenchmen.[8]

So Wordsworth's poem plays at putting brother and sister back together by blending separate memories, and the small yet telling shift from plural to singular—"pleasant were the days, / The time"—tries to conceive those days as one moment. But separation survives in the siblings' approach to the game they share: William fears what the object of his chase stands for (when faced by Frenchmen, it's kill or be killed); Dorothy runs toward the object of her fears (in another poem in the collection, "The Sparrow's Nest," her brother notes that "She look'd at it as if she fear'd it; / Still wishing, dreading to be near it").[9] In talking about their playful pleasures, brother and sister are talking about other things too.

Play isn't free play. It's more like a screen memory or a confession of dismay, as though the player knows (or half knows) that even one's visions of freedom are inexorable. Mary Midgley observed that "Compulsion can kill the game stone dead, which shows how much they matter."[10] And the fact that they matter so much suggests that games may themselves be compulsions. Wordsworth's lyric is one such game, and it came to him fast, as something that simply had to be entered into that very minute. On March 14, 1802, Dorothy recorded in her journal that instead of finishing another poem he'd started, "while we were at Breakfast . . . he, with his basin of broth before him untouched . . . wrote a Poem to a Butterfly! He ate not a morsel, nor put on his stockings, but sate with his shirt neck unbuttoned, and his waistcoast open while he did it."[11] He dashed off the lyric just a few days after the anniversary of his mother's death, and the poem he put aside was "Beggars," another work in which two children are watched "at play, / Chasing a crimson butterfly."[12] Those children also speak of their mother as dead, and although the narrator surmises that they are lying as "Off to some other play they both together flew," the pair captivate him. He seems to be gazing at an image of childhood from which he's now locked out—or which he never quite had.

The sister's trepidation in "To a Butterfly" keeps impending disaster at bay (no butterflies were hurt during the making of this poem). Yet it also breathes a hushed envy at everything her play might mean to her: "But She, God love her! feared to brush / The dust from off its wings."[13] The haunting nonevent is a mixture of the tactile and the tentative: not simply "off its wings" (as in Dorothy's account) or "from its wings" but "from off." A less intrepid writer would have tidied this up, but the wording captures a child's clumsy tenderness of touch; play suddenly comes up against the seriousness of the impulses that bring it into being. "Poetry is a game we play with reality," R. P. Blackmur observed, "and it is the game and the play—the game by history and training, the play by instinct and need—which make it possible to catch hold of the reality at all. Thus there is intimacy and irresponsibility, menace and caress, escape and aspiration, indigestion and sudden death: all this is in the play."[14] And all this is in something as seemingly airy as "To a Butterfly," a lyric that can be read as a primer in the quirks and questings of Wordsworthian playfulness.

*

Play is self-invention and self-exploration, and, for Wordsworth, it becomes a means by which he might compose himself by joining together two activities: the life of his reading and his reading of his life. But he wasn't playing in a vacuum, so before turning to his richest description of a child at play (in the Intimations Ode), I'd like to wander for a moment, to flit across other writings and sketch out some recurring associations, dilemmas, and values. The Greek *paizein* (play) is derived from *pais* (child), and serious play was a long-standing classical trope (later formulated by Renaissance theorists as *serio ludere*). One of Heraclitus's most renowned fragments—"a lifetime is a child playing games, moving pieces in a board-game; a child's is the kingship"[15]—casts long shadows, and Wordsworth's beloved Horace ("my great favourite," he said, the one who is "above all rivals, fit / To win the palm of gaiety and wit")[16] put play at the center of his poetics. "Haec ego ludo," he wrote in the tenth satire, and in the *Epistles* he envisaged children at play (*pueri ludentes*) as offering forms of oblique teaching for their superiors.[17] The odes are marked by a fondness for those moments "where grace is learned in the intricacy of play," and by a feeling that the poet's own learned folly is a version of such grace.[18] The ludic and the bardic are envisaged as a double act with the child as the intermediary between the two.

"The child is a poet in fact, when he first plays at hide-and-seek,"[19] suggested Hazlitt, and Shelley's *Defence* began by imagining a child "at play" with sense impressions: "In relation to the objects which delight a child these expressions are what poetry is to higher objects."[20] Coleridge observed that "Amid the profoundest and most condensed constructions of hardest Thinking, the playfulness of the Boy starts up, like a wild Fig-tree from monumental Marble,"[21] which allows for the possibility that the thinking is enhanced rather than compromised by the playfulness. This is in tune with Wordsworthian forms of seeing and being. He once noted that Charles Lamb's playfulness broke forth "As from a cloud of some grave sympathy,"[22] and for Lamb, just as for Wordsworth, play raises an urgent question about what you need from your childhood—and from other people's childhoods. While engaged in "grave speculations" at his writing desk, Elia says that he needs the sound of children "playing their own fancies . . . to modulate my periods," but he also has sense and humor enough to know that "I should but spoil their sport, and diminish my own sympathy for them, by mingling in their pastime."[23] As Eric Bentley observed: "No infant shares the grown-up's enjoyment in returning, or seeming to return, to infancy. Humour has a great deal to do with the distance between the infancy returned to and the point from which the return journey is undertaken."[24] Wordsworth shares Lamb's fascination with that distance—and with the odd humor that may arise from it.

It's noteworthy just how often Wordsworth depicts the blithe, beguiling weirdness of the child from an adult's perspective, and the child's refusal to play along with any design the adult might have on it. He is scornful of talk "about Good Boys and Girls, and bad Boys and Girls, and all that trumpery,"[25] and in "To H. C., Six Years Old," he marvels at the child's "unutterable thought."[26] (One senses that the more unutterable, the better; he would have enjoyed young Hartley's comment to his father, "I am always being a bad Boy, because I am always *thinking of my Thoughts*."[27]) Many of Wordsworth's strangely sane children are to be found playing up, and even the sudden death of parents doesn't interrupt the kids' true calling:

> The trouble of the elder Brood
> I know not that it stay'd
> So long—they seiz'd their joy, and They
> Have sung, and danc'd, and play'd.[28]

The lightest of pauses at the end of that second line is delectably sidelong—a coy understatement to placate any shocked parental sensibilities, and a reveling in the energy that quickly drops trouble to get on with the proper business of seizing transport. I'm reminded of something one child says to another in a poem by Robert Hass: "Let's play in my yard. It's ok. My mother's dead."[29]

Play is shameless, opportunist, resilient—something akin to what Wordsworth thought poetry should be: a way of doing your own thing, a riposte to things as they are, and a commitment to a pleasure that feels no need to justify itself. Elizabeth Barrett sensed this in his writing when she noted that he seemed "absorbed away from consideration of publics and critics as a child at play-hours."[30] Yet while absorbed, he's never entirely away, for play hours respond and call back to things beyond themselves. The player invokes by-players: in another poem, the child's gamesome teasing of the adult is a pretty set of "trespasses . . . affected to provoke / Mock-chastisement and partnership in play."[31] Play for Wordsworth often elicits partnership even as the rules of that partnership are not strictly codified; indeed, the rules are brought into question by the activity itself. And, by trusting to trespass, both poem and child have something to teach the adult-reader about how desire might be entertained in so-called maturity. Looking back to the comic theater he relished in London, Wordsworth recalled,

> how eagerly,
> And with what flashes, as it were, the mind
> Turn'd this way, that way! sportive and alert,
> And watchful, as a kitten when at play,
> While winds are blowing round her, among grass
> And rustling leaves.[32]

There's a lovely, light sense of danger here, for kittens are more than merely kittenish (small cataracts, Wordsworth said, should be called *kittenracts*, for they "remind a traveller of the Alps in the same way as a little kitten may suggest recollections of a full-grown tiger").[33] In "The Kitten and the Falling Leaves," having observed his child's delighted response to a kitten at play, the adult feels admonished and resolves to become

> Pleas'd by any random toy;
> By a Kitten's busy joy,
> Or an infant's laughing eye
> Sharing in the extacy,
> I would fare like that or this,
> Find my wisdom in my bliss;
> Keep the sprightly soul awake,
> And have faculties to take
> Even from things by sorrow wrought
> Matter for a jocund thought;
> Spite of care, and spite of grief,
> To gambol with Life's falling Leaf.[34]

As with *The Prelude's* pairing of "sportive and alert," the link between the "sprightly" and the "awake" suggests that play is not mere relaxation but an enhancement of perceptiveness. Yet there remains a sense that the poem's ostensible moral is being teased—gently, sadly—by the very fact of its having to be made: "Note to self: make a big effort to be more like the playful kitten and the laughing child." Fine, but if you wanted to be like either of them, it would really need to be effortless. As Coleridge once noted to his friend: "I find I cannot attain this innocent nakedness, except by *assumption.*

I resemble the Duchess of Kingston, who masqueraded in the character of 'Eve before the Fall,' in flesh-coloured silk."[35] Wordsworth plays on both the value and the absurdity of that assumption, and "The Kitten and the Falling Leaves" reads like a loving parody of one of his strongest convictions: that the mind needs to create something from time's sorrows. The call to "Find my wisdom in my bliss" wonderfully commits to the idea that gaiety is a form of acuity, but it also has the acuity to voice the call in the conditional, which is part of the grammar of experience. A similar feeling is present when Wordsworth proclaims that the child is father of the man: "And I could wish my days to be / Bound each to each by natural piety."[36] The manuscript reads "should wish" (as John Worthen nicely glosses it, "I am not certain, I am not certain that I even want it: I think I do.").[37] "Could wish" is no less unsure: "I might wish it, if I could. There's a version of me that could, I think."

A Wordsworthian commitment to play, then, is more than an unthinking, sentimental, or idealized attachment to a figure whom he is often credited with helping to invent: the Romantic child. This is no doubt why Coleridge was aggravated not by Wordsworth's detractors but by his "affected admirers," for whom he was "forsooth, a *sweet, simple poet*! and *so* natural, that little master Charles and his younger sister are *so* charmed with them, that they play at 'Goody Blake,' or at 'Johnny and Betty Foy'!"[38] Such insipid charm is far removed from the play Wordsworth depicts in *The Prelude*:

> A race of real children, not too wise,
> Too learned, or too good; but wanton, fresh,
> And bandied up and down by love and hate,
> Fierce, moody, patient, venturous, modest, shy,
> Mad at their sports like wither'd leaves in winds[39]

Given the motion on display, one senses a spry pun in "race", and, given talk of love and hate, perhaps there's more wordplay in "mad" (play sometimes makes the children furious, not simply obsessed). This is a version of the child that Adam Phillips sees in Wordsworth, a figure who is lost to himself in his absorption, marked by "his keen and amused hedonism, and his ruthlessness."[40] The fun here is also more than simply "fresh," for the children are like *withered* leaves. That beautiful touch speaks to a sense of play as aged—or, at least, already beyond its years. There's something poignantly adult about the child, as Wordsworth acknowledged in a draft fragment: "Children when they play / In those wild places, seem almost to lose / The quality of Childhood."[41] What children are doing when they play—and what the poet is doing when he admires or seeks to emulate them—is a fraught and pleasurable question, and a persistent means of addressing it is through a venturous yet modest mode (sometimes wanton, sometimes shy) that becomes a vital game for him: allusion. Whatever else it is, allusion is a form of play (from *allusio*, "game," and *alludo*, "to jest or sport with"), as Wordsworth intimated when he once spoke of "allusions suffused with humour."[42] Such suffusions can be found in unlikely places, and they shed light on the absorbed craft—and craftiness—of the Intimations Ode.

*

It is "a dismal truth," Wordsworth noted, "yet consolatory, and full of joy; that,—when a people are called suddenly to fight for their liberty, and are sorely pressed upon,—their best field of battle is the floors upon which their children have played."[43] And perhaps battle is sublimated sporting, for play itself is a fight for liberty. That possibility suggests why so much appears to be on the line when the poet puts the child at the center of his Ode:

> Behold the Child among his new-born blisses,
> A four year's Darling of a pigmy size!
> See, where mid work of his own hand he lies,
> Fretted by sallies of his Mother's kisses,
> With light upon him from his Father's eyes!
> See, at his feet, some little plan or chart,
> Some fragment from his dream of human life,
> Shap'd by himself with newly-learned art;
>   A wedding or a festival,
>   A mourning or a funeral;
>   And this hath now his heart,
>   And unto this he frames his song:
>   Then will he fit his tongue
> To dialogues of business, love, or strife;
>   But it will not be long
>   Ere this be thrown aside,
>   And with new joy and pride
> The little Actor cons another part,
> Filling from time to time his "humourous stage"
> With all the Persons, down to palsied Age,
> That Life brings with her in her Equipage;
>   As if his whole vocation
>   Were endless imitation.[44]

All the world's a stage (one contemporary said Wordsworth was "as much of a humourist, as the melancholy Jacques himself"[45]), but the part or tune that the writing plays is pleasurably tricky to describe. Wryly or ruefully amused?

Sadly or smilingly indulgent? Or both, plus something else? "Behold the Child" sets the lines going with an accent that could be wonderstruck, or ironic, or mock-heroic. The perspective is one of fond parental condescension, but "*new-born* blisses" accords the child respect by making him sound like the parent or carer of his own pleasures. And although talk of "some" little plan and "some" fragment casts a casual glance over the game playing from an uninvolved height, small excitations in the rhythm ("See, . . . See, at his feet") along with light vocal caresses ("his *own* hand . . . Shap'd *by himself*") provide momentary flickers of the child's pride.

The writing humors the boy, but it also allows for a sense of his pushing beyond or outgrowing the adults, of his thirst for independence even as he seeks to take his cue from them. "Fretted by sallies of his Mother's kisses" captures not just the child's vexation as he's smothered with love (mum always makes such a fuss) but somehow stays in touch with his conflicted need for that very fuss (to fret is to decorate, adorn, furnish, supply—as in *The Excursion*: "the cornice richly fretted"[46]—but also to eat, devour, wear away). As both enhancement and erosion, fretting tells of what love may give and take, and when Wordsworth later confesses "I love the Brooks which down their channels fret," he's recalling this earlier scene not just with fear for what the child loses as he grows up but with fondness for just how much energy the little Actor absorbs and augments.

The stanza has often been read as though it were the beginning of a tragedy. Many see the movement beginning "But it will not be long" as merely doom-laden, yet there's admiration here too, a sense of wonder at the child's hunger to extend his repertoire. Helen Vendler calls this scene the Ode's "center of despair," an "oppressive tableau of socialization," a moment of "satiric externality," with the child presented as a "repellent, if innocent, form."[47] But Wordsworth never sees innocence as repellent (nor does he always see it as innocent). Whenever I read the stanza, I think not of despair, oppression, and other big words that make us so unhappy but of Pontalis's reflections on play in *Love of Beginnings*:

> What self-denial more effective, for someone who wants to be himself, than the gift of mimicry! Thus one preserves a possibility, through conscious imitation and the deliberate accentuation of the model's traits, of not being the mere echo of admired voices. I'm nearly sure of not being the involuntary replica of the few people I know how to imitate—I shan't say who they are. . . . Nothing like make-believe, nothing like pretence, nothing like from time to time being an actor for exorcizing the actor in oneself. To go on stage and in that well-circumscribed space, the time of a performance, to give shape, demeanour, voice to the thousands of others embedded within us. The natural-

> ness that we envy in some children goes together with their taste for disguises, for play, for clowning.[48]

Yes—nothing like it, "from time to time" ("Filling from time to time his 'humourous stage'"). To give imitative shape, to give play, is to give things a go—and to give things to yourself.

The story of a life is linked here to a story about the poet's relationship to his own craft, for the making of the man is crucially bound up with the making of the lines. This is the only time that Wordsworth allows the word *imitation* into his poetry, and to rhyme it with *vocation* is to intimate a concern that one's designs and desires are borrowed. Yet the passage's own allusive force takes conned lines to new places. The most prominent allusion is one that Wordsworth decided to highlight; there were no quotation marks around "humourous stage" in manuscript, but they were added for publication and kept for all later editions.[49] The words are taken from Samuel Daniel's haunting prefatory sonnet to *Musophilus*, which Wordsworth had encountered in Robert Anderson's *The Works of the British Poets.* Daniel's "Tragi-Comedy" was important to him (his heavily annotated volumes of Daniel's poetry were, his grandson noted, "my Grandfather's especial favourites, and were frequently in his hands.")[50] Here is the sonnet in full.

> I do not here upon this hum'rous stage
> Bring my transformed verse apparelled
> With others passions, or with others rage;
> With loves, with wounds, with factions furnished:
> But here present thee, only modelled
> In this poor frame, the form of mine own heart:
> Where, to revive myself, my muse is led
> With motions of her own, t' act her own part,
> Striving to make her own contemned art
> As fair t' herself as possibly she can;
> Lest seeming of no force, of no desert,
> She might repent the course that she began;
> And, with these times of dissolution, fall
> From goodness, virtue, glory, fame, and all.[51]

This self-concentered resolution looks to its own frame while framing itself in that most bounded and borrowed of poetic forms. The Ode's child "frames his song" in a similar way, and Wordsworth is also paying his respects to Daniel's use of the verb in his "A Defence of Rhime": "All Verse is but a Frame of words . . . consisting of *Rithmus* or *Metrum* . . . disposed into divers Fashions according to the Humour of the Composer, and the set of the Time" (Daniel also spoke of "*Rhimes*, whose known Frame hath due stays for the mind.")[52] Wordsworth's stanza takes up Daniel's rhymes on *heart*, *part*, and *art* as due stays, yet even as his precursor uses those rhymes to insist on his originality, "these times" are felt as an informing pressure. Daniel's muse will *act* her part—fulfilling yet also fabulating a role. This is a poetry ghosted by loss, movingly uncertain of its own modest gains.

If Daniel's sonnet conjures up agency while hinting at the strain, the stanza from Wordsworth's Ode works in a conversely related way. The boy's play is always small ("little plan or chart . . . little Actor"), yet what could be smaller (or larger) than playing with syllables? In "A Defence of Rhime," Daniel had paid considerable attention to the importance of tiny adjustments in rhythm (elsewhere in *Musophilus* he had spoken of scanning "what defects his hum'rous breath obeyes"), so when Wordsworth flags up "hum'rous stage" and decides to let all the syllables in *humorous* breathe, the change is noteworthy. In the Ode, the word doesn't just fill the time or the line but exceeds its boundaries (this is the only occasion in his poetry that Wordsworth sees fit to use the word). Daniel was glancing at the physiology of four humors, and at "hum'rous" meaning "subject to or influenced by mood or humor; capricious, whimsical; odd" (*OED*, 3.a), but the modern definition, one that allows for something more active than simply being subjected to something—*humorous* as characterized by a sense of humor—had not yet come into being. Wordsworth's allusion doesn't merely submit to a script; it enjoins the play of language across the ages ("*from* time *to* time"). And while Daniel spoke of *this* humorous stage, the Ode revises to *his* stage. The game-playing child makes the passions of others his own, takes them on and takes them in, just as Wordsworth humors Daniel's lines. Richard Poirier once wrote of "the enriching effect that allusiveness can bring to poetry: of expanding a situation toward the simultaneous condition of pathos, because the situation is seen as recurrent and therefore possibly insoluble, and comic, because the recurrence has finally passed into cliché."[53] The Ode's newly learned art embodies this simultaneity even as it makes recurrence a potential source of pleasure.

Still, although Wordsworth needs to believe in the value of an antic childhood for an adulthood so earnestly in need of self-reinvention, the Ode acknowledges that maturity is never quite—or never only—child's play, and also that the play of children is not identical with the adult's fantasized conception of it. For as the adult yearns to be saved by the child, the child is dreaming of becoming an adult: both sides of the double act want to play each other's parts. As the next stanza points out, the child, "yet glorious in the might / Of untam'd pleasures," is just as desirous as the adult, just as keen to be something he's not:

> Why with such earnest pains dost thou provoke
> The Years to bring the inevitable yoke,
> Thus blindly with thy blessedness at strife?[54]

This vision of the child's blindness borders on the fancifully or willfully obtuse, tries to ignore the fact that the blindness is the blessedness. (As Wordsworth drolly puts it elsewhere: "O Man! that from thy fair and shining youth / Age might but take the things Youth needed not!"[55]) It may be just as erroneous to coddle the child for the purposes of one's self-pity as it is to romanticize their play as an escape from all the cares that beset the adult. The poem knows this, and what Coleridge famously referred to as "mental bombast"—the description of the child as "Mighty Prophet! Seer blessed!"'[56]—might rather be taken as a sign of the adult's own need to keep playing (as elsewhere in Wordsworth, hyperbole verges on bull). I think Geoffrey Hartman gets closer to the feeling of this moment when he describes the invocation as "sublimely absurd."[57] The commentary on bulls that Wordsworth marked up in his copy of *Biographia Literaria*—defined as "the bringing together two incompatible thoughts, with the *sensation*, but without the *sense* of their connection"—included the following example: "*I was a fine child, but they changed me.*"[58] The feeling that one both is and is not continuous over time can be sensed everywhere in the Ode and is central to Wordsworthian apprehensions of play. His poetry says "*I was a fine child, but they changed me*," but it also says "*I am the same as I was when I was different.*" The Ode's force comes not just from the grandness of its music or its ambitions but from its awareness of a necessary comedy of errors—or from a sense that error and intuition are hard to tell apart. As with its reworking of Daniel's lines, the poem's humorous stage allows its creator to restage and upstage his own yearnings—and to make a provisory peace with his ideals no less than with his demons.

*

Not that the peace is lasting, for other allusions are in play. Oliver Clarkson has suggested that many of the shorter lyrics in *Poems, in Two Volumes* possess "a self-performing over-insistence designed to give the impression of 'catching' at things which they know cannot really be caught," and the same is true of the Ode.[59] The poem was composed at a time when Wordsworth was preoccupied with the question of what sort of person and writer he wanted to be. If ludic forms of imitation provide not just evidence of the shades of the prison house but also opportunities for self-fashioning, then another poet hovering in the wings (the one who succeeded Daniel as Poet Laureate) casts further light on what is transpiring here. Anne Barton has argued that Wordsworth's reading of Ben Jonson early in 1802 was an influence on the revised preface to *Lyrical Ballads* as well as on the style of the new poems he was writing. The subtlety of Jonsonian sporting arrived in Wordsworth's life at just the right moment (he later acquired a laurelled portrait of Jonson, which still hangs at Rydal Mount).[60] Dorothy read him Anderson's biographical introduction along with many of Jonson's short poems in February, "which were too *interesting* for him, and would not let him go to sleep."[61] He was reading him again in early March (on the days around the anniversary of his mother's death and the composition of "To a Butterfly"), and on the first night of Coleridge's stay later that month when "they disputed about Ben Jonson."[62] The following week, he reread Jonson, and after discussion with Dorothy, he took the crucial decision on the twenty-second to see Annette and his daughter, Caroline, before marrying Mary. On the twenty-fourth he made some alterations to "To a Butterfly," and on the twenty-sixth he wrote to Annette. Childhood pasts and futures, family breakups and family planning, were intermingling with a new literary influence in his life. Thinking intensely about what it would mean to be a brother, a husband, and a father in new circumstances, Wordsworth kept being led backwards to what it meant to be a child—and to how much of his past he might need to take with him into the future. On the twenty-seventh, he began work on the Ode.

He would have found a model for the Ode's child in his own copy of Jonson's *Discoveries*:

> I have considered, our whole life is like a play: wherein every man, forgetful of himself, is in travail with expression of another. Nay, we so insist in imitating others, as we cannot (when it is necessary) return to ourselves: like children, that imitate the vices of stammerers so long, till at last they become such.[63]

Jonson's concern about imitation would come to be used as a weapon against him (in *Lectures on the Comic Writers*, Hazlitt claims that Jonson trusts to "imitation and custom," becoming merely "a great borrower" whose works "read like translations").[64] Anderson observed in his introduction that while the dangers of imitation were a threat to "unborrowed thinking," Jonson excelled in translation and forms of adaptive imitation: "he commonly borrows with the air of a conquerer, and adorns himself in their dress, as with the spoils and trophies of victory." On the same page, though, he censured Jonson's "poignant wit."[65] By poignant he meant sharp, piquant, stinging, but I think Wordsworth heard in that phrase another kind of poignancy, one for which he was seeking to find his own voice.

The crowning achievement of Jonson's collection, *The Underwood*, is his ode on the death of Sir Henry Morison. Wordsworth would later write loving parodies of Jonson,[66] and in his Ode he frequently draws on the Morison ode to eke out the larger significance of "Mock-chastisement and partnership in play."[67] While Morison's elegist seeks what "was left yet to mankind; / Where they might read, and find," Wordsworth girds himself to pronounce that "We will grieve not, rather find / Strength in what remains behind."[68] Jonson looks for a route through loss by seeing the march of time itself as a degradation, a process which turns an aging person's arts of imitation against them. He imagines another little actor who conned his part, somebody who "entered well, by virtuous parts, / got up and thrived with honest arts" before he stooped in his maturity

> To sordid flatteries, acts of strife,
> And sunk in that dead sea of life
> So deep.

Wordsworth alludes to these lines when he sees the child drawn "To dialogues of business, love, or strife," worrying about what it forsakes as it yearns for experience, when "custom lie upon thee with a weight, / Heavy as frost, and deep almost as life!"[69] Elsewhere, Jonson asks,

> What did this stirrer, but die late?
> How well at twenty he had fallen, or stood!
> For three of his four score, he did no good.

This writing contains what Wordsworth would have understood by the term *poignant wit*—witty because the satirical relish of the portrait is so determined to convert Morison's loss into a gain; poignant because the wordplay can't hide just how little its droll determination can change what's happened. It's akin to the wit that T. S. Eliot saw as part of Marvell's inheritance from Jonson, an "alliance of levity and seriousness (by which the seriousness is intensified)," something "rich in generations of experience. . . . It involves, probably, a recognition, implicit in the expression of every experience, of other kinds of experience which are possible."[70]

Such *generations* of experience (across ages, and across the life of an individual) are close to the play that Wordsworth was in need of when searching for a way of reconciling himself to himself. The Ode is part of that search, a quest for a Jonsonian liveliness of style that may answer back to what is taken away as life gets lived and lost. Coleridge later mocked a critic of Jonson's because "he has no notion of a jest, unless you tell him—*This is a joke!* Still less of that shade of feeling, the half-and-half."[71] These shades of feeling can be gleaned everywhere in Jonson, particularly in his ode:

Morison fell young:
He never fell, thou fall'st, my tongue.
He stood, a soldier to the last right end

Verbal dexterity both abides and resists physical frailty. Wordsworth's Ode contains more muted versions of Jonson's gambits—"Fallings from us," for example, are translated into "High instincts" that "Uphold us"[72]—but it sometimes finds itself drawn to the half-and-half, to expressions that countenance jokes even as they shy away from making them.

Nobody thinks the Ode is laugh-out-loud funny, but if, as Emerson suggested, the essence of comedy is "a well-intentioned halfness . . . a non-performance of what is pretended to be performed, at the same time that one is giving loud pledges of performance," then the poem has its own comic apprehensiveness.[73] In a line like "The fullness of your bliss, I feel—I feel it all,"[74] there's a strange enervation in the repetition, and although the words want to say "I feel it *in me*," they mean something closer to "I sense your bliss *in you*." "The Rainbow comes and goes, / And lovely is the Rose" has a wonderful flatness,[75] and toward the end, when Wordsworth wants it known that the brightness of the day "Is lovely yet,"[76] the phrasing gives pause: Just lovely? Lovely like that rose? The precariousness with which he tries to rally himself, the writing's combination of the blithe and the bereft, can be felt whenever the activity of playing reappears. Returning to that earlier image of the child-player conning his parts, he tells of how, when seemingly far from our childhood, in a moment we can call playful scenes to mind: "And see the Children sport upon the shore, / And hear the mighty waters rolling evermore."[77] Yet those waters threaten to engulf the sport, and a few lines later he proclaims, "We in thought will join your throng, / Ye that pipe and ye that play."[78] The distinctively Wordsworthian touch—not a joke, but not quite *not* a joke—is the half-and-half feeling he allows into the affirmation via "in thought." The moment contains what Lamb would later describe as that "finer species of humour" in Wordsworth, his "thoughtful playfulness," which involves the recognition that your thought may sometimes remove you from play even as it seeks to recommit you to it.[79]

*

What Wordsworth took from Jonson—or what Jonson's example encouraged him to develop—was an art of allusion and a sense of wit that could allow the simplest of utterances to become dramatic without becoming merely ironized. Another poet indebted to Jonson hovers in the margins of the 1807 volume, and his affinities with Wordsworth can perhaps suggest how even the renowned final lines of the Ode hazard a certain kind of wit. As one of the most playful "Sons of Ben," Robert Herrick lets the ludic instinct loose whenever he gets a chance, yet his writing also registers a sort of ache inside the need for play; he is the poet of the flying minute, the creature who must stay the time by luxuriating in the moment.[80] Wordsworth had reason to take personally one of several Herrick lyrics copied into his notebook ("To Primroses fill'd with morning-dew"), for the newborn flowers there were compared to "Orphans young." The speaker, after gently heckling the primroses (they should have no reason to weep because they're not "worne with yeares; / Or warpt, as we") ends by conceding

> No, no, this sorrow shown
> By your teares shed,
> Wo'd have this Lecture read,
> That things of greatest, so of meanest worth,
> Conceiv'd with grief are, and with teares brought forth.[81]

While all is grief stricken, the play of thought that brought forth this lyric allows for something other than grief. The conceit that thinks and speaks for the child-flowers, though itself worn with years, is still sprightly enough to know the limits of its lecturely wisdom. Readers are being asked to humor the speaker; he's using the primroses to console himself—and also to enjoy his own grief a little by fancifully elevating the stature of theirs.

Herrick's lines contain a quality Wordsworth smilingly refers to elsewhere when faced by images of decay and reminders of his own losses: "a not unpleasing sadness."[82] And if the passage above is heard playing in the background of the ending to the Ode, we may begin to hear an unlikely sort of play in the lecture that is read out:

> The Clouds that gather round the setting sun
> Do take a sober colouring from an eye
> That hath kept watch o'er man's mortality;
> Another race hath been, and other palms are won.
> Thanks to the human heart by which we live,
> Thanks to its tenderness, its joys, and fears,
> To me the meanest flower that blows can give
> Thoughts that do often lie too deep for tears.[83]

Are they too deep in the sense that when tears come to your eyes, you sometimes don't know exactly why they are there—as though the tears are brought on not solely by the thing that triggers them but by some other feeling you can't quite name? Or is it rather that, in such moments, the thoughts are so powerful that tears are out of the question? I say "you," but the very need to speak for more than the self *via* the self was what several early reviewers found ridiculous about Wordsworth—and about these last lines.[84] For many, the ending stood as the quintessence of his unwittingly comical egotism (when later copying out the Ode, Wordsworth gave himself a capital: "To Me.")[85] And then there's the play of vowel and consonant ("To **me** the **me**anest flower"), which speaks to the aggrandizement of "me" by means of apparent humility ("I, like the flower, have survived and flourished despite neglect").

The pronominal shift in the last four lines may suggest that the Ode's "we" holds only "me," but I think the lines know (with rueful embarrassment as well as with pride) that to you, such things may sometimes appear laughable—and that they *should* appear so (if he is to be him and you are to be you, differences of mood and opinion are preferable, desirable, vital). An important aspect of Wordsworthian fun, it seems to me, is the way the poet always seems to be imagining how his writing could be judged excessive even as we sense his distrust of received criteria for measuring excess. And at the end of the Ode, it's not even clear what we're measuring. Are the speaker's thoughts sadder than sad, or are the tears they surpass mixed with happiness? The thoughts may be within earshot of that complex pleasure Lamb discerned, one "far beyond the reach of all the world counts joy—a deep enduring satisfaction in the depths, where the superficial seek it not, of discontent."[86] Or perhaps they are within touching distance of that comic sadness Emerson described when reflecting on how the adult, as opposed to the child, can't *be* with nature: "The flowers jilt us, and we are old bachelors with our ridiculous tenderness."[87] The lines contain a kind of saddened wit, too, for they acknowledge, in the expression of this experience, other kinds of experience that are possible (note "can" in the penultimate line, and "often" in the last). Wordsworth's poetry both indulges and overhears itself, and the Ode's ending feels at once bold and modest in its claims, unabashed and mystified. It's as though the speaker knows his own mind yet can't quite be sure what he's thinking.

The thoughts are rendered even more complex (or wondrously nonsensical) by one other allusion that is put into play at this moment. The Ode's epigraph is from the opening of Virgil's fourth eclogue—"Paulò majora canamus" ("Let us sing somewhat of more exalted things"). That poem also dreams of a child's immense promise, envisaging a golden age attending his maturity while fearing that "a few traces of old-time sin will live on," and that poem, too, is sung by a poet whose aging and self-making is intimately bound up with the fortunes of the child ("I pray that the twilight of a long life may then be vouchsafed me, and inspiration enough to hymn your deeds!").[88] It ends with the most renowned and controversial reference to laughter in the classical canon—"Incipe, parve puer, risu cognoscere matrem"—one that makes it unclear whether the boy is being commanded to laugh at his mother or the mother is about to laugh at him.[89] This not yet laughed laugh is as difficult to decipher as Wordsworth's not wholly readable tears. To laugh or to cry would be a catharsis, something the Ode can't provide as it seeks to found an uncertain future on an ambiguous past.

What the Ode finally offers—or offers *un*finally—is a seriocomic fortunate fall, a mode of experiencing that Stanley Cavell terms "a happier disillusionment."[90] If an unlikely leap from Virgil to Wordsworth to Beckett might be permitted at this delicate moment, then I'd submit the exchange between Hamm and Clov in *Endgame*—"Do you believe in the life to come?" "Mine was always that"—and Cavell's comment on it: "We've heard it all, seen it all too often, heard the promises, seen the suffering repeated in the same words and postures, and they are like any words which have been gone over so much that they are worn strange. We don't laugh, we don't cry; and we don't laugh that we don't cry, and we obviously can't cry about it. That's funny."[91] Wordsworth's art of allusive play goes over past words like past lives and selves, wearing them strange even as it searches out connections. And while the writing hopes for replenishment via acts of remembrance, it is also aware of what *The Prelude* calls "the foolishness of hope,"[92] of just how much desire goes into memory, and of how the incessantness of one's dream for the life to come may counterfeit the past and sabotage the present. When Wordsworth spoke of "allusions suffused with humour,"[93] I think he was suggesting that, for him, *all* allusion approaches humor—or humoring—because it allows for the entertaining and qualification of one perspective from another vantage point. The Ode's playing off Daniel, Jonson, Herrick, and Virgil helps to make it funny in Cavell's sense, gives us a composite portrait of a poet who can't wholly give up on the need for the promises he can't quite make.

Allusion is repetition, but repetition is transformation, a way of reinventing the world. This is why the figure of the playing child is the heart of the Ode's secret longing and why it stands so eloquently for a dream of newborn blisses that Wordsworth's poetry often entertains. Walter Benjamin observed that, for a child, repetition is the soul of play, for nothing gives him greater pleasure than to "Do it again!": "And in fact," Benjamin added, "every profound experience longs to be insatiable, longs for return and repetition until the end of time . . . when a modern poet says that everyone has a picture for which he would be willing to give the whole world, how many people would not look for it in an old box of toys?"[94] Standing in the middle of the Ode—it's noteworthy that the line "Filling from time to time his 'humourous stage'" is placed at the *exact* center of the poem—this picture is the place where Wordsworth encounters his whole vocation. "See, where mid work of his own hand he lies." So play is also work, and the sentence depicting it is the work of Wordsworth's own hand as he pens the lines: what the poet-adult sees in his mind's eye is a version of what he's doing *right now*. (As Daniel had noted in "A Defence of Rhime": "if our Labours have wrought out Manumission from Bondage . . . we go at Liberty.")[95] Or, at least, we have a go at liberty, make a break for freedom via a process that takes us back to our roots.

In and beyond the Ode, Wordsworth keeps finding new ways to ask, How do you know when you're not playing? That question nurtures a sense of meanings, relations, and lives as yet to be decided—or ventured. And, in this particular case, it also implies that a poem is a toy. Whenever Wordsworth uses the word in *Poems, in Two Volumes*, he uses it to speak of something the *adult* is handling—as when he imagines an "old Man toying with his age," or when he hopes to become "Pleas'd by any random toy; / By a Kitten's busy joy, / Or an infant's laughing eye"[96] in lines that make the infant itself the poet's toy. That the toy could be *random* is an important part of its appeal and its value, for if the toy is our first possession, it is also the means by which we loosen hold of a cramped or confining self-possession. Elizabeth Bowen once wondered whether a toy given as a present should come as a complete surprise or should be the realization of a long-formulated wish. As the gift that Wordsworth gives to himself, the poem-toy fulfils both these requirements. "Should not all toys leave *something* to the imagination? Are we in danger of toys that forbid play?," Bowen goes on, before seizing on the most important class of toy:

> They are "things that one does other things with." Do these, perhaps, give the most pleasure—the most diversified, lasting pleasure—of all? . . . while Nature encourages us to meddle—while there are sands to dig in, undergrowths in which to make tunnels, and streams to dam—shall we not always love, above what is made already, that which we can make into something else?[97]

Wordsworth loves to meddle, loves to see meddling as a form of making, and to see the making as never quite finished. Play is an opaque sign of rapprochement between past and present, youth and age, unwitting pleasure and self-conscious toying, but distances and divisions don't simply vanish as a result of the spell cast by the poet's fanciful gaze. One of the pleasures of reading him is the feeling he gives that whenever he's watching another person at play (especially a child), he's relishing the privacy of their need to play, warming to a vision of the activity as an undivulged secret or mystery—to its participant as well as to its observer. Players are always becoming the playthings of their unconscious, never wholly in the know about what they're playing at. They have their reasons, no doubt, and their unreasons—as does the writer who plays with them.

Reprobates

the wantonness in which we play
With things we love
DRAFT MS FRAGMENT OF "NUTTING"[1]

I've been claiming that play—as both complex behavior and compositional practice—is central to Wordsworth's understanding of what poetry is: a form of negotiation between one's past and present; a means of coping that is also a mode of questing; a vision of potential being fulfilled even as a sense of potentiality is sustained. I want now to develop this line of argument but to change tack and tone, for critical commentaries are sometimes not wanton enough when playing with things they love. One root of *play*—*plegan*—means "to risk, chance, expose oneself to hazard," and play, after all, is sometimes foreplay. The lewdness of the ludic is age old; "*lechery*" is etymologically related to *leik* (another word for play), and in many languages play words are often used in reference to the erotic.[2] It's clear what Adam has on his mind when he turns to Eve in *Paradise Lost* to say "Now let us play,"[3] and from 1776, according to the *OED*, the verb also means "to engage in . . . sexual display." In eighteenth-century aesthetics, *play* does not play straight. Hogarth's line of beauty "gives play" to the imagination as "winding walks, and serpentine rivers, and all sorts of objects . . . *lead the eye a wanton kind of chace*,"[4] and in Burke the lines of a body become a "deceitful maze through which the unsteady eye slides giddily, without knowing where to fix, or whither it is carried."[5] Wordsworth is in the hunt for similar things—even in *The Excursion*, where a path "quits / The cultured fields,—and up the heathy waste / Mounts, as you see, in mazes serpentine."[6] A need to desert the cultured in favor of the curvaceous is everywhere in the writing, and it speaks of that within the poet which "takes its course / Along the line of limitless desires."[7]

A wanton, sexual, desirous Wordsworth admittedly seems an unlikely story. Shelley's accusations—"cold," "prude," "moral eunuch,"[8] and so on—die hard, and Camille Paglia's aversion remains representative; she notes that "a refusal to acknowledge the sex or cruelty in nature is one source of the palpable repression in his poetry, which constricts and weighs it down."[9] But how *palpable* does repression have to be before it ceases to be repression? Wordsworth conceives his medium itself as sexual. In the preface to *Lyrical Ballads*, the life of metrical language is linked to carnal pleasures: "From this principle the direction of the sexual appetite, and all the passions connected with it, take their origin: it is the life of our ordinary conversation."[10] If the ordinary contains the inordinate, then we can be talking about sex when we are not talking about it. And yet, if it's all about sex, what's the sex about? "The sexual appetite, *and all the passions connected with it*": the phrasing doesn't undertake to decide whether the appetite is an end—*the* end—in itself or a means to other ends. In his copy of Shaftesbury's *Characteristicks*, Wordsworth marked up the claim that "Everyone is a *Virtuoso*, of a higher or lower degree: Everyone pursues a GRACE, and courts a VENUS of one kind or another."[11] Perhaps his eye slid giddily from Shaftesbury's "or" to his "and": in some instances, it can be hard to tell the higher and lower apart (the act of "courting" a Venus sounds a little more courtly than all-out pursuit, while the need to "pursue" a Grace is a little less than graceful). Virtuosos are always virtuosos of more than one thing.

In a letter to George Beaumont in 1805, before settling down to discuss "the controul of good sense" and other sage matters, Wordsworth was sabotaged by his need to have fun. A winding path—what Proust called "that half-human part of nature"[12]—flashes into view:

> I am writing now rather for writing's sake than any thing else, for I have many remembrances beating about in my head which you would little suspect. . . . Last summer I had a charming walk along the River. . . . This Path winds on under the trees with the wantonness of a River or a living Creature; and even if I may say so with the subtlety of a Spirit, contracting or enlarging itself, visible or invisible as it likes. There is a continued opening between the trees, a narrow slip of green turf besprinkled with Flowers, chiefly Daisies, and here it is, if I may use the same kind of language, that this pretty path plays its pranks wearing away the turf and flowers at its pleasure. . . . You may guess that I was not a little delighted.[13]

We are on the path to the erotic, or the path *of* the erotic—"the intermittence of skin flashing between two articles of clothing," as Roland Barthes puts it, "the staging of an appearance-as-disappearance."[14] A slip of a thing, continually opening and contracting, it plays its pranks (perhaps with the older meaning in play: prank as "pleat or fold"). The writer writes for writing's sake in the same way that the path goes along "as it likes . . . at its pleasure," and play becomes a seriocomic flirtation with a reader. Wordsworth's correspondent knows him and he doesn't know him; he may guess his delight, but he would little suspect what's in his head.

Playing is a commitment to straying, but it heralds an agitated pleasure. The words allowed into a poem like "Nutting" (*erect, tempting, virgin, voluptuous, ravage, sullied, touch*) speak volumes, and Wordsworth's feeling that he's capable of anything is often mixed up with the fear of knowing what he's capable of.[15] Robert Hass's "Snow Egret" contains a suggestive translation of the kind of play I'm trying to get at, as the poem depicts a boy walking out one morning with a gun:

> He is of an age
> when the thought of winter is a sexual thought,
> the having thoughts of one's own is sexual,
> the two ducks muttering and gliding
> toward the deeper reeds away from him,
> as if distance were a natural courtesy,
> is sexual, which is to say, a mystery, an ache
> inside his belly and his chest that rhymes
> somehow with the largeness of the night.
> . . . He's of an age
> when the thought of thinking is, at night,
> a sexual thought.
> . . . He liked
> to practice stalking, and he raised his gun
> to his shoulder and crouched in the wet grasses
> and drew his bead just playfully at first.[16]

So the poem ends. Both boy and bird are stalkers (he's seen the egret, throat bulging as it swallows its prey, "a trickle / of blood just visible below the black beak"). In Wordsworth, too, there's an uncertainty about whether play is an imposition on nature or its fulfilment. The ache inside the boy's belly rhymes with the largeness of the night; he experiences himself as both outlaw and inmate, the inheritor of a bequest that commits him to trespass. A manuscript version of "Nutting" contains these lines:

> I would not strike a flower
> As many a man will strike his horse, at least
> If from the wantonness in which we play
> With things we love, or from a freak of power,
> Or from involuntary act of hand
> Or foot unruly with excess of life,
> It chanc'd that I ungently used a tuft
> Of meadow-lillies, or had snapp'd the stem

Of foxglove bending o'er his native rill,
I should be loth to pass along my way
With unreprov'd indifference,—I would stop
Self-question'd, asking wherefore that was done.[17]

"Self-question'd," not self-question*ing*. The compound is characteristically Wordsworthian: it's as though even the thought of such wantonness renders him a little less in control of himself.[18] Indeed, a claim about what he would not do turns into an admission of what he might, for where the poet wants to stand isn't exactly where his poetry wants to play. There is merely fine feeling in a phrase like "ungently used," but there's real pleasure in "snapp'd the stem," a pleasure not unrelated to Wordsworth's question to his brother when they were children: "Dare you strike your whip through that old lady's petticoat?"[19]

A few months before he wrote this passage, he began another work that confronted both the delight and peril of "excess of life," a work that, like "Nutting," revisited a primal Wordsworthian scene. In the middle of a wood, in "as sweet a scene / As ever human eye did view,"[20] someone gets caught up in a form of play that becomes as villainous as it is fanciful. When, in the lines above, Wordsworth's shady attraction to deflowering is entertained alongside the striking of horses, another opening comes to mind: "Said Peter to the groaning Ass, / 'But I will *bang* your bones!'"[21] For the remainder of this chapter, I want to read *Peter Bell* saunteringly, slowly—to delay the plot of my argument (not interminably, I hope), and to give this work's weird blend of humor and horror more attention than is usually deemed seemly. I do this partly because *Peter Bell*'s many lives in manuscript and print see Wordsworth stalking the meanings of *play* with particular fervor (the word and its cognates appear with more frequency than in any of his other writings), and partly because the poem is one of the most astonishing things he ever wrote.

*

Whatever else he is, Peter Bell is a player. The story he's in begins by taking a wrong turn, as Peter (a vagrant potter with no fewer than twelve wives) decides to take a shortcut down a serpentine woodland path, one that "might his steps betray."[22] He then comes across an ass standing over a stream in which, it transpires, the creature's former master lies drowned. Later, having brutally beaten the ass, Peter lets it take him where it will, and is led down yet another path. The poem knows that such paths must be followed, but it doesn't know—or is loath to state explicitly—the whys and hows of knowing. As the narrator admits, whether Peter was taking these routes in order to buy or sell, "or led / By pleasure running in his head, / To me was never known."[23] And the potter may well speak for the poet when he confesses that, while pleasure-seeking, he finds himself "Not knowing what I would be at."[24]

When not banging the bones of asses or telling them "You should have been a little fatter," Peter is messing around with maids; he "Had danced his round with Highland lasses; / And he had lain beside his asses / On lofty Cheviot Hills."[25] Layings are playings, and elsewhere one suspects something dubiously desirous in even his smallest actions: he taps on the lid of his tobacco box "in a light and careless way / As men who with their purpose play."[26] As the story unfolds, this purpose becomes hard to disentangle from Wordsworth's own purposes; appetites that are being repudiated seem to blend into those being gratified. One manuscript version includes the following speculations on just how wicked the potter might have been in the past:

> Did Peter e'er with club or stone
> Smite some poor traveller on the head,
> Or beat his father in a rage
> And spill the blood of his old age,
> Or kick a child till he was dead?
>
> Did Peter ever kill his man
> With fist or staff in single duel,
> Or stab with some inhuman wound
> A soldier bleeding on the ground?
> No—Peter never was so cruel.[27]

Just playing. Yet the last line is almost a disappointment and knows itself to be so. Wordsworth is tossing his readers questions that are also fantasies of what they—and indeed he—would like to encounter when reading about reprobates. Peter is like the character of the bigamist-rogue Wordsworth recalled from the comic theater he'd enjoyed in London: "the Spoiler came, 'a bold bad Man' / To God unfaithful, Children, Wife, and Home."[28] The scare quotes tell of something other than the scary, tell rather of a delight in what we affect to despise. "And Peter is a wicked man,"[29] the narrator will say in a moment (one is to imagine a gentle reader luxuriating in the stress on *is*).

The whole poem, in fact, is framed as a tale related to a well-heeled audience (the Vicar, his Dame, the Squire, Stephen Otter, and Little Bess). They interrupt the narrator by telling him he is sometimes too bold, he cunningly begs their indulgence, and so on, but just as the pivotal moment arrives when Peter gazes into the stream to see what's there, the poem suddenly turns on us: "You'd think that he was looking at you."[30] If he were, what would he see?

Is it a party in a parlour?
Cramm'd just as they on earth were cramm'd—
Some sipping punch, some sipping tea,
But, as you by their faces see,
All silent, and all damn'd![31]

It is as though *Alice's Adventures in Wonderland* has been crossed with the *Inferno*. Wordsworth thought this stanza "one of the most imaginative in the whole piece" but was persuaded to drop it from all later editions so as "not to offend the pious."[32] Many wanted to know what, precisely, the lines were playing at. "Is Mr Wordsworth in earnest or is he not?" asked Leigh Hunt; Southey felt that the words "seem placed as if to invite mockery," and another critic even ventured of the last line that it was "a pun on a water dam."[33] Charles Lamb seized on the spirit of the thing:

> I have sat at an Oratorio (that profanation of the purposes of the cheerful playhouse) watching the faces of the auditory in the pit, (what a contrast to Hogarth's Laughing Audience!), immovable, or affecting some faint emotion,—till . . . I have imagined myself in some cold Theatre in Hades, where some of the *forms* of the earthly one should be kept up, with none of the *enjoyment*; or like that—
>
> —Party in a parlor,
> All silent, and all DAMNED![34]

Wordsworth's stanza carries bite against those who merely affect fine feeling as well as those who deny emotion, but it carries its point by making it difficult to determine how much emotion is in the writing itself. Like much of his most provocative play with the ballad mode, it's as if the lines reserve the right suddenly to say "Only joking" while also making the reader unsure about whether they have got the joke. David Bromwich suggests that "It was the fault or freedom of Wordsworth when young to fret very little about the needs of the audience,"[35] to which it might be added that this freedom didn't preclude an interest in his readers, a drive to search for ways he might push his luck in relation to them, and a nagging desire to see their needs as somehow related to his. Peering into the poem and into the water, Narcissus-like, the gentle reader is invited to see his own reflection.

The next stanza returns us to Peter, but with a new sense of our relation to him.

A throbbing pulse the Gazer hath—
Puzzled he was, and now is daunted;
He looks, he cannot choose but look;

Like one intent upon a book—
A book that is enchanted.[36]

"He looks" bespeaks volition; "he cannot choose but look" is a reminder that choices may be compulsions. The revision within the line is a microcosm of a doubled perspective that can be sensed everywhere in *Peter Bell*, one that accounts for our sense that we are encountering not just a story but also, possibly, a blend of confession and interrogation. "He looks" describes Peter from the outside as the poet-narrator simply tells us what he witnesses, but the next phrase acts as witness in a more intimate way (he knows how Peter feels, as perhaps do we, for it takes one to know one). When the hero then faints as a result of what he sees and the poem's first part ends, the disturbing pause is passed on to the reader as the page's white space stares back at us in the 1819 edition. We look. We cannot choose but look.

As we come to our senses—and if we wish to turn over a new leaf—part 2 of the poem begins "We left our Hero in a trance."[37] This is the first time Peter has been called a hero, or described as ours. Speaking of the security with which, when we read, we follow the hero through perilous adventures, Freud suggested that the feeling could be summed up in one sentence: "Nothing can happen to you!" ("We have no difficulty in recognizing His Majesty the Ego, the hero of every daydream and every story.")[38] In which case, "in a trance" can surreptitiously refer to us as well as Peter. The poem keeps snatching us to the player with whom we thought we were playing, as though to read about him is to be read by him. When later discussing the Spirits of the Mind that act on Peter, the narrator returns again to the act of reading. He's heard of one, "a gentle soul,"

Reading, as you or I might read
At night in any pious book,
When sudden blackness overspread
The snow-white page on which he read,
And made the good man round him look.[39]

Wordsworth willingly risks offending the pious here ("any" has its glint: such books are ten a penny). The stanza is a conspiratorial, accusatory wink about the kind of books we really do read under cover of night, books like the one we're holding. A page as white as driven snow turns out to be the scene of another blackout, and what this gentle soul reads on the page, it transpires, is "a *word*" that remains unrevealed by Wordsworth's poem but that brings "full many a sin to light / Out of the bottom of his heart."[40] So, just as "a wicked man" isn't simply wicked, "a good man" isn't exactly good. Perhaps the men are related.

*

Peter Bell is relentless in its pursuit of things that are not meant to go together but that go together because they refuse to go away. While the forward movement of the plot sees Peter and the ass charting a course toward the home of the dead man's family, Peter's mind is—in Wordsworth's resonant phrase—"turn'd adrift into the past."[41] What he finds there is another unlikely couple: himself and someone with whom he used to play, "A sweet and playful Highland girl"[42] he left for dead once she became pregnant. Readers only learn about this girl, though, in the third and final part of *Peter Bell*, so the way the poem calls to its audience is analogous to the way Peter's unconscious calls to him: it keeps asking us not to forget what has gone before, keeps insinuating connections it can't wholly confirm. Small things start to play up by being replayed. As Peter plods through the wood, "A dancing leaf is close behind, / Light plaything for the sportive wind / Upon that solitary waste" ("The very leaves they follow me," the hero incredulously blurts out).[43] Recalling that he'd "danced his round with Highland lasses," and remembering this leaf when we are later told (twice in the space of a few lines) that one particular lass had "followed" him,[44] we begin to sense the tortuous toying of the hero's mind with itself. Elsewhere, "The dusty road is white as bone" initially comes across as mere balladic dressing, but when we later learn of the highland girl that "She to the very bone was worn,"[45] the road flashes back at us with belatedly proleptic force. When Peter, "Back-looking, sees upon a stone / Or in the dust, a crimson stain,"[46] we smell blood, for the whole poem is an uncanny echo chamber for "some strange world of silent pains."[47] "Blood drops—leaves rustle," Peter quips with what the narrator calls "wit mercurial," but the man's wit is in league with unwittingly associative forces in the center of his skull.[48]

Early reviewers were attentive—and resistant—to one particular association: the double act of ass and potter. "The ass is to Mr. Wordsworth's poetry what the *White horse* is to Wouvermann's paintings," one critic noted, "always in the fore-ground—or like the jack at bowls—no play without him."[49] The implications of this play are followed up after the hero has seen the dead man's body. In one manuscript Peter talks to the ass much as he might talk to a maiden he's deflowered or beaten:

> "I've played with you an ugly game,"
> Quoth Peter to the ass, "but still
> I did not mean to use you ill;
> You must allow you were to blame."[50]

This is hardly progress, but the fact that he now feels the need to justify himself is noteworthy. The later detail about the highland lass—"She to the very bone was worn"—travels in more than one direction, as the narrator intimates: "And not till now hath Peter seen / How gaunt the Creature is,—how lean / And sharp his staring bones."[51] It's as if a revelatory equation were being formulated: the ass is to the dead man as the highland lass was to Peter—abandoned yet faithful to a memory and the bond it recalls. This also echoes the position of the dead man's family, and when Peter and the ass return home, all the family's hopes seem to be thrust onto the animal. The wife "calls the poor Ass by his name,"[52] and for a moment the referent of "his" is brilliantly, comically, seriously uncertain; she may be calling out to her husband via the ass, loading all the feelings she has left onto the creature that stood by him.

Several readers were angered by the poem's horseplay. "He is too fond of the ass," one noted, "the incessant bursts of passion and regard directed towards the half-starved brute, and mixed with those of sorrow for the woman and her fatherless babes, only serve to break in upon our feelings, and to excite our disgust."[53] Yet Wordsworth was often drawn to combinations of excitement *and* disgust, and he insisted elsewhere that "the pathetic participates of an *animal* sensation."[54] *Peter Bell* pushes through the paraphernalia of sentiment to get at that sensation, breaks in on "feelings" in order to break them down. What, for example, might be extracted from such a trifling matter as *knees*? In the manuscripts, the hero talks to himself as the corpse comes into view:

> Those are, no doubt, a dead man's knuckles
> And there you see his brass shoe-buckles
> And there his breeches' knees.[55]

Wordsworth probably thought this too chipper; he subsequently revised so as to switch the owner of the knees: "So better to peruse the corse / He rises on his knees." Rising "on" (rather than "from") your knees is laughable in the wrong sort of way, so he dropped that idea and had another go: "a dead body there is lying / Face, feet and hands and knees."[56] Better, but still not satisfactory, so he gave up and cut the word altogether from that stanza. The editor of the Cornell edition notes that too often throughout the history of the *Peter Bell*, Wordsworth seems "uncertain of the boundary between the grotesquely effective and the busily ridiculous."[57] But it seems to me to be characteristic of Wordsworth to make that uncertainty into a source of his poetry's power, for he wants to know what it takes—and what it means—to be brought to your knees.

Toward the end, when Peter tries to hold the grieving widow together—"he held / Her body propp'd against his knee"[58]—the obdurate, awkward physicality of the action readies us for the moment a few stanzas later when Peter, stricken by his impotence in the face of her grief, goes outside to give her privacy:

> And Peter turns his steps aside
> Into a shade of darksome trees,
> Where he sits down, he knows not how,
> With his hands press'd against his brow,
> And resting on his tremulous knees.[59]

The lines are grotesquely effective on account of their connections with the busily ridiculous. In later editions, Wordsworth revised the last line to read "His elbows resting on his tremulous knees," perhaps because he was anxious to avoid the glimmer of absurdity in the first version: for a moment, readers might think that "resting" refers to the hands, not back to "he," before wondering how the hands can be in two places at once. But Peter is beside himself in the full sense of that term, doesn't even know how he sits down (can he be said to "sit" if he's on his knees?). The clumsiness of the lines tells of how in such agonizing moments a mind loses track of its body or feels separated from it. Wordsworth could easily have decided to describe Peter's knees as "trembling," but the very way that "tremulous" seeks to raise the tone a little, even as it unbalances the rhythm, speaks to the man's awkward struggle for self-command.

As Peter sinks down, it is "As if his mind were sinking deep / Through years that have been long asleep,"[60] and the sinking feeling alerts him once more to the inscrutable ass standing beside him. The moment reaches back to the instant when he first banged the animal's bones:

> What followed?—yielding to the shock
> The Ass, as if to take his ease,
> In quiet uncomplaining mood
> Upon the spot where he had stood
> Dropt gently down upon his knees.
>
> And then upon his side he fell
> And by the river's bank did lie
> And, as he lay like one that mourn'd,
> The patient beast on Peter turn'd
> His shining hazel eye.[61]

Do asses have knees? Wordsworth hardly ever refers to the knees of anything nonhuman, and the *OED* is similarly hesitant: "Knee: 4. a: A joint in an animal likened to, or regarded as corresponding in position or shape to, the human knee." The unruly comic potential of the appendages with which he had been playing in the manuscript now becomes a preparation for an insistence on what man and beast may share. The ass "lay like one that mourn'd," with "one" somehow conspiring to include the idea of both a person and an animal. The narrator later refers to "the animal within" when speaking of Peter's collapse into a new kind of "self-involv'd" wakefulness.[62] The animal has unwittingly shown the hero how to mourn—for himself as well as for others, for himself *via* others. Wordsworth takes a well-worn comic refrain—Falstaff sums it up with panache when he says "I do begin to perceive that I am made an ass"[63]—and puts pressure on it in order to trace links between subhuman passivity and a disorienting sense of humanity. To sink onto your knees like an ass is to plumb the depths of the comic, but Wordsworthian depths are often an intimation of dizzy heights. As he observed elsewhere, "The higher mode of being does not exclude, but necessarily includes, the lower; the intellectual does not exclude, but necessarily includes, the sentient; the sentient, the animal, and the animal, the vital—to its lowest degrees."[64]

The coalescence of the sentient and the intellectual in *Peter Bell* bears on the fact that our hero doesn't exactly choose a better life; he falls on it. As he watches the widow sit "In agony of silent grief—/ From his own thoughts did Peter start."[65] "From" (not, say, "At") is typical of Wordsworth's care with the smallest, blandest of words, and here it catches a mingled note of recognition and rejection, an uncertainty about whether Peter is ready to hear—and to bear—what his thoughts are telling him. The narrator may be viewing Peter from without or within (reading the state of his mind from his body language, or vice versa), but the feeling that the hero's voyage of self-discovery is in some obscure, half-buried way linked to Wordsworth's sense of his own life as a writer is strengthened by the decision to bring the vocabulary of fanciful play to the fore at a key moment. It's at this juncture that the narrator ventures the longest interruption to the main action of the poem. Addressing spirits "Whom in my fear I love so well," he says,

> I know you, potent Spirits! well,
> How with the feeling and the sense
> Playing, ye govern foes or friends,
> Yok'd to your will, for fearful ends—
> And this I speak in reverence!
>
> . . . .
>
> Then, coming from the wayward world,
> That powerful world in which ye dwell,
> Come, Spirits of the Mind! and try

To-night, beneath the moonlight sky,
What may be done with Peter Bell![66]

In the manuscript, Wordsworth claimed that these moods of the mind worked "for most gracious ends," but the revision to "fearful" stays true to his feeling that play is an unruly instinct before it is anything amenably moral. The question of what is to be done with Peter is related to the question of what the poet himself can do given his own propensity to go astray: "I feel that I am all unfit . . . I've play'd and danc'd with my narration— / I loiter'd long ere I began."[67] This last line may refer back to the lengthy prologue, or to the life the narrator-poet led before he sat down to write (in the manuscript he refers to himself as "a thoughtless man; / I've mov'd to many a giddy measure").[68] The poem isn't about to elaborate what this thoughtlessness entailed, although, like Peter, Wordsworth had been leading a wandering, wayward life in 1798 and had himself left both woman and child a few years earlier. If playing is a way of loitering with darkly delectable intent, and if it's associated with both emotional and poetic energy while rendering you somehow suspect, how is it to be handled or justified?

*

The man and writer who speaks most powerfully to Wordsworth about the needful, questionable relations between the ludic and the bardic—and about the force of a poetics that that is willing to countenance a risky kind of humor or lightness—is Robert Burns. Informing Coleridge in 1799 that he'd been hard at work on *Peter Bell*, Wordsworth paused to note that Burns "is energetic solemn and sublime in sentiment, and profound in feeling. His Ode to Despondency I can never read without the deepest agitation."[69] Burns's ode is spoken by an itinerant Peter Bell–like adventurer, a reprobate who laments that after early days spent "dancing thoughtless Pleasure's maze, / To Care, to Guilt unknown!" he is now "Unfitted with an aim": "Dim-backward as I cast my view, / What sick'ning Scenes appear!" Addressing the spirits of his youth, the "tiny elves that guiltless sport," he opines, "Ye little know the ills ye court."[70] The agitation Wordsworth felt on hearing such confessions is still present many years later in his *Letter to a Friend of Robert Burns* (1816). Casting a sly glance at "the rigidly virtuous" and speaking of "sensibilities which are the elements of genius," he praises Burns for trusting to "primary instincts." Burns's most celebrated hymn to such instincts, to lasses and asses, is *Tam o' Shanter* (Wordsworth would later question detractors of *Peter Bell* because their blood doesn't heat "at Tam o' Shanter's name").[71] His own blood is certainly up now:

> Who, but some impenetrable dunce or narrow-minded puritan in works of art, ever read without delight the picture which he has drawn of the convivial exaltation of the rustic adventurer, Tam o' Shanter? The poet fears not to tell the reader in the outset that his hero was a desperate and sottish drunkard, whose excesses were frequent as his opportunities. This reprobate sits down to his cups, while the storm is roaring, and heaven and earth are in confusion;—the night is driven on by song and tumultuous noise—laughter and jest thicken as the beverage improves upon the palate—conjugal fidelity archly bends to the service of general benevolence—selfishness is not absent, but wearing the mask of social cordiality—and, while these various elements of humanity are blended into one proud and happy composition of elated spirits, the anger of the tempest without doors only heightens and sets off the enjoyment within.—I pity him who cannot perceive that, in all this, though there was no moral purpose, there is a moral effect.
>
> Kings may be blest, but Tam was glorious,
> O'er a' the *ills* of life victorious.[72]

Given that this commentary is intended as a riposte to critics of Burns's life as well as his poetry, the narrow-minded puritan in works of art is now taken to be narrow minded in other areas too. In the next paragraph Wordsworth cools down and suggests that the lesson of Burns's poem is "charitable indulgence," adding that the moral effect is gleaned from how, "as far as he [Burns] puts the reader in possession of this intelligent sympathy, he qualifies him for exercising a salutary influence over the minds of those who are thus deplorably enslaved."[73] But the man who writes "deplorably enslaved" is giving a little too much back to the enemy, and he is not quite the same man who writes the words "conjugal fidelity archly bends to the service of general benevolence."

Lamb swooped on that last phrase in a letter to Wordsworth ("exquisite," he called it),[74] and it suggests that although the delight with which one reads *Tam o' Shanter* includes the pleasure of intelligent sympathy for a reprobate, it is not wholly accounted for by it. Wordsworth is not considering how to exercise a salutary influence over a man like Tam when he copies down the couplet that sings of his glory; he is intimating that one of "the *ills* of life" is the wish to tame such energies. Back in 1803, Lamb had copied out a large chunk of another poem that would become important to Wordsworth—Cotton's "Ode to Winter"—and sent it to his friend, asking "How could Burns miss the series of lines from 42–49?" Lest Wordsworth should miss the point, Lamb underscored the line "What would we be, *but what we are?*"[75] The seriocomic thrill of that question, its blend of the rueful, the consoling, and the incorrigible, lies at the heart of Wordsworth's poetry, and his love for

Burns's art is indebted to his feeling for how the work allows readers to glean connections (although not necessarily complete identifications) between the man who writes and the dubious players who inhabit the writing. Wordsworth notes that "On the basis of his human character he has reared a poetic one. . . . Burns avail[s] himself of his own character and situation in society, to construct out of them a poetic self,—introduced as a dramatic personage."[76] The terms here echo the point he had made to Coleridge many years earlier in the letter about *Peter Bell*: "Tam Shanter I do not deem a character, I question whether there is any individual character in all Burns' writing except his own. But every where you have the presence of human life. The communications that proceed from Burns come to the mind with the life and charm of recognitions."[77] The movement from Tam to "human life" is mirrored in the 1816 *Letter*, where there's a shift from talk of a sottish drunkard to that of "various elements of humanity," and the shift here from "communications" to "recognitions" is suggestive too.

The central terms of Wordsworth's appreciation of Burns are echoed in something Gilbert Burns said about his brother: "He frequently presents a caricature of his feelings, and even of his failings—a kind of mock-heroic account of himself and his opinions, which he never supposed could be taken literally [and] which the author evidently intends should be considered a mere play of the imagination."[78] The voices of *Peter Bell*'s fanciful hero and narrator bear a similar relationship to their creator, yet the mock-heroic impulse shouldn't be taken as a disclaimer for the feelings and failings it entertains. For both Wordsworth and Burns, play is never "mere" play in this sense. There are many moments of Burns-like play throughout *Peter Bell*, but one echo is particularly charged. What finally turns Peter adrift into his past is the moment at which he ambles—or stumbles—into a scene highly reminiscent of Burns:

passing by an inn
Brim-full of a carousing crew,
Making, with curses not a few,
An uproar and a drunken din.[79]

It's at this moment that Peter recalls the image of "A sweet and playful Highland girl, / As light and beauteous as a squirrel, / As beauteous and as wild!," the one who "put on her gown of green" and left her mother at sixteen (the Cornell editor notes, "A woman supposedly got a gown of green by tumbling in the grass; hence the phrase became a euphemism for loss of virginity").[80]

Close by a brake of flowering furze
(Above it shivering aspins play)

He sees an unsubstantial creature,
His very self in form and feature,
Not four yards from the broad highway[81]

What he sees next to this recollection of his past self is the highland girl at the moment of her death, crying out for her mother ("he beholds by the furze-brake / This miserable vision!"). One of Burns's most cherished visions of play is being superimposed over another, for the carousing crew gives way under the pressure of another poem that meant a great deal to Wordsworth. In "The Vision," Burns's speaker "backward mus'd on wasted time" just as Peter Bell does now, before he was suddenly accosted by an image of a highland girl from some "wild glen," "Her Mantle large, of greenish hue." This girl, it transpires, is the poet's muse, and—unbeknown to him—she's been musing too:

I saw thy pulse's maddening play,
Wild-send thee Pleasure's devious way,
Misled by Fancy's meteor-ray,
    By Passion driven;
But yet the light that led astray,
    Was light from Heaven.[82]

The cluster of feelings and forces on which Wordsworth places so much value (play, pleasure, fancy, passion) is sponsored even though—or, rather, *because*—it is acknowledged as maddening, wild, devious, misleading. In *Peter Bell*, the hero's stricken revelation about what his playful life entails is ghosted by Burns's inquiry into what goes into the making of a poetic vocation, as though one realm were being tentatively read as a key to the other.

"A Vision" closes with another stanza of charged play, one that Wordsworth committed to heart—he quotes it toward the end of a letter to Lady Beaumont in 1806 ("the longest letter I ever wrote in my life") and is still to be found chanting it in 1841 as he plants holly berries ("he was as earnest and eager about it," recalled an observer, "as if it had been a matter of importance"):[83]

"*And wear thou this*"—She solemn said,
And bound the Holly round my head:
The polish'd leaves, and berries red,
    Did rustling play;
And, like a passing thought, she fled,
    In light away.[84]

"Blood drops—leaves rustle," as Peter Bell would say. The stanza is, in Wordsworth's phrase, "energetic solemn." That the muse's blessing is received and remembered like a passing thought doesn't lessen its importance, and if Peter's miserable vision of the abandoned woman is informed by this one, then the crowning of a poet is somehow being used to comment on the transformation of a life.

For all his mockery in *Peter Bell the Third*, Shelley seized on something vital when describing the Wordsworthian way of seeing and thinking:

> An apprehension clear, intense,
> Of his mind's work, had made alive
> The things it wrought on; I believe
> Wakening a sort of thought in sense.[85]

This sort of thought is what Hass would call a sexual thought (which may or may not be a thought about sex)—somatic, involuntary, wrapped up in other thoughts it's not entirely sure it wants to have. And a sexual thought invites both a feeling of need and a feeling of shame—a feeling of shame *at* the need, coupled with a desire to overrule shame and to keep experiencing the thought regardless. Such thoughts are the mind's play as well as its work, a play that in some circumstances borders on modes of self-forgiveness and self-indulgence as well as on forms of guilt and remorse. "Who among philosophers," asks Stanley Cavell, "has a theory of forgiveness, and whether it is givable? It would be a theory of comedy."[86] And the theory would perhaps be comic, for the givable might well be risible, might well recommit you to the errors of your ways. If Wordsworth was drawing on Burns in order to apologize for libidinous energies by stressing how they shape artistic ones, trying to get the muse to forgive him for what he did to the maiden ("she fled, / In light away" reverses the contours of the situation, for it was he who fled her), then his writing is an act of sublimation, not simply an act of contrition. The poem sets things in defiance while setting them straight.

*

The Romantics didn't invent the unconscious, but they did christen it. The *OED* credits De Quincey for bringing *subconscious* into the language and Coleridge for inaugurating a specific valence of *unconscious*. The word is important for Wordsworth too; in *The Prelude* he tells of how Nature opened his eyes to a standard he then felt impelled to apply "Even when unconsciously, to other things / Which less I understood,"[87] and elsewhere he speaks of one "not unconscious of self-blame."[88] *Peter Bell* was an attempt to make something of such a feeling, and everywhere in it one glimpses shards of experience that Wordsworth was at the same time piecing together in early drafts of *The Prelude*, a poem whose roots in sensual life he would later stress when he spoke of its being composed "in Dythyrambic fervour."[89] The suggestion that Peter Bell is his creator's guileful, guilty double is also hinted at in the early manuscripts, where the narrator refers to "friend Peter." "But who is Peter?" asks one of the listeners to the tale, "'Tis a downright riddle!"[90] Wordsworth later told Isabella Fenwick that his potter was taken from "a wild rover with whom I walked from Builth on the River Wye downwards nearly as far as the town of Hay. He told me strange stories."'[91] Wordsworth was wildly roving himself, and another manuscript fragment tells an even stranger story:

I was foremost thou wert fore
The both hung back in murderer's
guize
Twas thou that were afraid of me
Twas I that was afraid of thee
We'd each of us a hundred eyes
. . . .
Ah Peter ~~peter well thou know'st~~
What tookst to lure my secret out
. . . .
Twas bullying now & now twas
crouching
Keen looks for a bards

[?]nd coaxing wheedling slyness
slouching
. . . .
But we were heroes both that
night[92]

One sometimes registers in Wordsworth a kind of eroticism of words, a feeling that he wants his poems to hide as well as to reveal things. Here, his self-portrait is very close to De Quincey's recollection of him as someone who bore "a natural resemblance to Mrs Ratcliffe's Schedoni and other assassins roaming through prose and verse."[93] Peter and Wordsworth are afraid of each other in the way that Peter may be "of himself afraid,"[94] or in the way that the narrator says of Peter that "To see him was to fear him."[95] And, when viewed in a certain light, everyone can see themselves in a murderous yet heroic guise.

If this meeting was the kernel of Wordsworth's poem, then the lines suggest that *Peter Bell* is both an attempted exorcism of demons and a defense of the need for them. And as the poet commits to retelling strange stories in print, he takes on something of his companion's slyness. In fact, the potter and his narrator face analogous difficulties when telling the story. Peter is "confus'd" as he tells the widow what's happened, is "pale as death; / His voice is weak with perturbation" and "from a thousand causes / Is crippled sore in his narration."[96] In the prologue the narrator "Limp'd on with some vexation" and with

> visage pale,
> And sore too from a slight contusion,
> Did I, to cover my confusion,
> Begin the *promised* Tale.[97]

Both men are driven to and from Wordsworth's founding scene of play, the scene in which you are compelled to revisit actions you find it difficult to disown (and, sometimes, to denounce) because they contain energies and experiences that have gone into the making of you.

In *Peter Bell*, nobody is allowed to escape from play unscathed or untutored, yet Leigh Hunt's mockery of the poem as a "didactic little horror"[98] misses its challenge by assuming that Wordsworth is championing a religious outlook. The Methodist sermon Peter chances to overhear is one factor among several that accompanies his change of heart, but the sermon arrives belatedly and is less the cause of his change than a desperately seized support for it. Besides, the change itself is handled in the last lines of the poem with a kind of deadpan polish that carries more than a hint of playfulness:

> And Peter Bell, who, till that night,
> Had been the wildest of his clan,
> Forsook his crimes, repressed his folly,
> And, after ten months' melancholy,
> Became a good and honest man.[99]

The lines are offered with a glint in the eye, like Burns's mock moral at the end of *Tam o' Shanter* ("Remember Tam o' Shanter's mare"). They also cast a side-glance at the poem to which *Peter Bell* alludes on several occasions and whose purported moral and ending feel equally strained ("A sadder and a wiser man / He rose the morrow morn").[100] Wordsworth noted elsewhere of one of his poems that, although a little out of love with it now, "I like, however, the beginning of it so well that, for the sake of that, I tacked to it the respectably tame conclusion."[101] The conclusion of *Peter Bell* might be read as an ironic concession to "the pious" or as further provocation to inauthentic pieties. As Walter Scott suggested, "The professed moral of a piece is usually what the reader is least interested in; it is like the mendicant, who cripples after some gay procession, and in vain solicits the attention of those who have been gazing upon it."[102] Imaginative play may have medicinal properties, but that's not the primary reason for swallowing it. A poem needn't enjoin what it espouses.

When someone complained that one of his poems had materials that "were without an arrangement as referring to an end," Wordsworth replied, "Oh, I don't care for that, if there are *good things* in a Poem."[103] The good things in *Peter Bell* are not exactly resistant to its status as conversion narrative but nor are they subservient to it. Defending the poem against possible objections, Jonathan Wordsworth admits that "To some it will seem gratuitous that Peter, having seen his double, and seen himself, should hear the words 'Repeat! Repeat!' echoing from the woods below, where a Methodist is preaching to his flock."[104] Indeed it will, primarily because the preacher says no such thing; his words are "Repent! repent!"[105] The critic's slip is exquisitely apt—a fortunate fall—because it unconsciously gets to the heart of this most unconscionable of poems. Walter Benjamin suggested that "The obscure urge to repeat things is scarcely less powerful in play, scarcely less cunning in its workings, than the sexual impulse in love,"[106] and that urge permeates *Peter Bell*, not least in a line Wordsworth thought so good that he has the narrator end the first stanza with it: "But I will *bang* your bones!"

Bang. Wordsworth's emphasis (at least in manuscript; the italics disappeared in the published version). The critics were either scandalized or sneering. John Taylor Coleridge felt the line was "inserted ornamenti gratiâ" in order to hint at "low and ridiculous associations" and wished that Wordsworth had "merely told us in his own person and in his own language, that Peter beat the ass very unmercifully."[107] (Partridge's *Dictionary of Slang* claims that, from around 1720, to bang someone could be to have sex with them.) The line is playing on an old comic trope in which the ass signifies the noble rider's relation to his own beastly, bodily pleasures. More specifically, it's playing on the moment in *Tristram Shandy* when Tristram's father speaks of how one man's flagellations were

> "the means he used, to make his *ass* (meaning his body) leave off kicking."
>
> It pleased my father well; it was not only a laconick way of expressing—but of libelling, at the same time, the desires and appetites of the lower part of us. . . . He never used the words *passions* once—but *ass* always instead of them—So that he might be said truly, to have been upon the bones, or the back of his own ass, or else of some other man's, during all that time.[108]

For Wordsworth to have his potter say the line at the outset is to take some risk, but then—like any truly treasured form of play—to allow the statement to return again some six hundred lines later is to commit to the body's most inveterate need: "Repeat! Repeat!"

In the prologue, the poet-narrator says to his audience, "To see how ye are all distrest, / Till my ribs ach'd, I'd laugh at you!"[109] The somatic, sadistic glee of this is close to the heart of the poem, and is in keeping with its hero's appetite for banging bones. It is also, crucially, imagined to be in keeping with the gentle reader's appetites. The Squire who listens to the narrator's tale notes that "Sure as Paradise / Was lost to us by Adam's sinning / We all are wandering in a wood."[110] One translation of this might be that Peter is to the narrator as the narrator is to Wordsworth and as Wordsworth is to anybody else who stays to watch:

> So from his pocket Peter takes
> His shining horn tobacco-box
> And in a careless way, as you
> Or I, good Mr. Swan, might do
> Upon the lid he knocks.[111]

Wordsworth cut the narrator's insinuating reference to "you or I" in the published version,[112] but the manuscript stays true to what the poem intimates: Peter and the poet tap on that tobacco box as though they were tapping on the coffin lid of their own pasts or of their most forbidden pleasures, and the invitation is left open to any reader who cares to inspect other pasts for themselves. When Wordsworth speaks elsewhere in the poem "Of all that *love* their lawless lives,"[113] he senses the difficulty of deciding who should be excluded from this group.

But *Peter Bell's* ending is not simply ironic even as it continues to play with its purposes while appearing to be intent on shipwrecking its hero into reality. Rather, the spruce summing up in which the wild man "Forsook his crimes, repressed his folly" is a kind of moral punchline. Manuscript versions tell us that he "forsook his folly," and in later editions Wordsworth revised it to "renounced his folly," but "repressed" is in tune with the irrepressible spirit of the poem because repressed folly is still very much a part of you, more likely to make a play for you when you're least expecting it (whatever else the poem says, it says that—for good and ill—the repressed *will* return).[114] This is the only occasion in his poetry that Wordsworth uses the word *repressed*, and it acts as a reminder that the hero is no more completely immunized against the "medley air"[115] that defines him than the poet-narrator is wholly rescued from the attractions and allegiances that helped to bring the poem into being.

Peter Bell is unnervingly, gloriously at play with two convictions—or intuitions—that Wordsworth held dear: the feeling that life teaches you how to live it, and the feeling that life is experienced most fully when lived without too much regard for any lesson it may provide. The poet-narrator began this tale, it will be recalled, "to cover" his confusion. The poem is one of Wordsworth's greatest cover stories, and it lures his secrets out: an unabashed yet conflicted appetite for trouble that plays with and against "the rigidly virtuous," and an enduring fear of his own relish for deviant delight. "Mr Wordsworth, how *could* you be so giddy?" Felicia Hemans once asked, before laughing at her surprise and adding, "He has, undeniably, a lurking love of mischief."[116] That love was still lurking when Mr. Wordsworth returned to his poem some thirty years after he wrote it. He was not claiming that he'd become "a good and honest man" when he confessed, "I am as much Peter Bell as ever."[117]

Idlers

> It seems they have no work to do,
> Or that their work is done.
>
> "THE IDLE SHEPHERD-BOYS"[1]

The play within the seriousness of the Intimations Ode and the serious play of *Peter Bell* exist in tandem—even in partnership: both poems are portraits of the artist as well as fantasies of connectedness between different parts of the self ("Children" and "Reprobates" are not so much polarities, but complements). But can these fantasies issue in connections between self and others? If Wordsworth is drawn to conceive the spirit of play as a form of recompense for personal losses or as a revaluation of his own fallings and failures, then how far might this spirit be imagined as interpersonal? Certain aspects of my discussion so far have conceived Wordsworth's poems as though they were something akin to private jokes, written to and for himself as a means of consolidating—or discovering—who he is. This is certainly an aspect of his poetry's opaque force, but private jokes are composed in a shared medium, for words are never simply private property. Language, like humor, is a social animal, and Wordsworth is mindful of the fact that composition is also a form of conduct. I now want to consider what sort of play is achievable—and, indeed, defensible—in that seemingly most nonludic of Wordsworthian modes: the poem of encounter.

On turning twenty-one, Wordsworth declared to a friend, "I am doomed to be an idler thro my whole life. . . . Yet with all this I am tolerable happy; do you think this ought to be a matter of congratulation to me, or no?"[2] Despite the drollery—or because of it—the question is a serious one for him. Lionel Trilling observed, "the will seeking its own negation—or, rather, seeking its own affirmation by its rejection of the aims which the world sets before it and by turning its energies upon itself in self-realization. Of this particular affirmation of the will Wordsworth is the proponent and the poet." This is absolutely true, although Trilling had noted earlier that the Wordsworthian moral essence resides in the interplay between the individual and other people, "between an awareness of the self that must be saved and developed, and an awareness that the self is yet fulfilled only in community."[3] Such an interplay makes play itself a negotiation with the world's aims, not a rejection of them. When the narrator of *The Idiot Boy* observes that "The world will say 'tis very idle,"[4] Wordsworth's enjoyment of the provocation issued to the world admits to his need to find—and to justify—his place in it.

Johan Huizinga suggested that "Romanticism was born in play,"[5] but there was nonetheless some debate about what play should be. Whether the apparent idleness of the activity might be conceived as a catalyst, not merely a luxury (or worse), was a recurring question in late eighteenth-century aesthetics. Building on lines of inquiry in Burke and Kant, Schiller saw the freedom of the play drive as the spur to aesthetic education; although the drive "tears itself away from the fetters of utility altogether, and beauty in and for itself alone begins to be an object," it also becomes a means of "making better insights effective for living."[6] (Poems are useless, A. R. Ammons would later note, but "only uselessness is empty enough for the presence of so many uses."[7]) So play may be both haven and testing ground—at once gratuitous and preparative—and Wordsworth's enduring fascination with the word often recalls this paradox. In the first book of *The Prelude* he hopes that "Not uselessly employ'd, / I might pursue this theme through every change / Of exercise and play,"[8] which hints at a concern about what should be considered gainful employment without renouncing the idea that the shaping of the ludic into language can be understood as a form of labor.[9] He likes to rhyme *play* with both *stray* and *prey*, and to inhabit a space where things can go either way. "We saunter'd, play'd, we rioted," he recalls elsewhere in *The Prelude*.[10] The verb feels languid yet strangely purposive in such company, and at other points in the poem it's associated with the partaking of strawberries and cream as well as with the revolutionary energy in France.[11]

Wordsworth adores those who play—"His fancy play'd with endless play / So full of mother wit was he"[12]—but should the endless be a means to an end? Sometimes, for him, this is not the right question; at other times it's the question that won't go away. A dual impulse can often be felt at his line ends, which allow for a glimpse of intransitive or self-enclosed meanings before the sense is gently expanded:

> Yet does she still all fondly play
> On scenes remote with smiling ray.[13]

> Among the hills the Echoes play
> A never, never ending song[14]

gladsome sounds,
That, from the rural School ascending, play
Beneath her, and about her.[15]

Then, chearful Flower! my spirits play
With kindred motion[16]

Play is just play, but it's also play *with*, or *on*, or *beneath*, or *about*. Neither wholly autotelic nor fully instrumental, it's on its way somewhere via a kind of improvised, fortuitous pleasure in the moment.

Wordsworth is often on the lookout for coalescences of work and play rather than oppositions between them. In *Evening Voluntaries* the dorhawk chases the white moth "with burring note, which Industry and Sloth / Might both be pleased with, for it suits them both";[17] in *Home at Grasmere* "a playful band" of birds is "at rest, / Yet not at rest."[18] When he turns to study human animals, though, things become more complex. In a fine discussion of georgic and pastoral impulses in the poetry, David Fairer suggests that the former becomes an element of unease placed within the *otium* of the latter, "as if allowing experience to shadow innocence . . . the text silently distances itself from georgic, but in a way that brings an unsettling georgic consciousness into being, haunting the scene much as we readers do as we watch and overhear it."[19] A crucial feature of Wordsworthian scenes of strange meeting is that they arise when the poet is not getting up to anything very much; lolling about is the founding condition of the poem's sense of the time it has on its hands—time to stop, stare, and reflect. And yet, this time (call it the time of idle, pastoral play) also becomes subject to the poet's inquiring gaze.

For the remainder of this chapter, I'll turn first to three poems of encounter before focusing in detail on "Resolution and Independence." As Fancy plays with endless play, we may recall Wordsworth's defense of the law under which the processes of this rival to Imagination are carried on, "as capricious as the accidents of things, and the effects are surprising, playful, ludicrous, amusing, tender, or pathetic, as the objects happen to be appositely produced or fortunately combined."[20] Talk of accidence and capriciousness should not be entirely dissociated from his anxieties elsewhere about language as "counter-spirit, unremittingly and noiselessly at work to derange, to subvert, to lay waste, to vitiate, and to dissolve."[21] The mixed fortunes of people's words—and of people at the hands of words—may lead to combinations of the ludicrous and the pathetic that feel inapposite. One way to face, if not necessarily to defeat, the risk of language as counterspirit is to build that risk into a poem's language. From which it may follow that a certain kind of wrong, or wrongness, is perpetrated in the very fabric of the writing, which can itself be more instructive than being in the right—if indeed that is a place where writing can be. Faced by certain versions of literary or ethical achievement, Wordsworth would I think have warmed to the serious comedy of Beckett's words: "Something there badly not wrong."[22]

*

Wordsworth's writing is frequently ghosted by an implicit questioning of its own fun—or a dramatizing of its own pleasure—as the poetry becomes drawn to wondering what it wants from people, why it wants to play around with them or to work them over. One of the "Poems on the Naming of Places" (sometimes called "Point Rash Judgement") recalls a time when Wordsworth, his sister, and Coleridge were sauntering in vacant mood, watching the "sportive wanderings" of dandelion seeds in the wind, "its very playmate":

> —Ill suits the road with one in haste, but we
> Play'd with our time; and, as we stroll'd along,
> It was our occupation to observe
> . . . .
> —And often, trifling with a privilege
> Alike indulg'd to all, we paus'd, one now
> And now the other, to point out, perchance
> To pluck, some flower or water-weed, too fair
> Either to be divided from the place
> On which it grew, or to be left alone
> To its own beauty.[23]

The lingering stress on "we" at the end of that first line revels in the self-indulgence of the mood, and one also notes the hazard of using a word like *occupation* at this moment. While idle talk about trifling with what "all" can enjoy isn't exactly treated ironically, the lines register what the route might feel like for others who have fewer privileges to play with. The writing is neither ambling nor analyzing; it is caught between the need to avoid taking things too seriously and the feeling that these matters are not unserious either. Can't plucking flowers simply be just plucking flowers? Yes and no. As so often in Wordsworth, the vignette has a kind of laconic shimmer. The memory of that day is shadowed by events that follow it, for even the fond recollection of pleasure is being asked to take on things that pleasure hadn't countenanced at the time.

The group continues in "happy idleness," listening to "the busy mirth / Of Reapers" (if "mirth" is pastoral, "busy" is georgic). They see a man fishing alone, and all agree that he must be "An idle man, who thus could lose a day / Of the mid-harvest." So idleness of one kind sees fit to berate idleness of another. But it turns out that he is "Too weak to labour." In fact, he is *at* labour:

> he turn'd his head
> To greet us—and we saw a Man worn down
> By sickness, gaunt and lean, with sunken cheeks
> And wasted limbs, his legs so long and lean
> That for my single self I look'd at them,
> Forgetful of the body they sustain'd.—

What looked like wasted time is a consequence of wasted limbs. The setting for the group's gentle stroll ("the lake that lay / Asleep in a dead calm") is the man's unyielding workplace; he's using "his best skill to gain / A pittance from the dead unfeeling lake / That knew not of his wants." It's as if the revelation is too much to bear, as if Wordsworth starts to see the pastoral calm of his own previous language as "unfeeling" and so transfers his lack of care onto the lake. The play of words starts to play against him: earlier, he had been "Feeding unthinking fancies" while the man looked for food; he'd let his eyes glance over "a thin veil of glittering haze" while other forms of thinness were passed over; he'd admired picturesque details ("wither'd bough . . . dry wreck") that gave the gaunt and lean an aesthetic sheen.

The line that strikes the arresting, disorienting Wordsworthian note in the passage above is not really about the worker. "That for my single self I look'd at them" has a somatic charge, speaks to the spasm or shudder you sometimes feel in your own legs when you catch a glimpse of weakness or decrepitude in somebody else's. "My single self": he means to stress that he doesn't want to speak for what the others saw or felt, but the phrase also implies that the narrator somehow finds himself staring for his own good, or that he arrives at a renewed sense of his own selfhood by momentarily apprehending the man as almost fractured into parts by the hardships he bears. The poem tries to recover from the shock of this by returning to community—"Nor did we fail to see within ourselves / What need there is to be reserv'd in speech, / And temper all our thoughts with charity"—but the collective moral doesn't come from quite the same place as the curious singularity of the former line. The old man has become an unnerving double of the flower that was earlier being played with (and "perchance" plucked): he's too astonishing a figure to be offered merely as a prompt for a moral lesson or "to be divided from the place" where he was trying to find his own means to grow; yet he's too uncanny a being "to be left alone" by the observer who senses the importance of trying to take the experience away with him. I say "flower," but the earlier line had in fact spoken of "some flower or water-weed." Wordsworth noted that "Weeds have been called flowers out of place. I fear the place most people would assign to them is too limited."[24] In trying to work out the man's place, the poem becomes unsure of its own.

"Nothing is so rare as to see misfortune fairly portrayed," Simone Weil observed. "The tendency is either to treat the unfortunate person as though catastrophe were his natural vocation, or to ignore the effects of misfortune on the soul, to assume, that is, that the soul can suffer and remain unmarked by it, can fail, in fact, to be recast in misfortune's image."[25] The sick man is gaunt and lean with wasted limbs, but he is worn down *by* sickness, not *with* it; the syntax avoids reducing him to his condition. "Forgetful of the body they sustain'd" acknowledges just how much the man has been remade in misfortune's image, but talking of the limbs as if they were somehow not entirely assimilable to the body refuses to naturalize catastrophe. The visceral shock of what the man has become is felt alongside the recognition that this is not the entirety of what he is. In 1802, defending himself against complaints from Mary and Sara Hutchinson about a phrase in an early version of "Resolution and Independence," Wordsworth wrote, "The poem is throughout written in the language of men—'I suffered much by a sickness had by me long ago' is a phrase which anybody might use, as well as 'a sickness which I had long ago.'"[26] "Had by me" is awkward, but the awkwardness defends the agency of the old man, tells of a precarious independence of the sufferer from his suffering (in a strange way, "by me" also allows for a spatial positioning of the sickness; he had it *by* him in the sense that it wasn't *in* him—or *of* him).

Despite the care Wordsworth takes with the smallest words, "Point Rash Judgement" remains mindful of the fact that any words may be a form of encroachment, or even of callousness (this is why the narrator initially says "I will not say / What thoughts immediately were ours"). "To be crisp even in praise of people's excellence is to make oneself a little the proprietor of their virtue," Hugh Kenner once noted, "the supreme insult to that which is other than we, that which, perceived by the eye, is *therefore* other: the supreme insult we can offer to the other is to have, on too little acquaintance, something to say 'about' it."[27] This is itself well said, but Wordsworth also senses that the minding of one's tongue may, in some situations, shade into a culpable minding of one's distance. To stay silent may be to duck the challenge of such a moment.[28] Not that the challenge is necessarily surmountable. The question of our answerability to others—and the limits of that answerability—is pushed further elsewhere via a curious mixture of the thoughtful and the thwarted.

In "The Old Cumberland Beggar," the narrator speaks in hushed appreciation of "that vast solitude to which / The tide of things" has led the beggar, a solitude in which he appears "To breathe and live but for himself alone" even as the narrator hopes that "while his life is his," the man may call forth a solicitude that brings him into connection with others.[29] But the poem cannot quite let him be:

> Then let him pass, a blessing on his head!
> . . . .
> Let him be free of mountain solitudes,
> And have around him, whether heard or not,
> The pleasant melody of woodland birds.[30]

So now Wordsworth appears to wish the beggar free of that vast solitude which he'd previously cherished as his right, not merely as his predicament. It's as though he confesses to a need to console *himself* (and also his readers) by blanketing the old man in companionable pastoral haze. Lamb's response to this was characteristically acute:

> The delicate and curious feeling in the wish for the Cumberland Beggar, that he may have about him the melody of Birds, altho' he hear them not.—Here the mind knowingly passes a fiction upon herself, first substituting her own feelings for the Beggar's, and, in the same breath detecting the fallacy, will not part with the wish.[31]

The fact that self-involved energies drive delicate feelings isn't necessarily a reason to suppress either the energies or the feelings. In its own way, the phrase "whether heard or not" actually leaves the beggar to his own devices—leaves him to and for himself—even as the lines confess to a concern about his being left alone.

Such poems of encounter frequently suspend or complicate the forms of community they hope to foster. Or, rather, they dream up community itself as a sort of attendance on difference and distance. Comparing Wordsworth with Goethe, Coleridge noted that "they both have this peculiarity of utter non-sympathy with the subjects of their poetry. They are always, both of them, spectators . . . feeling *for*, but never *with*, their characters."[32] This is true of the "The Old Cumberland Beggar," yet Wordsworth didn't want to disown that tempting, treacherous word *sympathy*. When the narrator speaks of the "mild touch of sympathy and thought"[33] that the beggar may awake in observers, "sympathy" and "thought" are conceived as allies even though they are called to monitor one another's activities. Similarly, when he hopes that the beggar will prompt the villagers "To tender offices and pensive thoughts,"[34] he is allowing for the possibility that one could have pensive thoughts about one's tender offices.

*

A lack of awkwardness often made Wordsworth feel uncomfortable. This suggests one reason why to read him is to feel compromised: we become involved in a perplexity about whether he and we are having the right feelings or the wrong ones—and about whether we know how to tell the difference. Resisting those critics—and there have been plenty[35]—who see only moral failure or escapism in Wordsworth's poetics of encounter, David Simpson has argued that many of his best poems stick in the mind precisely because they depict aporias of human interaction; they offer a kind of "epistemological uncanny," "a place of not knowing."[36] More recently, Peter Robinson suggests that the poetry is founded on "the inevitability of blunder" and that this is "the only route there can be to real, deepened insight."[37] This route is pursued through the playful pathos of the writing. A dual note—at once whimsical and haunted—becomes Wordsworth's means of exploring the discomforting connections between bad faith and responsible bafflement. The poetry often faces blunder by seeing it as implicated in wonder, yet without championing wonder as a neat solution to the difficulties being raised.

One poem in the 1807 volume, "Beggars," is characteristic in this respect, and it raises the stakes by having the objects of the idling poet's gaze actually demand something from him. The poem was based on an entry in Dorothy's journal that described a day when she encountered a beggar woman, gave her some bread, and then later came across two boys chasing a butterfly: "They continued at play till I drew very near and then they addressed me with the Begging cant and the whining voice of sorrow."[38] She is adamant that the boys are the sons of the lady she met, and so she tells them that she's already given their mother provisions. They reply that this couldn't be the case, since their mother is dead. Dorothy is fairly sure they are lying and so refuses to give them anything more (she later confirms that the boys were in fact lying). Something about this encounter stayed with Wordsworth. Two years later, "After tea I read to William that account of the little boy belonging to the tall woman, and an unlucky thing it was, for he could not escape from those very words, and so could not write the poem."[39]

Once he did escape them, "Beggars" took shape as something more playful—and more disorienting—than the journal entry. The narrator first encounters the lady begging ("Pouring out sorrows like a sea"), doesn't believe her tales of woe but gives her money anyway ("'for the Creature / Was beautiful to see; a Weed of glorious feature!")[40] He might be saying, not entirely without self-congratulation, "I give what help I can, regardless of desert." But would he have been so generous if he weren't so taken with her beauty? The very literariness of his tone, its luxuriant allusiveness, is hard to gauge: "a Weed of glorious feature" (from Spenser) almost voyeuristically writes her up, but it could also suggest that he's stooping (in the previous stanza she's like "a Queen" and then like a "ruling Bandit's Wife"). He walks on and encounters "A pair of little Boys at play, / Chasing a crimson butterfly." The poem ends,

> They bolted on me thus, and lo!
> Each ready with a plaintive whine;
> Said I, "Not half an hour ago
> Your Mother has had alms of mine."
> "That cannot be," one answer'd, "She is dead."
> "Nay but I gave her pence, and she will buy you bread."
>
> "She has been dead, Sir, many a day."
> "Sweet Boys, you're telling me a lie;
> It was your Mother, as I say—"
> And in the twinkling of an eye,
> "Come, come!" cried one; and, without more ado,
> Off to some other play they both together flew.

If the narrator was sure the lady was lying yet gave her money anyway, why not do the same now? We are not being invited to think that he's out of pocket but rather that he's done his good deed for the day. He's feeling pleased with himself about his earlier magnanimity, all bought and paid for, so he isn't feeling any particular pressure to be generous now. "Each ready with a plaintive whine" is trickier than it first sounds: "ready" could imply that the boys have spoken before we reach the next line, or that the speaker anticipates their beggars' patter before they open their mouths. He may, then, be keen to get the first word in, which casts new light on the word *each*: it would seem to refer primarily to the boys, but it could suggest that the narrator, too, is primed to make *his* plaintive whine: "Look, boys, before you say anything, not half an hour ago . . ."

The poem might have been shaped simply to highlight what Dorothy called "Begging cant," but—whether the boys are lying or not—these stanzas make space for the possibility that the beggars think *he* is guilty of cant. Their experience has made them all too aware of the chat a potential donor might come up with to fob them off ("I gave all my money to the last one"), so they have learned to develop strategies for this sort of thing ("If the old man says he's given money to mother—which is what the last one said, and he was lying—we need a quick answer this time"). Wordsworth's poems of encounter don't simply raise awkward questions about how their speakers (and their readers) are to see the objects of their gaze; they also contain hints that invite consideration of how those objects might see us. This poem isn't inclined—as Dorothy's journal entry was—to confirm whether the boys are in fact lying; "without more ado" even carries an envy at the boys' energy, an energy that makes a mockery of the narrator's shuffling ("you're very *sweet*, but . . ."). "Ado" could in fact refer to the fuss he's making, not just to their actions.

The resonant last line—"Off to some other play they both together flew"—doesn't undertake to separate admiration from suspicion. By "some other play" the speaker may mean that the boys are now in an irrepressible hunt for some other game (more butterflies, perhaps) or that they continue to hunt for a charitable dupe ("play" signaling pretense, "to deceive or betray . . . to fool, swindle . . . to play upon someone"; *OED*). There could also be an insinuation that the play in which the boys have just been involved was one in which the narrator played a feigned part as well. The boys become like those butterflies that can't be caught (they didn't "both" fly off or fly off "together," but *both together*—the possibility of tautology augments his sense of exclusion). Earlier, after giving money to the woman, the narrator tells us "I left her," but now it is he who is being left; the boys are other creatures "beautiful to see," yet their beauty is not there to be worked over. They run out of the poem, run out *on* it.

Wordsworth later told Crabb Robinson he wrote "Beggars" so as "to exhibit the power of physical beauty and health and vigor in childhood even in a state of moral depravity."[41] Behind "even in," I glean a suppressed "*especially* in." An easy phrase like "moral depravity" is uttered with a feeling for its limitations, for, like much of Wordsworth's poetry, what "Beggars" also exhibits is the depravity of morality (elsewhere, he has a character refer to "lazy charity,"[42] and in "The Old Cumberland Beggar" he casts side-glances on the "life of virtuous decency").[43] The poem is covetous of the boys' freedom and their fun, yearning for what Peter Sloterdijk has described in another context as "a sublime unemployment . . . an ecstatic unusability for any purpose."[44] Yet it knows that to envisage the boys as *only* free is itself to take a liberty, to rewrite their poverty as plenitude. The narrator both would and would not love to have what they have because he knows that beauty, vigor, and health isn't all that they have. "Beggars" can only be a selective reading of their situation, for the idle energies of play tell of an insatiability that needs feeding as well celebrating, and they tell, too, of the mind's need to relieve itself of its own burdens by watching how others relieve themselves of theirs. Writing to Sara Huchinson following her comments on "Beggars," Wordsworth spoke of the poem as "an affair of whole continents of moral sympathy,"[45] which makes it sound as though the poem is passed on to the reader as work in progress. The overseer will always have oversights; we are left with a sense of a poet who is himself still somehow troubled, still trying to come to terms with what has happened—and with what he's written.

*

You are never allowed to forget Wordsworth when you are reading Wordsworth—nor when he is reading other people. This awkward fact has often been used as a stick with which to beat him, but there are other ways of handling the situation. "All romantic otherness is accompanied in contemplation by a sense of incongruity which is a part of its saving power," John Bayley once suggested, adding that this power manifests itself in "a beautiful and mysterious hilarity. . . . What the poet creates, or feigns in creation, is always slightly ridiculous."[46] The work of Wordsworthian play is related, I think, to a sense of humor that recognizes both the ludicrousness and the pathos of our very need to be saved. The poet's most audacious experiment in mysterious hilarity, one that features him feeling "Perplexed, and longing to be comforted," is "Resolution and Independence," a work built around the relation created—or feigned—between a man who admits "The pleasant season did my heart employ" and a worker who faces "Employment hazardous and wearisome."[47] How—or how far—can these forms of employment speak to one another? Before considering that question, it should be said that when the speaker admits "My whole life I have liv'd in pleasant thought, / As if life's business were a summer mood," he is not necessarily undertaking to decide what life's business actually is.

Sensing both admiration and criticism in Lewis Carroll's superb parody of "Resolution and Independence," William Empson remarked, "If the meaning is not 'This poem is absurd' it must be 'In my present mood of emotional sterility the poem will not work, or I am afraid to let it work, on *me*.'"[48] He makes it sound like this is the only choice on offer, but what about this: "I might let the poem work on me by countenancing rather than denying its glimmers of absurdity; for, in some moods, I am afraid of absurdity itself, afraid of the way absurdity can expose me by making me less—not more—assured of the value of reasonableness." The manuscript version of the poem has the leech-gatherer saying things like "From house to house I go from Barn to Barn / All over Cartmell Fells & up to Blellan Tarn,"[49] a comment which sounds oddly chipper given his circumstances, and other lines that Wordsworth singled out for comment seem to parody a reader's expectations. As he explained to Sara Hutchinson, after a long buildup in which the speaker imagines the escape from his dejection "almost as an interposition of Providence," the reader is primed:

> A person reading this Poem with feelings like mine will have been awed and controuled, expecting almost something spiritual or supernatural—What is brought forward? "A lonely place, a Pond" "by which an old man *was*, far from all house or home"—not stood, not sat, but "*was*"—the figure presented in the most naked simplicity possible.[50]

The stressed "was," along with the comma, helps to accentuate the oddity of this insistence on thingness, hints at Wordsworth's interest in letting the rhythm play around, letting it place emphasis on seemingly wrong things—or on wrong things that are bound up with the right things.

I want now to attend to the poem as a form of acoustic play (as one might play on an instrument) and to keep in mind T. S. Eliot's claim that "versification is a definite concession to the desire to play,"[51] in order to rethink its strange resistances to legibility. In *Biographia Literaria*, Coleridge complained that in Wordsworth's poetry, "the metre merely reminds the reader of his claims in order to disappoint them; and where this defect occurs frequently, his feelings are alternately startled by anticlimax and hyperclimax."[52] The sound of "Resolution and Independence" startles in precisely this way:

> My old remembrances went from me wholly;
> And all the ways of men, so vain and melancholy.
>
> . . . .
>
> But there may come another day to me,
> Solitude, pain of heart, distress, and poverty.
>
> . . . .
>
> We Poets in our youth begin in gladness;
> But thereof comes in the end despondency and madness.

We may be tempted to voice "melan*cho*ly" to chime with the speaker's fleeting sense of joy, but it feels a little forced or willful (as the mood will prove to be). The half-hidden lilt in "pover*ty*" edges toward the luxuriatingly self-lacerating too, as though he's a little too determined to wallow in all the things that might never happen; part of him is feeling good about feeling bad. The mood is like that of the stock dove brooding over his own sweet voice in the first stanza; it's a beautiful line, but it's also a wry glance forward to other mellifluous brooders. The last couplet above contains the longest line in the poem; even an alexandrine isn't long enough here, and the thing sounds cumbersome even as the speaker searches for a polished aphorism. Anticlimax and hyperclimax are written into the verse structure before the leech-gatherer arrives on the scene.

When he does appear—"I saw a Man before me unawares: / The oldest Man he seem'd that ever wore grey hairs"—the meter plays up the perilous word: "wore" could appear twee, too casual almost (the man can take off and leave behind his condition, as though it were a costume or a choice). Even now, with the benefit of hindsight, the speaker can't find the right words, and seemingly innocent inversions are fraught with danger: a phrase like "he continuing motionless" threatens to turn oxymoronic, while "At length, himself unsettling" is shadowed by just how unsettling the man is to the speaker. A faux pas lies in wait around every corner:

> in his extreme old age:
> His body was bent double, feet and head
> Coming together in their pilgrimage;

Under pressure from the rhyme, the meter lends an odd lilt to "pilgrim*age*," a word that itself raises an awkward smile—awkward because we're not sure whether the long, pained haul of his body's motions should be talked about in this way. We see what the narrator means by "bent double," but "feet and head Coming together" brings the figurative very close to the ridiculously literal just at the moment that we are trying to visualize the old man in our mind's eye. In *The Simpliciad*, Richard Mant mocked "the solemn buffoonery" of "Resolution and Independence," and the phrase seizes on something important about the poem's mode of play in the act of dismissing it.[53] For Wordsworth, solemn buffoonery is a gaffe, or the possibility of one, but it's accompanied by the feeling that there are worse things to make than gaffes.

The slipperiness of the poet's words, the sense we have that they might let him down at any moment, is compounded by his not knowing what to say or do in the most quotidian of circumstances:

> And now such freedom as I could I took;
> And, drawing to his side, to him did say,
> "This morning gives us promise of a glorious day."

So it's taken ninety lines to prepare for a comment about the weather. (The slight tailing off in the last line's rhythm again lets the play of sound do a little of the poem's talking.) What is said is utterly banal, yet the greeting comes from a man who has just been worrying about an inglorious future, fretting about those like Burns, who walked "in glory and in joy" before taking a fall. The line is a comic anticlimax, but it also gains a force through the speaker's very need to maintain good form when he's at a loss: he's pouring all his worries into a social nicety as a way of putting them to one side. Commenting on this line, and also on "How is it that you live, and what is it you do?," A. C. Bradley observed,

> We find . . . lines of extraordinary grandeur, but, mingled with them, lines more pedestrian than could be found in an impressive poem from any other hand. . . . We meet also with that perplexed persistence, and that helpless reiteration of a question (in this case one already clearly answered), which in other poems threatens to become ludicrous, and on which a writer with a keener sense of the ludicrous would hardly have ventured. Yet with all this, and by dint of all this, we read with bated breath.[54]

Bradley's acute last sentence should prompt reconsideration of his preceding one, for only a poet with a keen sense of the ludicrous would know that the laughable can be a means of incitement and discovery. Writing to Robert Lowell, Elizabeth Bishop spoke of wanting to compose a certain kind of poem: "great clumsy structures like Wordsworth's Leechgatherer, that somehow lift the great sail and catch the wind."[55] She knew ("somehow") that the clumsiness was not easily separable from the greatness. When the speaker says "This is a lonesome place for one like you," a less reserved (or less self-composed) interlocutor might be tempted to reply "'One like me'? Pray tell me, stranger, who—or what—is it that you think I'm *like*, exactly?" Yet the speaker's clumsy stretch for intimacy, his need to reach across a gap to the old man, itself comes from a lonesome place, and he's trying to find a way of making things less lonesome for both of them.

"Like you," "Like one": these phrases occur often in Wordsworth's poetry, and they are fearful of precision as a form of encroachment, wary of claiming an omniscience that would be irresponsive and irresponsible. In "Resolution and Independence," just at the moment when the old man is felt to be linked to his spectator's own buried life, we learn

> And the whole Body of the man did seem
> Like one whom I had met with in a dream;
> Or like a Man from some far region sent,
> To give me human strength, and strong admonishment.

Given that "the whole Body" is initially the subject, we might have expected the phrase "Like one that." "Like one whom" is odd, makes the body itself seem like a person, not simply a synecdoche for a person. The analogical itch is a means of bringing the other person closer by placing him, but it may also render him more distant by placing him only in relation to what the speaker needs from him. He is both "the man" and "a Man," obdurate life and generalized figure. And because he is like one whom the speaker had met with in a dream, we get both a flash of uncanny recognition and a feeling that the speaker is not quite awake to what the man is, dreaming him up for his own purposes.

The poem keeps several relations or possibilities in play throughout its twisted, troubled course—especially, and crucially, those that hover around the word *play* itself. Wordsworth toys with anatomical feet as well as metrical ones, and Bradley's sense of the pedestrian line can be followed up by noting that, at the beginning, the poet tries to find a way out of his mood by attending to playful feet. "The Hare is running races in her mirth; / And with her feet she from the plashy earth / Raises a mist," he muses before sinking into sadness and then returning to a tentative hope: "I bethought me of the playful Hare: / Even such a happy Child of Earth am I." The resolution doesn't last long, but the hare becomes an unlikely prelude to—and preparation for—the leech-gatherer. When the speaker later repeats his questions to the old man, he watches him "stirring thus about his feet / The waters of the Ponds." The movement recalls the hare and signals the speaker's need to take admonishment and exemplars wherever he can get them, and this echoing occurs elsewhere. There are glimmers of both reverie and comedy in the opening confession that "I heard the woods, and distant waters, roar; / Or heard them not, as happy as a Boy." (The heedlessness of absorption often brings Wordsworth closer and less close to things: "Up the brook / I roam'd in the confusion of my heart, / Alive to all things and forgetting all.")[56] The distant waters again look forward to the leech-gatherer: "But now his voice to me was like a stream / Scarce heard." *Scarce* heard. Not quite listened to, then, but perhaps more fully heard in some deeper recess of the mind. In a manuscript version, the old man "seem'd like one who little saw or heard."[57] He's not the only one.

*

So where are we, exactly, once we've arrived at the poem's closing lines, lines that are by now so well known that it's hard to see or hear them? They constitute, in Bishop's terms, a great clumsy ending, and they bring with them a characteristic moment of Wordsworthian laughter, one that proves trickier to read the longer we look:

> I could have laugh'd myself to scorn, to find
> In that decrepit Man so firm a mind.
> "God," said I, "be my help and stay secure;
> I'll think of the Leech-gatherer on the lonely moor."

Critics have disagreed about whether these lines are good or bad—not just disagreed with each other, but with themselves—and the disagreements go to the heart of what it feels like to read Wordsworth. Lucy Newyln once saw the ending as indicative of "a curious indiscriminateness," a drop from the sublime to the inept as the poet becomes "blind to the sharpness and suddenness of changes in his writing."[58] But when revisiting the lines in a later study, she noted, "Even his wish to carry away a lesson from his experience is made faintly ludicrous, in a couplet whose ambiguities go on resonating beyond the poem's closure." If the ludicrousness is "made," then accusations of a poet's blindness may allow for a feeling that he is not blind to his blindness. Newyln continues: "we are left uncertain whose 'reality' is here affirmed. Is it that the resilience of the old man's mind causes the poet to laugh at himself for his fears about his own future? Or that the poet laughs at himself for finding reassurance in so unlikely a subject? Uneasily, we must acknowledge that the 'firmness' of the old man's mind is pure supposition."[59] These are good questions, although the slide from our being "left uncertain" to what we "must acknowledge" is notable—not least because *all* knowledge of what goes on in other people's minds is built on supposition. Pure supposition is always impure, and it runs deep—past fallible narrators, all the way down to bewildered readers. There remains the uncertainty regarding just how much of other people we need to fantasize or to make up in order to render our relations intelligible (or bearable), and the uncertainty regarding whether these fantasies should be courted as leaps of needful imaginative faith or resisted as narcissistic impositions. "*To deny our kinship is madness / to accept it is insanity.*"[60] Such quandaries put us in the odd position of being the laugher and the laughed at.

The closing couplet doesn't escape to safety either, but offers itself as an entanglement of the ponderous and the provocative:

> "God," said I, "be my help and stay secure;
> I'll think of the Leech-gatherer on the lonely moor."

The last line is the only one in the poem with exactly this metrical pattern (the extra syllable makes for a slightly forced feeling, unless we decide to gather up "gatherer" into a disyllable, which would be forced in another way). The syntax of the first line flirts with danger, as the decision to break up the speech allows the opening word, for a split second, to sound like an expletive, not a pious address. (Many years later, while considering another poem, Wordsworth worried about "the position of the two words By God in the beginning of a line which gives them the appearance of an oath, but I cannot alter it without weakening the passage."[61]) Encountering that penultimate line for the first time when I was at university, encouraged by what I took to be an imperative ("be"), I hastily wondered aloud at the oddity of ordering God to "stay secure." My tutor kindly pointed out the syntactical inversion. Having finally recovered from this some years later, I've started wondering about the line in another way. "Be" could be subjunctive, as though to say, "God! If my help and stay be secure, then I'll think of . . ." Whether one is guided by sound or syntax, the couplet is at once anticlimactic and effortful, a means of acknowledging both the force and fragility of the resolution.

To those who hear only bathos here, Stanley Cavell replies, "this is to forget that the writing of the poem is the keeping of that resolution, and that it is within the poem that the old man appears, hence appears after the poet's resolution has been taken."[62] One suspects, too, that the resolution will keep needing to be retaken. The conviction of the last couplet—like its form—seems liable to unravel at any moment, as it did before when the speaker quickly forgot about the hare: "I'll think of the Leech-gatherer" is awkwardly similar to "I bethought me of the playful Hare," for the realizations that "some people have it really hard!" and "there's joy all around me!" are both meant to serve as ways of making the speaker less self-conscious or self-pitying. There is an intrepid, uncertain humor at work and at play here, a sense that the explicitness of the resolution is part of the problem even though that resolution is still felt to be a valuable, necessary means of facing up to life. The ending dares us to laugh at it; it has a kind of fugitive yet undaunted banality which asks us what we want from poems while also implying that we are not as distanced from the narrator as we first think. "I could have laugh'd . . . I'll think": this is the characteristic rhythm of Wordsworthian comedies of encounter, one that includes the awareness that, once you've thought, you may well laugh. As Wordsworth remarked elsewhere, "The mind often does not think, when it thinks that it is thinking."[63]

What else might there be to laugh—or think—about? In his letter to Sara Hutchinson, Wordsworth dwelt on the audacity of his raising expectations early in the poem: he—and we—were about to face something to be taken "*almost* as an interposition of Providence," "expecting *almost* something spiritual or supernatural," only to be given just an old leech-gatherer. He added, "though I believe God has given me a strong imagination, I cannot conceive a figure more impressive than that of an old Man like this . . . carrying with him his own fortitude."[64] In the poem itself, he is very particular about the temptation to turn coincidence into providence—"Now, whether it were by peculiar grace, / A leading from above, a something given, / Yet it befel"—but he doesn't quite succumb to it. The old man's head and feet come together in "pilgrimage," but that word is knowingly figurative; he is later compared to "Religious men, who give to God and Man their dues" (*and Man*, note); and in the manuscript version the leech-gatherer says of his current occupation that "This is my summer work in winter time / I go with godly Books from Town to Town."[65] So he's been reduced to flogging religious conviction and consolation in a poem that seems hesitant, yet tempted, to accept it. When we finally face "'God,' said I, 'Be my help and stay secure,'" or when we come across Wordsworth's words in the letter to Sara ("But Good God! Such a figure, in such a place"),[66] the force of the moment is related to an obscure yet potent sense that God really has little place in what has transpired—or *shouldn't* have a place in it.

In his tract *Concerning the Convention of Cintra*, Wordsworth paused to interrogate the ease with which we seek out solace and the terms in which we couch it:

> Such is the burst and growth of power and virtue which may rise out of excessive national afflictions from tyranny and oppression;—such is the hallowing influence, and thus mighty is the sway, of the spirit of moral justice in the heart of the individual and over the wide world of humanity. Even the very faith in present miraculous interposition, which is so dire a weakness and cause of weakness in tranquil times when the listless Being turns to it as a cheap and ready substitute upon every occasion, where the man sleeps, and the Saint, or the image of the Saint, is to perform his work, and to give effect to his wishes;—even this infirm faith, in a state of incitement from extreme passion sanctioned by a paramount sense of moral justice; having for its object a power which is no longer sole nor principal, but secondary and ministerial; a power added to a power; a breeze which springs up unthought-of to assist the strenuous oarsman;—even this faith is subjugated in order to be exalted; and—instead of operating as a temptation to relax or to be remiss, as an encouragement to indolence or cowardice; instead of being a false stay, a necessary and definite dependence which may fail—it passes into a habit of obscure and infinite confidence of the mind in its own energies, in the cause from its own sanctity, and in the ever-present invisible aid or momentary conspicuous approbation of the supreme Disposer of things.[67]

If a call to God to be your "stay secure" may be a "false stay," a dire weakness, a cheap and ready substitute that covers for listlessness, indolence, or cowardice, and yet at the same time may breed a power that resists such tendencies, then one reason that Wordsworth "could" have laughed himself to scorn is that he can't always find it within himself to assent to the moral at the end of his poem—or, rather, finds himself unable to assent to everything the moral might entail. A faith in "miraculous interposition" from either God or the leech-gatherer is a mark of lamentable self-abnegation; the poem is just as committed to a line like "While I these thoughts within myself pursued" as it is to a line like "What kind of work is that which you pursue?" Wordsworth is a defender of "a habit of obscure and infinite confidence of the mind *in its own energies*" before he is a defender of anything else, and all this "in the cause *from its own sanctity*, and in the ever-present invisible aid or momentary conspicuous approbation of the supreme Disposer of things." The comma after *sanctity* makes what follows seem less than central, or merely a means to an end, an end that culminates with the Self. What I think Wordsworth warms to as he writes the sentence is the blasphemously blessed thought that the mind's infinite dispositions are more holy than any Holy Disposer.

*

Wordsworth's mind was made up when he wrote "Resolution and Independence," but he was also concerned about what his resolutions had committed him to. Drawing on Wordsworth's recollection that he met the old man described in the poem a few hundred yards from Town-End, while crossing over Barton Fell toward Askam, John Worthen observes that the last date he had taken this route before writing the poem was on his way to see Mary Hutchinson on his thirty-second birthday, April 7, 1802. The exhilaration of the narrator, then, in so far as it was rooted in the real, was that of a man traveling excitedly "to see the woman he would soon be marrying (although probably also extremely anxious about how they might manage financially), contrasted with the compelling image of the leech-gatherer, his wife dead and his children lost, broken down physically, living in absolute poverty, yet still firm-minded."[68] So Wordsworth registers two kinds of "Independence"—personal and financial—and a conflicted need to keep them separate even as he acknowledges their relation. But the poem's power is enhanced by a sense that the self can't stay on that lonely moor for long, that it has somewhere else to go, somebody else to be with—and to dream about. The poet's willingness to grant other people space stems from a need to defend *his* space.

"It is an attractive thing about Wordsworth," Trilling wrote, "and it should be a reassuring thing, that his acute sense of the being of others derives from, and serves to heighten, his acute sense of his own being."[69] The acuteness of that sense also keeps alive a feeling for the comedy as well as the urgency of one's need for reassurance, for your own being both imperils and inspires your most significant encounters with others. The sense Trilling describes can be compared with the capacity for play as Donald Winnicott conceived it:

> The thing about playing is always the precariousness of the interplay of personal psychic reality and the experience of control of actual objects. This is the precariousness of magic itself, magic that arises in intimacy, in a relationship that is being found to be reliable. . . . It is creative apperception more than anything else that makes the individual feel that life is worth living.[70]

Winnicott goes on to outline another mixture of precariousness and reliability: creative, playful looking. "When I look I am seen, so I exist. I can now afford to look and see. I now look creatively and what I apperceive I also perceive."[71] Wordsworth's poetry is always "seeing things"—as he once noted, "it is the *feeling* that instructs the *seeing*"—and in "Resolution and Independence," the verb *see* is used on three occasions.[72]

> I saw the Hare that rac'd about with joy
> . . . .
> I saw a Man before me unawares
> . . . .
> In my mind's eye I seem'd to see him pace
> About the weary moors continually

In each case, the verb is accompanied by an ambiguity about where the self ends and the other begins: joy could belong to either or both the I and the hare; the man may be unaware he's being seen, or the speaker may not be quite comprehending or consciously taking in the man he sees; "continually" may refer to the man's pacing or to the I's seeing. Fantasy is the very medium of thought—and of perception—for the mind is continually playing with its object, projecting and introjecting, and the final resolution to think of the leech-gatherer on the lonely moor is still informed by creative seeing (people, not moors, are "lonely" and "weary").

The final stanza's description of the old man's talk is at play, too, for "soon with this he other matter blended" is a quietly coy reminder that the leech-gatherer has himself always been blended with other matter and matters—a hare, a stone, a sea beast, a dream, a cloud, a moor, a sense of self. Trilling's intuition should be accompanied by the recognition that for Wordsworth, an acute sense of being is a sense of being's inscrutability, an awareness that one's own personhood, no less than other people, is an enigma—"a Being made / Of many Beings," as he put it elsewhere.[73] Wordsworth's encounters with others render both parties unfathomable. What "Resolution and Independence" describes as "blind thoughts" and "untoward thoughts" is not simply the poetry's way of saying how difficult it is to know people; it is also its method for defending our potential, a potential that resides in our not being knowable.

One of the best glosses on "Resolution and Independence" I've read—it contains glimmers of other poems by Wordsworth along with allusions to Lewis Carroll's parody—is Stevie Smith's "When Walking." "Far from the world I walk," Wordsworth had admitted in his poem, and Smith is strolling somewhere close by:

A talented old gentleman painting a hedge
Came suddenly upon my mind's eye when walking;
Forgive me for my sins
And bring me to everlasting life to be with thee in happiness for ever,
I wanted to say. But could not.
My heart leaps, I said. I am filled with joy
For your hedge. Nodding, he vanishèd.[74]

Lovely that the old gentleman should first come upon her mind's eye (not necessarily—or merely—her eye). Her heart leaps up when she beholds not a rainbow but a person doing—or being—something unaccountable. The closest (maybe) that she'll get to everlasting life is the joy she feels right now. "In my mind's eye I seem'd to see him pace / About the weary moors continually," Wordsworth had said. Certainly, but that was then, and his poetry is so often succumbing to a love of beginnings, to a temptation to move from past benedictions ("I saw the Hare that rac'd about with joy") to the rampant fun of the present tense: "The grass is bright with rain-drops; on the moors / The Hare is running races in her mirth."[75] To see the poet, in your mind's eye, simply luxuriating in grass, or hares, or hedges, or old men is to risk making him appear less responsible than he in fact is (or would like to be). Yet Wordsworth isn't averse to such risk-taking, and what he elsewhere calls "That soul of conscientious daring"[76] describes both the risk and everything else it puts into play.

It might sound daring (or flippant, or foolhardy) to suggest that the act of composing poetry is a kind of game for Wordsworth, but that's the word he chooses to describe his own acts of composition, and he is never more serious than when speaking of "the many games of life" and of "life's uneasy game."[77] Whether encountering or playing the child, the reprobate, or the idler, he is always alive to the sport that lies inside transport, always reading both activities as a birthright.[78] As Jean Piaget observed, to play is "both to imitate a real situation and to imagine a new one,"[79] which is a good description of how Wordsworth conceives the activity of the mind. The poet is driven by a need to indulge and to pass on this play of thought, energized by a hope—risible, yet vital—that we might encounter him as he encountered the leech-gatherer: as "a something given," where the *given* may signify both the fact of the matter, the stubbornness of what happens to be the case, and an offering, a gift, something to work and play with.

FOOLING

The men who could not make their hands meet around their objects, the rapt, the lost, the fools of ideas.

RALPH WALDO EMERSON

Vices

I found myself begirt with temporal shapes
Of vice and folly
THE PRELUDE[1]

"Why don't you hire somebody to abuse you?" Wordsworth asked Samuel Rogers in 1817. "For myself, I begin to fear that I should soon be forgotten if it were not for my enemies."[2] This is the poet's roundabout way of calling his critics fools, but he didn't always see the Fool as the enemy. Benjamin Haydon remarked on his good humor at a dinner a few months later—"giving in to all our frolics without affectation and laughing as heartily as the best of us"—as Charles Lamb played the jester to his king: "his fun in the midst of Wordsworth's deep & solemn intonations of oratory was like the fun & wit of the fool in the intervals of Lear's passion."[3] The fun isn't necessarily being had at the expense of the passion, for Lamb often drew attention to the hidden depths of such relationships: "the Grave-digger in Hamlet, the Fool in Lear, have a kind of correspondency to, and fall in with, the subjects they seem to interrupt."[4] Some years earlier, in 1798, when Klopstock complained about the impropriety of the Fool in *King Lear*, Wordsworth was quick in defense: "I observed that he seemed to give a terrible wildness to the distress."[5]

Over the next three chapters I'll circle back to the years leading up to 1798. The last section focused mainly on poems published after *Lyrical Ballads*. Having now conspired with a weirdly playful Wordsworth, I want to return to that foundational volume and to reconsider it in light of the fact that so many of his early abusers imagined him as playing a particular role, a role which has far-reaching implications for his self-conception—and for how we might yet conceive him. For *fun*, the *OED* suggests one possible root in *fon*, which signifies either "to be foolish; to act the fool; to become foolish," or "To befool, make a fool of," and the options provide a suitably equivocal gloss on a recurring aspect of Wordsworth's reception history. One critic referred to the poems as "motley productions," observing that "No folly was ever more foolishly boasted than that of this writer."[6] Others were more ambivalent: Byron pronounced Wordsworth "stupendous genius! damned fool!"[7] while William Jerdan was unnerved by the fact that even as he was "worshipped as an exalted Genius," he was "held up as a Zany with the cap and bells."[8] Yet the zany and his close relatives trade on mixed feelings, and curious versions of such figures appear throughout Wordsworth's writing. Robert, Margaret's broken-down husband in *The Ruined Cottage*, carves "uncouth figures on the heads of sticks," whistling flat "merry tunes" and "weaving bells and caps / Of rushes, play-things for his babes."[9] "Bells and caps" suggest that things have been woven round the wrong way, and we watch the character as we might watch a Fool who is no longer sure of his role. If, as Sianne Ngai has suggested, "the art of the zany is frantic and beset,"[10] the performance here is encountered less as an art and more as a chronic symptom. Robert oscillates between cruel verbal commentaries on his household—commentaries the poem does not care to repeat—and "wild freaks of merriment."[11] Whatever he does or doesn't say, his every gesture nurses some inward pain.

Accounts of the meeting between Wordsworth and Klopstock suggest that Wordsworth's praise of Lear's Fool was part of a larger debate. Coleridge remembered Klopstock taking issue with Shakespeare's absurdities and countered with a defense of the "exquisitely ludicrous" in his work; wisdom, he said, came "not only from the tragic characters but equally from Jacques, Falstaff, and even from the fools and clowns."[12] Coleridge had studied Karl Friedrich Flögel's compendious books on comedy and court fools in the 1790s, and Wordsworth echoes a comment made in Flögel's *History of Comical Literature* when responding to Klopstock's valuation of tragedy: "he seemed to rate too highly the power of exciting tears. I said that nothing was more easy than to deluge an audience. That it was done every day by the meanest writers."[13] One of the poems Wordsworth wrote during his stay in Germany ends on a similar note—"I feel more sorrow in a smile / Than in a waggon-load of tears"—and mourns the loss of his friend Matthew by playing on the links between folly and feeling:

> thou School of fair Glencarn,
> No more shalt thou in stormy weather
> Be like a play-house in a barn
> Where Punch and Hamlet play together.[14]

The double act isn't all that incongruous: Hamlet can play the Fool on occasion, and Punch harbors murderous desires.

As we've already seen, elegiac occasions led Wordsworth to new apprehensions of the comic. In *Essays upon Epitaphs* he recounts stories of two ancient philosophers who each stumbled across a corpse: the first buried the body and was praised for the piety of his act; the second "regarded the same with slight, if not contempt; saying 'See the shell of the flown bird!'"[15] The latter sounds like a prototype for a dark jester, a man who—given the right circumstances—would ask an erstwhile Yorick "Where be your jibes now?" or make puns over a grinning skull that lies "quite chapfallen."[16] Yet jokes at the body's expense bespeak a concern for the soul. Wordsworth notes:

> Each of these Sages was in sympathy with the best feelings of our nature; feelings which, though they seem opposite to each other, have another and a finer connection than that of contrast.—It is a connection formed through the subtle progress by which, both in the natural and the moral world, qualities pass insensibly into their contraries, and things revolve upon each other.[17]

This cognizance of alliance amid opposition—*coincidentia oppositorum*—had long been read as the founding trope of folly.[18] As James Spedding would later point out, the Fool's defining characteristic is "finding secret resemblances in things unlike."[19]

Folly itself compounds disparate objects and emotions. A folly may be a foible, a "deficiency of understanding," "an error," "a ridiculous thing," "an absurdity"; to be "foolish" is to be "ridiculous," "amusing," "insignificant," "trifling," and so on. But older meanings lurk in the word: "wickedness," "evil," "sin," "harm," "wrong-doing," "crime," "lewdness," "wantonness" (*OED*). From the French, *folie*, it may signal "madness, insanity, mania, rage, anger." The man who plays the Fool—and those who enjoy watching him do so—are engaging in more than light relief, and the links between the Fool and the Vice are long standing. The first signs of jesters in English drama were in the Vice characters like Fancy and Folly in Skelton; the Vice was established as a stage clown before he appeared in morality plays, and he often wore the dress of the Fool.[20] As well as the tricky servant (*callidus servus*) of Roman New Comedy, the Vice went into the making of Shakespeare's Fools (Feste compares himself to "the old Vice" with "dagger of lath / In his rage and his wrath").[21] Both figures played devil's advocate, challenged accepted moral standards, intertwined fury and fun. And both went into the making of Wordsworth's first major piece of writing. For the rest of this chapter, as a prelude to a return to *Lyrical Ballads*, I want to consider *The Borderers* (1796–1799). Any approach to the play risks becoming mired in its entanglements in the very process of drawing out their interest, and some of what follows has to be couched as a mode of storytelling. But I hope the details of the story are themselves telling when read through the lens of folly, for *The Borderers*'s meditations on foolery stage several issues that continue to resonate in the later writing. They also provide a space in which Wordsworth's attraction to the Shakespearean Fool is combined with a disturbing analysis of both himself and his imagined audience.[22] The play contains more instances of the word *fool* than the rest of Wordsworth's works put together. You might say that the apprentice-poet can't get the figure out of his head.[23]

*

In a note on the play, Wordsworth observed that "in the trials to which life subjects us, sin and crime are apt to start from their very opposite qualities."[24] The road to hell is paved with good intentions, but one also catches a Rochefoucauldian inflection and a glimmer of the Fool's cunning here: "hypocrisy is the homage vice pays to virtue," or—worse—"our virtues are generally but disguised vices."[25] As he would later admit in *The Prelude*, "from day to day / I live, a mockery of the brotherhood / Of vice and virtue."[26] That mockery runs deep, and an inquiry into the significance of the Fool offers Wordsworth a means to examine the motives for—and the possible effects of—his own creative maskings and machinations. In the preface to *The Borderers*, he speaks of his villain Rivers—Mortimer's servant—in ways that bring to mind the Fool's relish for inversion and perversion: the man is drawn to "fantastic obliquities," has "a low hankering after the *double entendre* in vice."[27] Low hankerings are usually a sign of unfinished business in Wordsworth, and besides, as he noted elsewhere, "genius is not incompatible with vice."[28]

The Borderers is structured around a lie. Rivers concocts a story about how an old man, Herbert, is planning to sell Matilda, the woman Mortimer loves, into slavery to the wicked baron Lord Clifford. As Mortimer is delaying and having doubts about whether he should kill Herbert, the terms in which Rivers censures him are revealing:

> We should deserve to wear a cap and bells
> Three good round years for playing the fool here
> In such a night as this.[29]

A Fool may be natural (somebody "deficient in judgement or sense") or artificial ("a jester, clown"; *OED*), and one punishment for being a natural fool, Rivers implies, is being forced to become an artificial one. But despite the character's apparent antipathy to both figures, Wordsworth's play thinks through what is gained and lost in the journey from one state to the other. The first time he is alone on stage, Rivers confesses to warring with "fools of feeling" within himself,[30] and in his last line in the play he speaks of the "Fool" he has helped to make of Mortimer.[31] Whatever he is trying to achieve or evade, the word is darkly dear to him. But in order to get closer to Rivers, and to the disturbing life of *The Borderers*, we need to step back and allow some other Fools take center stage for a while.

Wordsworth wasn't being fanciful when he spoke of playhouses where Punch and Hamlet played together. During his stay in London in 1792, Covent Garden put on a performance of *Hamlet* followed by the pantomime *Harlequin's Museum* in which Rayner took the part of Punch.[32] An evening at the Georgian theater was usually structured as a "serious" main piece followed by pantomime or farce, and the plot structure of pantomime reproduced this transition in miniature as the somber or mythological opening frame narrative made way for the harlequinade episodes. The other major presence in contemporary theater—the gothic—was also shaped as a potential tragedy averted by a romantic or a comic ending (usually the joining of two lovers after they had been kept apart by a tyrannical father figure). The increasing popularity of the pantomime exerted pressure on other parts of the repertory; a production of *Othello* in 1793 led a reviewer to note that one actor "descended into Buffoonery; in the dying scene of Roderigo he reminded us of the death of Clown in Harlequin Skeleton."[33] Given that Clown never dies—or dies only to jump up and start all over again—such performances threaten to remove the skeletons in tragedy's closet.

If tragedy is not being staged as an end in itself, but as an appetizer for a pantomimical-comical denouement, then the tragic may be laughed off as ludic and interludic. And even though comedy gets the final word, it may be cheapened by being conceived as a mode that absolves audiences from thought. When laughter is heard in *The Borderers*, however, it tends to increase rather than to lessen the tension; Mortimer appears to be yearning for as well as mocking a comic ending that is no longer available to him when, glancing at Matilda, he says, "That woman was to have been my wife. / [*Laughs hysterically*] Ha! ha!"[34] In this universe, a sense of humor is akin to a sense of horror; laughter is less a safety net than a trapdoor. By contemporary theatrical standards Wordsworth's play was deemed too fearfully foolish to be put on (it was refused by Covent Garden in 1797), and although he later said he wrote it with "no thought of the Stage," his thoughts often returned to it.[35] In March 1798 he wrote to a friend, "I am perfectly easy about the theatre, if I had no other method of employing myself Mr. Lewis's success would have thrown me into despair."[36] He's referring to one of the biggest hits of the age—Matthew Lewis's *Castle Spectre*—which debuted the day before Wordsworth left London having learned of the fate of his own play. *The Castle Spectre* stood as the pinnacle (or nadir) of gothic-pantomimic crossbreeding; one reviewer called it "a pantomimical exhibition of the most extravagant nature, and the whole may, with no breach of propriety, be termed a *Speaking Pantomime*, of which Kemble is made the Harlequin and Mrs Jordan the Columbine."[37] Wordsworth later saw *The Castle Spectre* in Bristol, and Hazlitt recalled his arch judgement: "He said 'it fitted the taste of the audience like a glove.'"[38]

In January 1798 Coleridge wrote to Wordsworth noting that the play's sentiments were "moral and humorous"'—by which he meant: cozy, second-hand, trite. "This Play proves how accurately you conjectured concerning *theatric* merit," he said, "The merit of the Castle Spectre consists wholly in its *situations*. These are all borrowed, and all absolutely pantomimical . . . the play is a mere patchwork of plagiarisms. . . . To admit pantomimic tricks the plot itself must be pantomimic—Harlequin cannot be had unaccompanied by the Fool."[39] Wordsworth was by no means against pantomime, but the Fool in *The Castle Spectre* (named Motley) is indeed a tepid figure. Although the play claims as part of its heritage "great Shakespeare's comic school / The gossip crone, gross friar, and gibing fool,"[40] Motley lacks the uncanny challenge of the Shakespearean fool and rarely threatens to disorient or derail his audience. None of the source texts that Shakespeare adapted contained a Fool; in Lewis's play, Motley is all too recognizable, safe, clubbable—himself a patchwork of plagiarisms.

Other fools, though, were loitering with delectably dubious intent at a little distance from the patent theaters. Wordsworth visited Sadler's Wells several times in the 1780s and 1790s,[41] and in *The Prelude* he remembered his delight in the "Clowns, Conjurers, Posture-masters, Harlequins" he saw there. "Nor was it mean delight," for Clown and his associates offered sidelong, satirical commentaries on "dramas of living Men / And recent things yet warm with life." Addressing Coleridge, Wordsworth recalls the antecedents of such activities: "Nor was it unamusing here to view / Those samples as of ancient Comedy" (in the revised *Prelude*, he writes, "Rough, bold, as Grecian Comedy displayed / When Art was young").[42] Coleridge speaks of the Fool as supplying the place of the ancient chorus in classical drama and notes that Vice and the Devil are "the genuine antecessors of Harlequin and the Clown. . . . I fully believe that our ancestors laughed as heartily as their posterity do at Grimaldi."[43] When audiences laughed at Joe Grimaldi, they were laughing at an altogether more primal, disturbing figure than Lewis's Motley.

Grimaldi's skills had been honed at the Wells, where Jean-Baptiste Dubois had taken over as Clown in 1787 and been celebrated for bringing out the troubling energies of the role. One contemporary spoke of Dubois's shift "from smiles to threats, from approbation to abhorrence."[44] Like Harlequin before him, Clown was metamorphosing from the lively into the lawless; at once roguish underdog and criminal overreacher, he became bent on "half-malicious, half-playful experiments in the inflicting of pain."[45] Grimaldi's first success, in 1794, was in fact as a Vice figure, and thereafter his Clown would not simply take joy in delinquency and collateral damage but seduce audiences into reconsidering the pleasure they took in watching him. As a reporter from the *Times* noted, "when he stole apples, we really doubted whether common honesty was not a kind of prejudice."[46] This Fool was increasingly likely to rebel against his master Pantaloon's orders and, rather than assisting him in the capture of the fleeing lovers Harlequin and Columbine, he often appeared to be in league with them. At other times, though, he took pleasure in disrupting Harlequin's dreams of a happy ever after, gleefully stealing the show, as though he couldn't bear to play second fiddle in either a tragedy or a comedy. One historian has noted how Grimaldi helped to turn clownery into an art of "grotesque leers and parodies of ardent love . . . the queasy prurience of one who uses obscenity to mask a deeper aversion to intimacy. Abandoned, isolated and incapable of passion, Joe was not an escape from the self, he was a confrontation with it."[47] Even when he is impersonating others, you feel that Clown might be offering self-caricatures: "For playing the fool I seem made; / But what's to become of poor me?"[48] Made for the role, or *forced* to play it? "Poor me" could be accompanied by either a knowing wink or a fading smile. At once Vice and victim, Clown refuses and solicits sympathy.

For Wordsworth, the experiments of Dubois and Grimaldi at Sadler's Wells would have been eerily, attractively familiar, in touch with the shady life of folly that he, Coleridge, and Lamb relished in Shakespeare. Robert Armin had helped to effect a shift of emphasis in Shakespeare's dramaturgy from the naive clown to the knowing Fool when he replaced Will Kemp in the Chamberlain's Men,[49] and he was first introduced to audiences (as Touchstone) by Jacques in *As You Like It*, who himself dreamed of donning the motley to "Cleanse the foul body of th'infected world / If they will patiently receive my medicine."[50] *If*. Although the Fool could be a medicine man, he also reminds us of the stubbornness of the symptoms. A trader in humiliation, he is the scourge of folly even as he has to watch his step, a man who might be treated as a criminal at any moment. Armin's Fool is still a servant, entertainer, performer, but he's also a separatist, a malcontent—or worse. The next time we see him in a comedy, it is as Feste, whose first words in the play, in response to a demand from his mistress, are noteworthy: "Let her hang me." This Fool is on the lookout for ways to tell his superiors to go to hell (or to lead them there), and his chilling last words while people are on stage tell of other roles he'd like to play: "thus the whirligig of time brings in his revenges."[51]

Like Dubois, Grimaldi, and their progeny, this character may be alienated, but he's not an alien. The comment made by Armin in his role as Lear's Fool ("this cold night will turn us all to fools"[52]) is a version of his earlier comment made as Feste ("Foolery, sir, does walk about the orb like the sun, it shines every where."[53]) The most common topic of the Fool's jokes and puns (sexual desire) suggests not so much that he is immune to the passions that everyone else feels but rather that he'd like to be. In response to Jacques's question, "Will you be married, motley?" Touchstone has to concede: "so man hath his desires; and as pigeons bill, so wedlock would be nibbling."[54] And even as the Fool tries to keep the show on the road, he is also, increasingly, the one who has that within which passeth show. When Viola says to Feste, "I warrant thou art a merry fellow and carest for nothing," he is quick to correct her: "Not so, sir, I do care for something."[55] Yet he is not about to divulge what that something might be.

*

This, then, is the opaquely antithetical figure Wordsworth has in his mind as he writes *The Borderers*—an unstable compound of servant, entertainer, medicine man, outlaw, trickster, satirist, and Vice. To return to Rivers, and to consider him as he orbits the other three main characters (Wordsworth stressed the importance of "the position in which the persons in the Drama stood relatively to each other"[56]), it's striking that the play offers an aggressive twist on the classic New Comic–pantomimic plot. Two young lovers (Harlequin/Mortimer and Columbine/Matilda) want to be together; the foolish old father (Pantaloon/Herbert) is the blocking figure against such a union; and a servant-messenger (Clown/Rivers) is friendly toward Pantaloon to his face but plots against him behind his back even as he sets about disrupting Harlequin's plans for a final union with Columbine.[57] *The Borderers* is a pantomime gone wrong—or a pantomime pushed to its logical, devastating conclusion. I think Wordsworth has surmised that the real subject and driving force of the mode, and of comedy itself, is wish fulfillment, a bid for a certain kind of freedom, and so he sets himself to write a play to see what happens when wishes are excessively fulfilled. Clown will persuade Harlequin that rather than merely triumphing over Pantaloon, it would be in everybody's best interests for Harlequin to kill him off—and, while he's about it, to drop his interest in Columbine and to aim for something more vertiginous than a happy ending. In act 3, Mortimer is pulled up short by a sudden awareness of the plot in which he's become enmeshed:

> if this be not enough
> To make mankind merry for evermore

Then plain it is as day—that eyes were made
For a wise purpose—verily to weep with![58]

You sense he would like to watch the comedy this situation reminds him of rather than having to play his ludicrous role in it to the bitter end.

Several of the most memorable moments of *The Borderers* come in Rivers's speeches, when he's driving Mortimer onward by urging him to resist the torpid acquiescence of those beaten down by "the tyranny / Of moralists and saints and lawgivers."[59] Geoffrey Hartman felt that because the strongest poetry goes to Rivers, "Wordsworth may have been of his party (and Nietzsche's) without knowing it."[60] But Wordsworth is unlikely to have felt the need for such protection, and *The Borderers* is more than willing to probe the genealogy of morality. When Rivers appears alone on stage, pondering his plan to lure Mortimer into knowledge of what Nietzsche would later call the comedy of our "old morality"—"the comedy of our existence!"[61]—he has one eye on the audience as he marvels "How many fools / Would laugh if I should say this youth may live / To thank me for this service!"[62] The plotter's relish for the apparently untenable, his self-delighting feel for the truth that may lie within the tendentious, is not to be dissociated from Wordsworth's willingness to play the demoralizer when it suits him. This is why it's often difficult to ascertain whether Rivers's utterances are risible or reasonable:

What? in this universe,
Where the least things controul the greatest, where
The faintest breath that breathes can move a world—
What, feel remorse where if a cat had sneezed,
A leaf had fallen, the thing had never been
Whose very shadow gnaws us to the vitals?[63]

Vehicle almost ambushes tenor: the sneezing cat has a superbly unanticipated comic vitality, threatening to sabotage the point Rivers is making even while exemplifying it. Nor does his Fool's question manage to sound as rhetorical as he'd wish, for he is still laboring under the feelings he's counseling us to abandon. Mortimer's immediate response to this speech sounds like a nervous joke even as it hits a nerve: "what is it that ails you?"

Much of *The Borderers* is ghosted by *Othello* (and, to a lesser extent, by *King Lear*), two of Shakespeare's boldest adventures in folly. The speech above, for example, contains something of Iago's resistance to qualms ("drown cats and blind puppies"), of Othello's hesitancy before he kills Desdemona ("Ah balmy breath, that dost almost persuade / Justice to break her sword!"), and of the inward gnawing that Iago confesses to feeling early in the play.[64] In the preface, Wordsworth likens Rivers to Ariosto's Orlando and Cervantes's Cardenio (both driven seriocomically mad because of spoiled love affairs) before adding that "there are particles of that poisonous mineral of which Iago speaks poisoning his inwards."[65] The allusion is to the moment when Iago vows to be evened with Othello, "wife for wife": "I do suspect the lusty Moor / Hath leaped into my seat, the thought whereof / Doth like a poisonous mineral gnaw my inwards."[66] Later he speaks of how love turns you into a "sick fool,"[67] and when Emilia tells him that somebody "turned your wit the seamy side without and made you suspect me with the Moor," he snaps back, "You are a fool, go to."[68] Iago cannot bear to think he's been made a fool of (either Emilia did it or somebody has fooled him into thinking she did) and so projects both the word and the condition outward (Othello's realization of what has happened to him leads him to cry "O fool, fool, fool!"[69]). Disgusted by the strength of his own feelings, by the way his feelings turn him into a dependent in more ways than one, Iago is revenged on that part of himself by taking revenge on others.

Othello meant a great deal to Wordsworth, and he took a lot from it—not least Shakespeare's sense of just how much was at stake in the word *fool* and its close relations.[70] Iago's quibble—"She never yet was foolish that was fair, / For even her folly helped her to an heir"[71]—bends *folly* from meaning *innocence* or *naivety* (Iago talks of "foolish honesty" elsewhere) toward its antonym: "lewdness, wantonness . . . A lewd action or desire" (*OED*, sense 3; Iago will later say "she turned to folly, and she was a whore").[72] The word *fool* contains a reminder of the body's desires and dependencies, and Iago plays on it in a clownishly calculated way to push the comedy toward tragedy. Later, when he accuses Emilia of lying, she snaps:

> By heaven I do not, I do not, gentlemen!
> O murderous coxcomb, what should such a fool
> Do with so good a wife?[73]

This is the first time that somebody calls Iago a fool in the play, and it drives him crazy enough to stab them to death. Emilia's appellation "murderous coxcomb" brilliantly seizes on the always exposed, potentially humiliating position of the Fool, the sense that the joker-trickster seeks to stage-manage situations in order to avoid becoming the butt of the joke—as though he were revisiting, with a view to mastery, a scene of trauma. One of the things *Othello* is intent on exploring is what it might feel like to be a Fool, what levels of rage and anxiety may underlie the role, and to what lengths the Fool might be driven given the right (or wrong) circumstances.[74] It was this interest of *Othello* that I think Wordsworth was responding to when he created Rivers.

His villain's first words alone on stage—like Iago's—make pointed reference to the Fool.[75] It's fitting that the word should arrive at such a moment in both plays because the trickster figure traditionally had a special relationship with the audience (in his frequent asides, he is honest with us about his lack of honesty to others). Rivers confesses to us his feelings about Mortimer:

> They chose him for their chief!—I had a gnawing
> More of contempt than hatred!—Shame on me,
> 'Twas a dull spark—a most unnatural fire.
> —It died the moment the air breathed upon it.
> —These fools of feeling are mere birds of winter
> That haunt some barren island of the north,
> Where if a famishing man stretch forth his hand
> They think it is to feed them.[76]

Rivers's first image toys with the etymological roots of folly: "*folle . . . follem, follis*, lit. 'bellows', but in late popular Latin employed in the sense of 'windbag', empty-headed person, fool" (*OED*). So he wants it known that his reason will not stoke but rather will put out the fire of these fools of feeling in himself. The second image, though, recalls the scene in Rivers's past when he was turned into a Fool through specious, pernicious appeals to his feelings. As he will later tell Mortimer, he was duped into becoming a murderer by a crew who falsely convinced him that the captain of his ship had wronged him. Rivers left the captain to die on "a bare rock, narrow and white and bare. / There was no food, no drink, no grass, no shade," and, as he confesses this, he thinks of other ways it might have turned out: "if a breeze had blown / It might have found its way into my heart / And I had been—no matter—."[77] Mortimer sees the wronged captain in his mind's eye, "famished . . . stretching forth his arms,"[78] and Rivers proceeds to tell of how he sank into despair after learning what he'd done, and then from despair he traveled to an awful comfort: "I saw that every possible shape of action / Might lead to good—I saw it and burst forth / Thirsting for some exploit of power and terror."[79] That exploit turns out to be his luring of Mortimer into a similar action in the hope of leading him to an analogous recognition. Rivers dreams of their both coming out through the other side of folly into a mood that knows no remorse, one that assures them that they differ from "common minds."[80] To do the very worst thing is to become free by embracing a lascivious, horrifying awareness of the self as nobody's fool.

And yet—to recall Rivers's initial aside—the eerie power of the image in which his resolution is couched suggests that the barren island and the famished man continue to pursue him. The image, in fact, implies that part of him *is* that man. Wordsworth noted in the preface, "His feelings are interested in making him a moral sceptic. . . . He is like a worn out voluptuary—he finds temptation in strangeness, he is unable to suppress a low hankering after the *double entendre* in vice."[81] So Rivers doesn't abandon his desire; he sublimates it. And double entendre—the key weapon of the Fool / Vice—speaks of the figure's own compulsions as he sets about compelling others through verbal manipulation. Behind Rivers's claim that "These fools of feeling are mere birds of winter," one catches an echo of Lear's Fool: "Winter's not gone yet, if the wild geese fly that way."[82] Barbara Everett observes that Lear's man brings with him from the Shakespearian comic world that bred him "an incurable ache," a sense of the submerged life of feeling, and she notes of the wild geese image that "the mesmeric power of such phrases derives from a quality of emotional, even sensual dread and yearning acted out at some level of the drama."[83] *The Borderers* acts out this yearning through Rivers; ashamed of emotion yet plagued by it, he is the Fool who would spectate on feelings the better to disown them.

Wordsworth's play is always looking for ways to suggest that folly is founded on relationships—and that relationships die hard. When Lear asks, "Who is it that can tell me who I am?" the Fool replies, "Lear's shadow."[84] The motion of thought here, if not the motive, may be related to Iago's comment on Othello: "In following him, I follow but myself."[85] Wordsworth discerned a connection between these two characters, and although Lear's long-suffering Fool lacks the concentrated malevolence of Iago, his mask slips at points. Immediately after Lear threatens him with the whip, he snaps back, "I had rather be any kind o'thing than a fool, yet I would not be thee. . . . I am better than thou art now. I am a fool, thou art nothing."[86] Rivers becomes a compound of Fool and Vice, fidelity and faithlessness, and when toying with options for his master, an inversion of the language of Lear's Fool and the twisted plotting of Iago come together in his aside: "What, have him whipped and howling? No, no, no . . . Henceforth I'll have him / A shadow of myself, made by myself."[87] *The Borderers* is a story of the revenge of the Clown. The force of that story, though, comes not just from Wordsworth's willingness to make us privy to Clown's secrets, but from the possibility that Clown's secrets may also be ours.

*

When conceiving Iago as the joker in the pack, W. H. Auden speculated, "If a member of the audience were to interrupt the play and ask him: 'What are you doing?' could not Iago answer with a boyish giggle, 'Nothing. I'm only trying to find out what Othello is really like'? . . . In that case, who are we to say to Iago—'No, you mustn't.'"[88] I'm not convinced that Iago would feel the need to hide behind a giggle, and his unerring line at the end of the play, "What you know, you know,"[89] is in no way boyish. But Auden does touch on a vital part of *Othello*'s power and Wordsworth's portrait of Rivers is in league with such provocations. (His antihero refers to his enterprise as a "game."[90]) "Such a mind cannot but discover some truths," Wordsworth notes of this kind of foolery in the preface, and while he admits that a man like Rivers may well "be furnished with sophisms in support of his crimes," he adds that they are nonetheless "difficult to answer."[91] The entwinement of the sophisticated and the specious is the Fool's privilege—and also the poet's. When Rivers says, "So meet extremes in this mysterious world, / And opposites thus melt into each other,"[92] he again sounds like his maker, the man who speaks elsewhere of how "both in the natural and the moral world, qualities pass insensibly into their contraries, and things revolve upon each other."[93] In which case, the question becomes, does such acuity offer a threat to morality, or a replenishment of it, or some other, as yet undiscerned option?

At one point, Mortimer seems to have learned Rivers's lesson almost too well. "Oh! fool," he calls himself, "Now could I laugh till my ribs ached,"[94] and with that laughter comes a new relish for ratiocinative game playing as he offers up a perverse parable and a question: "both fools, or wise alike, / Each in his way?"[95] That question resonates throughout *The Borderers*. Wordsworth notes in the preface that the moral of his play is obvious ("to shew the dangerous use which may be made of reason"),[96] and he ends by quoting the passage he will adopt as the play's epigraph (from Pope's *Moral Essays*, "Epistle to Cobham"):

> On human reasons reason though you can,
> It may be reason, but it is not man;
> His principle of action once explore,
> That instant 'tis his principle no more.[97]

In the same epistle, Pope notes that "Unthought-of Frailties cheat us in the Wise, / The Fool lies hid in inconsistencies."[98] The dangerous use of reason is a lesson not simply for those like Rivers, then, nor for those like Mortimer once Rivers has worked his equivocal magic on him, but for those rational creatures in the audience who know how to make infallible discriminations between folly and wisdom, vice and virtue, pleasure and responsibility. A closer translation of the play's moral—if we really must have a moral—might be George Eliot's comment, 'The great problem of the shifting relation between passion and duty is clear to no man who is capable of apprehending it."[99]

The Fool lies hidden in *our* inconsistencies, and, as Mortimer's men surround Rivers, crying "Dispatch him," his last words in the play manage to sound both omniscient and unknowing:

> If I pass beneath a rock
> And shout, and with the echo of my voice
> Bring down a heap of rubbish and it crushes me,
> I die without dishonour.—Famished!
> [*Smiles exultingly, his eyes fixed upon* MORTIMER.
> A Fool and Coward blended to my wish.[100]

This might be dismissed as the last laugh of the gothic villain cackling about how his plans have come to fruition even as he goes under. But the final line lingers in the mind's ear, becomes harder to gloss the longer you listen to it. Rivers has turned Mortimer the Coward into Mortimer the Fool, but he has also joined himself as Fool to Mortimer's Coward, forged a double act out of his own intolerable sequestration. Talk of the rock and famishment takes us back to Rivers's primal scene: the "bare rock" on which he left the captain for dead, "some barren island" where a "famishing man" may stretch forth his hand,[101] the place to which Rivers always returns whenever he tries to kill off fools of feeling. Yet this moment also enshrines the man's commitment to showing those in power just how little they differ from him. The feeling here is close to that which Empson brilliantly anatomized when arguing that we should see Iago both as wicked and as coarsely funny: "listeners are meant to feel a certain sting of truth in Iago's claim to honesty, even in the broadest sense of being somehow truer than Othello to the facts of life; and they are still meant to feel it even if it makes them hate Iago all the more, as indeed the play intends it to do."[102]

We love to hate those from whom we try and fail to distance ourselves. *Othello* is Shakespeare's only tragedy in which the villain survives at the end, and when Othello says to Iago, "If that thou be'st a devil, I cannot kill thee,"[103] he hints at how the Devil and his other archetypal associates—Trickster, Vice, Fool—cannot die because they always find a place in us. When Wordsworth came to revise *The Borderers*, he decided to have Rivers stabbed to death, but in the original version he is merely dragged off, his fate eternally postponed just as Iago's is. Critical responses to *The Borderers* have tended to conceive the link between Wordsworth and Rivers as if it were something the poet needed to surmount or to sever (and Wordsworth's own preface sometimes suggests as much), but the figure contains impulses and insights that he can't bring himself to bury (he insists at one point that Rivers "really *is* great").[104] Mortimer leaves the play to go forth "a wanderer on the earth, / A shadowy thing,"[105] thereby fulfilling Rivers's prophecy ("Henceforth I'll have him / A shadow of myself, made by myself"). He has graduated into a new kind of Fool, one who must now live "by mere intensity of thought." Such intensity confronts us with a disenchantment of morality in the name of ethics and with a vexed, compromised refusal of those people who live merely for "unmingled joy," a joy that Rivers sees as "the passion of fools and little fit / For such a world as this."[106]

Mortimer's blessing and his curse have been forged through his complicity with the trickster, the shaman, the medicine man, "the wounded wounder" who acts as the agent of healing. Rivers in fact makes his entrance into *The Borderers* by hinting at his links to this foolish archetype; he arrives holding a selection of plants and, when asked to name his favorite, replies, "That which, while it is / Strong to destroy, is also strong to heal."[107] Jung notes that although the trickster stands as the summation of all the inferior traits of character in individuals, he is—or should be—welcomed by each individual as something known to him: "I have, I think, found a suitable designation for this character-component when I called it the *shadow* . . . he is everything that a man can never get the better of and never finishes coping with."[108] From early on, Wordsworth recognized that an attempt to turn the trickster (and, indeed, the poet) into a figure of fun, a comic stooge, or a mere source of amusement is a means of keeping him at arm's length: what we are amused by we needn't acknowledge or take seriously.[109] And what he gleaned from Shakespeare, along with those contemporaries who created clowns who pushed their luck, was the force of our attraction to such figures and even our need to be taken in by them. This need is founded not only on our suspicion that such a motley crew may be less duplicitous than we are; it's fed by our desire to be reconnected to the thrill as well as the threat of our helplessness, to our sense of ourselves as beyond reproach because beyond responsibility. Reading *The Borderers*, you often get the uncomfortable feeling that Rivers understands you, even as you sense that you can't ever quite know him. He is like the unconscious, and, as Jung wryly observed, "nothing is corrected in the unconscious."[110]

One may wish to claim immunity from such provocation, and an exchange toward the end of the play should I think be read not only as an encrypted allegory of a gentle audience's take on Rivers (the kind of audience, you understand, that likes a play to fit its taste "like a glove") but also of its relations with the author. "We have been fooled—," one of Mortimer's men says of Rivers, to which another replies, "But for the motive?" The question is answered too quickly, too neatly by Lennox: "there needs no other motive / Than that most strange incontinence in crime / Which haunts this Rivers."[111] Wordsworth was never convinced by attributions of motiveless malignity (in

Iago or in anyone else), and his preface is witheringly incisive on this matter: "it must be observed that to make the nonexistence of a common motive itself a motive to action is a practice which we are never so prone to attribute exclusively to madmen as when we forget ourselves."[112] As the preface continues, he warms to his task:

> We all know that the dissatisfaction accompanying the first impulse towards a criminal action where the mind is familiar with guilt acts as a stimulus to proceed in that action. Uneasiness must be driven away by fresh uneasiness. . . . Besides, in a course of criminal conduct every fresh step that we make appears a justification of the one that preceded it; it seems to bring back again the moment of liberty and choice. . . . Every time we plan a fresh accumulation of guilt we have restored to us something like that original state of mind, that perturbed pleasure, which first made the crime attractive.[113]

What shouldn't be missed or downplayed is the venturesome, clinical glee of this passage, the pleasure one senses that Wordsworth takes in pitching what "we all know" in precisely this way. A phrase like "Every time we plan a fresh accumulation of guilt" means more than simply "every time we plan to do something we know will later cause us to feel guilt"; it whispers that we may even court and love the feeling of guilt so as all the better to love the feeling of ourselves defying it. Despite the claim elsewhere in the preface that, by exposing such murky psychological impulses, the poet equips his audiences with the tools to combat them, when reading a passage like this we do not feel—do not *want* to feel—that we are going to cease planning "fresh accumulations" anytime soon.

Perturbed pleasure at our criminality isn't simply Wordsworth's acknowledgment of the joy of transgression—an enjoyment of acting outside the law, or outside conventional wisdom, that merely confirms the value of such constraints. It also includes the pleasure we take in sensing that polite society's definition of criminal or questionable action is not the last word on such matters (David Bromwich is right to claim that the poet "was emphatic in supposing that no crime could be more original than the injustices of society"[114]). Wordsworth was driven as well as tormented by moments of "liberty and choice," and he wouldn't have had to look far when asked to give an example of an outlaw who had denounced the monarchy, who'd had children out of wedlock, and who would later proclaim that he had "no need of a Redeemer" (in 1796, Coleridge described his friend as "at least a *Semi*-atheist".[115]) All of which is not to say that Wordsworth approves of Rivers's actions; when he is writing this searchingly, he neither approves nor disapproves. It's rather that his intensely personal interest in the man as daemonic doppelganger is fed by a desire to investigate the very grounds of our rush to indict as well as our need to exculpate.

The poet talks to us confidentially, conspiratorially in the preface much as his character would do on stage, and Rivers is the only person who is repeatedly given the stage direction "*aside*" in *The Borderers*, a direction that presses home a long-recognised quality of the Vice/Fool: he stands on the threshold between play and community, continually prompting consideration of how his fictional antics are a part of life, part of the way in which people are tempted to make fictions out of their lives. As Robert Weimann observed, "as champion of 'sporte' and game, between the fiction of the moral action and the audience's festive expectations . . . he revealed the comic concurrence of audience and actor."[116] Such concurrence raises the nice question of how moral the festive expectations themselves are. (When Rivers says in the first scene of the play, "What strange pleasures / Do we poor mortals cater for ourselves!" his words are played at us, not merely for us.[117]) Audiences and readers are borderers, too, and in the very title of Wordsworth's play one detects a hint of the Fool's inclination toward wordplay—from *bourd* meaning "an idle tale, jest, or joke." The Trickster/Vice has ever been a borderer, for "the best way to describe trickster is to say simply that the boundary is where he will be found—sometimes drawing the line, sometimes crossing it, sometimes erasing it or moving it, but always there, the god of the threshold in all its forms."[118] Once this sense of the figure is combined with an awareness of him as someone we watch because we yearn to be made uncertain of where we stand, the play emerges as Wordsworth's first attempt to plumb the profound value of practical and impractical jokers. In composing *The Borderers*, the writer discovers himself *as* borderer, as trickster, as maker and spoiler of culture. And, recalling one older meaning of *fun* as "cheat, trick, hoax" ("an act of fraud or deception"), we may say that the poet-Fool can only have his perilous fun with us if we meet him half way. This is I think why, in *The Prelude*, Wordsworth refused to speak of his pleasure in the pantomime clowns at Sadler's Wells as a "mean delight." A fascination with such figures is not something for which anyone should have to apologize, for, as we watch them, he says, "How willingly we travel, and how far!"[119]

Naturals

Us, the fools of Nature.
"THE EGYPTIAN MAID"[1]

The Borderers was Wordsworth's apprenticeship in the dark arts of foolery, and the play's disturbing, vertiginous life provided him with more conjectures—and more kicks—than he'd perhaps anticipated. When Rivers tells Mortimer "You will be taught to think," the Vice/Fool could well be speaking for the poet as he would dream of addressing his audience, but he is also speaking from one part of the poet's self to the other, to that part of him who, like Rivers, sees intrepid thought as a way to "link / Pleasure with greatness."[2] This amalgamation of the will to pleasure and the will to power haunted Wordsworth—as thrill and as anxiety—and the question of whether the poet was to be the agent provocateur or the representative of his public, its unconscious or its conscience, continued to be a source of agitated fun for him.

The question is complicated by the sociopolitical commitments that helped to shape *Lyrical Ballads*, for Wordsworth was writing during a period in which those writers who wished to focus on the lower strata of society still tended to look to comedy or satire for their models; the real was the low and the low was the ridiculous. As a consequence, comedy influenced the development of the modern novel (particularly as practiced by those authors Wordsworth had adored as a child: Cervantes, Lesage, Fielding, Smollett).[3] Yet that development in turn allowed the low to be played for more than laughs. In Sterne's *Sentimental Journey*, Yorick says that his servant "La Fleur had a small cast of the coxcomb—but he seemed at first sight to be more a coxcomb of nature than of art; and before I had been three days in Paris with him—he seemed to be no coxcomb at all."[4] The longer such figures stayed around, the less straightforwardly comic they would come to appear—and the more they would raise the possibility that the master was the butt of the joke. "All men were created equally free and equally funny," remarked Robert Frost in 1937; "Before you laugh too much at that, take another look at it. Four hundred years ago the only people who were funny were yokels . . . today, even kings are funny. We've come a long way."[5] That eventuality hadn't quite come to pass at the end of the eighteenth century (especially not in poetry). When, in the advertisement to *Lyrical Ballads*, Wordsworth anticipated his audience's likely complaint that "the author has sometimes descended too low,"[6] he was saying that kings were not yet considered wholly funny, nor yokels wholly unfunny.

Before he was anything else, the lower-class person was a Fool, which is why Coleridge felt the need to stress that Wordsworth's focus on "low and rustic life" should be dissociated from "that pleasure of doubtful moral effect, which persons of elevated rank and of superior refinement oftentimes derive from a happy *imitation* of the rude unpolished manners and discourse of their inferiors." The pleasure is morally doubtful, he explained, because it arises from "the reader's conscious feeling of his superiority awakened by the contrast presented to him; even as for the same purpose the kings and great barons of yore retained, sometimes *actual* clowns and fools, but more frequently shrewd and witty fellows in that *character*."[7] If the artificial Fool originally took his lead from actual clowns (rustics and peasants) and from fools (Fools Natural), for whom does he really speak? Although he plays up to—and for—his patrons, could not his wit work against their sense of themselves as superior? And, more generally, if comedy had traditionally betokened privilege through its condescension to low subjects, how might this privilege be resisted—or rethought—in the act of being courted? These are questions a Fool-Poet might broach, and, for many early critics, Wordsworth was "the buffoon of Nature."[8] The Smith brothers prefaced their skit on the poet in *Rejected Addresses* with Richard Cumberland's lines:

> thou art Folly's counterfeit, and she
> Who is right foolish hath the better plea:
> Nature's true Idiot I prefer to thee.[9]

Preferences aside, an assurance about one's ability to spot the true from the false idiot, the "right foolish" from the wrong foolish, houses its own complacency. Among other things, *Lyrical Ballads* is meant as provocation to those who prefer to have their Fools wheeled on as light relief.

As I suggested in the introduction, Francis Jeffrey is helpfully (or unhelpfully) representative in this respect. Discussing "the new school" of poetry in 1802, he noted that the feelings of "a refined character" were very different from those of "a clown, a tradesman, or a market-wench." Poverty makes people ridiculous, and such people shouldn't be found in serious composition:

> A poet, who aims at sublimity or pathos, is like an actor in a high tragic character, and must sustain his dignity throughout, or become altogether ridiculous. We are apt enough to laugh at the mock-majesty of those whom we know to be but common mortals in private; and cannot permit Hamlet to make use of a single provincial intonation, although it should only be in his conversation with the grave-diggers.[10]

A constant wish to sustain one's dignity may itself become ridiculous—sometimes horrifyingly so (and who, exactly, can avoid being a "common mortal" in private?). The gravedigger's comments in *Hamlet*—"There is no ancient gentlemen but gardeners, ditchers and grave-makers"[11]—chime with Hamlet's musings on Yorick, which lead the prince to make connections between Alexander the Great and the loam that might stop a beer barrel. Elsewhere, Hamlet's appetite for infinite jest entails a recognition that a king may go a progress through the guts of a beggar, and Othello, Hamlet, Lear, and Macbeth all eventually use the word *fool* to describe themselves. Lear even admits that he is a "natural fool,"[12] and when Wordsworth refers to "us, the fools of Nature" in a late lyric he has Shakespeare in the back of his mind ("we fools of nature," says Hamlet to Horatio).[13] As one of the gravediggers snaps back at Hamlet "Every fool can tell you that" he is simply confirming the protagonist's own awareness of the word's fearful reach.[14] Coleridge observed that "In *Hamlet* the Fool is, as it were, divided into several parts, dispersed thro' the piece."[15] Not least Hamlet himself: he is "your only jig-maker," a jester who has walked into the wrong play, one who is trying—and failing—to jest himself out of it. He has of late lost all his mirth, but putting on an antic disposition is no cure; "My wit's diseased," he admits, and by the time folly makes its last appearance in the play, Hamlet's coda to his confession that all is ill about his heart ("but it is no matter . . . It is but foolery") exacerbates rather than lessens the Fool's tragedy.[16]

As well as setting the scene for the broader preoccupations of this chapter, a brief consideration of Wordsworth's poem "The Brothers" can serve to hint at the awkward, persistent presence of the Fool in *Lyrical Ballads* (and also at how—just as in *The Borderers*—the figure is given new life through recastings of Shakespearean folly). Readers initially encounter a stranger standing in a graveyard; he has just returned from a sea voyage, and he enters into conversation with a vicar in order to ascertain who lies in one particular grave. Recollections of the man's childhood then lead to a memory of his "Bearing his Brother on his back,"[17] and a question is raised about whether the person who is buried there committed suicide. To recall such details is to notice the shards of the scene from *Hamlet* that lie buried within the poem (Hamlet said of Yorick that "He hath bore me on his back a thousand times," and the gravediggers had been debating whether Ophelia took her own life).[18] The stranger, who is named Leonard, recalls Hamlet, but he comes from a very different world; a shepherd lad in his youth, he went on to try his fortune on the seas after he and his brother James were left destitute. We are introduced to Leonard through the vicar's perspective as he gazes at him from his cottage. The clergyman, it turns out, is the kind of person who knows a Fool when he sees one:

> at leisure, limb by limb
> He scann'd him with a gay complacency.
> Ay, thought the Vicar, smiling to himself,
> 'Tis one of those who needs must leave the path
> Of the world's business, to go wild alone:
> His arms have a perpetual holiday,
> The happy man will creep about the fields
> Following his fancies by the hour, to bring
> Tears down his cheek, or solitary smiles
> Into his face, until the setting sun
> Write Fool upon his forehead.[19]

Charles Lamb wrote to Wordsworth in praise of these lines ("that fine ShakespERIAN character of the Happy Man"),[20] and the fineness is enhanced by the way in which the languid, tactile force of the writing resists the official attitude of the vicar.[21] In his mind, "Fool" is fondly patronizing, but the intensity of the image that leads up to the word outbraves his condescension. Despite the furtiveness of "creep" and the way "following his fancies" makes Leonard sound rather in hock to them, there is a sense here that Nature is lured to rise to the level of sponsor for someone who is willing to go it alone (the act of writing on his forehead could be an obscure blessing or baptism). Other elements of the portrait return later in the poem and suggest that the vicar, mindful of the world's business, has been obtuse: tears don't roll down Leonard's cheek in a sort of unhinged, bumbling joy (he hides his face when he learns that the grave is his brother's, for "he felt / Tears rushing in"[22]); and the "happy man" will not in fact creep about these fields, for now the vale "where he had been so happy, seem'd / A place in which he could not bear to live."[23] Leonard will eventually go wild alone, but his experience is more like a memento mori than a perpetual holiday. To scan a Fool with a gay complacency, the poem intimates, is to presume to know too much—and to miss out on what the Fool knows.

Just as in *The Borderers*, those who insist on looking down on fools here are on the run from their complicity with them. The vicar is caught smiling fancifully to himself while foolishly diagnosing the meaning of the Fool's smiles and fancies, and he is "at leisure" even as he casts gentle aspersions on the holidaying of the other man's limbs. In his essay "All Fools' Day" (the piece contains supporting quotations from both Wordsworth and Shakespeare), Lamb praises one foolish figure who, despite (or because of) his "fantastic smiling to thyself," is "nothing inferior." He then turns to the gentle reader who might imagine himself as an amused spectator of such low-bred creatures: "and *you*, Sir . . . Do we not know one another? what need of ceremony among friends? we all have a touch of that same—you understand me—a speck of the motley . . . I love a *Fool*—as naturally, as if I were kith and kin to him."[24] Naturally, because a Fool Natural hints at unacknowledged family resemblances. The title of "The Brothers" refers primarily to Leonard and James, but it also gestures toward links between Leonard and the Vicar, brothers in folly.[25] Although the poem is one of the more somber pieces in *Lyrical Ballads*, it gives voice to a feeling that can be felt across the collection, one that is hinted at in a manuscript fragment of *The Prelude* when Wordsworth speaks of

> a bait
> Which cannot be resisted, at the close
> The simple reader, if he laugh not, looks
> Blank as an April fool.[26]

Poems act as similar baits, or as tests of our own simplicity and blankness when confronted by the complexly simple. In *Lyrical Ballads*, Wordsworth is not exactly playing practical jokes, but he is entertaining a far-reaching premise: the apparent ridiculousness of a person or object frequently exists as a marker of one's own ridiculousness before it.

One of the poet's avatars for the Fool was the balladeer or minstrel himself. In 1815, while gratefully acknowledging his debt to Percy's *Reliques*, Wordsworth lamented that Percy had been so abashed by ridicule that he would later alter his own style.[27] In the preface to the *Reliques*, however, Percy emphasized how the minstrel had at one time courted ridicule without necessarily being undone by it. His historical survey of the figure drew attention to "a jocose person exceedingly skilled in 'the Gests of the ancients,'" a person who, like the Fool, was "an attendant on a royal personage," granted license to satirize "kings and princes at pleasure." Minstrels were associated with "tumblers and posture-masters," with "Jongleurs (Lat. Joculator)," and with the "gleeman" (the last term also signified "*Jocista*, a Jester" and "*Scurra*, a saucy Jester"). "Their sportive talents rendered them generally obnoxious to the more rigid ecclesiastics," Percy observed, before charting their fall from grace by citing later decrees that led "all juglers, tinkers, pedlers, &c." to be deemed "rogues, vagabonds, and sturdy beggars, & c.," "idle persons, under colour of Mynstrelsie."[28]

For a lyrical balladeer to draw on such a model toward the end of the eighteenth century was to flirt with folly and to ask what had been gained and lost by dismissing the jester from the court of public opinion. At the heart of the minstrel controversy, Maureen McLane has observed, lies a question: "Was the minstrel a *poet*?"[29] And at the heart of this question lie a couple of others: Is the poet a Fool? If so, is his parodic, parasitical relation to culture the herald of an emergency or of an opportunity? When Wordsworth portrays minstrels directly—in "Song at the Feast of Brougham Castle," for example—he accords them a precarious position, brings them back to life as marginal presences. As McLane notes, "Not the glamor of minstrelsy and of medieval history but its bumptious tragi-comedy, its fatal aporias: this Wordsworth presents."[30] In *Lyrical Ballads*, tragicomedy becomes both symptom and resistance; the balladeer's willingness to entertain folly is shadowed by a sense that he can no longer hold an audience, yet his relish for the aporetic contains a hope for a new kind of readership. Before turning in the next chapter to one of Wordsworth's most enduring experiments in folly, I want to read another poem in *Lyrical Ballads*, slowly but unsurely, for it offers a key—or a clue—to the bewilderment that the Fool inspires in him.

*

The longer you look at "Simon Lee," the further away the poem seems to get. Andrew Griffin sees it as especially characteristic of *Lyrical Ballads*: "poems half serious and half mad, half story and half something else, conspicuously repulsive yet consciously inviting—obsessed with death, decay, and loss, yet full of a crazy glee."[31] Speaking of crazy glee, some aspects of the Fool as he was known at the early-modern English court are instructive here. He usually had a club, stick, or branch of wood that carried a phallic suggestiveness. He frequently combined an ability to amuse with the skills of a huntsman (there was an enduring link between hunting and fooling). He was sometimes rewarded for his service with a plot of land to cultivate on his retirement (Edward I's Fool was rewarded for the conduct of hounds). He was often a dwarf, or else associated with littleness or disfigurement. Last but not least, you would know him by his coat: "fooles," Thomas Nashe observed, "alwaies for the most part (*especiallie if they bee naturall fooles*) are suted in long coates," and one of the most famous Fools played by Robert Armin wore a long blue coat.[32]

Now consider old Simon Lee. He carries a mattock, but the implement totters in his hand. When "the chiming hounds" are out, they send his mind back to the good old days. He has a "scrip of land" but isn't really fit enough to tend it. He was a gleeman, once.

Simon Lee,
The old Huntsman,
with an Incident in which He was concerned.

In the sweet shire of Cardigan,
Not far from pleasant Ivor-hall,
An old man dwells, a little man,
I've heard he once was tall.
Of years he has upon his back,
No doubt, a burthen weighty;
He says he is three score and ten,
But others say he's eighty.

A long blue livery-coat has he,
That's fair behind, and fair before;
Yet, meet him where you will, you see
At once that he is poor.
Full five and twenty years he lived
A running huntsman merry;
And, though he has but one eye left,
His cheek is like a cherry.

No man like him the horn could sound,
And no man was so full of glee;
To say the least, four counties round
Had heard of Simon Lee;
His master's dead, and no one now
Dwells in the hall of Ivor;
Men, dogs, and horses, all are dead;
He is the sole survivor.[33]

Simon could be seen as a twist on the stock comic figure Wordsworth saw at the pantomime: "A scare-crow pattern of old Age, patch'd up / Of all the tatters of infirmity, / All loosely put together . . . Stumping upon a Cane."[34] But that man was the *senex iratus* (he liked to "Prate somewhat loudly"), and Simon is merry. Instead, I think two other stories are being entwined: the decline of the narrator's neighbor, and the decline of the Fool. There may be a tragic echo in the penultimate line ("And my poor fool is hanged! No, no, no life! / Why should a dog, a horse, a rat, have life"),[35] but, if it is an echo, it's hard to say what it's doing here. Maybe the narrator-balladeer is asking readers to countenance a world in which the tragedy of the master is replaced by that of his servant, insisting that tragedy can happen to servants. But to put it this way is to gloss over the eerie assurance of the writing (the neat grouping, for example, of "Men" with "dogs, and horses"). The sprightliness of the rhythm, the pleasure both teller and listener take in hearing the syllables fall into place, conspire to raise the question of how Simon is to be viewed, or of what tone one should take when approaching him. "Meet him where you will" conjures up a strolling reader in comfortable circumstances, one who is happy to be entertained by a Fool—provided that the figure doesn't get in his way.

John Danby nicely sums up the oddity of the situation: "Wordsworth, we feel, is watching our reaction, neither helping nor hindering us. . . . We have to reject the temptation to be sentimental as well as the temptation to laugh. The second half of the first stanza is deliberately intended to prevent a misplaced seriousness. We have as yet nothing to be serious about."[36] In fact, it's hard even to be sure about what is deliberately intended. "Of years he has upon his back, / No doubt, a burthen weighty": is "No doubt" merely a filler, or comically casual, or is it meant to intensify our sympathies? The narrator apparently possesses the authority to tell us about Simon—we are in safe hands—yet there are gaps ("*I've heard* he once was tall," "*He* says" he's seventy; others beg to differ). When recalling the man on whom he based the character, Wordsworth observed, "The expression when the hounds were out, 'I dearly love their voice,' was word for word from his own lips."[37] Yet Simon is never allowed to speak directly in the poem. The old huntsman is haunted by voices, senses that even animals have voices, but he doesn't have one.

We see "at once that he is poor," and the narrator goes on to repeat the word *poor* several times. What is all this pity doing? And what, if anything, does it want? Recalling one Mrs. Priscilla Pry, Lamb spoke of her delight at coming across specimens of poverty:

> Then does her sympathy burgeon, and bud out into a thousand flowers of rhetorical pity and wonder, . . . The word *poor* is her favourite; the word (on my conscience) is endeared to her beyond any monosyllable in the language. Poverty, in the tone of her compassion, is somehow doubled; it is emphatically what a dramatist, with some licence, has called *poor poverty*. It is stark naked *indigence*, and never in her mind connected with any mitigating circumstances of self-respect and independence in the owner, which give to poverty a dignity. It is an object of pure pity, and nothing else.[38]

The narrator of "Simon Lee" is not merely another version of Mrs. Priscilla Pry, but she might be a relation of his, and he keeps making it difficult for us to decide whether we care or not. "And, though he has but one eye left, / His cheek is like a cherry." Meter and rhyme serve to accentuate the challenge. Perhaps we are meant to think, "Oh well, that's some consolation; at least his cheek is bearing up." Simon sounds troublingly edible; it's as if he were being decked out for our consumption.

Comedy often secures its effect by preparing spectators for pity before then assuring them that they have no cause to be concerned. In that sense, it resembles certain aspects of the literature of sensibility of which Wordsworth was wary, a literature in which the gentle reader is allowed the pleasure of feeling involved in the pains of the lower classes while also being protected from the more discomforting implications of such feelings. Sensibility, like comedy, may turn poetry into an elegant pastime, an affluent spectator sport that has other people's sufferings packaged for the readers' entertainment. As Wordsworth drily noted elsewhere, "In the perusal of history, and of works of fiction, we are not, indeed, unwilling to have our commiseration excited by such objects of distress as they present to us."[39] Or, as he would have read in Rousseau's *Emile*, "Pity is sweet, because, when we put ourselves in the place of one who suffers, we are aware, nevertheless, of the pleasure of not suffering like him."[40] Wordsworth's blithe way with simile in "Simon Lee" (that cheek, that cherry) is an invitation to pleasure, and yet "one eye" is too close for comfort. The cherry casts back a grotesque glance to the preceding line, superimposes itself on the image of Simon's face, plants itself where the other eye should be. The poem seems both inclined and disinclined to imagine Simon as a cheerful, battered old codger (he can be that, on his good days, but he is never only that). It's as though the narrator had set out to paint a clown and got the proportions wrong.

In later versions of the poem, Wordsworth rearranged some of the early stanzas so as to "let the reader hear of Simon in his luckier days first, which I cannot but think is better than jumbling about, as is now done, the melancholy and chearful part."[41] The jumbling, though, was true to the delirium of Wordsworth's first instincts and to his interest in working through—without necessarily working out—the links between compassion and callousness.[42] These early moments in "Simon Lee" suggest that the narrator-balladeer isn't just depicting a Fool but acting like one (soon he will be taking the man's tool). As our joculator-minstrel, he's looking to provide some light entertainment to keep his patrons interested lest he should suffer the same fate as Simon. Yet the form into which he's been pitched sees him stumbling into unforeseen hazards. At several points, the Fool's greatest weapons (his puns and paradoxes) turn on him:

> His hunting feats have him bereft
> Of his right eye, as you may see:
> And then, what limbs those feats have left
> To poor old Simon Lee!

Something about the decision to use the man's name here to clinch the rhyme feels chillingly twee. "As you may see," placed so close to the loss of the man's eye, also seems infelicitous; and Simon lost his "right" eye, so talk of what he has "left" might have been better avoided. Given that we are about to hear that his poor old ankles swell, "feats" treads dangerously close to "feet." The Fool's performed puns have become unwitting ones. Words keep going awry.

Our foolish balladeer may guess as much—or, at least, he realizes that the performance isn't going to plan:

> Few months of life has he in store,
> As he to you will tell,
> For still, the more he works, the more
> His poor old ancles swell.
> My gentle reader, I perceive
> How patiently you've waited,
> And I'm afraid that you expect
> Some tale will be related.

Donald Davie's criticism of "Simon Lee" was based on his feeling that "Wordsworth sees no reason why swollen ankles should be vulgar or comical, and he is determined to write as if they are not."[43] It would be closer to the mark to say that Wordsworth does see the comic potential of swollen ankles but that he is determined to take risks and to lure the reader by means of comedy to a different kind of seriousness. The comedy of those swollen ankles tells of a grim liaison between delectation and revulsion, and the fact that the swelling is immediately followed by talk of a "gentle" reader (not just well born or cultivated, but also soft, tender, pliant, supple) also offers pause. The poem almost rebukes our suppleness, casts aspersions on the pliancy with which it has to bend to our need to avoid grotesqueries.

When the narrator speaks of his readers' patience, he implies that we have time to kill, but then we have just been told of Simon that "Few months of life has he in store," so our passing of the time may feel like a faux pas, or something worse. Where, then, are readers and the narrator to be placed? Danby notes that the speaker may stand for "the poet as ballad-retainer" or for "the poet as natural aristocrat," and the ambiguity of that standing is crucial.[44] The poem creates an uncertainty as to whether the narrator is speaking up to us or as one of us, refuses to confirm just how knowing he is. Maybe he oscillates between the acute and the obtuse. Only one thing is certain at this stage: if we can't gauge the narrator's level of awareness or authority, we don't know how to read the poem.

*

Once the "incident" is related, things become clearer—and less clear.

> One summer-day I chanced to see
> This old man doing all he could
> About the root of an old tree,
> A stump of rotten wood.
> The mattock totter'd in his hand;
> So vain was his endeavour
> That at the root of the old tree
> He might have worked for ever.

"About": how grimly, vividly impotent that word is here. The narrator handles the old tree like the old man: "a *tree* . . . well, no, more of a stump really" ("a little man, / I've heard he once was tall").[45] The able-bodied commentator accordingly steps up: "I struck, and with a single blow / The tangled root I sever'd." Acting as a would-be Alexander, he cuts the Gordian knot. The mattock that totters in Simon's hand is a poor substitute for the jester's phallic club, and Simon's weakness is driven home in the only moment of direct speech in the poem: "'You're overtasked, good Simon Lee, / Give me your tool' to him I said." The word is the right one—and the inopportune one: "tool: an unskilful workman; a shiftless person. *slang* or *dialect*" (*OED*, 3b). Worse, one feels "tool" edging toward another meaning, one the *OED* rather squeamishly refers to as "the male generative organ"; "1687 T. Shadwell tr. Juvenal *Tenth Satyr*: 'What pleasure can the weak Old Doting Fool, Expect from that infirm and Aged Tool?'"

After the narrator has jauntily hacked the tangled root—and the root of Simon's self-respect—the poem ends with a moral. At the risk of becoming foolishly ingenious or tortuous (although perhaps it's a little late to be worrying about that), I want to read the final stanza in slow motion in order to bring to a head the question of what, precisely, Wordsworth's poem is indicting—and what it's indulging. Recall that the narrator has already described Simon as a "*running* huntsman" with "one *eye* left" whose race "was *done*." My italics make heavy weather of something so covertly accomplished:

The tears into his *eyes* were brought,
And thanks and praises seemed to *run*
So fast out of his heart, I thought
They never would have *done.*
—I've heard of hearts unkind, kind deeds
With coldness still returning.
Alas! the gratitude of men
Has oftner left me mourning.

"Eyes," not "eye," coupled with thanks and praises that seem to run like his legs once did: the awkward matter of Simon's body can't be forgotten, keeps getting in the way, as the poem whispers things under the breath of its narrator's utterances. Maybe there's even a sense of disgust at the unseemly impropriety of the old man's body here. (The narrator's "mourning," on the other hand, is genteelly bodiless.)

It is not customary to read tactlessness into the ending of "Simon Lee." Speaking of the poem's "republican logic," David Bromwich's eloquent gloss is representative of many critical readings: "Gratitude (the poem is saying) can be redescribed as a vice, and ought to be a source of regret: it is a man like Simon Lee weeping tears of joy at what is in fact an absence of pleasure, an impotence that requires someone else to be an indispensable actor in his life. Wordsworth has the courage to mourn what others would admire with vicarious complacency as an occasion of 'sympathy.'"[46] Yet I think the last stanza contains another kind of courage, too, one that is willing to broach the question of why Simon is weeping—and why the mourning might itself be oddly vicarious, even a little sanctimonious in its very abjuring of sanctimony. Take, for example: "Thanks and praises seemed to run." *Seemed*? The narrator could be projecting, reading Simon's body language in a way that confirms gratitude even as the Good Samaritan in him feels embarrassed or admonished by that gratitude. "So fast out of his heart": is this tender outpouring, or are thanks and praises not in fact there or in the process of running out on him, deserting him? Simon could feel gratitude, but his impotence may also make him feel mortified, humiliated, enraged.

The scene is reminiscent of Yorick's charged encounters with "the sons and daughters of poverty" in Sterne's *Sentimental Journey*, particularly the moment when Yorick realizes he has overlooked one pauper on the road, a man "who had no one to ask a sous for him, and who, I believe, would have perish'd, ere he could have ask'd one for himself." So, in front of the others, Yorick atones and showers the man with even more money: "I could afford nothing for the rest. . . . The *pauvre honteux* could say nothing—he pull'd out a little handkerchief, and wiped his face as he turned away—and I thought he thank'd me more than them all."[47] Like Simon Lee, the man was done a charity, but not necessarily an honor, by Yorick's "eagerness of giving." As the benefactor raises the stakes from sous to livres as a way of combating his own guilt, he risks humiliating the man by turning him into a special case as well as sending the whole group a twisted rewrite of a paternalistic message ("Do *not* ask, and ye *may* receive"). Readers can't be sure whether the *pauvre honteux's* tears upon receipt of the money (if they *are* tears) express other things besides thanks. One suspects that both the man and Yorick are ashamed, but that Yorick is enjoying as well as enduring his own shame.

The ending of "Simon Lee" works in a similar way by hinting not just at the range of emotions Simon could be feeling but at the conflict of feelings in the narrator. "I thought / They never would have done": this sounds not just embarrassed, but oddly impatient, as though inwardly reprimanding Simon for not acting in a respectable manner—and it also sounds just a little pleased with itself (somewhere in the narrator's subconscious, he's commending himself for being so exquisitely understanding about the whole thing). Such flickering possibilities in the verse suggest that our guide is thoughtless when he thinks he's being thoughtful—and vice versa. His "mourning," resistant as it is to a cheap morality of charitable exchange, may itself be fawning. Lamb once seized on "the vanity of self-denial . . . the very coxcombry of charity"[48] and noted that "a man may be intemperate & selfish, who indulges in *good feelings*, for the mere pleasure they give him."[49] Elsewhere, he noted that "our delicacy forbids the dramatizing of distress at all. It is never shown in its essential properties; it appears but as the adjunct of some virtue, as something which is to be relieved, from the approbation of which relief the spectators are to derive a certain soothing of self-referred satisfaction."[50] Wordsworth's poem is fooling around with the narrator's need—and with *our* need—for such satisfaction.

None of this necessarily undoes what Bromwich and others have seen as the poem's "logic," but it does suggest how frequently that logic is subject to other considerations—and how difficult it is to maintain. "Alas! the gratitude of men / Has oftner left me mourning." *Oftner.* So this kind of thing has happened to the narrator more than once? Despite the potentially sadistic complacency of his good deed that day, nothing he did has stopped him acting similarly since then. Exclusive focus on individual acts of charity may of course preclude consideration of more systematic change (as Harold Laski put it, "Pity has no programme, because it is always an inadequate substitute for justice. It ignores relations and institutions in order to devote itself to the claims of persons").[51] Yet are the claims of persons to be disregarded? Is such devotion always an ignoring? And is our narrator to stop proffering help simply because he's become conscientiously (or preeningly) aware of how it might be taken as imposition or insult, or of how mixed motives may inform his wish to provide such aid? Elizabeth Bishop once noted "the ambiguous nature of all good deeds, the impossibility of ever knowing why they are being performed."[52] "Simon Lee" is knowingly unknowing in a similar way.

One way of handling this ambiguity is to stick with a conception of the poem that sees it as the narrator's attempt to atone for what happened that day by talking it all out.[53] Yet the narrator's very wish to generalize at the end (to slide from the particular incident with Simon to "Alas! the gratitude of *men*") edges toward a culpable thinning out of response, a kind of hankering for the panoptic instrumentality of the example. It tells of his need for a lesson and of his desire—along with his inability—to come up with a general code of conduct or morality. Besides, the lesson of the encounter with Simon Lee refuses to stay learned, for the only other time Wordsworth makes space in the poem for that word "Alas!" (so poetical, so tender, so easy a word) is midway through when the narrator explains how Simon and his wife struggle to tend their plot of land:

> Old Ruth works out of doors with him,
> And does what Simon cannot do;
> For she, not over stout of limb,
> Is stouter of the two.
> And though you with your utmost skill
> From labour could not wean them,
> Alas! 'tis very little, all
> Which they can do between them.

So the narrator is still tempted to speak like this even *after* what happened between him and Simon that day. He might be given the benefit of the doubt with "not over stout of limb" (a delicate understatement, perhaps), but what of talk of *weaning* them from work? References to our "skill" as distinct from their "labour" don't help, nor does the almost gloating proximity of "little" and "all." All this may be simply the narrator's trickery; he—and the poet behind him—play the Fool, miming our presuppositions all the better to unmask them. Or we may feel that the narrator is a natural fool, falling into old mistakes in new ways, heedless—for the moment, at least—of how care and complacency are implicated in one another and of how relieving the couple of their labor could relieve them of their dignity.[54] Reading this stanza, I'm reminded of the wisdom of Auden's dark joke: "We are all here on earth to help others; what on earth the others are here for, I don't know."[55]

*

"Simon Lee" is both a grim comedy of errors and a meditation on the error of a certain kind of comedy, comedy that would merely let us toy with humor before seeking to save us from error itself by offering us a moral (even a moral about the necessity of "mourning"). In a discussion of "the comic frame," Kenneth Burke noted,

> The progress of humane enlightenment can go no further than in picturing people not as *vicious*, but as *mistaken*. When you add that people are *necessarily* mistaken, that *all* people are exposed to situations in which they must act as fools, that *every* insight contains its own special kind of blindness, you complete the comic circle, returning again to the lesson of humility that underlies great tragedy.[56]

Wordsworth would I think have been inclined to draw from these wise words a further corollary: even the "lesson" of humility—the one that the narrator of "Simon Lee" proffers at the end of the poem—isn't immune from error, for it must contain the blindness of its insight (recall the poet's acute confession in *The Prelude* about moments in which "Humility and modest awe themselves / Betray me, serving often for a cloak / To a more subtle selfishness").[57] "Simon Lee" is characteristic of the strange humor—and the dark humorings—of the *Lyrical Ballads* in that it seems to dare a reader to take sides, which is perhaps why responses to the poem often feel inadequate rather than inappropriate. Heather Glen provides welcome resistance to some of the more cheerily moral readings, but when she claims that "the poem finally fails to explore or control that confusion of feeling which its 'incident' arouses. . . . It points away from the challenging fact of Simon's existence and into the world of essentially private feeling,"[58] something continues to nag. The poem has registered the fact of Simon's existence through the mawkish comedy of the narrator's attempts to rewrite or resist it, and that existence and the narrator's private feeling needn't be mutually exclusive. Feeling can be empty piety and also a catalyst for an enlarged sense of the complexity of social relations; it can be both an evasion and a mark of citizenship, a disingenuous substitute and an indispensable ground for ethics. The difficulty of calibrating the difference in any given situation is part of the challenge of "Simon Lee." It is not so much that the poem "finally fails to explore or control" its confusions, for an attempt to control the confusion here wouldn't necessarily be the best means of exploring it. Or maybe "Simon Lee" does fail—just not *finally*. Instead, it provokes doubt about what constitutes success in such matters.

A related doubt, it would now appear, was hiding in plain sight from the start: Simon is no longer a huntsman, yet the poem's oddly prolix title—"Simon Lee: The Old Huntsman, with an Incident in Which He Was Concerned"—tries to keep him as one, which either tells of the narrator's blithely wishful thinking or pays the man the respect of talking about him as he would wish to be talked about (when those hounds are out, it's as if he were his old self again: "And still there's something in the world / At which his heart rejoices"). Speaking of those weirdly foolish Old Persons in Edward Lear's limericks—poems indebted to the surreptitious simplicity of the *Lyrical Ballads*—James Williams asks, "is the Old Person's liveliness a spontaneous overflow of his inner life, or a kind of performance put on for our entertainment? How far are we to think he *knows* that he is a figure of laughter? And isn't that the question raised by court fools?"[59] These questions bear on our relations with Wordsworth's Old Huntsman of Cardigan. The Fool is always in one way or another raising the central concerns explored by "Simon Lee," issues of power and patronage, questions about the social responsibilities and performances of the self. The poem never quite claims authority for itself but seems to be in search of authority, or in search of its demise. Indeed, an authoritative reading is made even harder to establish when we consider a link between the poet's life and the one he detects in Simon Lee.

As Wordsworth's later comments suggest, his lyrical ballad struck close to home:

> This old man had been huntsman to the Squires of Alfoxden, which, at the time we occupied it belonged to a minor. The old man's cottage stood upon the common a little way from the entrance to Alfoxden Park. But it had disappeared. Many other changes had taken place in the adjoining village, which I could not but notice with a regret more natural than well-considered. Improvements but rarely appear such to those who, after long intervals of time, revisit places they have had much pleasure in. It is unnecessary to add, the fact was as mentioned in the poem, and I have, after an interval of 45 years, the image of the old man as fresh before my eyes as if I had seen him yesterday.[60]

The old huntsman was named Christopher Tricky. Wordsworth encountered him, as he notes, when he and Dorothy were renting at Alfoxden Hall (a "large mansion," Dorothy called it). The poem explains that Simon's "master's dead, and no one now / Dwells in the hall of Ivor," but in a way Wordsworth dwells there; he's a stand-in for the vanished owner, and yet he's also merely a tenant, a "no one" of sorts. Wordsworth was born the son of a man who worked for the richest landowner in England. He was cripplingly poor just before writing "Simon Lee," living on the produce from his own garden and worrying about his ability to pay for postage for letters (until he was in his midforties, he often lived from hand to mouth, frequently aware of his financial insecurity).[61] David Simpson has suggested that the predicament of the apprentice-poet in a world without patrons can be related to that of Simon Lee, for, as the narrator chops the tangled root, he finds a momentary freedom from an ongoing predicament that the old man must face—the predicament of one who cannot earn a living on his own. And this moment comes at a time when Wordsworth is discussing other people's freedoms in radical circles, finding himself caught between the feudal and democratic: "The instability of his position," Simpson notes, "makes him at once a man of the people—a man assisting a fellow man—and a proxy of the old hierarchy."[62]

To put it another way, Wordsworth sometimes feels like a fool—and never more so than when seeing versions of himself in decrepit old huntsmen or when speaking truth to power from a room within the castle walls, a room that is nevertheless not his own. Speaking of regrets "more natural than well-considered," Wordsworth again confesses to oversight as well as insight, resisting and pledging himself to folly once more as he digs about in his own roots. Years after the writing of the poem, Mary Wordsworth recalled how her husband would often make jokes out of "little matters"—not the least of which were jokes about his social standing:

> Your dear Father used to joke with me on the non arrival of the *expected Silver Coffee Pot* (which as that was the *marriage present* they sent to my cousin Hutchinson) I naturally thought would have been presented to me; at the same time I used to express a wish that something might come, to remember them by, more suited to our then Establishment. The *disappointment*, however, brought its reward, by the many jocund sallies your dear father used to launch upon my *blasted expectations*; and we have done very well without a *Silver Coffee Pot* to this day.[63]

Guy Davenport suggested that an informing principle of the comic spirit is "the ability of life to assert its claims no matter what social forms dictate."[64] Yet the defiant energy of comedic assertion knows, too, that social forms die hard—and that comedy itself is one of those forms. Comic instincts frequently thrive on the projection of disruptive experiences onto small or apparently insignificant objects (a coffee pot, or a poem about a running huntsman merry) just as they find new ways to play with expectation by making disappointments themselves a source of perplexed pleasure. All of which is not to say that those "jocund sallies" of Wordsworth's didn't nurse a serious grievance. The fact that he kept feeling the need to repeat the joke tells its own story.

Idiots

> Deep pools, tall trees, black chasms, and dizzy crags—
> I loved to look in them, to stand and read
> Their looks forbidding, read and disobey
>
> *HOME AT GRASMERE*[1]

The last chapter began by considering Wordsworth's relations with his audience and closed with the nonarrival of a coffee pot. One might read this as the occlusion or negation of the sociopolitical in the name of the personal, but the two categories are not always easily separable for Wordsworth and his writing often stages their entanglement through the dynamics of foolery. Even so, it's true that he is sometimes on the lookout for an escape route to a kind of embattled, brooding privacy. In 1805, while listening to his son with his friends ("little John's Visitors are playing below, equally noisy and happy"), he thought of the noise the newspapers were making: "I have asked myself more than once lately if my affections can be in the right place caring as I do so little about what the world seems to care so much for. All this seems to me 'a tale told by an Idiot full of sound and fury signifying nothing.'"[2] Wordsworth stood in need of a less worldly idiocy, elsewhere recalling his early fondness for George Crabbe's lines ("Far the happiest they / The moping idiot and the madman gay") and noting that in the district where he was brought up, such people were "too often the butt of thoughtless Children."[3]

"The Idiot Boy" was frequently the butt of that most thoughtless of children, contemporary opinion, but it was one of Wordsworth's most treasured possessions—the only poem he accorded the honor of a half-title page in *Lyrical Ballads*, and a poem he demanded be published in every subsequent edition of his work.[4] Idiocy and foolery have a long history. The "natural idiot" was closely linked to the "natural fool," for an idiot is not simply someone "profoundly mentally and intellectually disabled; exceedingly stupid"; the term has an older sense: "A man of low intelligence maintained as a source of amusement to others; a household or court fool; a professional fool or jester" (*OED*). Why such a figure was maintained—and what his patrons' amusement implies about both him and themselves—are questions the poem takes to be of more than historical importance. Wordsworth once wrote of "A face divine of heaven-born ideotcy!"[5] and he defended his own idiot boy, Johnny, in these terms:

> I have often applied to Idiots, in my own mind, that sublime expression of scripture that, *"their life is hidden with God."* They are worshipped, probably from a feeling of this sort, in several parts of the East. Among the Alps where they are numerous, they are considered, I believe, as a blessing to the family to which they belong.[6]

This points to the sanctity of true folly, for "hath not God made foolish the wisdom of this world? . . . God hath chosen the foolish things of the world to confound the wise." (1 Corinthians 1:20–27) So it betokens a certain kind of idiocy to shun the insights of the fool: "If any man among you seemeth to be wise in this world, let him become a fool, that he may be wise. For the wisdom of this world is foolishness with God." (1 Corinthians 3:18–19).

The grandeur of the lowly—and "the process where much is represented in little," as Wordsworth later put it—has several analogues in Christian thought.[7] He would have encountered such emphases in his reading of Desiderius Erasmus's *The Praise of Folly* ("nor is it merely an accident that fools are so extremely pleasing to God"),[8] and his letter also draws on other traditions, including the Greco-Roman view that misshapen and abnormal people, having already received all the bad luck that could be expected to befall them, were immune from divine punishment; they were therefore employed as mascots on the principle that contact with the lucky brings good luck.[9] The fact that Wordsworth's idiot is a boy, not a man, is also significant; as Erasmus noted, in Greek the "childish" and the "foolish" were etymologically related (in a book of proverbs Wordsworth owned, one encounters comments like "Children and fools speak truth," "Children and fools have merry lives," and so on).[10] "Happy, happy, happy John"[11] is never at risk of growing up nor of growing unwisely wise. Erasmus's Folly promises to restore Man to the happiest part of his life, claiming that he will enjoy perpetual youth. And, like Johnny, the Fool is "never restrained by any undertaking whatsoever—neither by modesty (because he has none), nor by danger (to which he pays no attention)."[12]

Johnny is also part of a long tradition of fools (holy and otherwise) who develop a partnership with donkeys and asses, from Christ to Don Quixote to Sterne's Yorick and beyond.[13] (Johnny's "steed and he right well agree, / For of this pony there's a rumour . . . He never will be out of humour."[14]) In folk tradition, the Fool also carried branches of wood, and Johnny too has "his holly-bough, / And with a hurly-burly now / He shakes the green bough in his hand."[15] The story begins as we learn that the boy is on a rescue mission. His mother, Betty, has asked him to ride through the forest at night to bring a doctor from the town, or her good friend Susan Gale will die.[16] Betty is aware that she may be sending Johnny on a fool's errand. He's a natural fool and probably can't (or won't) follow her orders because he's not able to comprehend the urgency of the situation. Her pride in Johnny, her worry for him, her "mighty fret" and "fiddle-faddle"[17] are never far from view, and even Wordsworth's supporters were unwilling to entertain the suggestion that she herself was anything but a fool. Coleridge later complained that "the idiocy of the *boy* is so evenly balanced by the folly of the *mother*, as to present to the general reader rather a laughable burlesque on the blindness of anile dotage, than an analytic display of maternal affection in its ordinary workings."[18]

"The Idiot Boy" is intent on resisting the separation of the laughable and the analytical, although it doesn't always foreground that intention—partly, I think, because Wordsworth sensed that the resistance would be more effective if undertaken by stealth, and partly because the poem was so entangled with events in his childhood that he probably wasn't entirely sure of his intentions when writing it. "The Idiot Boy" is not simply a critique but a comic apologia: a chronicle of Wordsworth's bafflement at his own thought processes and at the sources of his gratification. In this chapter, I want to approach the poem in the spirit analogous to that which J.-B. Pontalis approaches the trials of thought:

> If thought is to be set in motion again one first has to bring it to a halt. It has to be struck in fear or amazement, must allow itself to be *ravished* even at the risk of losing itself. . . . A thought that seeks to be constantly agile and which never undergoes the tribulation of failure, a kind of intelligence that fears idiocy, a kind of word that would never weaken, would ignore what was at the base of thought, of intelligence, of the word. It is what I am calling the *infans* or the silence of beginnings.[19]

This is very close to where "The Idiot Boy" begins—and where it ends. Unravished experts (adults, commentators, literary critics) do not generally pride themselves on their ability to fail, to lose themselves, to become beginners. Still, Wordsworth was wary of people who lacked inexperience.

*

If the tale is read from the mother's perspective, something more than "anile dotage" emerges. David Pirie notes of Betty that in entrusting Johnny with his errand, she wants to give him the responsibility, and the achievements, allowed to children who have developed normally.[20] This need can be felt in lovely, light touches. As she watches Johnny leave on his pony, she is "Proud of herself, and proud of him" (she'd find it hard to disentangle the two feelings).[21] Later, waiting by Susan's sickbed for Johnny to return, "She sits, as if in Susan's fate / Her life and soul were buried" ("as if": Susan isn't her main thought; Betty's life and soul are buried in her need for Johnny to do well at this).[22] "As sure as there's a moon in heaven," Betty reassures Susan, "he'll be back again; / They'll both be here."[23] That slip—"he"—is quickly corrected to "They," while the glancing stress on "both" hints at her attempt to undo the implication of her first thought; she was so wrapped up in thinking about Johnny, she'd forgotten the doctor with whom he's meant to be returning. She sits by the sickbed "Demure with porringer and plate":

> But Betty, poor good woman! she,
> You plainly in her face may read it,
> Could lend out of that moment's store
> Five years of happiness or more,
> To any that might need it.[24]

Betty is already dreaming up a future in which she will look back on this moment as one of her—and Johnny's—best achievements. The person in front of her would currently beg a little of such happiness (she may not have five hours to live), but the obliviousness to other people's sufferings that comes with your own surplus of pleasure is what the poem is asking us to recognize—and to enjoy. We are invited to indulge and to humor Betty but not to pretend that we'd feel any differently if we were her.

The poem's journey to the poignant via the ludicrous can be felt in one particular stanza that was mocked by reviewers. As the night rolls on with no sign of either Johnny or the doctor, Betty's worry gets the better of her, so she sets out to find her idiot boy. Several hours later, she spots him:

> She looks again—her arms are up—
> She screams—she cannot move for joy;
> She darts as with a torrent's force,
> She almost has o'erturned the horse,
> And fast she holds her idiot boy.[25]

For many critics, the simile was a miniature version of what was wrong with the poem: it made too much of Betty's feelings just as she made too much of her idiot boy.[26] Yet while the exaggerated notion that in Betty's keenness she could overturn the horse is laughable, to laugh here is to assent to the visceral rather than rational foundation of her love; the stanza is committed to portraying both the urgency and the idiocy of affection. "And fast she holds her idiot boy" is a wonderful condensation of her body's action in time and space; for a split second, "fast" means "quickly" before steadying itself to mean "firmly." Wordsworth would probably have been happy for readers to call this stanza comic provided they acknowledged that "All things are tragic / when a mother watches!"[27]

Before Betty finds Johnny, she has several misadventures of her own. She first searches for him at the doctor's house, and in her panic she forgets the reason for Johnny's errand: "Oh Doctor! Doctor! where's my Johnny?" The old man is not pleased to be woken up at this hour: "The Doctor, looking somewhat grim, / 'What, woman! should I know of him?' / And, grumbling, he went back to bed."[28] As it turns out, Johnny's nescience becomes a form of prescience, for it has the side effect of helping to bring about Susan's cure. Forced to wait for a doctor who never comes, her thoughts turn to Johnny and Betty lost in the wood: "many dreadful fears beset her, / . . . / And as her mind grew worse and worse, / Her body it grew better."[29] Two figures, then—a reckless, feckless Johnny and a selfish, unimpressionable doctor—are called on to steer everyone from tragedy to comedy, and the former comes good despite himself. Although their paths never cross, the two figures echo an old double act: the mountebank doctor and his zany servant-fool. *Zany*—the Italian word for Johnny—traditionally came with a partner; D'Avenant's masque *Brittania Triumphans* contained an antimasque featuring a mountebank in the habit of a grave doctor and a zany, and the saying "A mountebank without his fool / Is in a sorrowful case" stretched far back. The pair continued to thrive in fairs until the early nineteenth century, and the roles were sometimes blended or swapped, the figures being conceived as two kinds of Fool, one knowing and the other unwitting.[30]

With this partnership in mind, the line immediately following Betty's cry of "Oh Doctor! Doctor! where's my Johnny?" is suggestive: "I'm here, what is't you want with me?"[31] raises the possibility that the doctor could be Johnny's foil or double. The zany often undermined his master and his quack cures, deflating his claims and dignified poses (he could be found singing "he who is healthy, and cheerful and cool / Yet squanders his money on physic's a *fool.* / Fool, master, fool, fool.")[32] But he was also sometimes played as an honest worker, a man who created disasters unknowingly and with the best of intentions.[33] Wordsworth was clearly fascinated by the act and had seen some version of it; in his sonnet to Fancy he compares a wild rose to "a bonny Lass, who plays her pranks / At Wakes and Fairs with wandering Mountebanks, / When she stands cresting the Clown's head."[34] With this heritage somewhere in the shadows, the doctor's question to Betty—"What, woman! should I know of him?"—might prompt the answer "Quite a bit, only the story has been changed a little." Johnny the zany is the natural fool and errant servant who exposes the apparent expertise of his senior, thus becoming the catalyst for a different sense of what really matters (we see "Susan rise up from her bed, / As if by magic cured"[35]). Elsewhere, Wordsworth imagines a state and a place "Where Passion caught what Nature taught, / That all but Love is folly."[36] "The Idiot Boy" is his way of insisting that love is catching—and that what Coleridge would refer to as "affection in its ordinary workings" may lead to extraordinary outcomes.

But there are other, stranger affections lurking beneath this story, and the Fool lives more than one life in the poem. "The Idiot Boy" harks back to the thrilling trauma of Wordsworth's own boyhood, and to get closer to that trauma, we need to travel—like Johnny—via circuitous routes. Just as we've seen in *The Borderers*, "The Brothers," and other writings from the 1790s, Wordsworth's personal and authorial predicaments are often mediated through the example of Shakespearean folly. In *A Midsummer Night's Dream*, Peter Quince feels that the mechanics' comedy should be written in a traditional ballad meter of "eight and six," but Bottom suggests a slight tweak to the form: "No, make it two more: let it be written eight and eight."[37] Both their play and Shakespeare's are timed by the moon—this is important to Bottom: "look in the almanac. Find out moonshine"—and the action throughout is punctuated by "The clamorous owl that nightly hoots and wonders / At our quaint spirits."[38] "The Idiot Boy" is written in Bottom's preferred style, a version of "eight and eight," and its narrator immediately draws attention to "The owlet in the moonlight air" before reminding us toward the end that "The owls have hooted all night long, / And with the owls began my song."[39]

The trials and tribulations of the poem's Fool parallel those of Bottom: a journey into the wood, and a hazardous loss of bearings that may include both a meeting with spirits and strange, ass-like behavior (perhaps, readers are told, Johnny has been coaxed into "the goblins' hall," or "Perhaps he's turned himself about, / His face unto his horse's tail").[40] Bottom is himself a reincarnation of the clown (Oberon calls him a "fool"), and his most memorable speech is indebted to the ending of Erasmus's *The Praise of Folly*:

> "Eye has not seen, nor ear heard, nor has the heart of man conceived what things God has prepared for those who love him." And this is Folly's part. . . . Those who have the privilege of experiencing this (and it happens to very few) undergo something very like madness: they talk incoherently, not in a human fashion, making sounds without sense. . . . Soon after, when they come to themselves, they say they do not know where they have been, whether in the

> body or out of it, whether waking or sleeping. They do not remember what they heard or saw or said or did except in a cloudy way, as if it were a dream.[41]

"The eye of man hath not heard, the ear of man hath not seen . . . what my dream was," Bottom says as he comes to himself, talking incoherently about the privilege of his experience. "Man is but an ass if he go about to expound this dream. . . . Man is but a patched fool if he will offer to say what methought I had. . . . I will get Peter Quince to write a ballad of this dream."[42] Audiences never hear that ballad, just as they never quite get to the bottom of what the idiot boy has been doing all night when he was meant to be fetching the doctor, but Wordsworth's poem ends with a haunting echo of Bottom's language.

The weaver is inclined toward incongruity even in his more lucid moments. Singing to drown out the owls in the wood, Bottom thinks of "The ousel cock so black of hue," and then later, as a dying Pyramus, he addresses the moon: "Sweet Moon, I thank thee for thy sunny beams, / I thank thee, Moon, for shining now so bright."[43] "The Idiot Boy" closes when Johnny returns home from the wood, is asked by his mother to give his version of events, and replies, "The cocks did crow to-whoo, to-whoo, / And the sun did shine so cold."[44] This is almost goadingly frivolous, and yet, like Bottom's rapt nonexpounding of his dream, Johnny's metaphoric muddle is in tune with the foolish calling of the poet as Wordsworth conceives it. Elsewhere, he writes that even a thing which seems "for mockery combined . . . / Shows not a sight incongruous as the extremes / That everywhere, before the thoughtful mind, / Meet on the solid ground of waking life."[45] True thought renders reality itself incongruous, and folly becomes a form of replenished reasoning. In fact, Johnny's predilection for seeing extremes or opposites as coimplicated is of a piece with his poet-narrator's:

> Though Betty's in a mighty flurry,
> She . . . seems no longer in a hurry[46]
> . . . .
> Almost stifled with her bliss,
> A few sad tears does Betty shed.[47]
> . . . .
> She's happy here, she's happy there,
> She is uneasy every where[48]

The Bard "is half an idiot too,"[49] as Burns once put it. Poets, idiots, fools—they all talk funny.

The idiot boy's final words are the crowning example of such nonsense, and they exemplify what Betty refers to early in the poem as "Johnny's wit and Johnny's glory."[50] We need the words again—but slower this time, and in their setting—to register their limpid yet shrouded force:

> (His very words I give to you,)
> "The cocks did crow to-whoo, to-whoo,
> And the sun did shine so cold."
> —Thus answered Johnny in his glory,
> And that was all his travel's story.

Wordsworth "gives" us Johnny's words in the same way he gives us his own utterances: not simply as a fact, but as a gift or an inheritance. In the last line, there's a slight flicker of emphasis on "his," as though to say, "that's *his* story, and he's sticking to it." Alternatively, the stress on "all" may itself be a compacted, punning instance of wit, for it allows "that was all" to be registered in two ways: Johnny's story is at once something and nothing. The phrase is either bathetic or summative; hearing it as both, readers catch the sound of the poem's seriousness from within the provocations of its comedy.

The comedy is related to the glory, but what *is* glory? "I rather glory in my infirmities," writes Paul in Corinthians, "take pleasure in infirmities, in necessities, in persecutions, in distresses . . . I am become a fool in glorying" (2 Corinthians 12:9–11) The narrator gleefully noted earlier in the poem that "The moon that shines above his head / Is not more still and mute than he,"[51] which suggests another meaning of *glory* as "aureole, nimbus, or halo" (*OED*), and Wordsworth toys with this idea elsewhere ("circlet bright! / How glorious," he exclaims, on catching sight of snowdrops).[52] Nature is blessing the idiot boy, and the *OED*'s other definitions of glory are instructive too: "1. *subjectively*. The disposition to claim honour for oneself; boastful spirit"; "2. *objectively*. Exalted (and, in mod. use, merited) praise, honour, or admiration accorded by common consent to a person or thing." Johnny's glory, the poem's glory, is the dream of the subjective as the first and last authority for the objective, the dream of self-making that constitutes the world, a world in which whatever you feel disposed to claim for yourself becomes common consent.

Such gambits were a little too much for some. Early critics spoke of Wordsworth's poems as "nonsense" and of the way they "suppose folly to be feeling, and consider nature as synonymous with nonsense."[53] But Wordsworth felt that life's nonsense pierces us with strange relation, and the idiot boy stands somewhere close to where Wallace Stevens imagines the listener standing in "The Motive for Metaphor," amid the trees at night, listening to the way nature "repeats words without meaning":

The obscure moon lighting an obscure world
Of things that would never be quite expressed,
Where you yourself were never quite yourself
And did not want nor have to be,

Desiring the exhilarations of changes:
The motive for metaphor, shrinking from
The weight of primary noon,
The A B C of being[54]

*

The feeling one gets that Wordsworth is sponsoring Johnny, I've been suggesting, is related to a more unlikely feeling: Johnny is unknowingly sponsoring Wordsworth. The boy is partly imagined into existence as means for the poet to return to his past demons—and to his past delights. In reply to one critic of the poem, John Wilson, Wordsworth wrote,

> If an Idiot is born in a poor man's house, it must be taken care of and cannot be boarded out, as it would be by gentlefolks. . . . I have indeed often looked upon the conduct of fathers and mothers of the lower classes of society towards Idiots as the great triumph of the human heart . . . nor have I ever been able to contemplate an object that calls out so many excellent and virtuous sentiments without finding it hallowed thereby and having something within me which bears down before it, like a deluge, every feeble sensation of disgust and aversion.[55]

Wordsworth's simile ("like a deluge") recalls the sudden sense of "a torrent's force" within Betty as she almost overturns the horse. It could be said that he's telling Wilson he knows how Betty feels, but that wouldn't be quite right because he's admitting that he *does* feel a momentary sense of disgust and aversion (albeit a "feeble" one) whereas Betty does not. The syntactical knottiness of the closing comment gestures toward something weirder: "without finding it hallowed thereby and having something within me which bears down before it, like a deluge, every feeble sensation of disgust and aversion." The first "it" refers to the idiot (or to the heart?), and the second might refer to the "something within me" as well as to the idiot. Elsewhere in the letter Wordsworth talks of the process of "stripping our own hearts naked" when faced by such people,[56] and these comments are close to the fury of pleasure at the heart of his poem. When he later said of "The Idiot Boy" that "I never wrote anything with so much glee,"[57] he was pointing to another incongruous alliance with Johnny, for the narrator tells us that the boy's "heart it was so full of glee."[58] In the *Reliques*, Percy noted that the roots of *glee* lay in joy, mirth, gladness, cheerfulness, but observed that "the word still continues, though rather in a low debasing sense."[59] What might glee portend in a poem that is itself a riposte to those who see the low as synonymous with the debasing? And what was it about this particular poem that brought forth such a flood of feeling in its maker? Like all of Wordsworth's best writing, "The Idiot Boy" was something else before it was moral. It was personal.

At the center of the poem lies a silence. The narrator pauses to speculate on where the boy's glee might have led him before calling for help:

> I to the muses have been bound,
> These fourteen years, by strong indentures;
> Oh gentle muses! let me tell
> But half of what to him befell,
> For sure he met with strange adventures.
>
> Oh gentle muses! is this kind?
> Why will ye thus my suit repel?
> Why of your further aid bereave me?
> And can you thus unfriended leave me?
> Ye muses! whom I love so well.[60]

This is Wordsworth's way of teasing readers who are merely looking to tickle themselves with strange adventures, but it's also something more. The narrator, at the very moment when Betty feels bereaved and bereft of aid, obtrudes his own concerns about being left behind or left out. As Johnny is to his mother, so the poet's muses are to the poet: inscrutable, unaccountable, heedless. The poet, like Johnny, has forgotten any responsibilities he might have toward Betty and become waylaid by whatever the wood has to offer. He has—to borrow a phrase from De Quincey when he was thinking about Wordsworth—become lost in "the forest of his genius."[61]

Late in life, recalling his few fleeting memories of his own mother, Wordsworth spoke of a woman who worried about him:

> I remember my mother only in some few situations. . . . I remember . . . telling her on one week day that I had been at church. . . . The occasion was, a woman doing penance in the church in a white sheet. My mother commended my having been present, expressing a hope that I should remember the circumstance for the rest of my life. "But," said I, "Mama, they did not give me a penny, as I had been told they would." "Oh," said she, recanting her praises, "if that was your motive, you were very properly disappointed."
>
> My last impression was having a glimpse of her on passing the door of her bedroom during her last illness, when she was reclining in her easy chair. An

> intimate friend of hers, Miss Hamilton by name, who was used to visit her at Cockermouth, told me that she once said to her, that the only one of her five children about whose future life she was anxious, was William; and he, she said, would be remarkable either for good or for evil. The cause of this was, that I was of a stiff, moody, and violent temper; so much so that I remember going once into the attics of my grandfather's house at Penrith, upon some indignity having been put upon me, with an intention of destroying myself with one of the foils which I knew was kept there. I took the foil in hand, but my heart failed. Upon another occasion, while I was at my grandfather's house at Penrith, along with my eldest brother, Richard, we were whipping tops together in the large drawing-room, on which the carpet was only laid down upon particular occasions. The walls were hung round with family pictures, and I said to my brother, "Dare you strike your whip through that old lady's petticoat?" He replied, "No, I won't." "Then," said I, "here goes"; and I struck my lash through her hooped petticoat, for which no doubt, though I have forgotten it, I was properly punished. But possibly, from some want of judgment in punishments inflicted, I had become perverse and obstinate in defying chastisement, and rather proud of it than otherwise.[62]

There is a great deal going on here. Wordsworth remembers witnessing someone doing penance, and this leads to recollections of how he himself remained impenitent for his own transgressions. He remembers, for the rest of his life, not so much "the circumstance" his mother wants him to remember but her disappointed response to his demand that he put his own pleasure first. He remembers the visceral gratification at violence done in and to the home (the family pictures, the whips, the petticoats) but forgets the precise nature of the punishment he received. He remembers her death as a reclining in an "easy" chair, alongside his "stiff" moods and his unwillingness to put an end to his own life. He remembers her anxiety about how he would turn out alongside his pride in his perverseness. He remembers the emphasis around him on the proper ("properly disappointed," "properly punished") and his mother recanting her praises, and he remembers himself recanting nothing.

In the face of his mother's concerns, Johnny goes it alone. He "proudly shook the bridle,"[63] but only to signify his unbridled sense of joy at his own being, not to rein things in (he soon forgets the way he was meant to use his "holly whip").[64] Byron laughingly dismissed the poem:

> A moon-struck silly lad who lost his way,
> And, like his bard, confounded night with day . . .
> all who view the "idiot in his glory,"
> Conceive the Bard the hero of the story.[65]

This seizes on something important, for "The Idiot Boy" is the story of a self-conception, a comic bildungsroman in which traumatic possibilities become the catalysts for imaginative plenitude. It's as though Wordsworth were driven, with a kind of gleeful desperation, to read his own past *as* a comedy. The poem doesn't simply ask readers to admire a mother's love and to revise their own sense of what might be valuable through that love. It gives expression to a more inward, private need, one felt in Wordsworth's attraction to Johnny's being "As careless as if nothing were,"[66] a need to feel again the electrifyingly improper power of a boy's lack of consideration, his reckless sense of his own autonomy, his ability to survive anything.

A few months after writing "The Idiot Boy," Wordsworth began to compose the first spots of time in drafts of what would become *The Prelude.* One of these radiant moments tells of a horse ride he undertook when he was around six years old:

> While I was yet an urchin, one who scarce
> Could hold a bridle, with ambitious hopes
> I mounted[67]

He soon gets lost. In "The Idiot Boy," when Johnny gets lost, both his mother and the narrator speculate about the strange things that might have befallen him: he may have "joined the wandering gypsey-folk" or turned into something "like a silent horseman-ghost" or tried "To lay his hands upon a star" or galloped away like the devil "with head and heels on fire, / And like the very soul of evil" (as Wordsworth's mother said, he "would be remarkable either for good or for evil.")[68] What happened to the young Wordsworth on his horse ride wasn't any less strange: he came across an old gibbet where many years previously a man, "the murderer of his wife, was hung / In irons";[69] he gazed at a naked pool; he encountered a beacon on a summit; he watched a girl who bore a pitcher on her head struggling against the wind. The coalescence of these events composes a memory of visionary dreariness, records a loss of bearings in which he somehow found himself and discovered a sense of "power / Implanted in my mind."[70]

Somewhere close to the heart of Wordsworth's sense of the folly that constitutes the poetic instinct—and the folly that constitutes his life—stands the figure of the child who discovers his power amid peril. In "The Blind Highland Boy," the protagonist climbs into a washing tub and is carried away down river; like Johnny, he is the source of his mother's worry ("was she here, or was she there, / She thought of him with constant care"),[71] but then, who really wants *constant* care? Although the mother stands terrified on shore and the villagers try to rescue the boy before he is swept away to sea, he himself is triumphantly, ecstatically mutinous:

> "*Lei-gha—Lei-gha*"—then did he cry
> "*Lei-gha—Lei-gha*"—most eagerly;
> Thus did he cry, and thus did pray,
> And what he meant was, "Keep away,
> And leave me to myself!"[72]

To myself, not merely *by* myself. The poet is able to act as interpreter for the boy because he knows this feeling from the inside. It's the same one that animated Johnny as well as his younger self: a discovery of inner resources through an unsought exposure; a translation of the traumatic into the concentered; a defiance against the desolation of being rescued.

*

"Leave me to myself!" In other circumstances, such defiance could be a defense against the possibility that he might be left—or against the fact that he already had been. Early drafts of *The Prelude* speak of the child who "Doth gather passion from his Mother's eye!," a passion that gives him confidence to make his own way in the world, "No outcast he, bewildered and depressed" (the manuscript, tellingly, reads "*abandoned* and depressed").[73] And Wordsworth was abandoned not once but twice, which brings us to a question that should be asked of poems like "The Blind Highland Boy" and "The Idiot Boy": Where's the father? Readers are told early on that "Betty's husband's at the wood . . . / A woodman in the distant vale; / There's none to help."[74] At the crucial pause in the tale when the narrator worries about being bereaved of aid and left unfriended, the fact that Johnny has been wandering about in the moonlight "From eight o'clock till five"[75] is set aside for another time frame: "I to the muses have been bound, / These fourteen years, by strong indentures."[76] Apprenticeships are usually shorter, and some have suggested that the detail is intended to show that the narrator is a bit slow witted or even mentally impaired.[77] Perhaps, but there are other possibilities. "The Idiot Boy" was composed early in 1798; fourteen years earlier, Wordsworth's father died. To recall the specifics, he died of bronchitis as the result of a horse ride, a ride probably illuminated by a full moon, "in consequence of a cold caught on Coldfell, where he lost his way, and passed the night in the open air." He was buried in January 1784.[78]

In *The Prelude*, Wordsworth's recollection of his own youthful horse ride, the one in which he himself lost his way and as a result discovered new powers, immediately leads him to recall the death of his father: "I and my two Brothers, orphans then, / Followed his body to the grave."[79] He remembers that the death appeared "A chastisement" and was somehow linked in his mind with the day he'd waited with "such anxiety of hope" for his father's horses to collect him from school.[80] The poem seems unwilling to clarify exactly what the boy has to feel guilty about. David Ellis suggests that Wordsworth experienced hostility toward his father for keeping him waiting, and that the situation becomes "analogous to that where one might write a reproachful letter to a friend for his failure to get in touch and then discover that he has been very ill." Ellis's recourse to George Moore's comments on the death of his own father are instructive: "I loved my father, and yet my soul said, 'I am glad' . . . My father's death freed me, and I sprang like a loosened bough up to the light. His death gave me the power to create myself."[81] Wordsworth's guilt, then, may be related to what Freud called the "omnipotence of thoughts" and to a vague sense that some part of him longed for this even as he feared it. Recalling his father's death, he ponders a strange kind of exhilaration:

> I do not doubt
> That in this later time when storm and rain
> Beat on my roof at midnight, or by day
> When I am in the woods, unknown to me
> The workings of my spirit thence are brought.[82]

"The Idiot Boy" puts him in those woods again. Wordsworth's father was called John; as Johnny, the poet takes his father's last perilous ride and survives it, and in doing so he fathers himself, fathers his own creative sovereignty and his resilience. Ghosted by an anxious mother who worried about how her son would turn out and by the death of a father whose own night journey created an orphan who was forced to take his life into his own hands, the poem is Wordsworth's portrait—or fantasy—of the artist as an idiot boy.

He once observed that "he never wrote anything more currently than this poem, nor when he was in a happier & more poetical state of feeling."[83] "The Idiot Boy" is a comedy to the extent that it makes us believe in happiness—or makes us believe, at least, in a particular version of it ("happiness itself is a forest in which we are bewildered, turn wild, or dwell like Robin Hood, outlawed and at home").[84] For all the seductiveness of this dream, the poem remains aware of its own wishful thinking. Even though he celebrates a need to go wild, Wordsworth returns his hero to the fold and into the arms of the waiting mother (just as he did in "The Blind Highland Boy"). From this perspective, another small detail matters: Betty's age. At one point she says "I'm almost three-score";[85] in her mid- to late fifties, then. Had Wordsworth's mother not died, she would have been in her fifties when her son composed the poem.

"The Idiot Boy" resurrects a version of her so that, despite her worries, she can be allowed to see that it all comes good in the end. The two of them are a company of fools, for "Johnny's in a merry tune" in the same way that Betty "Is in the middle of her story" (the stress on "in" tells of joyous states of immersion and absorption, ones that will finally be protected by the tale).[86]

Even so, the poem is never simply a comic parable about a person's capacity to be loved no matter how unworthy, or wayward, or foolish he is. When "Johnny burrs and laughs aloud, / Whether in cunning or in joy, / I cannot tell,"[87] the narrator isn't necessarily saying that he doesn't know the reason for the laughter but rather that he doesn't want to spell it out. I think he feels a little nervous about directly admitting that he has felt such glee—a joyful cunning that revels in its own conflicted wish to be free of the family, of care, of the constringent demands of sympathy. As Sidney Keyes recognized in his sonnet-portrait "William Wordsworth":

> No room from mourning; he's gone out
> Into the noisy glen, or stands between the stones
> Of the gaunt ridge, or you'll hear his shout
> Rolling among the screes, he being a boy again.[88]

Part of what poetry and idiocy mean, for Wordsworth, is the wish for—and the fear that attends—privacy of experience. *Idiot,* as the *OED* notes, is derived from the Greek *idios,* meaning "private," "peculiar," "one's own," "separate," "distinct." It could also signify a common man or plebian, and was sometimes linked to a natural state of ignorance into which people were born; before you were a citizen, before you were educated to become part of the public, you were an idiot. Later, the *idiotes* became a comic type in classical drama, someone characterized by self-centeredness. When Wordsworth speaks in *The Prelude* of his early life and of "the absolute wealth / Of my own private being,"[89] he is treating such character traits fondly even as he knows they will make way for other feelings he will come to cherish. Elsewhere in *The Prelude,* between the memories of his horse ride and of his father's death, he makes a confession: "I am lost . . . / . . . the hiding-places of my power / Seem open; I approach, and then they close."[90] "The Idiot Boy" was his first attempt to search those hiding places by committing to the folly of getting lost to get found, and it helped free him up to write his great epic of the private, foolish, idiotic self.

*

Wordsworth was alert to the fact that you may sometimes pity people in order not to confess to yourself that you need their example—or that you envy them (in an early fragment, he wrote of a "strange comparison / Of Envy linked with pity").[91] Being a "fool of Nature" means knowing that what you are—or want—is tied to something you can't always quite admit to, and that your most cherished version of fun is somehow feral:

> It's a pity that nature no longer means
> The woods, nor the wilds, not even our own
> Worst behavior, nor the behavior of
>
> Certain creatures.[92]

Mark Strand writes these words immediately before allowing some of Wordsworth's words into his poem in support of them, and elsewhere he suggests that there is, in Wordsworth, "a presumption about Being that no contemporary poet, so far, has been able to make. It is not merely that Nature is good . . . but that Being is an adequate reflection of Nature. . . . For Wordsworth the self precedes experience. . . . It makes a silent claim for primacy, and we almost feel that Nature is its invention."[93] When reading Wordsworth, we *almost* feel that. The claim for primacy, the very strength of the need to make it, gestures toward a sense that the self is made rather in its resistance to experience, in its refusal to be defined by—or to be beholden to—what has happened to it. A presumption about Being is fed by a prior sense that something has been escaped or repelled.

There are only two stanzas in "The Idiot Boy" where the narrator claims to know what Johnny is feeling: the one in which readers learn that "His heart it was so full of glee" and the one when he is first placed on the pony. Our worst-best behavior and the behavior of "Certain creatures" come together as Johnny suddenly realizes he is about to be freed from his mother's watchful eye:

> But when the pony moved his legs,
> Oh! then for the poor idiot boy!
> For joy he cannot hold the bridle,
> For joy his head and heels are idle,
> He's idle all for very joy.[94]

Poor boy! This is the poem's way of mocking any gentle, pitying readers who would claim that they don't covet such a feeling. Given that the puckish spirit of *A Midsummer Night's Dream* elsewhere informs the poem, it's worth recalling the name of the magical flower that causes all the delectable havoc in the play: "love-in-idleness." (Incidentally, but perhaps not coincidentally, it has two other names among many others: Johnny-jump-up and Heart's ease.) Johnny's jumped-up ease comes from the utterly incredible fact that "the pony moved his legs" ("his," not "its"): this personalizes the pony a little while creating a slight ambiguity ("his" refers primarily to the pony's legs but may also extend to include Johnny's). Johnny couldn't or wouldn't want to make a distinction, for the joy of the thing is bound up with the way they move together as one. The moment is one of the poem's most self-pleasuring, self-amazed examples of Being that is not simply "an adequate reflection of Nature," but Being that feels its own nature as something animatedly animal—an agency miraculously encountered at the center of passivity, a freedom that has not so much been worked for but given in to.

Wordsworth's own discoveries lie behind these lines. The delight at rhyming "bridle" with "idle," the very feeling of discovering "idle" within the longer word, tells of a sense of Being arising from a comic capacity to take your chances. The stanza again looks forward to *The Prelude* while looking back into Wordsworth's past—to the young child as "one who scarce / Could hold a bridle," and to the man who would later confess that, when young, he "loved idleness and joy."[95] When Johnny is finally found in the poem, it is the narrator (and therefore the reader), not Betty, who finds him first: "Who's yon," he asks, "near the waterfall?": "'Tis Johnny! Johnny! as I live."[96] In its casual yet reverberating way, the last phrase lets slip one of Wordsworth's secrets: he has lived like that too, and will continue to do so whenever he gets the opportunity. And he writes about the boy at this moment—currently, happily, poetically—as though his life depended on it.

HUMORING

Perhaps, after all, the best way of talking about what you love is to speak of it lightly.

ALBERT CAMUS

Oddities

'Tis an odd thought—I like the color of it.
RIVERS, *The Borderers*[1]

Johnny is resplendent because alone, the blind highland boy demands to be left to himself, and throughout his work Wordsworth is compelled to restate the pleasurable oddness of singleness. It's "The Solitary Reaper," not "The Reaper," and lest readers miss the point, in the first five lines we are told that she is "Single," "solitary," "by herself," and "alone."[2] He could be impatient with those who missed or glossed over such emphases; Aubrey De Vere once recalled Walter Scott's misquoting a line from "Yarrow Unvisited" as "The Swans on sweet St Mary's lake," and Wordsworth pounced: "'The *swan* on *still* St Mary's lake.' Never could I have written 'swans' in the plural . . . there was *one* swan, and one only."[3] "Never could *I* . . .": you sense that he also means that there is *one* Wordsworth, and one only. Before turning in the final chapters to his most sustained attempt to humor himself—*The Prelude*—I want to lead up to it by considering how Wordsworthian fun can be gleaned from the values and dangers that circle around singularity. When one contemporary noted that Wordsworth seemed "to pique himself upon eccentricity . . . and to chuckle in secret,"[4] he was raising questions that have proved hard to shake for many readers: What's the poet up to? Is there a joke we're not getting? And is his eccentricity something that needs to be made comprehensible, or is it rather our response to it that we need to comprehend?

The person who notices odd things does so because he is odd himself. De Quincey spoke of his friend's "extreme, intense, unparalleled one-sidedness, (*einseitigkeit*)"—"*einseitig* in extremity," the most *einseitig* man "that ever lived."[5] Wordsworth's love of the object's "sole seat / In singleness" is born of his own feeling of apartness (as he put it in *The Excursion*, such a life or impulse is "Free as the Sun, and lonely as the Sun").[6] In draft lines for *Michael*, the shepherd

> Yielding to the bent
> Of his peculiar humour, would let loose
> His tongue, and give it the mind's freedom, then
> Discoursing on remote imaginations, strong
> Conceits, devices, day-dreams, thoughts and schemes,
> The fancies of a solitary Man![7]

This gestures toward the older meaning of *humour* as an aberration from the norm—defined by William Congreve as "a singular and unavoidable manner of doing or saying anything, Peculiar and Natural to one Man only"[8]—but it takes care to humor the character by avoiding any glimmer of gentlemanly condescension. We are not being invited to feel sorry for Michael or to sense that his conceits, devices, and fancies diagnose a plight.

Eighteenth-century commentators had spoken of "the Follies, the Singularities, and Humors; in a word, it is the Human Heart in its odd Variety, pleasantly represented, that makes up the elegant Entertainment of Comedy."[9] John Hughes's comment was representative of a larger shift, one that gathered pace as the century progressed, from the pathological to the "pleasant" oddity. Hobbes's emphasis on comic humor as the singular thing that is beneath you, the wayward thing that needs to be whipped back into line through the social corrective of laughter, was resisted by several writers to whom Wordsworth was indebted. Swift defended "Humor" as winningly "odd, grotesque, and wild"; in *Tom Jones*, when Fielding speaks of a barber as "a Fellow of great Oddity and Humour," he is paying him a compliment; and Tristram Shandy feels similarly well disposed when noting of his Uncle Toby that "His humour was of that particular species, which does honour to our atmosphere."[10] Humors are amiable foibles, marks of distinction. In this light, comedy is the art of the exception to which you needn't take exception.

Clearly, several felt that Wordsworth had taken the personally stylized a step too far. One critic labeled him as "the Sterne of poetry":

> He has like his predecessor, endeavoured to extract sentiment where nobody else ever dreamt of looking for it, and has often exalted trifles into a consequence which nature never intended them to occupy; and may therefore be said to have, with Sterne, lent his aid to implanting, in certain literary departments, a tone not always auspicious to true and genuine feeling.[11]

For "true" and "genuine," read "general" and "representative" ("nothing odd will do long," as Samuel Johnson put it).[12] The natural is the ordered, and a good sense of humor is a clear sense of proportion. Jeffrey set the tone for this kind of response to Wordsworth when he charged him with "ludicrous and affected singularity,"[13] receiving him, first and foremost, as a humorist in the older sense of the term: compulsively sui generis, unwittingly laughable. But Coleridge ventured an alternative vision of the singular when he noted that "There always is in a genuine humour an acknowledgement of the hollowness and farce of the world, and its disproportion to the godlike within us":

> You cannot conceive a humorous man who does not give some disproportionate generality, or even a universality to his hobby-horse, as is the case with Mr. Shandy; or at least there is an absence of any interest but what arises from the humour itself, as in my Uncle Toby, and it is the idea of the soul, of its undefined capacity and dignity, that gives the sting to any absorption of it by any one pursuit, and this not in respect of the humourist as a mere member of society for a particular, however mistaken, interest, but as a man . . . every man is more or less a humourist. And, indeed, to be a little more subtle, the propensity to notice these things does itself constitute the humourist.[14]

Such characters have degenerated into types, become their own self-parody through too faithful an adherence to what makes them tick; yet the defiant intensity of their passion, the force with which they commit to being themselves, vouches for their unplumbed depths. We may read Wordsworth, as we read Uncle Toby, with a sense of his "one pursuit" *and* with a relish for his "undefined capacity." In the rest of this chapter I'll explore mixtures of the egotistical and the sublime, the humorous and the wondrous, first by looking at the behavior of some words and tropes across a range of his writings before then turning to "The Thorn." That poem was, he said, always "a favorite with me,"[15] and as Hugh Sykes Davies has noted, "in the course of writing it, he developed, almost for the first time, what was to become the basic characteristic of his whole handling of words for poetic purposes."[16] Those purposes were personal as well as social, obscurely connected to the dream of a man who could become "sole keeper of his own intent."[17]

✶

Wordsworth's fragmentary essay on "The Sublime and the Beautiful" emphasizes two things: the sublime object "suspends the comparing power of the mind," and the object is not sublime *in itself*. The observer should therefore not waste time trying to convince others of its sublimity but instead "look into his own mind & determine the law by which he is affected.—He will then find that the same object has the power to affect him in various manners at different times; so that, ludicrous as it . . ."[18] Tantalizingly, the manuscript breaks off here, but a few pages later the thought returns:

> many of the forms before his eyes, by associations of outward likeness, merely may recal to his mind mean or undignified works of art; & every where might

> he be haunted or disturbed by a sense of incongruity, either light & trivial, or resembling in kind that mixture of the terrible & the ludicrous which dramatists who understand the constitution of the human mind have not unfrequently represented[19]

Wordsworth conceives the human constitution itself as tragicomic. He stresses elsewhere just "how strict is the connection between the ludicrously, and the terribly fantastic,"[20] and that connection can be variously elaborated. Both feelings register an incomparable singularity; as Emerson would later note: "Separate any part of Nature and attempt to look at it as a whole by itself, and the feeling of the ridiculous begins . . . contemplate the object alone, standing there in absolute nature, it becomes at once comic; no useful, no respectable qualities can rescue it from the ludicrous.'[21] Both feelings also confront observers with an incongruity without confronting them with an insurmountable threat. In his discussion of the sublime, Kant focuses on the object that is perceived to be "beyond all comparison" and adds that we can only entertain this disposition "as long as we find ourselves in safety."[22] Compare Coleridge on a widely celebrated definition of the comic: "Aristotle's definition is as good as can be: Surprise at perceiving any thing out of its usual place, when the unusualness is not accompanied by a sense of serious danger."[23] In some circumstances, a feeling for sublimity is a similarly charged mixture of vertigo and pleasure.

When observing objects with Wordsworth (a tree, say), one becomes aware of just how recurrent this feeling is. In his *Guide to the Lakes*, he speaks smilingly of "separate individual trees, obstinately presenting themselves as such," or of a tree that stands by itself "somewhat fantastically."[24] In *The Prelude*, he is enraptured by "A single Tree . . . with outlandish grace."[25] There's often a kind of ecstatic obstinacy in Wordsworth that perceives the ludicrous and the wondrous as secret sharers, as Henry Crabb Robinson appreciated:

> I had been in the habit when reading this marvellous Ode to friends, to omit one or two passages—especially that beginning
>
> But there's a tree, of many one,
>
> lest I shd. be rendered ridiculous, being unable to explain precisely *what* I admired—not that I acknowledged this to be a fair test. But with Blake I cd. fear nothing of the kind, & it was this very Stanza which threw him almost into an hysterical rapture. His delight in W.'s poetry was intense.[26]

Robinson's embarrassment is understandable; Wordsworth has already said that it's "a" tree, so "of many one" only restates the obvious. What he is admiring, though, is the poet's feeling for how, under certain conditions, the obvious turns both numinous and nebulous. Blake gave Robinson permission to admire something without having to give a reason for that admiration; he allowed him to wonder at the lines just as Wordsworth wondered at the tree. Wonder (*admiratio* in Latin) is a form of esteem that can't quite be accounted for; it throws observers into confusion even as they feel convinced that they have touched upon something significant. Sublime specificity needn't preclude embarrassment and may well be a catalyst for it. Some forms of wonder cannot be reached without running the risk of being rendered ridiculous.[27] As another contemporary noted, when reading Wordsworth you are often faced by something so odd "that it is impossible not to laugh outright, whilst you are compelled to wonder at the marvellous incongruity."[28]

The line from the Ode is a compacted version of a less well-known poem in the 1807 volume, one whose vertiginous sense of scale treads another path to ludicrous sublimity. In *Gulliver's Travels*, what Gulliver refers to as "the *singularity* of my Humour" is frequently sensed and measured against the singularity of trees: in Lilliput he is shocked to discover "Their tallest Trees are about seven Foot high"; in Brobdingnag the trees are "so lofty that I could make no Computation of their Altitude"; elsewhere he makes jokes about "Dwarf apple-trees," and on one occasion he looks at trees "with a Sort of Wonder . . . I often seemed hardly able to contain my Laughter; which he [the Captain] knew not well how to take, but imputed it to some Disorder in my Brain."[29] This is Wordsworth's version of a related disorder:

> "Beloved Vale!" I said, "when I shall con
> Those many records of my childish years,
> Remembrance of myself and of my peers
> Will press me down: to think of what is gone
> Will be an awful thought, if life have one."
> But, when into the Vale I came, no fears
> Distress'd me; I look'd around, I shed no tears;
> Deep thought, or awful vision, I had none.
> By thousand petty fancies I was cross'd,
> To see the Trees, which I had thought so tall,
> Mere dwarfs; the Brooks so narrow, Fields so small.
> A Juggler's Balls old Time about him toss'd;
> I looked, I stared, I smiled, I laughed; and all
> The weight of sadness was in wonder lost.[30]

There's a lovely, lithe comedy here even before the final recognition. The poem's first four words record a drop in temperature from the apostrophe to the reporting clause and, in doing so, tell of other oddities to come. A poem like this, apparently disappointed by lack of awful thought or vision, could be read as an exercise in the antisublime, but it's more an encounter with the oddity of the sublime, part of what Wordsworth elsewhere calls "a new mission to extend its kingdom, and to augment and spread its enjoyments."[31]

Kant speaks of the sublime as an initial feeling of our own limitation in the face of a huge or immeasurable object before Reason steps in: "it is a law (of reason) for us and part of our vocation to estimate everything great that nature contains as an object of the senses for us as small in comparison with the ideas of reason."[32] So the shrinkage of the trees to dwarfs from the adult's perspective follows the contours of the Kantian narrative, rolling out the sublime moment across a lifetime. But the last two lines go a step further, as if to say "I was lost, then found . . . *then lost again.*" Being beside yourself with laughter and being lost in wonder are analogous states. The lines don't quite fit a story about rediscovered "vocation" but rather speak to an enduringly strange feeling of pain and pleasure: "and all / The weight of sadness was in wonder lost" says less that the sadness has vanished or evaporated and more that it has been sunk and dissolved into wonder, has become an informing yet barely perceptible part of the feeling. It's as though, in deciding to write the poem, Wordsworth had planned to finesse this state of laughable sublimity into shapely, manageable form by putting it into the past tense—putting it beneath him, or behind him—but that, through the act of writing, he finds himself accosted by the oddity of the feeling once more. Singular objects or experiences won't stay put, and those trees—"Mere dwarfs"—may well change shape again.

*

For Wordsworth, singularity is crucially related to the difficulty of establishing a scale—and to an awareness that our very demand for a scale shields us from a disorientation of which we stand in need. This awareness is close to the heart of Wordsworthian humoring as I'm conceiving it, and his comedy of oddity—alongside the oddity of his comedy—is particularly apparent in two recurring tropes or tics: acts of comparison and acts of enumeration. For the Ode doesn't simply say that it's one tree, but "of many one": the object is *surrounded* by what it could be and yet what it is not. What *The Prelude* describes as "the strife of singularity" is a feeling for oddity that makes itself felt through analogy.[33] This helps to account for the superbly tendentious behavior of Wordsworth's similes; *The Prelude*, for example, is populated by "Sheep like Greenland Bears" and "open fields . . . shaped like ears."[34] This poet tends to use *like* with a sense not just of the comic, grotesque incongruities it creates (Harry Gill's "jaws and teeth they clatter, / Like a loose casement in the wind"),[35] but with a feeling for how the word keeps failing us: one sound he describes is like an ordinary cry, “Like—but oh how different!”[36] The analogical itch is always humored a little, smiled at for the effortfulness of its approximations (the idiot boy’s burr is “As loud as any mill, or near it”).[37] Elsewhere he asks: “But to what object shall the lovely Girl / Be likened?”[38] Whether it be an extravagant or ingenious liberty, or a near miss, or an unforthcoming revelation, Wordsworth is fascinated by similitude that owns up to incompleteness. Poetic fun is likened to “the humour of the game” as he likes to “sit, and play with similes / Loose types of Things through all degrees.”[39] As Coleridge noted in *Biographia Literaria*: “it is with similes, as it is with jests at a wine table, one is sure to suggest another.”[40]

The link between similes and jokes hints at a larger debate that informs Wordsworth’s feeling for the humorous oddity at the center of poetic endeavor. To his contemporaries, the phrase “similitude in dissimilitude” in the preface to *Lyrical Ballads* would have been most immediately recognizable in relation to debates about wit and humor, for the incongruity theory of humor evolved from eighteenth-century discussions about wit. Locke saw wit as “the assemblage” of differing ideas to give a sense of “resemblance or congruity,”[41] and, following Hutcheson’s work on laughter, James Beattie envisaged the affect as a response to “similarity and dissimilitude.”[42] When Hazlitt delivered his *Lectures on Comic Writers* in 1819, he adopted Wordsworth’s formulation: “the ludicrous is here blended with a certain beauty and decorum . . . from the principle of similitude in dissimilitude.”[43] Some critics tended to make clear distinctions between the fanciful wit of incongruity (the “laughable”) and the real wit of congruity (the “serious” or “sublime”)[44] and to stress the difference between the sublime and the ridiculous (Hutcheson claimed that acts of comparison should generally “separate what is great from what is not so”).[45] But, from the very start, Wordsworth’s similes are less able, less willing, to tell the great from the not great. *Descriptive Sketches* speaks of “mountains, glowing hot, like coals of fire,”[46] and in the first review of Wordsworth poems ever published (in the *Analytical Review* of March 1793), the critic complained, “We fancy there are few readers, whose imagination will be sufficiently flowing, to bear this last image, without pronouncing it extravagant.”[47]

If similes in Wordsworth conjure up sublime oddities, acts of numbering are engaged in a related process, for while his forms of enumeration assume a similarity in the objects they collect to be counted—and, to that extent, tell of an inclination toward the general—they also highlight a refusal of some things to add up. Eighteenth-century debates on the sublime were founded on a related tension.[48] In his essay on Cowley, Johnson had asserted that “sublimity is produced by aggregation”—“great thoughts are always general, and consist . . . in descriptions not descending into minuteness"—which is no doubt why, as Imlac points out in *Rasselas*, the poet remarks general properties, "he does not number the streaks of the tulip."[49] The sublime, in this view, is also the serious; Jean Paul Richter observed that "the serious always emphasizes the general," while comedy "individualizes to the smallest detail"; comic writers will always "give definite quantities in allusions to money, numbers, and all magnitudes, where one expects the indefinite."[50] On occasion, Wordsworth suggests that Imagination doesn't descend to counting; she would definitely *not* "tell you that her gigantic Angel was a tall as Pompey's Pillar; much less that he was twelve cubits, or twelve hundred cubits high . . . because these, and if they were a million times as high it would be the same, are bounded."[51] Yet his imagination sometimes delights at the bounded; discussing Burns's "Death and Mr. Hornbrook," he remarks, "with what lively humour does he describe the disorder of his senses and the confusion of his understanding, put to test by a deliberate attempt to count the horns of the moon! 'But whether she had three or four / He could na' tell.'"[52] Wordsworthian counting is often an *attempt* at counting, a marker of the oddity of trying to translate disorder into order, a way of signaling the strain of understanding before a recalcitrant object or experience. Harry Gill's "voice was like the voice of three,"[53] and where another poet might have plumped for "many" or "sev'ral," Wordsworth gives definite quantities. Gazing at the Farmer of Tilsbury Vale, "a Poet might spy / The image of fifty green fields in his eye."[54]

When reading Longinus, Wordsworth would have noted that sublimity can be produced by "instances in which singular forms are seen on reflection to be plural in sense," or, conversely, by "the contraction of plurals into singulars" through phrases that compress "separate individuals" into "corresponding unity."[55] Wordsworth is alert to this effect in Milton (he remarks on how in *Paradise Lost*, "the fleet, an aggregate of many ships, is represented as one mighty person"),[56] but when he himself makes similar maneuvers, the writing contains a half-comic lilt:

> The cattle are grazing,
> Their heads never raising;
> There are forty feeding like one![57]

"Forty" isn't necessarily a placeholder for "many"; you can't rule out the possibility that he's counted them, just to make sure.[58] The line speaks not just to the miraculous sense of individualities in unison but to individualities in their own right. In the preface to *Poems* (1815), he writes, "the Imagination also shapes and *creates*; and how? By innumerable processes; and in none does it more delight than in that of consolidating numbers into unity, and dissolving and separating unity into number."[59] It is tempting to say that, in "We Are Seven," the child does the consolidating while the adult narrator does the separating, but this would be misleading:

> "Their graves are green, they may be seen,"
> The little Maid replied,
> "Twelve steps or more from my mother's door,
> And they are side by side."[60]

Twelve steps "or more": the girl is an astute counter of people as well as paces. She has realized that her questioner is a stickler for facts, but she is also aware—perhaps without being aware that she's aware—that number is invention, not simply discovery, and that the facts will be different depending on whose shoes you are standing in ("Twelve steps for you," she means, "but more for me; my legs are shorter"). The little maid is a poet of sorts, consolidating into unity by insisting that "we are seven," separating unity into number with asides like "Twelve steps or more," and her words—although dismissed as merely ridiculous by the narrator—haunt both him and us because of the different kinds of truth they keep on registering. "Sublimity will never be wanting," Wordsworth claimed, "where the sense of innumerable multitude is lost in, and alternates with, that of intense unity."[61] The innumerable needn't always be registered as an overwhelming, seemingly endless magnitude; it may be felt as both the fact and the factitiousness of number, a sense of how things will and will not tally. For the innumerable to be "lost in" unity is not the same as its being "alternated" with it; the former movement is usually a very serious business indeed in Wordsworth, but the latter process approaches something more disorienting: the seriously funny.

*

Peculiar humors, weird trees, strange similes, irregular scales, singular approaches to number—all these oddities come together in "The Thorn." The poem is Wordsworth's most Swiftian creation, and, as well as containing allusions to past and contemporary balladry, the grotesqueries of Swift's "On Cutting Down the Thorn at Market Hill" are in the background too:

> But Time with Iron Teeth I ween
>   Has canker'd all its Branches round;
> No Fruit or Blossom to be seen,
>   Its Head reclining tow'rds the Ground.
>
> This aged, sickly, sapless Thorn
>   Which must alas no longer stand[62]

From the start, though, Wordsworth's thorn refuses to lie down:

I

There is a thorn; it looks so old,
In truth you'd find it hard to say,
How it could ever have been young,
It looks so old and grey.
Not higher than a two-years' child,
It stands erect this aged thorn;
No leaves it has, no thorny points;
It is a mass of knotted joints,
A wretched thing forlorn.
It stands erect, and like a stone
With lichens it is overgrown.

II

Like rock or stone, it is o'ergrown
With lichens to the very top,
And hung with heavy tufts of moss,
A melancholy crop:
Up from the earth these mosses creep,
And this poor thorn they clasp it round
So close, you'd say that they were bent
With plain and manifest intent,
To drag it to the ground;
And all had joined in one endeavour
To bury this poor thorn for ever.[63]

The thing is at once insinuating and bewildered. That casual yet faintly wheedling "you" ("In truth you'd find it hard to say . . . you'd say that they were bent") seems to call us to be witnesses—or accomplices—even as the narrator struggles to set the scene. The tree is "like a stone": no, not exactly; more "Like rock or stone" (a little mound of moss nearby "Is like an infant's grave in size / As like as like can be").[64] But how like *can* like be? Numbers, too, loiter with dubious intent; this is the only poem in *Lyrical Ballads* whose stanzas are numbered, and a two-years' child feels unnervingly specific. The poem's metrical numbers are also up to something: the tree is "overgrown" and in the next line "o'ergrown." The adjustment is of course needed to preserve syllabic decorum, but one has the awkward feeling that the narrator isn't quite up to the job of being poetical—or that the poetical isn't up to the job of saying what needs to be said on this occasion. "This poor thorn . . . this poor thorn": the insistence is a laughably misplaced sympathy, but as *dis-*

placed sympathy it's more than laughable. You sense that the narrator fixates on the thorn because something else is bothering him.

The next stanza contains the most ridiculed lines Wordsworth ever wrote:

> Not five yards from the mountain-path,
> This thorn you on your left espy;
> And to the left, three yards beyond,
> You see a little muddy pond
> Of water, never dry;
> I've measured it from side to side:
> 'Tis three feet long, and two feet wide.[65]

Keston Sutherland has surveyed critical responses to the couplet, the long history of derision, equivocation, and apology that includes treating the poem as though it were a satirical dramatic monologue (obtuse or idiotic by design) or as though such moments are in fact reasonable (the speaker is trying to ascertain whether the abandoned woman on the mountaintop could have drowned her infant in the pond). Sutherland reads the lines rather as a sign of Wordsworth's tenacity, "a deeply unfamiliar flourish of *intransigence*" that marks his commitment to "wrong poetry," a form of expression that is "extremely hard to get into any sort of right focus. If it means anything, 'wrong poetry' means just that: a trial of doubt that confounds identification, the perdition of confidence in being right, passionate unease about what will qualify or matter."[66] In which case, the couplet allows the poet's trial to blend with that of his narrator—and of his reader. Our relation to the passage mirrors the narrator's relation to the pond; we scan it or try to find another way of sizing it up, but our decision to take such measurements is a sign that we don't know what to do with it.

The itch to itemize—like the line itself—is ridiculous, yet the strength of the comedy tells of how strong the sublimity might be. The speaker makes too much out of too little, but he also makes too little out of too much; his very attempts at accuracy point to his sense that something big is escaping him. When Wordsworth observes in his note to the poem that words "ought to be weighed in the balance of feeling, and not measured by the space which they occupy upon paper,"[67] he is wryly alluding to his speaker's attempts at spatial measurement, asking readers to sense the emotions that feed—and the forces that resist—such acts of allotment. We may call this tedious, and it's true that the poem wouldn't necessarily be rescued by knowingly ironizing its most disturbing wrongnesses (it would perhaps be worsened), but when Coleridge dismissed the lines on the grounds that "it is not possible to imitate truly a dull and garrulous discourser, without repeating the effects of dullness and garrulity,"[68] much hinges on his word *truly* and on his confidence that the dull and the interesting are mutually exclusive categories. Wordsworth is less sure about what the effects of this combination might be—and more interested in finding out.

The note to "The Thorn" has often been read as a disingenuous, post hoc evasion of the poem's strangeness, as though, pressurized by the critics' mockery, the poet hid behind what he refers to as "the character of a loquacious narrator."[69] But in the note Wordsworth takes pains to say that he wants readers to feel the narrator's passion even though they "are not accustomed to sympathize with men feeling in that manner, or using such language" (he was, he says, aiming for "a picture which should not be unimpressive yet consistent with the character that should describe it").[70] The suspicion that Wordsworth is having fun with the danger of uncertainty is strengthened by the very specificity of his portrait; the speaker might be "a Captain of a small trading vessel for example, who being past the middle age of life, had retired upon an annuity or small independent income to some village or country town of which he was not a native, or in which he had not been accustomed to live."[71] Some have at least taken this seriously enough to sense a parodic allusion to the Ancient Mariner,[72] but I think Wordsworth has another figure in mind too.

The best criticism I have encountered on the spirit in which the "The Thorn" was written comes from De Quincey. The criticism is so good it hardly matters that he's not talking about the poem:

> Gulliver's style is purposely touched slightly with that dullness of circumstantiality which beset the excellent, but somewhat dull, race of men, old sea-captains. Yet it wears only an aerial tint of dullness; the felicity of this colouring in Swift's management is, that it never goes to the length of actually wearying, but only of giving a comic air of downright Wapping and Rotherhithe verisimilitude. All men grow dull, and ought to be dull, that live under a solemn sense of eternal danger, one inch only of plank (often worm-eaten) between themselves and eternity; and also that sea for ever one wilderness of waters—sublime, but (like the wilderness on shore) monotonous. All sublime people, being monotonous, have a tendency to be dull, and sublime things also. Milton and Æschylus the sublimest of men, are crossed at times by a shade of dullness. So is Bilidulgerid, so is the Sahara, so is the sea. Dulness is their weak side. But, as to a sea-captain, a regular nor'-nor'-wester, and sou'-sou'-easter, he ought to be kicked out of the room if he is *not* dull. It is not "ship-shape," or barely tolerable, that he should be otherwise.[73]

Like Wordsworth's narrator, Gulliver was a stickler for measurements ("The great gate fronting to the north was about four feet high, and almost two feet wide, through which I could easily creep"),[74] and De Quincey's own self-delighting play with number here—from "one inch only" to "one wilderness of waters"—has a Wordsworthian sense of both the modesty and magnitude of oneness. "The Thorn" is a standing affront to the mirage of the "ship-shape" because of its very fascination with those who try to make things so.

In search of a word and a mood that blends dullness with sublimity, stupefaction with astonishment, Sianne Ngai offers *stuplimity*—the synthesis of awe with what refuses awe.[75] She suggests that the feeling often leads to repetition and refrain, adding that stuplimity "paradoxically strengthens an affective link between text and reader, transferring the text's 'stupor' to him or her."[76] The narrator of "The Thorn" has good claim to being the most repetitive speaker Wordsworth ever conceived, and part of the poem's stuplimity lies in the way in which the structure of the woman's agonized refrain on the mountaintop ("Oh misery! oh misery! / Oh woe is me! oh misery!")[77] is infectiously catching, first in the narrator's own need to keep repeating things from the outset ("it looks so old . . . it looks so old . . . this aged thorn"), and then in our need to repeat him. As the speaker's interpolated readers, we reiterate what he's already told us, and then ask

> And wherefore does she cry?—
> Oh wherefore? wherefore? tell me why
> Does she repeat that doleful cry?[78]

Like her words and his, our broken-backed triads keep coming back: "But what's the thorn? and what's the pond? / And what's the hill of moss to her?"[79] And what are they to him and to us, the poem asks. De Quincey suggested that "far more of our deepest thoughts and feelings pass to us through perplexed combinations of *concrete* objects, pass to us as *involutes* (if I may coin that word) in compound experiences incapable of being disentangled, than ever reach us *directly*, and in their own abstract shapes."[80] In Wordsworth's writing the involute is experienced as a sort of failing, flailing wit. Dissimilar objects are brought together in one unlikely "assemblage" (in Locke's term), yet the combination misses its target or punchline and keeps speaker and reader perplexed. The thorn, the pond, and the moss play on the sometimes gruesome comedy of associationism, the incongruity of everybody's experience to themselves as well as to each other. Our coherences are like our confusions, and our revelations are like our repetitions—as like as like can be.

*

Talk of "everybody's experience" doesn't account for—or shake off—the nagging question of what "The Thorn" is to Wordsworth. As an eerie form of self-humoring, a tale about a woman who became pregnant and whose lover then abandoned her sounds familiar, and some have seen it as evidence of Wordsworth's guilt for having left Annette Vallon and his daughter. That story is lurking somewhere within the poem, but I want here to consider his choice of name for the bereft woman—Martha Ray—in relation to some other details. "The Thorn" was begun in the same month that Wordsworth started another tale about a distraught mother and a lost child, "The Idiot Boy," and elsewhere he talked about the poems as though they were a pair.[81] One sign that "The Thorn" is especially, bewilderingly personal for him is that it came quickly ("I composed it with great rapidity," he recalled).[82] The real Martha Ray was the mother of one of Wordsworth's best friends, Basil Montagu. Dorothy and William had undertaken to look after Basil's son, also called Basil, during his infancy: he was the first child Wordsworth ever cared for, and he came to live with them in 1795, when he was four years old. Brother and sister were walking with the young Basil in March 1798 when Wordsworth saw the thorn tree that, he claimed, inspired his poem.

Commentators have expressed uncertainty about what the poet was up to when he made use of Martha Ray's name.[83] As far as I know, nobody has yet pointed out that Montagu père, his son Basil, and Wordsworth all have something important in common: each of them had lost their mother by the time they were eight years old. At the very moment he introduces the mother's name into the poem, the narrator tells us that it's been "some two and twenty years"[84] since Martha Ray gave herself to her lover. "Two and twenty" is oddly precise, and in later versions Wordsworth would draw less attention to the time passed by revising to "twenty years,"[85] but when he first composed the poem, something in him needed that specific number. Readers are told that the couple subsequently fixed a wedding day, but the groom-to-be jilted Martha Ray, and then "full six months after this" it became clear to observers that she was pregnant.[86] After reaching term and giving birth, no one knew for certain what became of the child; all they know is that, from "about this time," Martha began to go up the mountain to cry out her misery.[87] So that would be close to twenty years ago. If the act of narration is equated to the time of composition (March 1798), this dates Martha's first treks to around March 1778, which was the month Wordsworth's mother died (he began writing the poem, in fact, a week after the anniversary of her burial). The woman in this poem has been voicing her misery for the same length of time that Wordsworth has been without a mother. "The Thorn" was written when the young Basil was seven, the age Wordsworth was when he lost his own mother. Whatever is lurking beneath the thorn tree, Wordsworth's past is buried somewhere nearby.

A young child's response to the death of his parent may include, among other things, rage at the fact that he has been abandoned, guilt as he mulls over what he did to deserve it, and envy because he wishes that he were dead instead. A fantasy that could stem from such feelings would be a reversal of roles in which the mother is watched while grieving over the loss of her child. "What if I were dead and she had to mourn me?" the child might wonder. Rage could then be assuaged by the recognition that the mother suffered too (the separation wasn't easy for her either); guilt and envy would be lessened by means of the child's potently paradoxical claim, "Well, I didn't *choose* to die; and besides, I'm no longer alive to feel guilty." In "The Thorn," the villagers gossip about what happened to the child—"some will say / She hanged her baby on the tree, / Some say she drowned it in the pond"[88]—but it can also be ventured that, in the terms of the fantasy being dreamt up here, the mother left Wordsworth for as good as dead when she died. The narrator's response to the gossip—"But kill a new-born infant thus! / I do not think she could"[89]—is an answering cry of sorts: "It wasn't her fault; she wasn't to blame for what her dying would do to me."

All this no doubt is too neat, too measured from side to side. And it's complicated by the fact that when Wordsworth thought about the death of his mother, he often thought about the death of his father. The first thorn tree to appear in his poetry comes in an early manuscript fragment of "The Vale of Esthwaite": he recalls "the wintry blast / Through the sharp Hawthorn whistling pass'd" when he was waiting at school "For little Horse to bear me home" just a few weeks before his "sorrow o'er a Father's bier."[90] The narrator of "The Thorn" may be confused, but he is very clear about some things: he climbs "the mountain's height: / A storm came on, and I could see / No object higher than my knee";[91] "'Twas mist and rain . . . And then the wind!," but on the mountain's "highest ridge," "This thorn you on your left espy."[92] The 1798–1799 version of *The Prelude* recalls the day Wordsworth waited at school for the horses: climbing to "the highest summit," "'twas a day / Stormy, and rough, and wild," everywhere "the wind, and sleety rain," "eyes intensely straining as the mist / Gave intermitting prospects," and "one blasted tree," "A whistling hawthorn on my left."[93] Long afterward, he says, all these things "were spectacles and sounds to which / I would often repair, and thence would drink / As at a fountain."[94] "The Thorn" is one such return: a journey back to the site he associates with the death of his father in order to watch the endlessly mourning mother.

There is much to untangle here—and much that refuses to be untangled. From one perspective, "The Thorn" becomes a way for Wordsworth to spectate on the sources of his own miseries. In "The Vale of Esthwaite" he wrote,

For much it gives my soul relief
To pay the mighty debt of Grief
With sighs repeated o'er and o'er
I mourn because I mourn'd no more
For ah! the storm was soon at rest
Soon broke the Sun upon my breast
Nor did my little heart foresee
—She lost a home in losing thee
Nor did it know—of thee bereft
That little more than Heav'n was left.[95]

If he is talking about the passing of the storm at school that day, then he is saying something like: "Ah, little did I know that, although the sun had come out, you, father, were at home, dying." But the writing also says something less predictable, less safely moral: "I mourn now because I didn't mourn for very long then; the storm of my feelings passed, and I didn't feel all that much, didn't see back then how much I *would come to feel*." Not that his feeling now is necessarily all that guilty; as Thomas Weiskel astutely observes, "grief is a 'mighty debt'—something owed, not felt, or felt only because it is owed."[96] Maybe he was too shocked to grieve, or too shocked to know that his apparent nonfeeling—a sort of stuplimity—was itself a stage of grieving, and still is. And maybe he really felt and continues to feel untrammeled. As the Sun broke, the Son broke free. "Free as the Sun, and lonely as the Sun."

"With sighs repeated o'er and o'er / I mourn because I mourn'd no more": the boy may mourn in the way Martha Ray mourns in "The Thorn," mourning for *herself* ("Oh woe is me") and not merely for someone else. If the creation and handling of Martha Ray's predicament is a way for Wordsworth to recast his own sufferings, then certain flashes of grotesque humor signal his commitment to live with his emotion as well as to cast quizzical side-glances at it—to live with it, in fact, *by* casting such glances. Northrop Frye once observed that "Repetition overdone or not going anywhere belongs to comedy,"[97] and, in keeping with the spirit of this claim, it could be asked, How many times—or for how many years—does the narrator have to repeat himself, or Martha Ray have to say "Oh woe is me! oh misery!," before it becomes funny? This unanswerable question prompts another: If they each said everything only once, would the reader be inclined to take them seriously? To imagine "The Thorn" as written by a grief-stricken man who feels guilt for having not always cared enough (but who is honest enough with himself to acknowledge his own disdain for the fact that he *does* feel guilty) is to see how the restaging of these mixed feelings becomes a way to humor them by having them tell against each other. The writing speaks of the comic redundancy of grief, and of its need to survive itself, while also speaking for all those who know that their grief has helped to make them what they are. Like Martha Ray, the narrator feels the need to return to the spot—and, crucially, to send us there, as though we might be able to help him out with some problem he's having: "But if you'd gladly view the spot, / The spot to which she goes."[98] The poem, like the spot, continues to nettle, not least because we sense that its almost but not quite comic tone is a cover story of sorts.

*

In Wordsworth's favorite work of Swift's—*A Tale of a Tub*—the narrator hopes that we may approach "the very *bottom* of all the *sublime* throughout this treatise" and later notes "how near the frontiers of height and depth border on each other."[99] "The Thorn" is written in the same key. When complaining about the unevenness of the poem, Coleridge said that it subjected readers to "sudden and unpleasant sinkings from the height to which the poet had previously lifted them."[100] But then, highs and lows are everywhere part of the content as well as the form of Wordsworthian pleasure: the narrator is obsessed by something "High on a mountain's highest ridge,"[101] yet when he gets there he tends to look only below waist height: close beside the thorn is "a hill of moss, / Just half a foot in height" (in our mind's eye we look up then down as hill turns tiny over the line end).[102] The lover who lets Martha Ray down is called Stephen *Hill*, and, while on the summit, the narrator looks up and spots a crag toward which he runs for shelter, yet "Instead of a jutting crag, I found / A woman seated on the ground."[103] Something about Wordsworth's bathos is hard to get to the bottom of. His sinkings plumb new depths.

And the thorn, finally, is a singular, odd, lowly thing that won't be laid low: "Not higher than a two years' child, / It stands erect." As an uncanny blend of the old and the childlike, as "a wretched thing forlorn," it will not consent to be abandoned or buried. In many ways, it stands as the involute of the poet himself. You'd say that the mosses "had joined in one endeavour / To bury this poor thorn for ever," but in an early manuscript fragment Wordsworth suggested that necessity might be the mother of invention:

> It stands upon that spot so wild;
> Of leaves it has repaired its loss
> With heavy tufts of dark green moss,
> Which from the ground in plenteous crop
> Creep upward to its very top
> To bury it for ever-more.[104]

In that first line, it's as though the thorn steals "wild" as an adjective that was meant to refer to the hostile environment, converting it into an adverb in order to celebrate how the tree itself stands in resistance to that environment. It repairs its losses in a manner akin to that in which Wordsworth repairs to images of loss as a means of reinterpreting his life, and although the "plenteous" means of repair may threaten to bury it, it's not dead and buried yet.

"The Thorn" leads Wordsworth toward himself via his enigmatic connections with others (his various selves as griever, as carer, as explorer; via his parents, Basil Montagu father and son, and others), and the poem is characteristic of his oddity primarily through the way it conceives estrangement as a kind of homecoming. That conception extends to the unfinished business of how the poet finds himself placed before his readers—and how we find ourselves placed before him—for Wordsworth has a fantasy of oddity as a singularity so concentrated that it becomes a microcosm of everything else. In *The Prelude* he writes:

> Points have we all of us within our souls,
> Where all stand single; this I feel, and make
> Breathings for incommunicable powers.[105]

The repeated stress on "all" is played off against the "I" (he resisted the temptation to write "we feel"), yet he stands for us by standing single; our isolation, our sense of ourselves as an anomaly, is what we have in common. To apprehend this shared singularity is to sense a predicament, but it is also to cultivate a kind of fun, a potential and a prowess at once egotistically sublime and ridiculous—a sublime self-unimportance, even. "A sense of humour," Auden once wrote, "develops in society to the degree that its members are simultaneously conscious of being each a unique person and of being in common subjection to unalterable laws."[106] Wordsworth's poetry is founded on this consciousness and remains deeply beholden to it. He always wanted to be the odd one in.

Medleys

> that motley imagery,
> A vivid pleasure of my youth
> *THE PRELUDE*[1]

It would appear to be a large leap from the balladic deliria of the last two chapters—"The Idiot Boy" and "The Thorn"—to *The Prelude.* Yet Wordsworth began composing his epic just a few months after those poems were written, and years later, as he came to the end of it, he recalled walking

> Murmuring of him who joyous hap! was found,
> After the perils of his moonlight ride
> Near the loud Waterfall; or her who sate
> In misery near the miserable Thorn[2]

I've already suggested what the finding of Johnny might have to do with the loss of Martha Ray, and allusion to both poems at this climactic moment in book 13 speaks to Wordsworth's need to bind his days each to each—and to put different moods and modes into conversation with one another. Talk of "joyous hap!" and "misery" initially suggests a contrast, yet it's not so much that "The Idiot Boy" is simply comic and "The Thorn" simply tragic but that each poem—like *The Prelude* itself—is a medley. For all the differences between the balladic and the blank-verse Wordsworth, that he should find himself recalling his earlier work here raises some possibilities—or questions. Can "the history of a Poet's mind" continue the process of self-humoring in a new form?[3] If so, what would the new form do to the process?

"And he shall howl, and I will laugh, a medley / Most tunable.—What say you to it?" asks Mortimer in *The Borderers.*[4] The medleys had started early, for a young man who titles one of his first poems "The Dog—An Idyllium" may be howling or laughing or both. (The dog apparently had a "sportive smile," so he and his master must have made quite a pair.)[5] Many have expressed reservations about this sort of thing. Bemoaning the fact that we sink "almost as in a *medly*," Coleridge noted that "A portion of that awkwardness is felt which hangs upon the introduction of songs in our modern comic operas."[6] But Wordsworth never uses the word *medley* in a wholly negative sense. In *The Prelude* he recalls a "promiscuous rout, / A medley of all tempers"[7] that kept him up until dawn, and elsewhere the word tells of a foolishness he would not want to be without. One *OED* definition of *medley* is "motley," and Wordsworth is happy to appear in his poetry dressed in "Motley accoutrement"[8] or to roam the streets "Delighted, through the motley spectacle."[9] Most instances of *motley*, in fact, turn up in the longer blank-verse poems. They are works in search of what *The Prelude* calls "Some variegated story,"[10] one that allows space for medleys most tunable.

It's fitting that the best parody of Wordsworth's blank verse ever written, by James Hogg, should focus on "The Flying Tailor," a leaping yet low-down marvel who works among "shreds and patches . . . bestrew'd / With various colours, brightening gorgeously / The board all round him."[11] Although the lines poke fun at Wordsworth's motley insistence on dressing up shreds and patches, they have a gorgeousness that extends beyond the mockery. When the parodist tells readers that the tailor is "Apt to perceive in slightest circumstance / Mysterious meaning,"[12] he is reading the lowly workman as a surrogate for his author, but not suggesting that such instincts are always misplaced. Whatever else Wordsworth is committed to, he's committed to inaptness. The *OED* credits him with the invention of the word ("inaptness to perceive"),[13] and his writing seeks to show how a demand for the merely apt can itself become a bar to perception.

Upon first hearing *The Prelude*, Coleridge called it "An Orphic song indeed, / A song divine," but he later had second thoughts and spoke of "A tale *obscure* . . . / To a *strange* music chaunted."[14] As something *told*, as something not always quite sung, the poem's strangeness is voiced through diversity, not divinity. Although *The Prelude* was meant to prepare for the philosophical hymn to Oneness that, according to Coleridge, would save Wordsworth from himself by saving him from sudden dips in form, sometimes the poet doesn't want to be saved. On occasion, he tries his best to resist sinkings of heart:

> not yet tamed
> And humbled down—Oh! then we feel, we feel,
> We know where we have friends.[15]

The stress on "then," the defiant repetition, the timing of the pauses—all build toward an uplifting insistence on what we *know*. But elsewhere in *The Prelude*—more often, I think, than is generally acknowledged—there's a strange fascination with "a swell of feeling follow'd soon / By a blank sense of greatness pass'd away,"[16] and this sense creates a different kind of sound:

> weight and power,
> Power, growing with the weight: alas! I feel
> That I am trifling[17]

Wordsworth noted that, when composing and reading blank verse, he allowed for a short pause at the end of the line regardless of whether it was punctuated or not.[18] The chiastic drumroll of "weight" and "power" makes "I feel" sound momentarily impressive (something like "I feel—I feel it all" in the Intimations Ode), but the moment passes and the run-on tilts into bathos. In such surroundings, *trifling* is adjective as well as participle—not just what the poet does, but what he is.

While parodies like Hogg's are alert to the play of aggrandizement and abasement in Wordsworth's style, they also realize that blank verse is itself something of a risk (as Samuel Johnson had warned: "If blank verse be not tumid and gorgeous, it is crippled prose").[19] *The Prelude*'s humoring of its own trifling is a development of earlier dalliances in Thomson, Young, and Cowper (Wordsworth refers to *Night Thoughts* and *The Task* as forms of "composite order").[20] Thomson and Young had helped to shape a mode that Marshall Brown terms "the urbane sublime," one that combines the rapturous and the lightly satirical. The style is best summed up by an adjective that Thomson coined in *The Seasons*: the *amusive* (Wordsworth was struck by the word, marking it up in his own edition).[21] Signifying the "illusive," "recreative," "engaging," or "risible" (*OED*)—or a medley of these qualities—the amusive embodies what I. A. Richards called a "*slightly* whimsical" poetics, "a social, urbane, highly cultivated, self-confident, temperate and easy kind of humour."[22] This is a poetry that plays by the rules of the game even when it's playing things down, one that rarely allows the whimsical to become anything more than slight. And yet, as Brown notes, Cowper likes to test the limits of the mode's decorums.[23] The reference to horse dung in *The Task* as a "stercorarious heap"[24] is both mock-heroic periphrasis and self-mocking squeamishness, but it also contains a delightfully improper glee, a relish for the disorientation of values that follows from an insistence on polishing turds.

The Task's shifts down the scale hint at a related loss of bearings. Cowper doesn't simply toy with tender solicitations ("The nurse sleeps sweetly, hir'd to watch the sick / Whom snoring she disturbs"); he can't resist telling readers a few lines later that the nurse "snores the sick man dead."[25] Such jokes linger, as though their speaker senses he might have told them in the wrong place or in the wrong form, and I suspect that they are not what Coleridge had in mind when praising Cowper's "divine Chit chat."[26] In *Biographia Literaria* he spoke of the excellence of *The Task*, but he also complained about its "abrupt and arbitrary" transitions in much the same way as he had complained about Wordsworth's sinkings.[27] Cowper was aware of these qualities in his temperament and writing, although his bafflement at himself also included a certain abandon: "I wonder that a sportive thought should ever knock at the door of my intellect," he confessed; "It is as if harlequin should intrude himself into the gloomy chamber where a corpse is deposited in state."[28] This confession speaks of a hankering for disorder within "composite order," and Wordsworth's search for a form that might contain flights of fancy even as it sought to stay true to his appetite for sinking follows Cowper's resistance to the controlled proprieties of the amusive and the urbane. When praising Wordsworth's "finer species of humour" and his "thoughtful playfulness," it's telling that Charles Lamb thought not of his experiments in lyric and ballad but of his blank verse, adding that the allegedly non-Wordsworthian qualities he'd singled out were ones "in which the author more nearly perhaps than in any other quality resembles Cowper."[29] Wordsworth spoke of knowing Cowper "by heart," and the writer he had taken to heart was the one who had insisted that "All my poems are serio-comic."[30]

As Coleridge was bemoaning the fact that his friend wasn't being epic enough, others were having fun with Wordsworth by suggesting that his strengths lay elsewhere. One critic made this observation of *Benjamin the Waggoner*:

> Throughout the piece, or at all events very frequently, we perceive a sly covert sort of irony, an *under-tone* of playfulness, smiling at the mock heroics of the author; and preserving that difficult but exact spirit of bombast, which betrays a consciousness of misapplied sublimity, without rendering it quite gross and ridiculous . . . from the strong spirit of humour evidently displayed in this memorable passage, we more than suspect where Mr. Wordsworth's real *forte* lies: we exhort him to cultivate his talent for the ridiculous; and we earnestly request him no longer to *laugh in his sleeve* at his "solemn, vacant" admirers, but to come forth in that character for which nature has plainly designed him, "the Prince of Poetical Burlesque."[31]

This commentary has a sly irony of its own, of course, but its presuppositions are revealing: talk of *misapplied* sublimity assumes that discerning readers always know the difference between what is and what is not sublime. A *princely* poetical burlesque is a little too self-satisfied for Wordsworth's tastes; he did not conceive the ridiculous as a regal talent to be cultivated or dispensed but as a doubtful, equivocal impulse to be explored—and *The Prelude* became an important place to explore it.[32]

*

"9,000 lines . . . an alarming length! and a thing unprecedented in Literary history that a man should talk so much about himself."[33] Wordsworth is confessing, without quite apologizing for, the mock-heroic nature of his undertaking, for the story of the self as an epic event is always a mock-heroic story.[34] Many years later he observed that "a first rate Ode or Elegy, or a piece of humour even, is better than a poorly or feebly executed epic Poem."[35] What place, then, can humor have in epic? And might epic be enfeebled without it? For guidance in these tricky matters, Wordsworth turned to Pope. The two poets are worlds apart in many ways, but when Wordsworth said that "I could repeat with a little previous rummaging of my memory several 1000 lines of Pope," he was offering more than faint praise.[36] In the preface to *Lyrical Ballads* he notes that "Pope by the power of verse alone, has contrived to render the plainest common sense interesting, and even frequently to invest it with the appearance of passion,"[37] and his precursor turns up at other significant moments (in the epigraph to *The Borderers*, for example). Even the renowned Wordsworthian commitment to "a sinking inward into ourselves from thought to thought"[38] recalls the moment in *The Dunciad* when Pope positions Cibber in mock-heroic relation to Satan by reimagining his flight through Chaos, laughing at him "Sinking from thought to thought, a vast profound!"[39] Wordsworth transfigures the art of lamentable sinking into a voyage toward the depths of the psyche, and yet, hearing Pope alongside Wordsworth, one discerns in the earlier line a kind of delighted shock at how so little might portend so much.

Neoclassical rules for epic did not always tally with the works from which those rules were supposedly derived. In the preface to his translation of *The Iliad* Pope speaks of the poem as a "wild paradise,"[40] and in his Postscript to *The Odyssey* he supports Longinus's reading of the epic as a kind of comedy, asking, "how far a Poet, in pursuing the description or image of an action, can attach himself to *little circumstances*, without vulgarity or trifling? what particulars are proper, and enliven the image; or what are impertinent, and clog it?"[41] (Wordsworth later considered the same issue: "Happy is he who can hit the exact point, where grandeur is not lowered but heightened by detail, and beauty not impaired, but rendered more touching and exquisite by Passion."[42]) Pope's responses to such questions have different inflections at different times. Reading Homer is like "travelling along the ridge of a hill; which is not half so agreeable as sometimes gradually to rise, and sometimes gently to descend."[43] This sounds like a most civilized, unthreatening modulation (*amusive*, one might say). But a page later, when he adds, "Let it be remembered, that the same Genius that soar'd the highest . . . was also he who stoop'd the lowest,"[44] it is clear that neither the soaring and stooping need take place gradually or gently, and elsewhere Pope praises both Homer and Milton for their risky experiments in the ludicrous.[45]

In *Peri Bathous*, the narrator's irony cuts both ways. He laughs at dullards who don't (or won't) observe neoclassical standards, but he also knows that genius will bend or flout the rules ("A receipt to make an epic poem"[46] is a joke whatever your conception of an epic poem is). Later he archly claims that "A genuine writer of the profound will take care never to magnify any object without clouding it at the same time. His thought will appear in a true mist, and very unlike what it is in nature," yet he quotes from Milton to show up—and to show off—what can be achieved in such a mode: "No light, but rather darkness visible."[47] Since Pope thinks Milton no dunce (he makes use of "darkness visible" to laugh at dullness in *The Dunciad*),[48] it follows that daring dunces may sink as well as rise to the true sublime. In *The Prelude*, Wordsworth recalls a summer night spent outdoors when he was struck by "The breathless wilderness of clouds"[49] and by mountains that could be discerned "more by darkness visible / And their own size than any outward light."[50] The darkness visible of Milton's hell "Serv'd only to discover sights of woe," but Wordsworth experiences such sights as "food."[51] The allusion (along with the image of the moon in the water, "changing oftentimes its form / Like an uneasy snake")[52] tells not so much of either heaven or paradise lost but of a precious taste of knowledge and experience gained. The lines do not cloud the object; rather, they apprehend and express the unclear clearly, allow the wilderness of the natural to invade both the thought and the writing.

By suggesting that *The Prelude* is permeated by mock-heroic impulses—and by the influence of Pope as well as Milton—I don't mean to imply that such impulses necessarily lighten the tone or the load of the poem. In *Peri Bathous* Pope's narrator imagines two objects that all sons and daughters of dullness should aim for ("to depress what is high" and "to raise what is base and low to a ridiculous visibility"), adding that "When both these can be done at once, then is the *bathos* in perfection."[53] Yet this nadir is the perfection of the mock-heroic. A simple—or, more precisely, a dull—conception of mock-heroic would insist that the pleasure we take from the mode is based merely on our knowing what is base and low and what is high; we laugh because we are assured of the hierarchy on which the incongruities are built. But many eighteenth-century readers sensed a more disorienting mischief lurking in the mode; George Sewell suggested that "we are betrayed into a

Pleasure that we could not expect; tho,' at the same time, the Sublimity of the Style, and the Gravity of the Phrase, seem to chastise the Laughter they provoke."[54] I think Wordsworth would have warmed to the idea of our being *betrayed* into pleasure—especially a pleasure that draws out ambivalence. As Claude Rawson has noted, when reading Dryden, Pope, and those who learned from them, "the parodic derision could naturally be mistaken for genuine eloquence at first reading . . . it acquires a heroic bravura which shadows forth the aspiration of mock-heroic to transcend its parodic element." We could call this "mock-mock-heroic," or "unparodying," and "there is a sense in which mock-heroic parody, in its more ambitious forms, is always striving to un-parody itself."[55] When Pope opens *The Rape of the Lock* by joyfully lamenting "What dire Offence from am'rous Causes springs, / What mighty Contests rise from trivial Things,"[56] the force of the couplet is founded partly on the wit that situates the battle of the sexes in relation to other kinds of epic contest and partly on its delight at how, for those who care to look, the trivial really can be seen to reside in the mighty—and vice versa (the sublimation of aggression into the niceties of social ritual, for example). Indeed, for a mock-epic like *The Dunciad* to score its point, readers have to believe that the apparent triviality of the dunces is a looming cultural and sociopolitical menace; they are at once small fry and a big deal.

These vertiginous double-dealings are a formative influence on Wordsworth's sense of what an epic of the individual life might look and feel like, for if mock-heroic's central impulse is the consideration of the minute alongside the mighty, epic founds and licenses this impulse. In his copy of *Paradise Lost*, Wordsworth marked up the phrase, "if great things to small may be compar'd." The formula had a distinguished heritage (it had appeared in Virgil's *Eclogues* and *Georgics*),[57] but by the time the poet was poring over his Milton, it was also a signature phrase of comic modes: "if small things we may compare with great," as Beattie's *Grotesquiad* has it,[58] while Peter Pindar (Wordsworth called him "the redoubted Peter")[59] wrote in *The Lousiad*, "Good Lord! (as somebody sublimely sings) / What great effects arise from little things!"[60] *The Prelude*'s aspiration to "build up greatest things / From least suggestions" is the ordination of the inordinate, and the longer you listen to a phrase like "all the mighty world / Of eye and ear" (note the play of expectation at the line end), the more it can be heard both as quintessentially Wordsworthian and as a new turn on the mock-heroic.[61] It's as though he has made a joke without being aware that there is a joke to be made, or, rather, as though he were aware of just how much some jokes might contain.

Wordsworth apprehends size not as a property of objects but as a perspective on them. "There littleness was not," he writes in *The Pedlar*, "the least of things / Seem'd infinite,"[62] which is a version of Coleridge's jottings on Jean Paul Richter's theory of humor.[63] Richter's claim ("Humor thus annihilates both great and small, because before infinity everything is equal and nothing") led him to conceive the mode as an "inverted sublime,"[64] probably because the mind that can dream up infinity as an obliteration of size may be suddenly inclined to see the world as laughable. And if, as John Limon has suggested, the sublime—like the ridiculous—is an amplification of the paltriness of things, then the self that apprehends the world may be one of those things.[65] Coleridge captures something of this feeling in a superb letter to Southey:

> What a wonderful City Edinburgh is!—What alternation of Height & Depth! —a city looked at in the polish'd back of a Brobdignag Spoon, held length-ways. . . . When I first looked down on it, as the Coach drove in on the higher Street, I cannot express what I felt—such a section of a wasp's nest, striking you with a sort of bastard Sublimity from the enormity & infinity of its littleness—the infinity swelling out of the mind, the enormity striking it with wonder.[66]

Versions of this odd sublimity can be felt throughout *The Prelude*—not least when, just before turning to indulge in "shifting pantomimic scenes," Wordsworth celebrates a miniature model, a "life-like mockery," of "Edinburgh throned / On Crags."[67] Elsewhere, looking back through the years and gazing down on people at a "Summer Festival, a Fair,"[68] he admits "How little They, they and their doings seem," before admitting something else: "and yet how great! / For all things serve them."[69] The very way in which the poet offers himself a reprieve from the need for any settled perspective becomes the means by which *The Prelude* effects its strange mixtures of the whimsical and the revelatory, the outlandish and the charged.

⁎

Medleys of tone and outlook are attempts to master strife. Before it is anything else, a medley is "The mixing or mingling of people in combat . . . a war, battle; tournament; a quarrel," and, among other, older meanings, the *OED* gives "A mixed or blended colour." Book 3 of *The Prelude* turns from discussion of manners "finely spun, the delicate race / Of colours, lurking, gleaming up and down" to another memory:[70]

> At this day
> I smile in many a mountain solitude
> At passages and fragments that remain . . .
> Of that inferior exhibition play'd
> By wooden images, a theatre

For Wake or Fair. And oftentimes do flit
Remembrances before me of old Men,
Old Humourists who have been long in their graves,
And, having almost in my mind put off
Their human names, have into Phantoms pass'd,
Of texture midway betwixt life and books.
I play the Loiterer: 'tis enough to note
That here, in dwarf proportions, were express'd
The limbs of the great world, its goings-on
Collaterally pourtray'd, as in mock fight,
A Tournament of blows, some hardly dealt,
Though short of mortal combat[71]

Wordsworth humors the humorists and smiles at his own loitering yet defends himself by seeing much in little. The writing also willfully envisages life itself as an exercise in mock-heroic (nobody dies in the "mock fight" of mock-heroic, for everything falls short of mortal combat). While all this sounds dreamy enough, the passage is recalling a nightmare that didn't quite make it into the poem. Among Wordsworth's earliest fragments is a prose account of visions that plagued him when he stayed at Ann Tyson's cottage as a boy. In bed, alone in the darkness, he saw the gloom peopled with shapes, and since then, he says, "have the forms of Fear been dear to me."[72] Several years later, when composing the first fragments of *The Prelude* in Germany, he returned to the medleys of clashing colors and armies:

arrayed in hues more bright
Than flowers or gems or than the evening sky:
Processions, multitudes in wake or fair
Assembled, puppetshews with tru[m]pet, fife,
Wild beasts, and standards waving in the [?field],—
These mounting ever in a sloping line.
These vanishing, appear'd another scene—
Hounds, and the uproar of the [?chase], or [?steeds]
That galloped like the wind through standing corn;
Then came a throng of faces all [?arranged],
Unutterably horribly arranged,
In parallel lines, in feature and in look
All different, yet marvellously akin;
Then files of soldiery with dazzling arms,
Still mounting, mounting upwards, each to each
Of all these spectra, every band and class,
Succeeding with fantastic difference
And instant, unimaginable change.[73]

The "Wake or Fair" mentioned in the 1805 *Prelude* is a kind of screen memory for those other things he saw, the theater of the absurd inside his own head. Spectating on the capacities of his mind, revolted by yet reveling in what it can do, he senses the turbulence that lies within any mock-heroic indulgence of one's demons. The feeling here is similar to Lamb's self-diagnosis in "Witches, And Other Night-Fears" when he longs for the terrors he's put to bed: "For the credit of my imagination, I am almost ashamed to say how tame and prosaic my dreams are grown. . . . The poverty of my dreams mortifies me."[74] *The Prelude* puts these medleys in touch with the poet's present, and its own art of parallel lines ("All different, yet marvellously akin") embodies what its creator can barely speak of—the fear and the frisson of a self he can't understand.

The poem actually founds itself on a majestically bold yet bewildered mock-heroic note. The 1798–1799 version begins midline—"Was it for this . . . ?"—and continues on its winding way: "For this didst thou / O Derwent . . . ?"[75] Pope's Belinda had cried, "Was it for this you took such constant care / With bodkin, comb, and essence to prepare?" The phrase is repeated a few times in *The Rape of the Lock*, yet one can also catch within Wordsworth's use of it a Miltonic inflection ("For this did the angel twice descend? For this / Ordained thy nurture holy . . . ?"), along with the words "*Hoc erat . . . ?*," from Virgil's *Aeneid*, when Aeneas rebukes Venus for not helping him ("Was it for this, fostering parent, that you brought me through spears, through fire?").[76] In *The Prelude*, the question somehow manages to sound incredulously knowing (All that effort, care, thought, merely for *this*? So much for so little?) even as it remains open to possibility, ready to be surprised (Did so many little things lead me here? And where—or what—is here, exactly? A mood, a dream, a vocation?). The poem's first words are a medley of sorts, rendering a kind of bathos that is also a kind of buildup. Christopher Ricks observes that "Wordsworth is at his best not when he toys with the mock-heroic but when he reverses such an impulse. He restores. Often it is dignity that he restores" (for Ricks, the restorative is the opposite of the "ridiculous" and the "demeaningful," "a reversal of the parodic").[77] But this underplays the unparodying instincts at the heart of mock-heroic, for one cannot easily reverse an impulse that is itself ambivalent. At certain moments, Wordsworth sees the apparently ridiculous as restorative of a dignity that is in touch with the undignified.

The card game in *The Prelude* is "strife too humble to be named in Verse," but, in verse that somehow conspires to be both hesitant and intrepid, Wordsworth goes on to name it anyway:

Or round the naked Table, snow-white deal,
Cherry, or maple, sate in close array,
And to the combat, Lu or Whist, led on
A thick-ribb'd Army, not as in the world
Neglected and ungratefully thrown by
Even for the very service they had wrought,
But husbanded through many a long campaign.
Uncouth assemblage was it, where no few
Had changed their functions, some, plebean cards,
Which Fate beyond the promise of their birth
Had glorified, and call'd to represent
The persons of departed Potentates.
Oh! with what echoes on the Board they fell!
Ironic Diamonds; Clubs, Hearts, Diamonds, Spades,
A congregation piteously akin;
Cheap matter did they give to boyish wit,
Those sooty Knaves, precipitated down
With scoffs and taunts, like Vulcan out of Heaven,
The paramount Ace, a moon in her eclipse,
Queens, gleaming through their splendour's last decay,
And Monarchs, surly at the wrongs sustain'd
By royal visages. Meanwhile, abroad
The heavy rain was falling, or the frost
Raged bitterly, with keen and silent tooth,
And, interrupting the impassion'd game,
From Esthwaite's neighbouring Lake the splitting ice,
While it sank down towards the water, sent,
Among the meadows and the hills, its long
And dismal yellings, like the noise of wolves
When they are howling round the Bothnic Main.[78]

If this is Wordsworth "toying" with the mock-heroic, then it tells of just how much some toys can mean. The scene has Belinda's game of ombre in the background, and, behind that, a recollection of epic: "Those sooty Knaves . . . like Vulcan out of Heaven" was a late addition to the passage, recalling Milton's comparison of Satan and Vulcan in book 1 of *Paradise Lost.* The allusion is a way of expressing how seriously children take games even as it smiles at such seriousness (the postlapsarian adult knows what a real fall feels like). But the adult hasn't wholly surmounted those earlier feelings; the way the boys used the cards—not overly concerned by hierarchy, permitting some to change their functions as the tattered pack required, raising them "beyond the promise of their birth"—is an emblem of how Wordsworth fantasizes the action of his life and his poem, elevating cheap matter to high station. *The Prelude* is both an uncouth assemblage and a vision of the poet's own long campaign.

To appreciate the subtlety and the tenacity of Wordsworth's medleyed way of being in the world, it's important to recognize that what happens on the board here prefigures—or takes its bearings from—what happens abroad. The indoors *contains* the outdoors: the deal is "snow" white; the paramount Ace is a "moon" in her eclipse. The card game offers an escape from the elements but also a microcosm of them, a sublimation of their energies: cards fell inside as "heavy rain was falling"; the sooty knaves "precipitated down" as the splitting ice "sank down"; monarchs are surly and the frost rages bitterly; the cards land with echoes while the ice sends forth long and "dismal yellings." (Given that they are playing whist, the splitting ice even glances back to the possibility of other kinds of splitting; see Charles Cotton's *Complete Gamester*: "If the Honours are equally divided among the Gamesters of each side, then they say Honours are *split*.")[79] The poem is not saying that nature trumps culture; it's alluding to how much of the former feeds into the latter. As De Quincey noted when praising Pope's card game in *The Rape of the Lock*, "the depth of agitation on such occasions, whether at chess, at draughts, or at cards, is not measured of necessity by the grandeur of the stake."[80]

The depth of the Bothnic main isn't necessarily more impressive than the depth of agitation in the impassioned game. The simile that closes the passage is a wonderfully knowing—or half-knowing—exaggeration; it comes across as a piece of free indirect style, as something the children might have thought or said because they'd read it in a book. It is, as it were, *deliberately* impressive, literary, far-fetched in the sense that none of the children has actually heard wolves howling round the Baltic sea (nor, one suspects, has the narrator). In *Paradise Lost*, we would take such a simile straight and grant the narrator a little epic license; in *The Prelude*, the lines may still be moving even as—and because—they conspire to let us in on the glimmer of a joke, let us catch a tinge of melodrama or "boyish wit" that the poet can't quite put behind him. The dismal yelling of the splitting ice is astonishing in the particular way that Wordsworth can be astonishing, whereas the noise of the wolves that follows it is a great touch, but it is only that—a flourish, not quite a sublimity.[81] I'd be tempted to say that the lines in this passage are themselves "Ironic diamonds," but only on the condition that irony isn't seen to be at the expense of the imaginative relish of child's play, or indeed at the expense of anything. The animation and animus that make up the game, the game's blend of the aleatory and the skillful, the way love for the game allows you to get carried away—all these things are a part of adult experience too. The felt fabrication of Wordsworth's memory is a testament to what it feels like for him to be living his life, which includes the very way he lives it through the composition of this poem. "I have play'd with times," he observes later, "And accidents as children do with cards."[82]

*

Other accidents of circumstance in *The Prelude* shed further light on Wordsworth's attraction to medley, an attraction that becomes the means through which he both humors compromising feelings and honors how such feelings generate renewed yet perplexed commitments. Just as at the very center of his Intimations Ode we encounter a playing child ("Filling from time to time his 'humourous stage'"), so at the center of *The Prelude* (by which I mean the *exact* center of its middle book, lines 370–71 of book 7), he recalls another scene of child's play. At a theater in London, two figures—a prostitute and her child—are spotted among the spectators of a pantomime: "Child as beautiful / As ever sate upon a Mother's knee!"[83] It's a shock for him to see the kid there, among "a Ring / of chance Spectators, chiefly dissolute men / And shameless women," playing with the fruit and glasses

> While oaths, indecent speech, and ribaldry
> Were rife around him as are songs of birds
> In spring-time after showers
> . . . .
> Like one of those who walk'd with hair unsinged
> Amid the fiery furnace. He hath since
> Appear'd to me oft-times as if embalm'd
> By Nature; through some special privilege,
> Stopp'd at the growth he had; destined to live,
> To be, to have been, come and go, a Child
> And nothing more, no partner in the years
> That bear us forward to distress and guilt,
> Pain and abasement, beauty in such excess
> Adorn'd him in that miserable place.[84]

As so often in Wordsworth, the unconscionable is the compelling. Alongside the child's vulnerability there is a feeling for his strength—not just because he is magically protected from experience but because his appetite, his curiosity, is itself a marker of potency (as Robert Lowell put it when studying a young girl who was recovering from a nasty encounter with fire: "Though burned, you are hopeful, accident cannot tell you / experience is what you do not want to experience").[85] Not unrelated to Wordsworth's cherishing of this child is the fact that he was himself rarely "miserable" at the pantomime (when he speaks years later of "the patient curiosity and contagious acclamations" of those in the theater, he speaks as one of the "chance Spectators").[86] The simile at the opening of the passage above, with its daring yoking of urban and pastoral, inhabits the child's experience from within (although he couldn't understand what the adults were saying, he was in love with the sound, the energy, the motion of it all), but it also knows that strangely exorbitant beauty can emerge from such a place and not simply adorn it.

The lines catch the spirit of Lamb's vignette of London, delightfully painted in the first letter we have from him to Wordsworth:

> I have passed all my days in London, until I have formed as many and intense local attachments, as any of you Mountaineers can have done with dead nature. . . . Coaches, waggons, playhouses, all the bustle and wickedness round about Covent Garden . . . drunken scenes, rattles . . . the impossibility of being dull in Fleet Street, the crowds, the very dirt and mud . . . steams of soup from kitchens, the pantomimes, London itself, a pantomime and a masquerade, all these things work themselves into my mind and feed me without a power of satiating me. . . . I often shed tears in the motley Strand from fullness of joy at so much *Life*.[87]

Lamb goes on to twit his friend for having "rural emotions," but the motley setting speaks to something in Wordsworth too. Elsewhere in book 7, when he tells of how "shifting pantomimic scenes / Together join their multifarious aid / To heighten the allurement,"[88] he echoes Lamb's 1802 essay on "The Londoner" (which had included details from his letter to Wordsworth) and his love of "the shifting scenes of a skilful Pantomime."[89] These scenes often pop up in unlikely places: Dorothy's journals tell of the beauty of a rural scene as something for "a London pantomime-maker . . . with all its beautiful colours," and elsewhere she enjoys "The grandeur of nature strangely mixed up with Stage effects."[90] Wordsworth delights in weather that appears "with the suddenness of a Pantomime trick," and in his edition of Drayton's *Poly-Olbion* he marks up lines that speak of how "The dales do overspread, by them like motley made."[91] Whatever else *The Prelude* may be, it is a love affair with pantomimic shape-shifting, a vision of medley and motley not as perversions of nature but as embodiments of it.

This vision is a way for Wordsworth to reclaim past experience, but it also stakes a claim for what the future of poetry might be. In *Peri Bathous*, Pope had read the explosion of "harlequins and magicians on our stage" as a baleful influence on modern poetics,[92] and the final version of *The Dunciad* took special note of the ubiquity of "motley Images" and affronts to decorum ("How Tragedy and Comedy embrace; / How Farce and Epic get a jumbled race").[93] By 1800, Friedrich Schlegel could suggest that "The pantomimes of the ancients no longer exist. But, in compensation, all modern poetry resembles pantomimes."[94] A few years later one contemporary joked about how "Epic and Pantomime for mastr'y thrive / Till Momus cries, 'My sons, ye both my thrive.'"[95] Pantomime itself thrived as a mock-heroic medley: the harlequinade section stood as a parody of the "serious" opening story, and Harlequin often stood as a burlesque of (and compliment to) Perseus, Hercules, and other heroes from classical epic. When Garrick's Harlequin announced that "I am nobody and came from nowhere," some members of the audience may have heard Odysseus's trickery of the Cyclops in the background (and some probably also enjoyed the fact that one nobody—a mere servant—could aspire to become a truly epic Nobody).[96] The celebrated "dark scenes" of pantomimes echoed classical descents to the underworld; as Pope navigated the shady depths in *The Dunciad* and as Umbriel entered "the gloomy Cave of Spleen"[97] in *The Rape of The Lock*, they were undertaking pantomimic motions. When in book 7 of *The Prelude* Wordsworth descends to the capital's low-down places, condescending to name the "Lowest of these . . . Yet richly-graced," the home of pantomime at "Sadler's Wells," he is not being dully ironic.[98] Book 7 has often been described as satirical, but as Wordsworth recalls how in the theaters, "the laugh, the grin, the grimace / And all the antics and buffoonery, / The least of them not lost, were all received / With charitable pleasure,"[99] he is being charitable to his own pleasure too.

The pleasure runs deep. When Hazlitt spoke of the child as becoming a poet when he first plays hide and seek, he added, "or when he repeats the story of Jack the Giant-Killer."[100] The specific pantomime Wordsworth recalls—*Jack the Giant Killer* by Charles Dibdin—was labeled "serio-comic" on its title page, and the poet strikes a similar tone:

> How willingly we travel, and how far!
> To have, for instance, brought upon the scene
> The Champion Jack the Giant-Killer, Lo!
> He dons his Coat of Darkness; on the Stage
> Walks, and atchieves his wonders, from the eye
> Of living mortal safe as is the moon
> "Hid in her vacant interlunar Cave,"
> Delusion bold! and faith must needs be coy;
> How is it wrought? His garb is black, the word
> *Invisible* flames forth upon his Chest![101]

To quote a line from *Samson Agonistes* so audaciously out of context (Samson is bereaved, mourning the loss of his sight) and to turn it to the advantage of a less than grand hero is to protect the young man from the bloody possibilities of epic itself. In the pantomime's recitative the Goblin sings to Jack, "This *Coat of Darkness* wear, it will / Make you all *invisible*,"[102] so, given the allusion to Milton, readers are being invited to imagine another lowly prince of darkness resisting giant-size tyranny. Here is a personification of a "darkness visible" who, rather than serving "only to discover sights of woe," is watched with a certain delight. The actor playing Jack is a figure for the mode he inhabits, for pantomime was still considered so disreputably low that Sadler's Wells and other theaters were not granted licenses for speaking parts.[103] This knowledge turns the bathos of "on the Stage / Walks" into a rich kind of joke; in answer to an incredulous reader's question, "Of course he *walks*; what else would he do?" one could reply, "He might talk—if he were allowed. The actor can't *say* 'Invisible'; the invisible must be seen." And Jack stands for the lower orders too—those who are invisible, or who do not have a voice, but who will have their day.

Yet what the hero stands for most—or, rather, what both poet and audience want him to stand for most—is captured in one word in the passage above: "safe." Dickens would later note that in the world of pantomime,

> there is no affliction or calamity that leaves the least impression; where a man may tumble into the broken ice, or dive into the kitchen fire, and only be the droller for the accident; where babies may be knocked about and sat upon, or choked with gravy spoons, in the process of feeding, and yet no Coroner be wanted, nor anybody made uncomfortable; where workmen may fall from the top of a house to the bottom, or even from the bottom of a house to the top, and sustain no injury to the brain, need no hospital, leave no young children; where every one, in short, is so superior to all the accidents of life, though encountering them at every turn, that I suspect this to be the *secret* (though many persons may not present it to themselves) of the general enjoyment which an audience of vulnerable spectators, liable to pain and sorrow, find in this class of entertainment.[104]

Wordsworth was in on this secret (not least, I suspect, on account of pantomime's fascination with saving parents so that they need "leave no young children"). It's of a piece with the way he describes his pleasurable memories of the pantomime itself—"The least of them *not lost*," for nothing you need is ever truly lost in this realm. In book 5 he speaks warmly of the child-reader's identification with Jack and "the invisible Coat,"[105] and here the fact that he walks in safety across stage is quietly aligned with "How willingly *we* travel." The figure of the child facing down dangers, using magical resources to get the better of a hostile world, is the figure for the poet who saturated himself in his childhood and who survived it to write the lines we read. Just like the child he saw in the audience at the theater, surrounded by hazards even as "beauty in such excess / Adorn'd him in that miserable place,"[106] in *The Prelude* Wordsworth can often be caught gazing at versions of himself both on- and offstage, imagining himself into being as someone who, in his own pantomimic way, achieves his wonders. The scene from *Jack the Giant Killer*—and the wish fulfilment it embodies—is "Delusion bold," but it's the boldness that Wordsworth doesn't want to renounce. The bravery of delusions, the very capacity to have them, is the mark of a vitalizing escape artistry, and this artistry promises to take poetry—not simply the poet—to new places.

*

As with the card game, the wonder of the pantomime stretches outdoors. In *Peri Bathous*, Pope's narrator glances at Bartholomew Fair as a notorious site for the medleys he is discussing, and *The Dunciad* begins with "The Smithfield Muses."[107] These Muses prided themselves on their shifts of mood (shows titled "Monk and Murderer!" were followed by "Mirth and Magic!"),[108] and early fragments from the mid-1790s see Wordsworth referring to Smithfield's mixed blessings.[109] When Lamb took Wordsworth to the Fair in 1802, he helped to sow the seeds for one of the most extraordinary medleys he ever wrote, the mock-epic catalog near the end of book 7. The passage takes us back once more to the boy in the darkened bedroom at Ann Tyson's (certain phrases from that suppressed, early fragment are directly repeated). It's hard to know when to stop quoting, so I'll simply quote it in full:

> For once the Muse's help will we implore,
> And she shall lodge us, wafted on her wings,
> Above the press and danger of the Crowd
> Upon some Show-man's Platform: what a hell
> For eyes and ears! what anarchy and din
> Barbarian and infernal! 'tis a dream
> Monstrous in colour, motion, shape, sight, sound.
> Below, the open space, through every nook
> Of the wide area, twinkles, is alive
> With heads; the midway region and above
> Is throng'd with staring pictures, and huge scrolls,
> Dumb proclamations of the prodigies!
> And chattering monkeys dangling from their poles,
> And children whirling in their roundabouts;
> With those that stretch the neck, and strain the eyes,
> And crack the voice in rivalship, the crowd
> Inviting; with buffoons against buffoons
> Grimacing, writhing, screaming; him who grinds
> The hurdy-gurdy; at the fiddle weaves;

Rattles the salt-box; thumps the kettle-drum;
And him who at the trumpet puffs his cheeks;
The silver-collar'd Negro with his timbrel,
Equestrians, Tumblers, Women, Girls and Boys,
Blue-breech'd, pink-vested, and with towering plumes.
—All moveables of wonder from all parts
Are here, Albinos, painted Indians, Dwarfs,
The Horse of Knowledge, and the learned Pig,
The Stone-eater, the Man that swallows fire,
Giants, Ventriloquists, the Invisible Girl,
The Bust that speaks, and moves its goggling eyes,
The Wax-work, Clock-work, all the marvellous craft
Of modern Merlins, wild Beasts, Puppet-shows,
All out-o'th'-way, far-fetch'd, perverted things,
All freaks of Nature, all Promethean thoughts
Of man; his dulness, madness, and their feats,
All jumbled up together, to make up
This Parliament of Monsters: Tents and Booths,
Meanwhile, as if the whole were one vast Mill,
Are vomiting, receiving, on all sides,
Men, Women, three years Children, Babes in arms.[110]

Commentators have often been unwilling to admit what demonic fun it must have been to write this passage. Peter Stallybrass and Allon White quote the first five lines and claim that Wordsworth "flees in panic from the festive scene."[111] But he doesn't flee anywhere; the muse "shall lodge us, wafted on her wings, / *Above* the press and danger of the Crowd / *Upon* some Showman's Platform." Earlier in *The Prelude* he recalls that he "wish'd to be a Lodger in that house / Of Letters, and no more,"[112] so the epic call to the muse to lodge him lowers the tone of the verb a little, makes it pleasurably insecure (he's just passing through). He flirts for a moment with the idea of transcendence, but as "Above" gives way to "Upon," he opts for a station that is, crucially, *part* of the show. The poet is playing to the crowd, not away from it. Milton's Pandemonium meets Pope's "dulness" meets something else entirely: "the open space, through every nook / Of the wide area, twinkles, is alive / With heads" is a brilliant medley of the beguiling and the grotesque. Like the "many-headed mass / Of the Spectators . . . each little nook" at the pantomime earlier, the many-headed monster isn't only a swinish multitude. The scene brings with it Wordsworth's love of Hogarth's crowd scenes (he spoke elsewhere of Hogarth's works as one of "the higher kinds of comedy"), scenes in which people literally and figuratively play with fire.[113] In *The Pre-*

lude's rendition of such play, words like *twinkles* or *nook* make it hard for anyone to be afraid or disgusted.

As monstrous compulsions meet "marvellous craft," the poet-showman becomes a modern Merlin, cracking his voice in rivalship. He, too, turns "Ventriloquist," sounds more like a hawker than a watcher when he cries, "All moveables of wonder from all parts / Are here." *Here* points to the poem, too, not simply to what its creator remembers ("Roll up, roll up, ladies and gentleman. Don't leave without seeing the Albinos, or the Dwarfs"). It's hell for eyes and ears, but Wordsworth can't get or give enough—from the man who swallows fire to Promethean thoughts of man (Wordsworth's only other use of "Promethean" in his poetry speaks of a person who, "kindling with a poet's soul / Hast loved the painter's true Promethean craft / Intensely").[114] The man who swallows fire harks back to the boy at the pantomime; in retrospect, the boy who is "Like one of those who walk'd with hair unsinged / Amid the fiery furnace" starts to sound like a panto act ("For one night only—The Amazingly Unburnable Kid"). Tents and booths "Are vomiting, receiving, on all sides, / Men, Women, three years Children, Babes in arms," and although the first verb almost steals the show, there's a strangely warm welcome in "receiving" (Wordsworth could have gone for *swallowing* there, but didn't). Of arms and the babes he sings. Nothing is being disowned or disallowed.

While humoring the horror, one is momentarily brought up short before the uncanny thrill of the phrase "staring pictures," which insists that viewing such a scene means being viewed by it. The urban medley drags you into a kind of staring competition in which you daren't look away for fear of missing out. Whenever I read it, I think of Winnicott on another child of pantomime and carnival: "One is at a music-hall and on to the stage come the dancers, trained to liveliness. One can say that here is the primal scene, here is exhibitionism, here is anal control, here is masochistic submission to discipline, here is a defiance of the super-ego. Sooner or later one adds: here is LIFE. Might it not be that the main point of the performance is a denial of deadness."[115] This is close to the spirit in which Wordsworth yearned for—and continues to yearn for—the pantomime hall:

> A yearning made more strong by obstacles
> Which slender funds imposed. Life then was new,
> The senses easily pleased; the lustres, lights,
> The carving and the gilding, paint and glare,
> And all the mean upholstery of the place
> Wanted not animation in my sight . . .
> Romantic almost, looked at through a space
> How small of intervening years![116]

The very site is a version of the mock-heroic (the gilding and paint are polished-up versions of the low), while "animation" hints, pantomimically, at upholstery's vitality. (The heroes of pantomime could make even furniture come to life; one reviewer would later note that objects in Wordsworth's writings are always "sure to be animated at once, as with the touch of Harlequin's wand.")[117] Book 7 is all luster and light; nowhere else is *The Prelude* more outrageously committed to its own monstrous appetite for color, motion, shape, sight, sound; to pleasures it can't separate from confusion; and to what Wordsworth elsewhere describes as "the vulgar light / Of present actual superficial life."[118]

Denials of deadness here, along with reduction of the space between intervening years, are related to the other show mentioned in book 7: Dibdin's burletta *Edward and Susan*, which played alongside *Jack the Giant Killer* and told the story of Mary Robinson, a woman from Buttermere in the Lake District whom Wordsworth had known (she had been seduced into a bigamous marriage by one John Hatfield). He briefly outlines the story and is about to move on when something odd happens:

> These last words utter'd, to my argument
> I was returning, when, with sundry Forms
> Mingled, that in the way which I must tread
> Before me stand, thy image rose again,
> Mary of Buttermere![119]

The rising of the image followed by the bathos of the name is itself medley of sundry forms (Wordsworth lost his nerve in the 1850 version and revised to "Maiden of Buttermere").[120] The lines answer back to the process in which the person's sufferings were turned into a theatrical performance by turning her back into a person again, yet they are a performance too, and they take their bearings from pantomime, the form in which nobody really gets left behind. "Mary of Buttermere" is addressed, not simply recalled; the apostrophe brings her back from the past. In late eighteenth-century pantomime, the division between the opening and second section was known as the "transformation scene"; it occurred when the conflict between the characters in the serious plot was interrupted by a benevolent supernatural being, almost always female, who intervened to save the lovers.[121] Mary's arrival here is the transposition of that rhythm into the workings of memory and the poet's hopes for his future. She is "in the way," but without her he cannot be on his way, for she silently speaks of what *The Prelude* and pantomime have in common: a need to believe that the sufferings that go into a life are not the last word on it, and a feeling that the incredible revises one's sense of the conceivable.

Yet that feeling is itself a mixed one. Of the many sundry forms Mary is mingled with at this moment, one is the image of the prostitute's child at the pantomime, another person seemingly embalmed by a denial of deadness. There's something disturbing about how Wordsworth speaks of Mary and her own dead baby as "Happy," and how he then imagines the child at the pantomime as having grown up: "he perhaps, / Mary! may now have liv'd till he could look / With envy on thy nameless Babe."[122] Whether this is palliation or insolence—or both—it's certainly a risky twist on a happy ending. It's as though Wordsworth can't quite decide which version of his wishfulness to humor: are you better off experiencing and surviving your suffering or dying young and avoiding all the ills the flesh is heir to? That unanswerable question is perhaps best left alone, but the fact that it can even be broached here speaks to the trepidation that can frequently be sensed in *The Prelude*'s medleyed essayings on life. While Wordsworth watches himself and others as if they were part of a stage show, he knows that he and they are not always bound by the parts they play. In knowing this, he sometimes gives the impression that he's committing himself to a peculiar kind of comedy, one in which a feeling that all's well that ends well jostles alongside an apprehension that the end is not yet in sight.

This commitment often comes as a shock to him, arrives with a sense that he can hardly believe what he's seeing or saying. In a manuscript, he speaks of the child at the pantomime as "a miracle . . . An infant Hercules,"[123] and such a figure is a miracle of the mock-heroic, both apparition and aberration, an act you could imagine appearing on stage or at Bartholomew Fair. One of Wordsworth's phrases in the passage on the fair—"freaks of Nature"—appears to be of his own invention (it predates the *OED*'s first instance by over forty years),[124] and these freaks are not distinct from other conceptions of nature he cherishes. Book 7 closes with the poet surprised at himself, surprised that from the pantomime, the fair, and other "least things" he is provided with "An under sense of greatest":[125] "The Spirit of Nature was upon me here."[126] That last word needs to be heard with the most incredulous, grateful of stresses ("*here*, of all places"). The stress stands in defiance of the subsequent critical tendency to read book 7 as a mere interlude, a series of digressions or "episodes," before readers get on with the real business of "Love of Nature Leading to Love of Mankind."[127] The book is in fact the heart of *The Prelude*, the one in which he chooses to tell us of how he became stalled on his poem ("stopp'd for years") before taking it up again after a break.

And the current urge was renewed, he explains at the beginning of the book, "yester even" as he was "Sitting within doors betwixt light and dark."[128] This motley betwixt and between time is an apt prologue for where the poem is headed.

For Wordsworth, a medley is a reminder—or an insistence—that only one sort of feeling about a subject isn't enough. As Hazlitt observed,

> The great difficulty in serious pantomime, is to avoid perplexity between the real seriousness of certain combinations, and the absurdity and foolery to which they are to lead; which is like reconciling a contradiction. Minor chords have a severe meaning in them . . . In fact, it is hard to keep a joke in reserve behind particular musical ideas, and to prevent ourselves from becoming in earnest.[129]

The Prelude is a serious pantomime, one that conspires to keep jokes in play, not primarily in order to resist earnestness (although it does do that on occasion) but rather to enlarge one's sense of what earnestness sounds like and to raise one's expectancy for the sheer range of places it can be encountered. In a manuscript for book 7, Wordsworth likens the rush of recollections in his poem—and his manner of handling them—to a "toy of many coloured beads" with which he used to play as a child. Such colorful medleys, he admits, "Appear to some not dignified enough,"[130] and the same could be said of both mock-heroic and pantomime. But he refuses to outgrow them, not least because they multiply the meanings of his life by recalling him to the perplexed pleasures of his fun.

Selves

when baffled most
Not least delighted
DRAFT MANUSCRIPT LINES FOR *THE PRELUDE*[1]

Wordsworth never quite relinquishes his delight at bafflement, always remains within touching distance of what A. R. Ammons calls "the *I's* and *am's* that make a harlequin of any head."[2] I want now to range more widely across *The Prelude* in order to consider how forms of selving and humoring speak to one another—and how they speak to a vision (or version) of Wordsworth I've been arguing for over the course of this book. In the year in which he completed the thirteen-book *Prelude*, he remained ruefully cognizant of the strangeness of a life lived through writing. "I am now writing in the Moss hut, which is my study," he noted to George Beaumont:

> I cannot however refrain from smiling at the situation in which I sometimes find myself here; as, for instance, the other morning when I was calling some lofty notes out of my harp, chaunting of Shepherds, and solitude, etc., I heard a voice, which I knew to be a male voice, whose also it was, crying out from the road below, in a tone exquisitely effeminate. . . . Guess who this creature could be, thus speaking to his Lap-dog in the midst of our venerable mountains? It is one of two nondescripts . . . who go about parading the valley in all kinds of fantastic dresses.[3]

In another letter, the figure is described as a "harlequin,"[4] a motley Fool of sorts—male yet effeminate, man yet creature, exquisite yet nondescript. Poet and harlequin aren't exactly an odd couple; the fun of the situation, for Wordsworth, is bound up with his awareness that "chaunting of Shepherds, and solitude, etc." is no less absurd an activity than parading the valley in fantastic dress. The figure reminds the poet that anything can happen, including any odd thing he himself might attempt.

The feeling that what is laughable may be akin to ourselves extends to a feeling for the self *as* other. Sterne observed that each person "may be as unlike . . . the man he was twenty or thirty years ago, as he ever was from any thing of his own species,"[5] and Coleridge would remark that "My Neighbour is my *other* Self, *othered* by Space—my old age is to my youth an other Self, *othered* by Time."[6] As Wordsworth remembers his past, he confesses,

> so wide appears
> The vacancy between me and those days,
> Which yet have such self-presence in my mind
> That, sometimes, when I think of them, I seem
> Two consciousnesses, conscious of myself
> And of some other Being.[7]

"Sometimes"—and sometimes not. Elsewhere, such confessions are allowed to speak to and for the peculiar ridiculousness at the heart of Being. "Strange rendezvous my mind was at that time," he writes in book 4, "A party-colour'd shew of grave and gay."[8] "At that time" suggests he's older and wiser now, but the parti-colored poem knows that the show isn't over yet.

Comic instincts have long gravitated toward the idea that there is something silly about the self's not being wholly identical with itself. Hobbes's notion that laughter is a sign of one's feeling of superiority over others needs to be read alongside his coda: "Laughter is nothing else but sudden glory stemming from sudden glory arising from some sudden conception of some eminency in ourselves, by comparison with the infirmity of others, *or with our own formerly: for men laugh at the follies of themselves past.*"[9] Incongruity theorists who later resisted Hobbes were, in fact, following one of his leads. Kant suggested that when we laugh at past naivety, "the joker in ourselves is exposed";[10] Richter observed that "No man's actions can appear ridiculous to himself, except an hour later, when he has already become a second self and can attribute the insights of the second to the first."[11] Wordsworth doesn't need the full hour. While working on *The Prelude*, he penned a lyric beginning "These chairs they have no words to utter," only to follow it with a poem titled "Half an Hour Afterwards" in which he smiled at the mood he no longer inhabited.[12] Composition encourages what Richter described as "that paternalistic smile at oneself,"[13] an activity close to that which Freud conceived as the most primitive, significant situation of humor. Although he concedes that it never issues in laughter, this situation does provide a valuable if nonintense kind of pleasure:

> Someone directs the humorous attitude against his own person, as a way of defending himself against the possibilities of his suffering. Is it meaningful to say that someone is treating himself as a child and at the same time playing the

> role of the superior adult towards that child? . . . If it is really the superego that speaks with such loving consolation to the intimidated ego, we should bear in mind that we still have a great deal to learn about the superego.[14]

Humoring yourself is like parenting yourself. Self-mockery becomes a form of self-care by establishing a framework for how you wish to be mocked, which is itself a confession about the person you want to be. When, in 1826, Wordsworth says that "I laugh full as much as ever, and of course talk more nonsense,"[15] or when, at the tender age of seventy-one he says that "if these Poems do not benefit some minds here and there, I shall reproach myself for playing the Fool at my time of life in such a way,"[16] his reproaches are rapprochements.

To play the fool is to become subject to your own folly even as you seek some distance from it. James Thurber's claim that "humour is emotional chaos recollected in tranquillity" is an astute comment about Wordsworth as well as about humor,[17] and *The Prelude* opens with a kind of half joke that sets a very particular tone and timescale—from "Oh there is blessing in this gentle breeze" to "Now I am free" to "The earth is all before me" to "I cannot miss my way" to "this hour / Hath brought a gift" and onward. But, it transpires, this grand entrance is not emotion, but recollection:

> Thus far, O Friend! did I, not used to make
> A present joy the matter of my Song,
> Pour out, that day, my soul in measur'd strains,
> Even in the very words which I have here
> Recorded[18]

One way to account for this shift in tense and emotional temperature is to recall the precise terms of Wordsworth's views on emotion recollected in tranquility:

> The emotion is contemplated till by a species of reaction the tranquillity gradually disappears, and an emotion, similar to that which was before the subject of contemplation, is gradually produced, and does itself actually exist in the mind. In this mood successful composition generally begins, and in a mood similar to this it is carried on.[19]

From this perspective, the beginning of *The Prelude* enacts the successful mood by playing memory as present event. When Wordsworth later recalls that day and speaks of how, "being not unwilling now to give / A respite to this passion, I paced on,"[20] he recommits to the process via the duality of the stressed "now." Now means then, yet recollection is again morphing into presentness.

This process is subject to constant slippage, for nobody's past is certain (if, as Wordsworth claims, "Each man is a memory to himself," the self is only as reliable as the memory).[21] *The Prelude* is a study in its maker's fabrication of the past as a means of holding himself together (he poured out his thoughts that day "Even in the very words which I have here / Recorded"'; the *very* ones?). He is on a journey to himself, but the self is never transcendent when seeking to become its own parent; it must both humor and hesitate over its need to turn emotional chaos into story. In response to a reviewer who had labeled the *Critique of Pure Reason* a work of higher idealism, Kant remarked, "By no means 'higher.' . . . My place is the fruitful bathos of experience."[22] This is Wordsworth's place in *The Prelude*; the man who says "it is shaken off, / As by miraculous gift 'tis shaken off, / That burthen of my own unnatural self,"[23] knows that the unnatural self is part of the natural one. Miracles can happen, but other things keep happening too, things that make the very desire to believe in miracles a kind of avoidance and a kind of necessity.

Later, Wordsworth calls the opening lines of the poem a "Dythyrambic fervour, deep / But short-liv'd transport."[24] The enjambed line's syntax, the lovely duplicity it gives to "deep," marks the speaker's immersion in the fruitful bathos of experience. Some of the poem's most subtle, wryly wondrous effects come from the way it cannot say things, yet says them anyway:

> That day consummate happiness was mine,
> Wide-spreading, steady, calm, contemplative.
> The sun was set, or setting, when I left
> Our cottage door[25]

For the briefest of moments as we read, and as the writer thinks, the sun has already dropped out of sight, before being raised a little only to begin a stately, delectable descent, as though to match the recollected mood (the man who feels "wide-spreading" happiness would not have wanted to miss the sunset). We do not believe in the happiness any less, but simply note the wishfulness that goes into memory. Wordsworth's need to let desirous recollection both anchor and unhinge even the smallest details of his past lends such moments a flickering humor.

Throughout *The Prelude*, the image of the river becomes a locus of such recollection, keeps returning as an image for the self (in book 4, "I saunter'd, like a river murmuring / And talking to itself").[26] Returning home to the lakes from university, he revisits Ann Tyson's cottage and thinks about his current situation as he gazes at the water:

> And that unruly Child, of mountain birth,
> The froward Brook; which, soon as he was box'd

> Within our Garden, found himself at once,
> As if by trick insidious and unkind,
> Stripp'd of his voice, and left to dimple down,
> Without an effort, and without a will,
> A channel paved by the hand of man.
> I look'd at him, and smil'd, and smil'd again,
> And, in the press of twenty thousand thoughts,
> "Ha," quoth I, "pretty Prisoner, are you there?"
> And now, reviewing soberly that hour
> I marvel that a fancy did not flash
> Upon me, and a strong desire, straitway
> At sight of such an emblem that shew'd forth
> So aptly of my late course of even days
> And all their smooth enthralment, to pen down
> A satire on myself.[27]

This is Wordsworth's take on the fact that you can't step in the same river twice. Self-parody becomes a means of casting aspersions on the self without disowning it. The mood is closer to burlesque than to satire, and, as R. P. Blackmur noted in another context, "There is a certain immediate protection afforded to this insufficiency by the surface toughness, by the convention of burlesque; as if by mocking oneself one made sure there was something to mock."[28] The passage is not simply a recollection, but the recollection of a recollection; the benefit of hindsight in Wordsworth is always shadowed by the feeling that the current sense of benefit will soon become subject to *more* hindsight (and besides, what right does our present have to speak of our past?).[29] The reason he resisted the temptation to pen a satire on himself back then, and the reason he resists it now, owes to his suspicion that the self has not changed all that much—has changed least, in fact, when most assured that it *has* changed.

Such passages gently tease what they appear to be saying ("better to be young and free, an unruly Child of nature, than to be boxed in," and so forth). The self, like the river, isn't merely lost through submission to form; for a brief moment, a phrase like "found himself at once" announces self-arrival, but then the syntax unwinds ("found himself at once / . . . / Stripp'd of his voice"). That brief moment, though, whispers another comical secret about the "I": like syntax itself, it can only be apprehended *as* shaped, and as shaped in time. The undulating yet boxed-in lines the poet writes are yet another "channel paved by the hand of man" and offer a means of penning down by penning in. "Are you there?" is a question that can only be asked of a self—and *by* a self—that is not entirely in flux. "I look'd at him, and smil'd, and smil'd again": does the second smile register the same feeling as the first, or does it come as though from another self, one that knows (or suspects) its own continuing thrall to smooth enthrallment? Moments like this in *The Prelude* contain rich ironies—rich because they don't succumb to the temptation to think of irony itself as the last word. When Wordsworth is ironic, he is so in the sense that Robert Lowell understands the mode: "Irony is being amusing about what we can't understand."[30]

*

If, as I have been suggesting, *The Prelude* is never quite a progress narrative, it is nonetheless in search of a humored self that would mark a progress of sorts. Wordsworth is resistant to the person who "must live / Knowing that he grows wiser every day,"[31] but then he himself does want to grow, to imagine a self emplotted if not exactly improving. When he was looking around for epic-mock-epic models for the romancing of the self, certain writings, cherished from his childhood, would have come readily to mind, ones that should be kept in mind when reading him: eighteenth-century novels; behind them, Cervantes; and behind him, Ariosto. Wordsworth claimed to Mathews in 1791 that *Tristram Shandy* was the only modern literature he'd read, and it appears he was rereading it in 1796 and again in 1805–1806.[32] He'd adored Fielding as a boy—read "all" of him, he recollected—and was reading *Tom Jones* again with his sister in 1800.[33] De Quincey remembered his friend confessing how much he loved "Smollett, Fielding, and Le Sage . . . read and remembered with extreme delight,"[34] and *The Prelude's* opening mock-heroic spin on Milton—"The earth is all before me . . . whither should I turn"—is also a nod to Fielding, who in *Tom Jones* tells of how the young hero "began to debate with himself whither he should go. *The World*, as *Milton* phrases it, *lay all before him*."[35] Fielding's defense of "prosai-comi-epic Writing" was a restatement of his intent, expressed in the preface to *Joseph Andrews*, to create "a comic Romance . . . a comic Epic-Poem in Prose."[36] Sterne took these combinations further, pushing Fielding's intermittent authorial digressions into full-blown first-person pyrotechnics. From *Gil Blas* onward, the fiction adopted by the picaresque novelist is usually that of a man recalling—and sometimes satirizing—his early life.[37]

A major precedent for these adventures in identity was Ariosto, the writer whom Friedrich Schlegel praised in 1799 for a "happy mixture of jest and earnest" that made him "the master and archetype in relaxed storytelling and sensual fantasies."[38] Ariosto exerted a formative influence on the experiments of both Fielding and Sterne,[39] and while writing *The Prelude* Wordsworth rekindled his love affair with the poet: "I can translate, and have translated, two books of Ariosto at the rate nearly of 100 lines a day," he told George Beaumont in 1805.[40] He'd also been translating him in 1802 and back in the early 1790s.[41] Ariosto's insistence on going astray stylistically, on indulging in transitions from high to low, had long been associated with his frequent allusions to sexuality (Coleridge, for example, censured "the disgusting licentiousness . . . which poisons Ariosto").[42] Such desertion of purpose, registered in the poem's willingness to turn chivalric quest narratives into pretexts for delectable deviation, was what captured Wordsworth's attention and imagination. In his personal copy of *Orlando Furioso*, the gloss on book 11—"we may see that things done in jest, ofte turn to earnest"—receives the commendation of a tick in the margin, and one of the most earnestly jest-like things in Ariosto's universe is desire itself.[43]

An early manuscript version of "Nutting" refers to the ruination of the bower in these terms: "From such rude intercourse the woods all shrink / As at the blowing of Astolpho's horn."[44] One wonders a little at "horn" (the *OED* records the slang use of the word to mean sexual excitement from 1785). In *Orlando Furioso*, Astolfo's magic horn isn't obviously sexual, but it's very obviously potent. When, in *The Prelude*, Wordsworth speaks of one who, "like a Hero in Romance / He winds away his never-ending horn,"[45] he gestures toward other forms of never-ending desire, and the figure for embodied desire in Ariosto is of course Angelica, the maiden who both drives and derails the plot as knight after knight chases her through the forest. She's still running in *The Prelude*, flashing past unexpectedly in book 9 as Wordsworth recalls how, when walking through forests in France, he "From earnest dialogues . . . slipp'd in thought":[46]

> if a devious Traveller was heard
> Approaching from a distance, as might chance,
> With speed and echoes loud of trampling hoofs
> From the hard floor reverberated, then
> It was Angelica thundering through the woods
> Upon her Palfrey[47]

She wasn't likely to be caught. When dwelling on the pleasures of romance, drafts of *The Prelude* tell of "talismanic rings,"[48] and in the prologue to *Peter Bell*, a poem shot through with allusions to Ariosto, Wordsworth speaks again of "the magic ring."[49] He was probably thinking of the ring Angelica uses to render herself invisible so as to escape the clutches of Orlando.

Ariosto plays with desire by repeatedly staging foilings of consummation, and surviving fragments of Wordsworth's translations continue that game.[50] Like Orlando, Wordsworth is always at the beginning of everything he means to be—and have. Eros is error, but error is errancy, and errancy is possibility. One of Wordsworth's distinguishing characteristics as a writer is the joy he senses *in* desire, as though to have desire were to have everything. In *The Prelude*, whenever happiness beckons, some obstacle appears. "The mind itself," he admits, "hath less quiet instincts, goadings-on / That drive her, as in trouble, through the groves,"[51] and she is driven through these groves—the "groves of Chivalry"[52]—as through a book she never wants to end. Granted, Wordsworth sometimes conceives such goadings-on as predicaments. In the tract *Concerning the Convention of Cintra*, when speaking of both public and personal moods, "vanishing and reviving and piercing each other like the Northern Lights," he observes,

> the long calenture of fancy to which the Lover is subject; the blast, like the blast of the desart, which sweeps perennially through a frightful solitude of its own making in the mind of the Gamester; the slowly quickening but ever quickening descent of appetite down which the Miser is propelled; the agony and cleaving oppression of grief; the ghost-like hauntings of shame; the incubus of revenge; the life-distemper of ambition;—these inward existences, and the visible and familiar occurrences of daily life in every town and village; the patient curiosity and contagious acclamations of the multitude in the streets of the city and within the walls of the theatre; a procession, or a rural dance; a hunting, or a horse-race; a flood, or a fire; rejoicing and ringing of bells for an unexpected gift of good fortune, or the coming of a foolish heir to his estate;—these demonstrate incontestibly that the passions of men (I mean, the soul of sensibility in the heart of man)—in all quarrels, in all contests, in all quests, in all delights, in all employments which are either sought by men or thrust upon them—do immeasurably transcend their objects. The true sorrow of humanity consists in this;—not that the mind of man fails; but that the course and demands of action and of life so rarely correspond with the dignity and intensity of human desires.[53]

The decision to couch this extraordinary passage as omniscient narration doesn't hide—intensifies, rather—its personal investments. (A few years earlier, Wordsworth had spoken of himself as having "loiter'd, and frequented night by night / Routs, card-tables, the formal haunts of men"[54] and as having "coasted round and round the line / Of Tavern, Brothel, Gaming-house, and Shop."[55]) Even "The true sorrow of humanity," though, has a humorous edge; in fact, the last sentence of the passage reads like a definition of comedy. Alenka Zupančič asks, "Is not the very existence of comedy and of the comical telling us most clearly that man is never just a man, and that his finitude is corroded by a passion which is precisely not cut to the measure of man and of his finitude? . . . *Not only are we not infinite, we are not even finite.*"[56]

This failure of finitude needn't be a source of disillusionment, and the figure that sets off Wordsworth's voyaging in the Cintra tract—the vanishing and reviving Northern Lights—is used in *The Prelude* to speak of those dreamers and "Forgers of lawless Tales" who "charm away the wakeful night / In Araby, Romances, Legends."[57] Such lawlessness involves "adventures endless," and those who commit to it are blessed for their ability to create "Space like a Heaven fill'd up with Northern lights, / Here, nowhere, there, and everywhere at once."[58]

Wordsworth's wish to be the poet of his life keeps involving him in a wish for that nowhere-and-everywhere experience—and in a craving to become more than he is. One response to this strand of feeling would be to say that he is so aware of the past and present degradations of need, so haunted by the exposed, exposing nature of long-held desires and hopes, that he tries to turn his pain into a form of pleasure by *asserting* the value of nonconsummation. Certainly, *The Prelude* is caught between two ways of imagining the self's relation to its own desire: the poet adores an "insuperable look / That drinks as if it never could be full,"[59] but he longs for answers, staring at a world "that seem'd / To have some meaning which I could not find."[60] The poem is often very close to a kind of confusion that Thoreau describes in "Walking" when, looking at the natural world, he confesses "I do not know whether I heard the sounds of a suppressed hilarity or not."[61] It's a state that Emerson describes in "Nature" as he senses "something mocking" in the natural world, something that won't keep faith with us:

> There is in woods and waters a certain enticement and flattery, together with a failure to yield a present satisfaction. This disappointment is felt in every landscape. I have seen the softness and beauty of the summer clouds floating feathery overhead, enjoying, as it seemed, their height and privilege of motion, whilst yet they appeared not so much the drapery of this place and hour, as forelooking to some pavilions and gardens of festivity beyond. It is an odd jealousy, but the poet finds himself not near enough to his object. The pine-tree, the river, the bank of flowers before him, does not seem to be nature. Nature is still elsewhere. This or this is but outskirt and far-off reflection and echo of the triumph that has passed by and is now at its glancing splendor and heyday, perchance in the neighboring fields, or, if you stand in the field, then in the adjacent woods. The present object shall give you this sense of stillness that follows a pageant which has just gone by. What splendid distance, what recesses of ineffable pomp and loveliness in the sunset! But who can go where they are, or lay his hand or plant his foot thereon? Off they fall from the round world forever and ever. It is the same among the men and women as among the silent trees; always a referred existence, an absence, never a presence and satisfaction.[62]

This is what it feels like for Wordsworth to be in the forest of himself—and what it feels like to read Wordsworth. But then, if the poet is forever the suitor of ways in which he needn't coincide with himself—always in search of a stranger past, always putting off his consummations to an even stranger future—in what sense does identity stake its ground, and stake a claim? To answer this question—or to hear it asked in a way that makes it disappear—I'd like to open just one more book, the book Wordsworth often returned to as he thought about the rueful, risible tragicomedy of the self.

*

When, as he wandered in the woods in France, Wordsworth heard footsteps and then dreamt up an Angelica, he was having fun with a recurring trope of Ariosto's poem: the blurring of the real and the fantastical (his metrical emphasis makes the point, for the trampling hoofs "From the hard floor reverberated, then / It **was** Angelica thundering through the woods")."[63] The earliest of Wordsworth's translations on record, a lone stanza from book 1 of *Orlando Furioso*, reads,

> Nor wants within for traveller hither led
> Such turf and may invite to sweet repose
> In closest covert on that flowery bed
> She drops and slumber came her eyes to close
> Nor had she rested long her weary head
> Ere at the coming sound of feet she rose
> Softly she rose and near the river side
> Between the trees and armed knight espied.[64]

Wordsworth's version accentuates the possibility that Angelica wakes *into* dream, not *from* it, as though even she, so often the object of desire, is no less subject to fantasy than her pursuers, unconsciously looking to find ways of making others fall into the script that her fantasies have written for them. In his essay on "The Romantic School," Heinrich Heine imagines a lady of high degree who has to help her pedantic middle-class husband in his affairs ("or even in his cheese store"): "But sometimes, at night, when her spouse is snoring peacefully with his cotton nightcap on his head, the noble lady arises from the confining conjugal bed, mounts her white steed, and once more gallops as joyously as before in the enchanted forest of romance."[65] So maybe she becomes the lady of her husband's dreams—or leaves his dreaming far behind. Within the space of a page, this flight of fancy carries Heine to another figure: "It is quite amusing that it was precisely the Romantic School that provided us with the best translation of a book in which its own folly is exposed so very delightfully. For this School was deluded by the same madness that inspired the noble man of La Mancha to all his follies."[66]

When Sterne speaks of "my beloved Cervantes" in *Tristram Shandy*, and when Fielding says on the title page of *Joseph Andrews* that it is "Written in Imitation of the Manner of Cervantes," they are paying their respects to a Quixotism that Ariosto had helped Cervantes to create, one that they would in turn pass on to their Romantic inheritors.[67] As Stuart Tave has observed, Fielding was the first writer in England to make Don Quixote a symbol of nobility, not merely a figure of fun, and Sterne would take up the baton; to Tristram Shandy, "the peerless knight of *La Mancha*" is someone whom, "with all his follies, I love more, and would have gone further to have paid a visit to, than the greatest hero of antiquity."[68] The shift from satirical to sympathetic readings of Don Quixote had of course first appeared in Cervantes's novel itself, for while Sancho Panza begins by laughing at his master, he soon falls in love with him. Smollett noted at the beginning of his translation of *Don Quixote* that the knight should not be seen merely as "an ordinary madman" nor should Sancho's actions be conceived as "affected buffoonry."[69] Quixote's quest is some form of sublimation of his unrequited feelings for Aldonza Lorenco, the peasant girl with whom he had once been in love, as the first chapter explains.[70] He is knowingly unknowing, and his stubbornness is tied to his creativity, for his knack of finding ways to resist those who gainsay his delusions is his means of keeping the show on the road. (When he says of Aldonza that "I paint her in my imagination as I desire her," he admits as much.) Quixote is humored—for laughs, and because people sense that he needs to be in his own little world to avoid his suffering—but he also humors the world, reminding those who watch him that they have become estranged from their lives by relinquishing or denying the fantasies that go into the making of the real. When it is put to him that Dulcinea is just an illusory image, his reply shows how an apparent avoidance of tricky questions can be the route to wisdom: "There is much to say about that . . . these are not the kinds of things whose verification can be carried through to the end."[71]

Wordsworth acknowledged his debts to Ariosto and Cervantes when shaping the character of Rivers in *The Borderers*, and Cervantes was an enduring preoccupation for him.[72] He kept all his life his father's beloved Smollett translation of *Don Quixote* and also sought out other valuable editions, including the first scholarly version (it's worth stressing that Cervantes was the only author Wordsworth ever showed a marked interest in "collecting" in this way).[73] His appetite for blendings of solemnity, quixotry, and quest romance would also have been fed by his visits to the London theaters. The customary transformation scene in pantomime, which we encountered earlier, saw the young suitor transformed into harlequin and sent on a knight-errant quest,[74] and Wordsworth was in London in late 1797 when performances of *King Lear* at Covent Garden were followed by *Barataria; or, Sancho Turned Governor.*[75] (Another double act may have caught his attention: *The Orphan*, followed by *Harlequin and Quixote.*)[76] Several early observers discerned a resemblance between Wordsworth and the Knight of the Sorrowful Countenance; in addition to Hazlitt's description of his friend as "Don Quixote-like," with "an air somewhat stately and quixotic," Ellen Ricketts spoke later of "our dear old Poet's *Quixotic* appearance . . . we were saucy enough to laugh at him repeatedly, which seemed much to divert him."[77]

Those responding to Wordsworth's poetry were saucy enough to pursue the analogy. J. T. Coleridge spoke of his "Quixotism" in which "there is nothing too trifling for grace, too disgusting for pleasant speculation." Walter Scott referred to "an amiable Quixotry." De Quincey, in less amiable mood, asked him, "Would you, as Sancho says, have 'better bread than is made of wheat'?" And Hazlitt said of Wordsworth that "His nature is a mere Dulcinea del Toboso . . . he would make a Vashti of her."[78] From the start, he seemed willing to provoke such associations. In the preface to *Lyrical Ballads* Wordsworth notes that he might, to some, appear to be "like a man fighting a battle without enemies"[79] before speaking of the poet as

> a man pleased with his own passions and volitions . . . delighting to contemplate similar volitions and passions as manifested in the goings-on of the Universe, and habitually impelled to create them where he does not find them. To these qualities he has added a disposition to be affected more than other men by absent things as if they were present; an ability of conjuring up in himself passions, which are indeed far from being the same as those produced by real events.[80]

His quixotic precursor in knight-errantry and errancy is somewhere in the background, and in *The Prelude* he is permitted to step forward into the light.

Coleridge read Sancho and Quixote as two parts of the same mind, with the former as "common sense without reason or imagination" and the latter as the opposite: "Put him and his master together, and they form a perfect intellect. . . . These two characters possess the world, alternately and interchangeably the cheater and cheated."[81] I think Wordsworth conceived the double act in a similar way, although he had begun to explore this dynamic as a key to one's apprehension of the self over time. Sancho sometimes treats Quixote like a child before realizing that this is no reason to dismiss him. *The Prelude* takes this prompt and turns it into the comic-epic story of the child who is father of the man, the man who cannot help but play Sancho to his own past Quixote and who, while doing so, comes to discover that the knight is never wholly past.

The rhythms of this dizzying form of self-encounter are present in the famous dream in book 5. The episode is couched in the third person in the 1805 version, related by "a Friend" of Wordsworth's who fell asleep having been reading "The famous History of the Errant Knight, / Recorded by Cervantes."[82] One suspects a splitting or evasion of the self, a self that doesn't feel at liberty to say to what extent his vision belonged to him. In the dream, he meets a rider on a quest: "A wish was now engender'd in my fear / To cleave unto this Man, and I begg'd leave / To share his errand with him."[83] (The wish is engendered *in* the fear, we note, not merely *by* it.) The dreamer adopts the position of Sancho Panza, all the while having to admit that the man he follows was sometimes "the very Knight / Whose tale Cervantes tells, yet not the Knight."[84] So readers are privy to a half-desired, half-resistant identification, and the dreamer is in fact not permitted to follow his man for long; he is outpaced by him, left behind, and wakes in terror as he imagines the sea is about to engulf him.

As so often in Wordsworth, the aftermath is even more startling than the event:

> Full often, taking from the world of sleep
> This Arab Phantom, which my Friend beheld,
> This Semi-Quixote, I to him have given
> A substance, fancied him a living man,
> A gentle Dweller in the Desart, craz'd
> By love and feeling and internal thought,
> Protracted among endless solitudes;
> Have shap'd him, in the oppression of his brain,
> Wandering upon this quest, and thus equipped.
> And I have scarcely pitied him; have felt
> A reverence for a Being thus employ'd;
> And thought that in the blind and awful lair
> Of such a madness reason did lie couch'd . . .
> I, methinks,
> Could share that Maniac's anxiousness, could go
> Upon like errand. Oftentimes, at least,
> Me hath such deep entrancement half-possess'd,
> When I have held a volume in my hand,
> Poor earthly casket of immortal Verse![85]

Upon waking, he recommits to dream via daydream. He embodies as well as depicts the Knight of La Mancha, because to give a substance to a dream, to fashion a living thing from your fancy, is itself a commitment to the quixotic ("craz'd" in this passage could refer to the "I" as well as to his imagined quest figure). Yet the poet is "*half*-possess'd," just as the figure is a "*Semi*-Quixote." He announces the highest hopes for the effects of poetry, while gently acknowledging the limits of what is hoped for: "I, *methinks*" might be proud or slightly hesitant; "*could* go" is not "will go"; "Oftentimes, *at least*" hovers between self-assertion and concession. The grand Miltonic cadence of "Me hath such deep entrancement half-possess'd" comes across as oddly inflated when followed by the more plainspoken "When I have held a volume in my hand." The whole passage—like much of the best writing in *The Prelude*—is both aspiring and wryly self-watchful, and the assonance of that last line beautifully captures the sound of the poem thinking to itself. By drawing "earthly" and "Verse" closer together and by pulling "immortal" and "Poor" into each other's orbit, Wordsworth creates a space in which the egotistical sublime is shadowed by an earthly ruefulness.

As Coleridge noted of "frequently ironical" images in dreams, it is "as if the fortunes of the Ego diurnus appeared exceedingly droll and ridiculous to the Ego nocturnus."[86] Wordsworth's dream and its aftermath contain a comedy of self-apprehension, a conflict between avowal and disavowal, and these mixed feelings are linked directly to his feelings about his own childhood. Immediately after the Don Quixote episode, he admits that he's been detained from other thoughts and switches his attention to

> the lisping time of Infancy,
> And later down, in prattling Childhood, even
> While I was travelling back among those days,
> How could I ever play an ingrate's part?[87]

One answer to his question might be offered via Sándor Ferenczi's thoughts on laughter:

> The essence of laughing: How much should I like to be as imperfect as that! The essence of laughing at: How satisfactory it is that I am so well behaved, not so imperfect as that! . . . Behind every laughing at there is concealed unconscious laughing. . . . Remaining serious is successful repression. . . . We are always delighted by the naïve (the childish) element in the comic and it rouses the unconscious child in us. . . . Why must I emphasize that I am *not* like that? Because I *am* like that![88]

The child in me is mad, maddening, but also, as Smollett would put it of Quixote, "a medley of sense and madness" (Quixote's own favorite phrase for this is *la razón de la subrazón*—"the reason of unreason").[89] Throughout *The Prelude*, the child's experience is indulged and humored in mock-heroic, Romantic-chivalric terms even as the aftershock of the memory translates that indulgence into a haunted series of identifications. The boy who steals the boat and finds the cliff striding after him "like a living thing" might as well be fighting windmills,[90] but the "dim and undetermin'd sense / Of unknown modes of being" that follows is still very much with the adult *now*.[91] When the child's kite pulled "at its rein, like an impatient Courser," or when he felt "Gleams like the flashing of a shield," or when he stared at stones and "saw them feel," or when he looked at something that was "doubtless nothing more / Than a black rock" only to see "it was a burnish'd shield . . . Suspended over a Knight's Tomb . . . some magic cave," at all these points he committed himself to the quixotic instinct that remains part of the poem's unfolding eventfulness.[92] "What I saw," Wordsworth admits, "Appear'd like something in myself, a dream, / A prospect in my mind"[93] ("Some call'd it madness," or saw him as "craz'd in brain").[94] Perhaps so, but, as Erich Auerbach put it, "if Don Quijote had not gone mad, he would not have left his house."[95]

Wordsworth's reading and rereading of his experience by the light of *Don Quixote*, his absorption of his precursor's own need to read his life as a story, is hiding in plain sight throughout *The Prelude.* (When, later in book 5, he praises "adventures endless, spun / By the dismantled Warrior in old age," he might well be speaking of Cervantes, and when he says that such adventures are first dreamed up in childhood, a time when we "make our wish our power," he is turning Cervantes loose again on his own past.[96]) Even Wordsworth's coming of age finds itself harking back to such models; accompanying him through the Alps in 1790, along with his treasured copy of Ariosto, was one of his closest friends, Robert Jones, and the pair looked like an odd couple to those who saw them ("Our appearance is singular," Wordsworth dryly remarked).[97] He later recalled that Jones had a "calm and even temper so enviable compared with mine";[98] he was "fat and roundabout and rosy, and puffing and panting," according to Dorothy, and "a most affectionate man," according to Wordsworth.[99] He plays Sancho to his friend's Quixote as they wander through the mountains in search of adventure:

> Nor, side by side
> Pacing, two brother pilgrims, or alone
> Each with his humour, could we fail to abound
> (Craft this which hath been hinted at before)
> In dreams and fictions pensively composed,
> Dejection taken up for pleasure's sake,
> And gilded sympathies[100]

Faced by the bathos of experience—"we had cross'd the Alps"—this Quixote will soon call out to "Imagination!"[101] to gird him up, and we surmise that, despite differences in each man's "humour," Sancho's calm, even temper would make allowances for such flights of fancy (Sancho, after all, has his own dreams and fictions). As Wordsworth looks back now, he watches himself with something of the mood with which his friend would have watched him then, and he has not yet desisted from fabulating for pleasure's sake. That pleasure is also a pledge, a commitment to the belief that certain things are all the more real *because* purely ideal. As that lovely, quickening shift from "Pacing" to "abound" suggests, the composition and crafting of their dreams is as actual, as physical, as anything else they do.

*

I want to end by looking at another crafted dream, a primal scene that serves to bring together all the others, one that shows what Wordsworth makes of comedy—and what comedy makes of him. It turns on that most Wordsworthian of moments, plays on his appetite for an encounter for which he has often been mocked—an appetite, in fact, that he mocked in himself ("chaunting of Shepherds, and solitude, etc."). In book 8 of *The Prelude*, in the middle of nowhere, its author suddenly stops and finds himself staring at a shepherd who is apparently more than a shepherd. "It is unusually plain that Wordsworth has nothing to say," Jonathan Wordsworth claims; this is just "triumphant irrelevance," the poet is "talking nonsense."[102] The nonsense he's talking, though, is best approached via the story that stands behind it. Late in *Don Quixote*, the hero returns home with a new plan; he shall become Shepherd Quixotiz, and Sancho will become Shepherd Pancino (the project is described as "a new madness" by the villagers).[103] Maybe he's trying to make up for his past adventuring, for, in one of the novel's most celebrated episodes, he gets shepherding brilliantly wrong. In book 1, his view obscured by "great clouds of dust," Quixote mistakes a flock of sheep for an enemy horde of "knights and giants." Despite Sancho's best efforts at dissuasion, his master fixes his lance in its socket and charges, is beaten back by angry shepherds, and then turns to his astonished sidekick and gives a small oration on the glories of God's mercies ("there were knights errant in past times who would stop and give a sermon or a talk in the middle of the field of battle just as if they were graduates of the University of Paris"):

> God, who provides for all things, will not fail us, especially since we are so much in His service, when he does not fail the gnats in the air, or the grubs in the earth, or the tadpoles in the water; He is so merciful that He makes His sun to shine on the good and the evil and His rain to fall on the unjust and the just.

To which Sancho replies, "Your grace would do better as a preacher than as a knight errant."[104]

In *The Prelude*, having recalled a long-forgotten story about shepherds on a "devious quest,"[105] Wordsworth remembers seeing "a pastoral Tract . . . where Fancy might run wild,"[106] a place where the poet-traveler may "pursue at will / His devious course."[107] This brings him back to childhood memories, where he found himself watching a shepherd and feeling awestruck without knowing why.[108] (The 1850 version hints at links to the episode from Cervantes by describing how the shepherd moves on with "His staff portending like a Hunter's Spear.") Wordsworth later acknowledges that some may see his vision as mere delusion, but he commits it to paper nonetheless.[109]

suddenly
Surpriz'd with vapours, or on rainy days
When I have angled up the lonely brooks
Mine eyes have glanced upon him, few steps off,
In size a Giant, stalking through the fog,
His Sheep like Greenland Bears: at other times,
When round some shady promontory turning,
His Form hath flash'd upon me, glorified
By the deep radiance of the setting sun:
Or him I have descried in distant sky,
A solitary object and sublime,
Above all height! like an aerial Cross,
As it is station'd upon some spiry Rock
Of the Chartreuse, for worship . . .
. . . .
hence the human form
To me was like an index of delight,
Of grace and honour, power and worthiness.
Meanwhile, this Creature, spiritual almost
As those of Books; but more exalted far,
Far more of an imaginative form,
Was not a Corin of the groves, who lives
For his own fancies, or to dance by the hour
In coronal, with Phillis in the midst,
But, for the purposes of kind, a Man
With the most common; Husband, Father; learn'd,
Could teach, admonish, suffer'd with the rest
From vice and folly, wretchedness and fear:
Of this I little saw, cared less for it;
But something must have felt.[110]

Cervantes's novel ends in disenchantment; Quixote recovers his senses and realizes the error of his ways. Sancho tries to rally him back to a life of fantasy ("let's go to the countryside dressed as shepherds, just like we arranged"),[111] but the joke—and the sublime energy that informed it—has run out. Wordsworth's vignette begins by paying oblique homage to Cervantes as the poet seeks to reenchant the world: the "great clouds of dust" in book 1 of *Don Quixote* are swapped for "fog" and "vapours"; talk of rain and sun in Quixote's sermon, along with good and evil, are given new expression. The poet internalizes the knight's high spirits, keeps those spirits up, by experiencing the shepherd as Giant and the sheep as gloriously absurd Greenland bears before then offering his own sermon on the man as aerial Cross. And yet *The Prelude*'s version of quixotic pastoral isn't merely naive. Creative and recreative exaltation now include an acknowledgment of Sancho Panza's relish for life as lived through vice and folly, a life "most common."

Auden suggested that while Quixote is comically mad, Sancho is comically sane: "If madness says 'windmills are giants,' sanity says 'windmills are only windmills.' If madness confuses analogies with identities, philistine realism refuses to recognize analogies and only admits identities; neither can say, 'Windmills are like giants.'"[112] *The Prelude* knows the value of *like* and employs the word carefully: sheep are only like Greenland bears; a shepherd is only like an aerial Cross; the human form is only like an index of delight. But Wordsworth also senses that *like* risks becoming too balanced, too sane, and when he speaks of glorification and sublimity "Above all height!" he means it. Or, rather, he is helping to make an ideal more actual by assuming that it already exists, sensing that one can't believe in something so passionately without some of it coming true. For Wordsworth, true experience is blind (often blindly comic) for the experiencer is so immersed in experience, so accosted by feeling, that he cannot be cognizant of all that he knows. As "Of this I little saw, cared less for it" is answered by the insistence of "But something must have felt," the poet testifies once more that child is the father of the man. Yet that "something" is important, speaks of a gap, tells of a feeling that can only occur *through* reflection. The sane man smuggles as many of the child's quixotic instincts into his adulthood as he can, but only in his adulthood can he comprehend just how much quixotry is there for the taking.

In the middle of a field, Quixote thought of Paris University; in the middle of another field, Wordsworth thought of "some spiry Rock / Of the Chartreuse." An adult's memory—another moment from Wordsworth's knight-errantry with Jones—is being superimposed onto a child's experience here; as Dorothy recalled of her brother's recollections of the monastery, "I do not think that any one spot which he visited during his youthful Travels with

Robert Jones made so great an impression on his mind: and in my young days he used to talk so much of it to me."[113] The particular images that stayed with him were those "crosses seen on the tops of the spiry rocks of the Chartreuse, which have every appearance of being inaccessible":

> The cross with hideous laughter Demons mock,
> By angels planted on the aëreal rock.[114]

That laughter has been replaced in *The Prelude* by something altogether less mocking. The vision of the shepherd as aerial cross somehow combines affection with sublimity, and the figure is conceived in this way because Wordsworth now needs to sense something of himself in the man he watches. "His Form hath *flash'd* upon me, *glorified* / By the deep radiance of the setting sun": mention of the sun, along with the pun on *glory* ("aureole, nimbus, or halo" [*OED*]), recalls that other seriously comic alter ego who is so important to Wordsworth: Johnny, the idiot boy, who answered in his glory about the sun that shone so cold. And as one reads again that "His Form hath flash'd upon me, glorified," there's a brief moment—the moment it takes to pause at the line end—in which one senses that the *me* is glorified too. Early in the poem, Wordsworth had described himself as like "a shepherd on a promontory, / Who, lacking occupation, looks far forth / Into the endless sea, and rather makes / Than finds what he beholds."[115] This vision of childlike, quixotic shepherdhood is again ghosted by Cervantes and allows for a humoring of the self as another, another who is nonetheless the self's deepest wish.

For Wordsworth, no less than for Quixote, fiction will always extend beyond books and into life. In *The Prelude*, when thinking about how the people he cares for keep changing over time, how they appear not to stay still *as* themselves, he is led to a realization that he has changed too (this is precisely why he is able to see them in more than one way):

> A freshness also found I at this time
> In human Life, the life I mean of those
> Whose occupations really I lov'd.
> The prospect often touch'd me with surprize,
> Crowded and full; and changed, as seem'd to me,
> Even as a garden in the heat of Spring,
> After an eight days' absence . . .
> . . . .
> Yes, I had something of another eye,
> And often, looking round, was mov'd to smiles,
> Such as a delicate work of humour breeds.[116]

Comedy was ever the mythos of spring, and light springings of surprise can be felt in the smallest words: Harlequin "I"s and "me"s sometimes do and sometimes don't take metrical stress, and "Yes" is also a lovely touch ("Humor in Mr. Wordsworth?" "Yes, even in him"). I think there's also a quiet pun in that line, because Wordsworth's eye has long been drawn to seeing things as having something of another I. The pun—like the self—houses a cherished need to mean at least two things at once. The passage is an invitation to the reader to return to Wordsworth just as he returns to the people he thinks he knows: touched with surprise, moved to smiles.

The work of humor as this poet conceives it is close to what Gillian Rose once described as love's work, which involves a willingness to be "bounded and unbounded, selved and unselved, 'sure' only of this untiring exercise. This sureness of self, which is ready to be unsure, makes the laughter at the mismatch between aim and achievement comic, not cynical."[117] To be moved to the kind of smile that Wordsworth is talking about is to know that humor, like a good joke, is always only half true. We humor a joke played on ourselves or on those we care about, but in finding it funny we survive the joke, gesture toward a sense of selfhood that doesn't feel the need to know itself wholly. The first fragments of *The Prelude* were composed during a cold, isolating winter in Goslar—Wordsworth told Coleridge in December 1798 that "as I have had no books I have been obliged to write in self-defence"[118]—and, as the poem took shape as a defense and anchoring of the self, it also became a means of disorienting it. In writing, Wordsworth makes himself up as he goes along, and in doing so gets closer to the self that he really feels himself to be. The untiring exercise, the endless play of possibility, is what humor breeds from him and for him. Humor is his self-cure for radical confoundedness, but the cure is always a catalyst for yet another self, a self that is still to be made, found, and lost.

Acknowledgments

Grants from The Leverhulme Trust gave me precious time to work on this book, and I'm grateful to the Trust for supporting the research. I'd also like to thank the editors of *Essays in Criticism*, *The Wordsworth Circle*, and *Raritan* for permission to reuse material that first appeared in their journals, and Jeff Cowton for permission to quote from manuscripts at the Jerwood Centre in Grasmere. Colleagues and students at the Universities of York and Oxford, along with lecture and seminar audiences at Harvard, Cambridge, Birkbeck, and Pittsburgh, asked questions that pushed me to rethink what I was trying to say. At the University of Chicago Press, I am indebted to Alan Thomas for his belief in the idea, to the two anonymous readers for their heartening and searching reports, and to Steve LaRue, Susan Karani, and Randy Petilos for guiding me through the final stages.

This book started life some years ago as a speculative essay, and I'm thankful to Hugh Haughton for responding to that piece with such enthusiasm and imagination. Don Bialostosky, Daniel Karlin, Angela Leighton, Seamus Perry, and Peter Robinson read material and provided valuable feedback on my early thinking. Toward the end, I benefitted a lot from the sharp-eyed comments of Rebecca Bevis, David Dwan, Kathryn Murphy, and Robert Stagg on various draft chapters. Several others gave advice and support along the way: Ruth Abbott, Laura Ashe, Derek Attridge, Colin Burrow, Matthew Campbell, James Castell, John Creaser, David Fairer, Rachel Falconer, Marilyn Gaull, Julian Gewirtz, Stephen Gill, Michael Hawcroft, Jean Holloway, Alex Houen, Hermione Lee, John Lennard, Maureen McLane, Michael O'Neill, Simon Palfrey, Adam Piette, Claude Rawson, Spencer Reece, Daniel Robinson, David Russell, Erica Sheen, Fiona Stafford, Peter Swaab, David Francis Taylor, Bart van Es, Marcus Waithe, and Michael Wood.

Oliver Clarkson, Barbara Everett, Patrick Mackie, Adam Phillips, Jenny Uglow, and James Williams made a big difference. Each of them generously read a draft of the whole manuscript with great care and insight, and I'm very grateful for their thoughts and suggestions.

I'd especially like to thank James Longenbach and Adam Phillips; their writing, conversation, and friendship have been vital.

This book is dedicated to Rebecca, who makes everything possible—and to Noah and Rosa, who keep offering me new meanings of fun.

M. B.

Notes

A Note on Citations and Abbreviations

Unless stated otherwise, quotations from frequently cited works are from the editions listed below (writings are by Wordsworth unless otherwise indicated). For quotations from shorter poems, I give page number only at the first citation. With the exception of *Peter Bell* and *Benjamin the Waggoner* (for which page numbers will be used), quotations from longer poems include line and/or book numbers for every citation. Quotations from *The Borderers* give act, scene, and line numbers.

BL Coleridge, Samuel Taylor. *Biographia Literaria, or Biographical Sketches of My Literary Life and Opinions.* Edited by James Engell and Walter Jackson Bate. 2 vols. Princeton, NJ: Princeton University Press, 1984.

Bord *The Borderers.* Edited by Robert Osborn. Ithaca, NY: Cornell University Press, 1982.

BW *Benjamin the Waggoner.* Edited by Paul F. Betz. Ithaca, NY: Cornell University Press, 1981.

CH Woof, Robert, ed. *William Wordsworth: The Critical Heritage.* London: Routledge and Kegan Paul, 2001.

CLC Coleridge, Samuel Taylor. *The Collected Letters of Samuel Taylor Coleridge.* Edited by Earl Leslie Griggs. 6 vols. Oxford: Clarendon, 1956–71.

CN Coleridge, Samuel Taylor. *The Notebooks of Samuel Taylor Coleridge.* Edited by Kathleen Coburn and Merton Christensen. 4 vols. Princeton, NJ: Princeton University Press, 1957–90.

CO *The Critical Opinions of William Wordsworth.* Edited by Markham L. Peacock. New York: Octagon, 1969.

CP Coleridge, Samuel Taylor. *Samuel Taylor Coleridge: The Complete Poems.* Edited by William Keach. London: Penguin, 2004.

DS *Descriptive Sketches.* Edited by Eric Birdsall and Paul M. Zall. Ithaca, NY: Cornell University Press, 1984.

EPF *Early Poems and Fragments, 1785–1797.* Edited by Carol Landon and Jared Curtis. Ithaca, NY: Cornell University Press, 1997.

EW *An Evening Walk.* Edited by James Averill. Ithaca, NY: Cornell University Press, 1984.

EY Wordsworth, William, and Dorothy Wordsworth. *The Letters of William and Dorothy Wordsworth.* Vol. 1, *The Early Years, 1787–1805.* Edited by Ernest de Selincourt. 2nd ed. edited by Chester L. Shaver. Oxford: Clarendon, 1967.

Exc *The Excursion.* Edited by Sally Bushell, James Butler, and Michael C. Jaye. Ithaca, NY: Cornell University Press, 2007).

FN *The Fenwick Notes of William Wordsworth.* Edited by Jared Curtis. London: Bristol Classical Press, 1993.

HG *Home at Grasmere: Part First, Book First, of The Recluse.* Edited by Beth Darlington. Ithaca, NY: Cornell University Press, 1977.

HW Hazlitt, William. *The Complete Works of William Hazlitt.* Edited by P. P. Howe. 21 vols. London: Dent, 1930–34.

JDW Wordsworth, Dorothy. *Journals of Dorothy Wordsworth.* Edited by Ernest de Selincourt. 2 vols. London: Macmillan, 1952.

LB *Lyrical Ballads, and Other Poems, 1797–1800.* Edited by James Butler and Karen Green. Ithaca, NY: Cornell University Press, 1992.

LL Lamb, Charles, and Mary Ann Lamb. *The Letters of Charles and Mary Lamb.* Edited by Edwin W. Marrs. 3 vols. Ithaca, NY: Cornell University Press, 1975–78.

LP *Last Poems, 1821–1850.* Edited by Jared Curtis, Apryl Lea Denny-Ferris, and Jillian Heydt-Stevenson. Ithaca, NY: Cornell University Press, 1999.

LS Wordsworth, William, and Dorothy Wordsworth. *The Letters of William and Dorothy Wordsworth: A Supplement of New Letters.* Edited by Alan G. Hill. Oxford: Clarendon, 1993.

LW Lamb, Charles, and Mary Lamb. *The Works of Charles and Mary Lamb.* Edited by E. V. Lucas. 7 vols. London: Methuen, 1903–5.

LY Wordsworth, William, and Dorothy Wordsworth. *The Letters of William and Dorothy Wordsworth: The Later Years.* Edited by Ernest de Selincourt. 2nd ed. edited by Alan G. Hill. 4 vols. Oxford: Clarendon, 1978–88.

MY Wordsworth, William, and Dorothy Wordsworth. *The Letters of William and Dorothy Wordsworth: The Middle Years.* Edited by Ernest de Selincourt. 2nd ed. edited by Mary Moorman and Alan G. Hill. 2 vols. Oxford: Clarendon, 1969–70.

OED *Oxford English Dictionary.* http://www.oed.com.

PB *Peter Bell.* Edited by John E. Jordan. Ithaca, NY: Cornell University Press, 1985.

P2V *Poems, in Two Volumes, and Other Poems, 1800–1807.* Edited by Jared Curtis. Ithaca, NY: Cornell University Press, 1983.

PrW *The Prose Works of William Wordsworth.* Edited by W. J. B. Owen and Jane Worthington Smyser. 3 vols. Oxford: Clarendon, 1974.

RCP *The Ruined Cottage and The Pedlar.* Edited by James Butler. Ithaca, NY: Cornell University Press, 1979.

SP *Shorter Poems, 1807–1820.* Edited by Carl H. Ketcham. Ithaca, NY: Cornell University Press, 1989.

SPP *The Salisbury Plain Poems.* Edited by Stephen Gill. Ithaca, NY: Cornell University Press, 1975.

SSIP *Sonnet Series and Itinerary Poems, 1819–1850.* Edited by Geoffrey Jackson. Ithaca, NY: Cornell University Press, 2004.

TCV *Translations of Chaucer and Virgil.* Edited by Bruce E. Graver. Ithaca, NY: Cornell University Press, 1998.

Tuft *The Tuft of Primroses, with Other Late Poems for The Recluse.* Edited by Joseph F. Kishel. Ithaca, NY: Cornell University Press, 1986.

WD *The White Doe of Rylstone, or The Fate of the Nortons.* Edited by Kristine Dugas. Ithaca, NY: Cornell University Press, 1988.

1799 *The Prelude, 1798–1799.* Edited by Stephen Parrish. Ithaca, NY: Cornell University Press, 1977.

1805 *The Thirteen-Book Prelude.* Edited by Mark L. Reed. 2 vols. Ithaca, NY: Cornell University Press, 1991. Citations are to the reading text in vol. 1 unless otherwise indicated.

1850 *The Fourteen-Book Prelude.* Edited by W. J. B. Owen. Ithaca, NY: Cornell University Press, 1985.

Facing Him

1. *LB*, 238.

2. Cited by H. D. Rawnsley, in "Reminiscences of Wordsworth among the Peasantry of Westmoreland," in *Wordsworth*, ed. Peter Swaab, Lives of the Great Romantics by Their Contemporaries 3 (London: Pickering and Chatto, 1996), 451.

3. Walter Bagehot, cited in *Tennyson: The Critical Heritage*, ed. John Jump (London: Routledge and Kegan Paul, 1967), 237.

4. William Hazlitt, "My First Acquaintance with Poets," *HW*, 17:118.

5. Hazlitt, "Mr Wordsworth," *HW*, 9:91.

6. Thomas Carlyle, cited in Swaab, *Wordsworth*, 414.

7. *LB*, 212.

8. *P2V*, 529.

9. *P2V*, 530.

10. Henry James, preface to *The Golden Bowl*, ed. Ruth Yeazell (London: Penguin, 2009), 19.

11. *LB*, 49; *P2V*, 65; *1805*, I. 389–90.

12. *LB*, 739; *P2V*, 527.

13. For a study of the communal and sociopolitical dimensions of pleasure, see Rowan Boyson, *Wordsworth and The Enlightenment Idea of Pleasure* (Cambridge: Cambridge University Press, 2012).

14. *P2V*, 229–30.

15. *P2V*, 233. See also Simon Jarvis, *Wordsworth's Philosophic Song* (Cambridge: Cambridge University Press, 2009), who writes of "a wish which animates the whole authorship: for an unconscious reciprocity of excess" (106).

16. James Elkins, "What Is a Face?," in *The Object Stares Back: On The Nature of Seeing* (New York: Harcourt Brace, 1997), 182, 192–93.

17. *HW*, 17:118.

18. *PB*, 68.

19. Percy Bysshe Shelley, *Peter Bell the Third*, in *The Major Works*, ed. Michael O'Neill (Oxford: Oxford University Press, 2003), 433.

20. *LB*, lines 225–31.

21. *PB*, 90.

22. On Wordsworth's negatives, his "dark comedy," and moments of "triumph in comic

timing," see Oliver Clarkson's excellent essay, "Wordsworth's Negative Way," *Essays in Criticism* 67, no. 2 (April 2017): 116–35.

23. *PB*, 124.

24. Arthur Schopenhauer, *The World as Will and Idea*, cited in *The Philosophy of Laughter and Humor*, ed. John Morreall (New York: State University of New York Press, 1987), 62.

25. *1805*, IV. 58–9.

26. Thomas De Quincey, "On Wordsworth's Poetry," reprinted in in *Romantic Critical Essays*, ed. David Bromwich (Cambridge: Cambridge University Press, 1978), 155.

27. Thomas De Quincey, "John Paul Frederick Richter," *London Magazine* 4, no. 24 (December 1821): 608.

28. *SSIP*, 584.

29. *P2V*, 582.

30. *P2V*, 191.

31. *LB*, 539.

32. Basil Montagu, *Thoughts on Laughter* (London: William Pickford, 1830), 57.

33. In have in mind something akin to Anne Boyer's approach to the matter: "There are faces which, like avant-garde literature, must at once create their own texts and their own theories of reading them." Such faces, she adds, "do not reveal the person but rather the conditions in which all things are the opposite of what they appear to be." See "Erotology III: Categories of Desires for Faces," in *A Handbook of Disappointed Fate* (New York: Ugly Duckling Presse, 2018), 93–96.

34. See Stanley Jones, "B. R. Haydon on Some Contemporaries: A New Letter," *Review of English Studies* 26, no. 102 (May 1975): 189. See also Sara Hutchinson's account of the difficulties one artist had when trying to paint Wordsworth's portrait in 1817: "Mr Carruthers has nearly finished one picture of Wm—but he is not satisfied himself . . . this was not the Artist's fault for Wm himself sate, as Joanna told him, in 'a *perpetual smirk*,'" cited in *Wordsworth: A Life in Letters*, ed. Juliet Barker (London: Penguin, 2007), 132.

35. Benjamin Haydon, cited in *William Wordsworth: Interviews and Recollections*, ed. Harold Orel (Basingstoke: Palgrave Macmillan, 2005), 149–50.

36. *1805*, VIII. 784.

37. *LP*, 222.

38. *HW*, 9:90–1.

39. *CH*, 58.

40. David Ferry, *The Limits of Mortality: An Essay on Wordsworth's Major Poems* (Middletown, CT: Wesleyan University Press, 1959), 98.

41. Donald Davie, "Dionysus in *Lyrical Ballads*," in *Wordsworth's Mind and Art*, ed. A. W. Thomson (Edinburgh: Oliver and Boyd, 1969), 120.

42. Christopher Ricks, "In Conversation," interview by Cal Revely-Calder and Anne M. Stillman, *Cambridge Humanities Review*, no. 15 (Easter 2017): 36. Elsewhere, Ricks notes a "severe variety of wit" in *The Prelude*; see *The Force of Poetry* (Oxford: Oxford University Press, 1995), 108.

43. Early explorations include R. F. Storch, "Wordsworth's Experimental Ballads: The Radical Uses of Intelligence and Comedy," *Studies in English Literature* 11, no. 4 (Autumn 1971): 621–39, and John Jordan, "Wordsworth's Humor," *PMLA* 73, no. 1 (March 1958): 81–93. See also David Perkins, *Wordsworth and the Poetry of Sincerity* (Cambridge, MA: Belknap Press of Harvard University Press, 1964), 178–86. Elsewhere, critics have spoken in passing of the poet's "habitual

irony" and his "vein of parody" (Richard Gravil, *Wordsworth's Bardic Vocation, 1782–42* [Basingstoke: Palgrave Macmillan, 2003]), 93–99); his glimmers of "poker-faced fun" (Michael O'Neill, *Romanticism and the Self-Conscious Poem* [Oxford: Clarendon, 1997], 36); his abilities as "a great comic poet" (Peter Swaab, "'Wonder' as a Complex Word," *Romanticism* 22, no. 1 [October 2012]: 279); and his inclination toward "half-parody of poetic mannerism" (J. H. Prynne, *The Solitary Reaper and Others* [Cambridge: Barque Press, 2007], 72.) I engage with related observations from other commentators throughout this book, and I should also note here my debt to John F. Danby's superb study *The Simple Wordsworth: Studies in the Poems 1797–1807* (London: Routledge and Kegan Paul, 1960), in which he argues that "fun never falls outside Wordsworth's major convictions concerning what being human entails" (53).

44. Basil Bunting, cited in *The Star You Steer By: Basil Bunting and British Modernism*, ed. James McGonigal and Richard Price (Amsterdam: Rodopi, 2000), 256.

45. M. H. Abrams, "Two Roads to Wordsworth," in *Wordsworth: A Collection of Critical Essays* (Englewood Cliffs, NJ: Prentice-Hall, 1972), 5; I. A. Richards, *Coleridge and Imagination* (London: Routledge and Kegan Paul, 1962), 192. More recently, in the last of his Oxford Lectures on Poetry, Geoffrey Hill wondered what revelations might occur "once we've finished laughing ourselves egotistically naked" over some lines in "Simon Lee" ("I Know Thee Not, Old Man, Fall to Thy Prayers," May 5, 2015, http://www.english.ox.ac.uk/professor-sir-geoffrey-hill-lectures).

46. *CLC*, 2:1013.

47. *1805*, VII. 463–66.

48. *1805*, VII. 496–500.

49. *1805*, VII. 672–73.

50. *CN*, 1:1546.

51. *BL*, 2:121–22.

52. *PrW*, 2:346.

53. "Happiness Equally Dispensed to the High and Low," *Sporting Magazine* 46 (April 1815): 12.

54. *CH*, 154, 158, 186.

55. Behind such strictures lies an anxiety about loss of decorum and deference; the vulgar is not only an ungenteel display of manners and behavior but a public danger, a republican threat, a smack of the people's uprising. Jeffrey's public criticisms—and the politics they enshrine—are infamous, but less well known are his comments in private. In 1799 he admitted he was enchanted by *Lyrical Ballads*, and a few years later he made an intriguing confession to Francis Horner: "I am almost as great an admirer as Sharpe. The only difference is, that I have a sort of consciousness that admirers are ridiculous, and therefore I laugh at almost everything I admire, or at least let people laugh at it without contradiction. You must be in earnest when you approve, and have yet to learn that everything has a respectable, and a deridable, aspect" (*CH*, 128).

56. See David Bromwich, "How Moral Is Taste?," in *Skeptical Music: Essays on Modern Poetry* (Chicago: University of Chicago Press, 2001), and *The Intellectual Life of Edmund Burke: From the Sublime and Beautiful to American Independence* (Cambridge, MA: Harvard University Press, 2014), 59–96.

57. Edmund Burke, *A Philosophical Enquiry into the Origin of Our Ideas of the Sublime and Beautiful*, ed. Paul Guyer (Oxford: Oxford University Press, 2015), 40. As Bromwich notes, this claim comes as the summation of "the most controversial passage on aesthetics in the eighteenth century" (*Intellectual Life*, 68).

58. See Ronald Paulson, *Don Quixote in England: The Aesthetics of Laughter* (Baltimore: Johns Hopkins University Press, 1998).

59. "New Books and Pamphlets; With Remarks," *Gentleman's Magazine* 37 (1767): 75.

60. Samuel Taylor Coleridge, *Table Talk*, ed. Carl Woodring, 2 vols. (Princeton, NJ: Princeton University Press, 1990), 1:428.

61. Friedrich Schiller, "On Naïve and Sentimental Poetry," in *German Aesthetic and Literary Criticism*, ed. and trans. H. B. Nisbet (Cambridge: Cambridge University Press, 2009), 177–233.

62. *PrW*, 1:103.

63. *1805*, II. 381–85.

64. *1805*, V. 567–68.

65. *LY*, 2:454.

66. *LY*, 4:8.

67. *LB*, 738.

68. *CO*, 169.

69. Max Eastman, *Enjoyment of Laughter* (1936; repr., New Brunswick, NJ: Transaction, 2009), 41.

70. *MY*, 1:155.

71. *LY*, 2:324.

72. Elizabeth Barrett, "William Wordsworth's *Poems*," *Athenaeum*, August 27, 1842, 757; Robert Frost, cited in John Evangelist Walsh, *Into My Own: The English Years of Robert Frost* (New York: Grove, 1998), 236–37.

73. Edward Quillinan diary (hereafter Quillinan diary), ref. WLMS 13/3/1, entry for September 1, 1836, Jerwood Centre, Grasmere.

74. I'm reminded of a comment by John Kerrigan in another context: "These protestations would seem hollow did they not so honestly betray the fascination of what they reject," in "Wordsworth and the Sonnet: Building, Dwelling, Thinking," *Essays in Criticism* 35, no. 1 (January 1985): 46.

75. Quillinan diary, entry for September 3–4, 1836.

76. *PrW*, 3:372.

77. *EY*, 55–57.

78. See Chester and Alice C. Shaver, *Wordsworth's Library: A Catalogue* (New York: Garland, 1979), 11, 89, 164, 173, 204, 209, 277.

79. *CLC*, 2:1017.

80. DCMS 26, item no. 17, Jerwood Centre, Grasmere.

81. Robert Pinsky, *Landor's Poetry* (Chicago: University of Chicago Press, 1968), 114.

82. Geoffrey Hartman, *Wordsworth's Poetry 1787–1814* (New Haven, CT: Yale University Press, 1964), 141, 150.

83. David Bromwich, *Disowned by Memory: Wordsworth's Poetry of the 1790s* (Chicago: University of Chicago Press, 2000), 126; introduction to *Selected Poetry of William Wordsworth*, ed. Mark Van Doren (New York: Modern Library, 2002), xix; *Moral Imagination* (Princeton, NJ: Princeton University Press, 2014), 8–13.

84. Maureen McLane, "Wordsworth now," in *William Wordsworth in Context*, ed. Andrew Bennett (Cambridge: Cambridge University Press, 2018), 78.

85. J. K. Stephen, "A Sonnet," quoted in *Parodies: An Anthology from Chaucer to Beerbohm*, ed. Dwight MacDonald (London: Random House, 1960), 75.

86. See, for example, W. W. Robson, "Ordinary Sights and Visionary Gleams," *Times Literary Supplement*, August 1, 1980, 864, and Harold Bloom's claim that "Wordsworth's Copernican

revolution in poetry is marked by the evanescence of any subject but subjectivity, the loss of what a poem is 'about'"; see Harold Bloom, "The Internalization of Quest-Romance," in *Romanticism and Consciousness: Essays in Criticism*, ed. Harold Bloom (New York: W. W. Norton, 1970), 8.

87. Friedrich Nietzsche, *The Gay Science* (1887), trans. Walter Kaufmann (New York: Vintage, 1974), 20.

88. Luigi Pirandello, *On Humor*, trans. Antonio Illiano and Daniel P. Testa (Chapel Hill: University of North Carolina Press, 1960), 94.

89. John Bayley, "Family Man: William Wordsworth," in *The Power of Delight: Essays 1962–2002* (New York: W. W. Norton, 2005), 125.

90. *MY*, 2:547.

91. *BW*, 44. Because I refer at various points to both the manuscript and the first published edition (1819), for all quotations for *Benjamin the Waggoner*, I give page numbers from the Cornell edition (*BW*).

92. *BW*, 48.

93. *BW*, 48.

94. *BW*, 74.

95. *BW*, 78.

96. *BW*, 74.

97. *BW*, 108–10.

98. The earliest fragments of *Benjamin the Waggoner* date from around May to June 1802 (see *BW*, 5–11). This was also the period in which Wordsworth had decided to meet Annette Vallon and his daughter Caroline in Calais before marrying Mary later that year.

99. *1805*, XI. 336–38.

100. *BW*, 72.

101. *BW*, 52.

102. *BW*, 117.

103. *BW*, 145.

104. *EPF*, 699.

105. *Bord*, 2.3.227–28.

106. Hugh Kenner, "The Man of Sense as Buster Keaton," *Virginia Quarterly Review* 41, no. 1 (Winter 1965): 77.

107. Kenner, "Man of Sense," 89–90.

108. *P2V*, 123. As Wordsworth notes of the line elsewhere, the bird is imagined as "participating of a still and quiet satisfaction, like that which may be supposed inseparable from the continuous process of incubation" (*PrW*, 3:32).

109. *P2V*, 205.

Laughing—Echoes

1. *1805*, I. 64–65.

2. James Beattie, *Essays on Poetry and Music, as they Affect the Mind; On Laughter and Ludicrous Composition; On the Usefulness of Classical learning* (London: Dilly, 1779), 403. The idea that the laugher should not be an ungentlemanly threat to polite society was also implicit in discussions about the ethics of comedy; Wordsworth had, for example, encountered Hugh Blair's insistence that the mode be conducive to "the progress of refinement" and "promote attention to the proper decorums of social balance"; see Hugh Blair, *Lectures on Rhetoric and Belles Lettres* (London: Strahan & Cadell, 1783), 2:550, 528.

3. *1805*, V. 306–7.

4. *DS*, 295; *LP*, 366.

5. *P2V*, 207–8.

6. *CH*, 221.

7. See Stephen Halliwell, *Greek Laughter: A Study of Cultural Psychology from Homer to Early Christianity* (Cambridge: Cambridge University Press, 2008), 13.

8. *P2V*, 155; *EPF*, 660.

9. Cited in Henry Crabb Robinson's diary, in *Wordsworth*, ed. Peter Swaab, Lives of the Great Romantics by Their Contemporaries 3 (London: Pickering and Chatto, 1996), 310.

10. Stevie Smith, *Me Again: The Uncollected Writings of Stevie Smith* (London: Virago, 1983), 115.

11. Water Pater, "Wordsworth," from *Appreciations* (1889), in *Selected Writings of Walter Pater*, ed. Harold Bloom (New York: Columbia University Press, 1974), 137.

12. *JDW*, 1:131–32.

13. Samuel Johnson, "Good Humour," in *The Speaker*, ed. William Enfield (London: Johnson, 1774), 70.

14. Samuel Johnson, *The Idler*, no. 64 (1759), in *The Yale Edition of the Works of Samuel Johnson*, ed. W. J. Bate, J. M. Bullitt, and L. F. Powell (New Haven, CT: Yale University Press, 1963), 2:199.

15. Samuel Johnson, *The Lives of The Poets: A Selection*, ed. Roger Lonsdale and John Mullan (Oxford: Oxford World's Classics, 2009), 220–21.

16. See *PrW*, 3:79.

17. DCMS 26, item no. 17, Jerwood Centre, Grasmere.

18. *CH*, 251.

19. *LY*, 4:396.

20. *LB*, 76.

21. *BL*, 2:121–22.

22. See Marjorie Levinson, "Of Being Numerous: Counting and Matching in Wordsworth's Poetry," *Studies in Romanticism* 49, no. 4 (Winter 2010): 636.

23. Geoffrey Willans and Ronald Searle, *Molesworth* (London: Penguin, 2000), 34.

24. Ovid, *Metamorphoses*, trans. Mary M. Inners (London: Penguin, 1955), 84–86.

25. *MY*, 1:194.

26. Ovid, *Metamorphoses*, 84.

27. For Wordsworth's early passion for Ovid's *Metamorphoses*, see *SP*, 544. In his personal copy of Robert Anderson's *The Works of the British Poets*, 14 vols. (Edinburgh: Bradfute and Mundell, 1792–1807), Wordsworth marked up this couplet from *The Franklin's Tale* for special notice: "And die he must, he said, as did Ecco / For Narcissus that dorst not tell hire wo" (1:101); ref. 1995.R171, Jerwood Centre, Grasmere. Elsewhere, he is entranced by the cuckoo, "invisible as Echo's self" (*SSIP*, 766).

28. Leonard Barkan, *Gods Made Flesh: Metamorphosis and the Pursuit of Paganism* (New Haven, CT: Yale University Press, 1990), 49.

29. Christopher Ricks, *Allusion to the Poets* (Oxford: Oxford University Press, 2002), 272.

30. *EY*, 627.

31. *JDW*, 1:131.

32. Ovid, *Metamorphoses*, 87.

33. *Bord*, 4.2.53–55.

34. *1805*, IV. 333.

35. Thomas De Quincey, *Confessions of an Opium-Eater and Other Writings*, ed. Robert Morrison (Oxford: Oxford University Press, 2013), 135–36.

36. Elizabeth Bishop, *Poems, Prose, and Letters* (New York: Library of America, 2008), 205; John Ashbery, "The Big Cloud," in *April Galleons* (New York: Farrar, Straus and Giroux, 1984), 58–59.

37. *SSIP*, 58.

38. *CH*, 793.

39. John Hollander, *The Figure of Echo: A Mode of Allusion in Milton and After* (Berkeley: University of California Press, 1981), 26.

40. *CLC*, 2:844.

41. *JDW*, 1:226.

42. Robert Rose, "A Lyrical Ballad,"' in *Parodies of the Romantic Age*, ed. Graeme Stones and John Strachan, 5 vols. (London: Pickering and Chatto, 1998), 2:67.

43. Wordsworth, cited in *Letters of John Wordsworth*, ed. Carl Ketcham (Ithaca, NY: Cornell University Press, 1969), 96.

44. On Wordsworth as "in some incongruous sense, his own best parodist," see Nicola Trott, "Wordsworth and the Parodic School of Criticism," in *The Satiric Eye: Forms of Satire in the Romantic Period*, ed. Steven E. Jones (New York: Palgrave Macmillan, 2003), 72. For an overview of more recent literature, see Brian R. Bates, *Wordsworth's Poetic Collections, Supplementary Writing, and Parodic Reception* (London: Routledge, 2012), 14–15.

45. James Williams, "Echo and Narcissus in Victorian Poetry," *Essays in Criticism* 69, no. 2 (April 2019).

46. *LB*, 244.

47. *LL*, 1:265.

48. *BL*, 2:102.

49. See, for example, *Odyssey* (IX. 391–96) and *Aeneid* (III. 432; VII. 563). In Thomas Love Peacock's *Crotchet Castle*, Harry "burst into a flood of tears, and blubbered till the rocks re-echoed"; *Crotchet Castle*, ed. Freya Johnston and Matthew Bevis (Cambridge: Cambridge University Press, 2017), 117, 295n4.

50. *LB*, 246.

51. Hollander, *Figure of Echo*, 8.

52. Denise Riley, *Selected Poems* (London: Reality Street Editions, 2000), 95.

53. It is telling that Wordsworth should choose this precise moment to notice—to *admit* to noticing—that she is "fair," as Joanna Hutchinson herself appreciated when discussing various poems in *Lyrical Ballads*. Noting that Wordsworth was a "canny" man, she asked, "what do you think of the *fair* Joanna—it is thought a very capital one—but I like any of them as well." Cited in Thomas H. Schmid, "Strained Tenderness: Wordsworth, Joanna Hutchinson, and the Anxiety of Sister Resistance in 'To Joanna,'" *Studies in Romanticism* 40, no. 3 (Fall 2001): 423. Elsewhere in her correspondence, she talks of jokes that "rais'd a laugh" at Wordsworth, and Schmid's description of her makes her sound like a modern-day version of Echo: "From a nineteen-year-old girl with a propensity for fun and laughter, Joanna became early on a self-reliant woman . . . fated never to marry" (419–20).

54. *1805*, V. 310–18.

55. Henri Bergson, *Laughter* (1900), in *Comedy*, ed. Wylie Sypher (Baltimore: Johns Hopkins University Press, 1980), 64.

56. Bergson, *Laughter*, 64.

57. *LB*, 398.

58. René Girard's view on why "the inclusion of a laughing spectator is a major procédé of comic writers" is relevant here and seems to me to be in tune with Wordsworthian provocations: "As this spectator laughs, he falls into the very trap which has already swallowed his victim and he becomes laughable in his turn. The loss of autonomy and self-possession which is present in all forms of comedy must be present, somehow, in laughter itself. Laughter, in other words, must never be very different from whatever causes it. . . . As an assertion of superiority, in the more intellectual forms of the comic, laughter really means a denial of reciprocity. . . . As I laugh, I mimic and repeat the whole process I have been watching, both the attempt to establish mastery and its failure, both the dizzy feeling of superiority and the loss of balance which comes with the dizziness, the disintegration of self-control which is always creeping upon us in the wild reactions and uncontrolled convulsions of laughter itself." René Girard, "Perilous Balance: A Comic Hypothesis," *MLN* 87, no. 7 (December 1972): 819–20

59. Clarice Lispector, "The Smallest Woman in the World," trans. Elizabeth Bishop, in Bishop, *Poems, Prose, and Letters*, 306–7.

60. Adam Phillips, *Missing Out: In Praise of the Unlived Life* (London: Penguin, 2013), 47.

61. *LB*, 140.

62. John Milton, *Paradise Lost*, ed. Alastair Fowler (London: Longman, 1998), XII. 57–61.

63. Wordsworth, cited in *The Romantics on Milton: Formal Essays and Critical Asides*, ed. Joseph Anthony Wittreich (Cleveland: Case Western Reserve University Press, 1970), 109.

64. Ovid, *Metamorphoses*, 87.

Laughing—Fits

1. *LY*, 1:246.

2. *Tuft*, lines 181–84.

3. *SSIP*, 364.

4. Euripides, *Bakkhai*, trans. Anne Carson (New York: New Directions, 2017), 3.

5. *CP*, 165.

6. *CLC*, 2:521.

7. *EPF*, 534–35.

8. *EPF*, 501.

9. *EPF*, lines 150–53.

10. *EPF*, 843.

11. David Hartley, *Observations on Man*, cited in *The Philosophy of Laughter and Humor*, ed. John Morreall (New York: State University of New York Press, 1987), 41–4.

12. See Duncan Wu, *Wordsworth's Reading*, 2 vols. (Cambridge: Cambridge University Press, 1993), 1:101. Beddoes's translation of Kant appeared in the May issue of 1796.

13. Immanuel Kant, *Critique of the Power of Judgment*, ed. Paul Guyer, trans. Paul Guyer and Eric Matthews (Cambridge: Cambridge University Press, 2000), 208–11.

14. Wu, *Wordsworth's Reading*, 1:44.

15. *EY*, 199.

16. Erasmus Darwin, *Zoonomia; or The Laws of Organic Life*, 2 vols. (London: Johnson, 1794–96), 1:426, 2:325.

17. *CLC*, 1:647.

18. See Coleridge, *Marginalia*, ed. George Whalley, 6 vols. (Princeton, NJ: Princeton University Press, 1980–2001), 2:191: "It is the Law of Pleasure to pass into Pain. . . . Laughter is the nascent Convulsion by which Nature brings off the train of sensations before they reach a pain-

ful state. Hence it is, that the suppression of Laughter is always painful, and sometimes even dangerous."

19. *PrW*, 1:146–47.

20. *PrW*, 1:146–48.

21. Darwin, *Zoonomia*, 1: 426, 429.

22. Thomas Beddoes, *Notice of some observations made at the Medical Pneumatic Institution* (Bristol: Biggs and Cottle, 1799), 9.

23. Davy often uses the word *fit*; see *Researches, Chemical and Philosophical, Chiefly Concerning Nitrous Oxide* (London: Johnson, 1800), 475, 513, 527, 540. See also Beddoes, *Notice of some observations*, 13, 17, 20.

24. *BL*, 2:65.

25. *PrW*, 1:148.

26. See Susan Wolfson, "Romanticism and the Measures of Meter," *Eighteenth-Century Life*, 16 (November 1992): 221–46, and Brennan O'Donnell, *The Passion of Meter: A Study of Wordsworth's Metrical Art* (Kent, OH: Kent University Press, 1995).

27. *PrW*, 3:29–30.

28. *EPF*, lines 150–51.

29. Tendering a case study of a man with "rampant high spirits," Coleridge asked Davy, "Does it not seem here, as if Nature herself had elaborated the nitrous oxyde out of the common Air?" A week later he spoke of his son: "Hartley is a spirit that dances on an aspin leaf—the air, which yonder sallow-faced & yawning Tourist is breathing, is to my Babe a perpetual Nitrous Oxyde. Never was more joyous creature born" (*CLC*, 1:605–6, 612).

30. Duncan Wu gives a suggested date of reading as "26 Jan. 1801 onwards"' (*Wordsworth's Reading*, 2:71), although it could have been earlier. Coleridge's involvement with Davy is likely to have led to discussion about the scientist's ideas from late 1799.

31. Davy, *Researches*, 460, 488.

32. Davy, *Researches*, 496, 501, 505.

33. "The Pneumatic Revellers: An Eclogue," *Anti-Jacobin Review and Magazine* 6 (May 1800): 113.

34. Davy, *Researches*, 489, 524.

35. Davy, *Researches*, 494–95.

36. *PrW*, 1:126. On links between Davy and Wordsworth, see Noel Jackson, *Science and Sensation in Romantic Poetry* (Cambridge: Cambridge University Press, 2008), 44–45; Maurice Hindle, "Humphry Davy and William Wordsworth: A Mutual Influence," *Romanticism* 18, no. 1 (2012): 16–29.

37. *PrW*, 1:152.

38. Davy, *Researches*, 489–92.

39. *LB*, 161–62.

40. *CH*, 226–28.

41. *LB*, 162.

42. Milton, *Paradise Lost*, X. 626–27.

43. Thomas Percy, *Reliques of Ancient English Poetry*, 3 vols., 4th ed. (London: Nicols, 1794), 2:184–87. For Wordsworth's reading of *Reliques*, see Mark L. Reed, *Wordsworth: Chronology of the Early Years 1770–1799* (Cambridge, MA: Harvard University Press, 1967), 253, 257.

44. Paul Fry, *Wordsworth and the Poetry of What We Are* (New Haven, CT: Yale University Press, 2008), 97, 95.

45. *LP*, 363.

46. *BW*, 46.

47. See James Williams, "The Jokes in the Machine: Comic Verse," in *The Oxford Handbook of Victorian Poetry*, ed. Matthew Bevis (Oxford: Oxford University Press, 2013), 817–33.

48. Abraham Cowley, "On Liberty," in *The Works of Abraham Cowley* (London: Herringman, 1700), 77.

49. *LS*, 109–10.

50. Percy, *Reliques*, 3:178–79.

51. *CP*, 121.

52. *CLC*, 1:490.

53. Thomas De Quincey, *Recollections of the Lakes and the Lake Poets*, ed. David Wright (London: Penguin, 1978), 163.

54. John Ashbery, "Retro," in *Notes from the Air* (New York: Ecco, 2008), 339.

55. I am quoting from Beddoes's translation in *Monthly Magazine*, May 1796, 267.

56. *CH*, 462.

57. *MY*, 2:238.

58. *CN*, 1:1533.

59. See *P2V*, 530.

60. See Winifred Milius Lubell, *The Metamorphosis of Baubo: Myths of Women's Sexual Energy* (Nashville, TN: Vanderbilt University Press, 1994), and Catherine Conybeare, *The Laughter of Sarah: Biblical Exegesis, Feminist Theory, and the Concept of Delight* (Basingstoke: Palgrave Macmillan, 2013). Wordsworth's *Book of Proverbs* (ref. 2003.82, Jerwood Centre, Grasmere) includes the following: "A maid that laughs is half taken" (16).

61. See Richard Holmes, *The Age of Wonder* (London: HarperCollins, 2009), 273.

62. Gavin Budge, "Darwin and the Poetics of Wordsworth: 'Excitement without the Application of Gross and Violent Stimulants,'" *British Journal for Eighteenth-Century Studies* 30, no. 2 (2007): 279–308.

63. The Preface to *Lyrical Ballads* draws attention to "the truth that the power of the human imagination is sufficient to produce such changes even in our physical nature as might almost appear miraculous" (*PrW*, 1:150).

64. Thomas Beddoes, "Essay on the Nature and Prevention of Some of the Disorders Commonly Called Nervous," in *Hygëia, or Essays Moral and Medical on the Causes Affecting the Personal State of Our Middling and Affluent Classes*, 3 vols. (Bristol: Mills, 1802–3), 3:15.

65. On seeing Coleridge having a fit, Charles Lloyd began to have fits "as if in sympathy." See Richard Holmes, *Coleridge: Early Visions* (London: Hodder and Stoughton, 1989), 127.

66. Rachel Hewitt, *A Revolution of Feeling: The Decade That Forged the Modern Mind* (London: Granta, 2017), 364–65.

67. *1805*, V. 310, 318–19.

68. John Banville, *The Book of Evidence* (London: Picador, 2014), 217.

69. *RCP*, 49.

70. *1805*, I. 146–48.

Laughing—Pains

1. *EPF*, 396.

2. *EY*, 236.

3. *MY*, 1:96.

4. *P2V*, 72.

5. *CH*, 219.

6. Hazlitt, "Gravity" (1830), in *New Writings of William Hazlitt*, ed. Duncan Wu, 2 vols. (Oxford: Oxford University Press, 2007), 2:416.

7. *CH*, 771.

8. William Blake, *The Marriage of Heaven and Hell*, in *Blake: The Complete Poems*, ed. W. H. Stevenson (Harlow: Pearson Longman, 2007), 114; Percy Bysshe Shelley, "To A Skylark," in *The Major Works*, ed. Michael O'Neill (Oxford: Oxford University Press, 2003), 466; John Keats, *The Letters of John Keats*, ed. Hyder Edward Rollins, 2 vols. (Cambridge, MA: Harvard University Press, 2002), 2:79.

9. John Keats, "Why did I laugh tonight?," in *Complete Poems*, ed. Jack Stillinger (Cambridge, MA: Harvard University Press, 2003), 243.

10. Immanuel Kant, *Critique of the Power of Judgment*, ed. Paul Guyer, trans. Paul Guyer and Eric Matthews (Cambridge: Cambridge University Press, 2000), 208.

11. See Duncan Wu, ed., *Wordsworth's Poets* (Manchester: Carcanet, 2003), 169, 271.

12. *LY*, 2:237.

13. Catherine Clarkson, quoted in John Worthen, *The Gang: Coleridge, the Hutchinsons, and the Wordsworths in 1802* (New Haven, CT: Yale University Press, 2001), 30.

14. *CP*, 125.

15. Horace Walpole, quoted in *The Idea of Comedy: Essays in Prose and Verse*, ed. W. K. Wimsatt (Englewood Cliffs, NJ: Prentice-Hall, 1969), 193; *CP*, 61.

16. *CP*, 287.

17. *CP*, 252–53.

18. *LB*, 116.

19. *BL*, 1:26–27.

20. Thomas Love Peacock, *Nightmare Abbey*, ed. Nicholas Joukovsky (Cambridge: Cambridge University Press, 2016), 56.

21. Laurence Sterne, *The Letters of Laurence Sterne*, ed. Lewis Perry Curtis (Oxford: Clarendon, 1935), 401.

22. Henry Brooke, *The Fool of Quality*, 3 vols. (Philadelphia: Robert Campbell, 1794), 2:31.

23. *CN*, 1:62, 87.

24. *1805*, VIII. 532.

25. *PrW*, 1:140.

26. *SP*, 243.

27. *SPP*, 139.

28. *LB*, 88.

29. *LB*, lines 171–74.

30. William Shakespeare, *As You Like It*, ed. Juliet Dusinberre (London: Arden, 2004), 4.1.97–99.

31. *LB*, 176.

32. *RCP*, 51.

33. Marianne Moore, *The Poems of Marianne Moore*, ed. Grace Schulman (London: Penguin, 2005), 82.

34. *Bord*, 3.3.14–19.

35. *CH*, 45.

36. *1805*, III. 277–79.

37. All quotations are from Wordsworth's version; *TCV*, 56–60.

38. *CP*, 400.

39. *CH*, 142.

40. *LB*, 163.

41. Geoffrey Hartman, *The Fate of Reading and Other Essays* (Chicago: University of Chicago, 1975), 158–59.

42. Samuel Butler, "Quis Desirderio . . . ?," in *The Humour of Homer and Other Essays*, ed. R. A. Streatfield (London: Fifield, 1913), 99–103.

43. F. W. Bateson, *Wordsworth: A Re-Interpretation* (London: Longman, 1963), 31–32.

44. Mark Jones's comments on "A Slumber did my spirit seal" could be applied to "She dwelt among th' untrodden ways" and to other poems in the collection. He stresses just "how much the poem makes the reader invent. The very ease and subtlety with which we 'half-create' this poem tends to make us oblivious to the extent of our own activity. . . . One cannot read it without making more questionable assumptions than there are lines"; *The Lucy Poems: A Case Study in Literary Knowledge* (University of Toronto Press, 1995), 34.

45. *CLC*, 2:976.

46. *PrW*, 2:63.

47. *PrW*, 2:68, 70–55.

48. *EY*, 236.

49. Richard Lovell Edgeworth and Maria Edgeworth, *Essay on Irish Bulls*, 4th ed. (London: Hunter, 1815), 93.

50. *CLC*, 6:1015; *BL*, 2:136.

51. *BL*, 1:72. Wordsworth's copy of *Biographia Literaria* is at the Jerwood Centre, Grasmere (ref. 1995.R.33).

52. *BL*, 1:72.

53. Mary Shelley, *The Last Man*, 2 vols. (Philadelphia: Carey, Lea and Blanchard, 1833), 1:47.

54. Frances Ferguson, *Wordsworth: Language as Counter Spirit* (New Haven, CT: Yale University Press, 1977), 184.

55. Quintilian, *Institutio oratoria*, 8.6.76. "There is little need to advise me against publishing," Wordsworth wrote to James Tobin in 1798; "it is a thing which I dread as much as death itself. This may serve as an example of the figure by rhetoricians called hyperbole" (*EY*, 211).

56. *PrW*, 2:67–68.

57. See, for example, the Solitary's claim in *The Excursion* that "I entertain / The antiquarian humour" as he goes about commenting on "Pompey's pillar; that I gravely style / My Theban obelisk" (*Exc*, III. 135–38). See also Steven Matthews, *Ceaseless Music: Sounding Wordsworth's* The Prelude (London: Bloomsbury, 2017): "We mustn't, in the earnestness of such decoding of the words . . . blind ourselves to the wittiness also on display, a wittiness that has something to do with that overloading of even such a key passage as this at the gibbet-side with puns precisely about the 'graveness' of the moment. There is a humour in much of this which counters the normal sense of the serious sage" (51–52).

58. James Beattie, *Essays on Poetry and Music, as they Affect the Mind; On Laughter and Ludicrous Composition; On the Usefulness of Classical learning* (London: Dilly, 1779), 336.

59. Henry Crabb Robinson, diary entry (September 10, 1816), cited in *Wordsworth: A Critical Anthology*, ed. Graham McMaster (Harmondsworth: Penguin, 1972), 145.

60. *LP*, 82.

61. See Brennan O'Donnell, *The Passion of Meter: A Study of Wordsworth's Metrical Art* (Kent, OH: Kent University Press, 1995), 152, and 268n35.

62. In early fragments, and in some early poems (*An Evening Walk* and *Descriptive Sketches*),

Wordsworth makes use of the elision "th' un," but, as far as I'm aware, at no other time after those poems—apart from here—does he do this.

63. *LY*, 4:492–93.

64. *1805*, X. 870–71.

65. G. K. Chesterton, "The Optimism of Byron," in *Byron: The Critical Heritage*, ed. Andrew Rutherford (New York: Routledge, 2010), 484.

66. *DS*, 74.

67. Thomas Percy, *Reliques of Ancient English Poetry*, 4th ed. (London: Nicols, 1794), 2:169

68. Percy, *Reliques*, 2:328.

69. Bateson, *Wordsworth*, 33–34.

70. *LP*, 395.

71. *1805*, I. 246–48.

72. J.-B. Pontalis, *Love of Beginnings*, trans. James Greene with Marie-Christine Réguis (London: Free Association, 1993), 164–65.

73. I'm borrowing Ridgeon's words from George Bernard Shaw's *The Doctor's Dilemma* (1906), cited in Michael Holroyd, *Bernard Shaw* (London: Vintage, 1998), 345.

74. *HW*, 9:87.

75. *CH*, 460.

76. Stevie Smith, *Me Again: The Uncollected Writings of Stevie Smith* (London: Virago, 1983), 300.

77. *RCP*, lines 220–21.

Playing—Children

1. *LB*, 647.

2. *CH*, 678, 734, 740.

3. *PrW*, 3:36.

4. *CH*, 308. For a wide-ranging study of the topic, see Jeffrey C. Robinson, *Unfettering Poetry: Fancy in British Romanticism* (New York: Palgrave Macmillan, 2006).

5. *CLC*, 2:812.

6. *P2V*, 203–4.

7. *P2V*, 418.

8. *JDW*, 1:123.

9. *P2V*, 213.

10. Mary Midgeley, "The Game Game," in *Heart and Mind: The Varieties of Moral Experience* (London: Routledge, 1983), 163.

11. *JDW*, 1:123.

12. *P2V*, 113–15. Wordsworth's mother died on March 8, 1778, and was buried on March 11.

13. In one manuscript, Wordsworth wrote "his" wings; the revision heightens the butterfly's unknowability.

14. R. P. Blackmur, "Lord Tennyson's Scissors," in *Form and Value in Modern Poetry* (Garden City, NY: Doubleday, 1952), 370.

15. On play in classical literature, see Stephen Halliwell, *Greek Laughter: A Study of Cultural Psychology from Homer to Early Christianity* (Cambridge: Cambridge University Press, 2008), 19, 21, 38, 289, 349–50.

16. *CO*, 283; *LP*, 208.

17. Horace, *Satires, Epistles and Ars Poetica*, trans. H. Rushton Fairclough (Cambridge, MA: Harvard University Press, 1991), *Satires* 1.9.37, *Epistles* 1.1.59.

18. Horace, *The Odes*, trans. David Ferry (New York: Farrar, Straus and Giroux, 1998), 31, 89.

19. *HW*, 5:2.

20. Percy Bysshe Shelley, *The Major Works*, ed. Michael O'Neill (Oxford: Oxford University Press, 2003), 675.

21. *CN*, 4:4777. On Coleridge's engagement with "play," see John Beer, *Coleridge's Play of Mind* (Oxford: Oxford University Press, 2010).

22. *LP*, 300.

23. *LW*, 2:53.

24. Eric Bentley, *The Life of the Drama* (London: Methuen, 1966), 231.

25. *MY*, 1:286–87.

26. *P2V*, 100.

27. *CLC*, 2:1014.

28. *SP*, 48.

29. Robert Hass, *The Apple Trees at Olema: New and Selected Poems* (Tarset, UK: Bloodaxe, 2011), 112.

30. Elizabeth Barrett, "William Wordsworth's *Poems*," *Athenaeum*, August 27, 1842, 757.

31. *SP*, 118.

32. *1805*, VII. 469–74.

33. *EY*, 250.

34. *P2V*, 97.

35. *CLC*, 1:379.

36. *P2V*, 206.

37. John Worthen, *The Gang: Coleridge, the Hutchinsons, and the Wordsworths in 1802* (New Haven, CT: Yale University Press, 2001), 135

38. *BL*, 2:158–59.

39. *1805*, V. 436–40.

40. Adam Phillips, *Unforbidden Pleasures* (London: Hamish Hamilton, 2015), 153.

41. *LB*, 328.

42. *LB*, 398.

43. *PrW*, 1:336.

44. *P2V*, lines 85–107.

45. *CH*, 1020.

46. *Exc*, VIII. 471.

47. Helen Vendler, "Lionel Trilling and the Immortality Ode," *Salmagundi* 41 (Spring 1978): 75–76.

48. J.-B. Pontalis, *Love of Beginnings*, trans. James Greene with Marie-Christine Réguis (London: Free Association, 1993), 136.

49. See Jared Curtis, *Wordsworth's Experiments with Tradition: The Lyric Poems of 1802* (Ithaca, NY: Cornell University Press, 1971), 167; see also *P2V*, 367.

50. The words are inscribed in Wordsworth's volumes of *The Poetical Works of Samuel Daniel*, 2 vols. (London: Gosling, 1718). The books are housed at the Jerwood Centre, Grasmere (ref. 1995.R.40). For Wordsworth's praise of Daniel's "Tragi-Comedy," see *Poetical Works*, 1:86.

51. The poem was included Robert Anderson, *The Works of the British Poets* 14 vols. (Edin-

burgh: Bradfute and Mundell, 1792–1807), 4:209. Wordsworth's copy is in the Jerwood Centre, Grasmere (ref. 1995.R171).

52. Daniel, *Poetical Works*, 1:7.

53. Richard Poirier, *The Performing Self: Compositions and Decompositions in the Languages of Contemporary Life* (New Brunswick, NJ: Rutgers University Press, 1971), 120.

54. *P2V*, lines 124–28.

55. *P2V*, 210.

56. *P2V*, line 114.

57. Geoffrey Hartman, *The Unremarkable Wordsworth* (London: Methuen, 1987), 115.

58. *BL*, 1:72–73.

59. Oliver Clarkson, "Wordsworth's Lyric Moments,"' *Essays in Criticism* 65 (April 2015): 129.

60. See Anne Barton, "The Road from Penshurst: Wordsworth, Ben Jonson, and Coleridge in 1802," *Essays in Criticism* 37 (1987): 209–33; see also Jared R. Curtis, "William Wordsworth and English Poetry of the Sixteenth and Seventeenth Centuries," *Cornell Library Journal* 1 (1966): 28–40.

61. *JDW*, 1:110.

62. *JDW*, 1:127.

63. Ben Jonson, *The Complete Poems*, ed. George Parfitt (London: Penguin, 1996), 407. Wordsworth's copy of Jonson's *Discoveries* is at the Jerwood Centre, Grasmere (ref. 1995.R.153).

64. *HW*, 6:38–40.

65. Anderson, *Works*, 4:529.

66. Dorothy writes to a correspondent about a poem that "William and Sara threw off last Sunday afternoon. . . . The first stanza of Ben Jonson's poem slipped from W's lips in a parody—and together they finished it with much loving fun—Oh! how they laughed"; *LY*, 1:88.

67. *SP*, 118. Colin Burrow has suggested that "Building Jonson's poetic identity out of destruction, basing vitality upon ephemera, seems to be one function of *The Underwood*"; "Ben Jonson," in *The Cambridge Companion to English Poets*, ed. Claude Rawson (Cambridge: Cambridge University Press, 2011), 135. Wordsworth's 1807 collection makes him a cobuilder of sorts. Anne Barton notes an affinity between Jonson's ode and Wordsworth's (she suggests that the "timely utterance" mentioned early in Wordsworth's poem may be a reference to Jonson's ode), but she tends to discuss that affinity in broad terms rather than specific allusions. In addition to the echoes I discuss below, there are several others: Jonson's sense that a "lily of a day, / Is fairer far, in May" can be heard alongside the Ode's awareness of "This sweet May morning"; Jonson's dream of "bright eternal day" is translated into Wordsworth's "innocent brightness of a new-born Day," and so on.

68. Jonson, *Complete Poems*, 211; *P2V*, lines 44, 182–83, 197.

69. *P2V*, lines 130–31.

70. T. S. Eliot, "Andrew Marvell," in *The Annotated Waste Land with Eliot's Contemporary Prose*, ed. Lawrence Rainey (New Haven, CT: Yale University Press, 2006), 150–56.

71. Cited in *Coleridge on The Seventeenth Century*, ed. Roberta Florence Brinkley (Durham, NC: Duke University Press, 1955), 642, 648. For a suggestive reading of Jonson's style alongside a consideration of "jokes" in poetry, see Robert Pinsky, "Poetry and Pleasure," in *Poetry and the World* (Hopewell, NJ: Ecco, 1988), 30–46.

72. *P2V*, lines 146, 149, 156.

73. Ralph Waldo Emerson, "The Comic," (1843) in *Theories of Comedy*, ed. Paul Lauter

(New York: Doubleday, 1964), 378. Michael O'Neill has noted "a delicately calculated over-insistence" and "lines that border with dramatic art on the over-protesting"; see his excellent essays on the poem, "'The Trembling from It Is Spreading': A Reading of Wordsworth's 'Ode: Intimations of Immortality,'" *Charles Lamb Bulletin*, n.s. 139 (July 2007): 77, and "Ode: Intimations of Immortality," in *The Oxford Handbook of William Wordsworth*, ed. Richard Gravil and Daniel Robinson (Oxford: Oxford University Press, 2015), 252.

74. *P2V*, line 41.

75. *P2V*, lines 10–11.

76. *P2V*, line 198.

77. *P2V*, lines 168–70.

78. *P2V*, lines 174–75.

79. *CH*, 413.

80. See, for example, "Let us now take time, and play, / Love, and live here while we may," or "Why then, since life to us is short, / Let's make it full up, by our sport," in Robert Herrick, *The Complete Poetry of Robert Herrick*, ed. Tom Cain and Ruth Connolly, 2 vols. (Oxford: Oxford University Press, 2013), 1: 126, 226. See also John Creaser's illuminating essay "Herrick at Play," *Essays in Criticism* 56, no. 4 (October 2006): 324–50.

81. Herrick, *Complete Poetry*, 1:99. For the Herrick lyrics in the Wordsworth notebook, see DCMS 131, Jerwood Centre, Grasmere.

82. Wordsworth uses this phrase in his *Guide to the Lakes*, *PrW*, 2:187; see also *P2V*, 412.

83. *P2V*, lines 205–6.

84. See, for example, *CH*, 221, 336, 527, 584.

85. See the fragmentary manuscript bMS Eng 327 (7), Houghton Library, Harvard University, Cambridge, MA.

86. *LW*, 2:273.

87. Ralph Waldo Emerson, *Essays* (New York: Library of America, 1996), 547–48.

88. Virgil, *Eclogues, Georgics, and Aeneid I–IV*, trans. H. R. Fairclough, rev. G. P. Goold (Cambridge, MA: Harvard University Press, 1999), 49–53. On Wordsworth's seriocomic play with Virgil elsewhere, see Rachel Falconer, "Wordsworth unEnglished," in *Englishness and Nationalism: Festschrift in Honour of Margaret Trudeau-Clayton*, ed. Rahel Orgis and Matthias Heim (Basingstoke: Palgrave Macmillan, forthcoming).

89. Mary Beard gives a sharp account of the complexity of the moment in *Laughter in Ancient Rome: On Joking, Tickling, and Cracking Up* (Berkeley: University of California Press, 2014), 81–85.

90. Stanley Cavell, *In Quest of the Ordinary: Lines of Skepticism and Romanticism* (Chicago: University of Chicago Press, 1988), 75.

91. Stanley Cavell, "Ending the Waiting Game," in *Must We Mean What We Say? A Book of Essays* (Cambridge: Cambridge University Press, 1976), 121.

92. *1805*, I. 513.

93. *LB*, 398.

94. Walter Benjamin, "Toys and Play: Marginal Notes on a Monumental Work," in *1927–1930*, vol. 2, pt. 1 of *Selected Writings*, ed. Michael Jennings, Howard Eiland, and Gary Smith; trans. Rodney Livingstone et al. (Cambridge, MA: Belknap Press of Harvard University Press, 1999), 120.

95. Daniel, *Poetical Works*, 1:13–14.

96. *P2V*, 209, 97.

97. Elizabeth Bowen, "Toys," in *People, Places, Things*, ed. Allan Hepburn (Edinburgh: Edinburgh University Press, 2008), 179–82.

Playing—Reprobates

1. *LB*, 549.

2. See Diane Ackerman, *Deep Play* (New York: Vintage, 1999), 7–8.

3. Milton, *Paradise Lost*, IX. 1027.

4. William Hogarth, *The Analysis of Beauty*, ed. Ronald Paulson (New Haven, CT: Yale University Press, 1997), 33.

5. Edmund Burke, *A Philosophical Enquiry into the Origin of Our Ideas of the Sublime and Beautiful*, ed. Paul Guyer (Oxford: Oxford University Press, 2015), 93.

6. *Exc*, VII. 45–49.

7. *Exc*, IV. 183–84.

8. Percy Bysshe Shelley, *The Major Works*, ed. Michael O'Neill (Oxford: Oxford University Press, 2003), 428.

9. Camille Paglia, *Sexual Personae* (London: Vintage, 1991), 300.

10. *PrW*, 1:148.

11. Wordsworth's edition of Anthony Ashley Cooper Shaftesbury, *Characteristicks of men, manners, opinions, times*, 3 vols., 3rd ed. (1723), is at the Jerwood Centre, Grasmere (ref. 1993.16). The marginal mark is made at 1:138 ("An Essay on the Freedom of Wit and Humour").

12. Marcel Proust, *Within a Budding Grove*, vol. 2 of *In Search of Lost Time*, trans. C. K. Scott Moncrieff and Terence Kilmartin, rev. D. J. Enright (New York: Modern Library, 2003), 572.

13. *EY*, 625–28.

14. Roland Barthes, *The Pleasure of the Text*, trans. Richard Howard (New York: Hill and Wang, 1975), 9–10.

15. *LB*, 218–20.

16. Robert Hass, "Snow Egret," in *The Apple Trees at Olema: New and Selected Poems* (Tarset, UK: Bloodaxe, 2011), 34–35.

17. *LB*, 312.

18. The *OED* has no entry for *self-question'd* even though Wordsworth uses it on more than one occasion (he never uses *self-questioning*). Coleridge also uses *self-questioned* in a sonnet dated 1796 (*CP*, 121).

19. *PrW*, 3:371–72

20. *PB*, 74. As I cite from a range of published and manuscript versions of *Peter Bell*, for all references I will give page numbers in the Cornell edition.

21. *PB*, 59.

22. *PB*, 71.

23. *PB*, 71.

24. *PB*, 128.

25. *PB*, 77, 63.

26. *PB*, 125.

27. *PB*, 116.

28. *1805*, VII. 323–24.

29. *PB*, 117.

30. *PB*, 61, 92, 123.

31. *PB*, 91.

32. *LY*, 1:646.

33. *CH*, 648, 653, 1024.

34. *LW*, 2:39–40.

35. David Bromwich, *Disowned by Memory: Wordsworth's Poetry of the 1790s* (Chicago: University of Chicago Press, 2000), 127.

36. *PB*, 91.

37. *PB*, 95.

38. Sigmund Freud, "Creative Writers and Daydreaming," in *The Uncanny*, trans. David McLintock (London: Penguin, 2003), 30

39. *PB*, 119.

40. *PB*, 118.

41. *PB*, 131.

42. *PB*, 130.

43. *PB*, 113, 115.

44. *PB*, 133.

45. *PB*, 114, 132.

46. *PB*, 115.

47. *PB*, 114.

48. *PB*, 123.

49. *CH*, 723.

50. *PB*, 100.

51. *PB*, 85.

52. *PB*, 145.

53. *CH*, 706–7.

54. *PrW*, 3:82.

55. *PB*, 96.

56. On these manuscript changes, see John E. Jordan, "The Hewing of *Peter Bell*," *Studies in English Literature* 7, no. 3 (Autumn 1967): 587.

57. Jordan, "Hewing of *Peter Bell*," 577.

58. *PB*, 143.

59. *PB*, 149.

60. *PB*, 149.

61. *PB*, 81–83.

62. *PB*, 139, 149.

63. William Shakespeare, *The Merry Wives of Windsor*, ed. Giorgio Melchioro (London: Arden, 1999), 5.5.119.

64. *PrW*, 1:340.

65. *PB*, 147.

66. *PB*, 121.

67. *PB*, 123.

68. *PB*, 122.

69. *EY*, 256.

70. Robert Burns, "Despondency, an Ode," in *Poems and Songs*, ed. James Kinsley (Oxford: Oxford University Press, 1989), 186–87.

71. *CH*, 770.

72. *PrW*, 3:124.

73. *PrW*, 3:124–25.

74. *CH*, 599.

75. *LL*, 2:98–106. Wordsworth celebrates the poem in his 1815 preface, and he compares Burns to Cotton elsewhere in the *Letter to a Friend of Robert Burns* (*PrW*, 3:120).

76. *PrW*, 3:123–25.

77. *EY*, 256.

78. Gilbert Burns, cited in Alexander Peterkin, *A Review of the Life of Robert Burns* (Edinburgh: Macredie, Skelly and Muckersy, 1815), lxxxi.

79. *PB*, 129.

80. *PB*, 131–32.

81. *PB*, 135.

82. Burns, "The Vision," in Kinsley, *Poems and Songs*, 89.

83. *MY*, 1:119–20; Stephen Gill, "Wordsworth and Burns," in *Burns and Other Poets*, ed. David Sargeant and Fiona Stafford (Edinburgh: Edinburgh University Press, 2012), 158.

84. Burns, "The Vision," in Kinsley, *Poems and Songs*, 90.

85. Shelley, *Major Works*, 427.

86. Stanley Cavell, *A Pitch of Philosophy: Autobiographical Exercises* (Cambridge, MA: Harvard University Press, 1994), 87.

87. *1805*, VI. 122–23.

88. *WD*, 122.

89. *1805*, VII. 5.

90. *PB*, 61.

91. *FN*, 17.

92. *PB*, 371–79.

93. Thomas De Quincey, *The Collected Writings of Thomas De Quincey*, ed. David Masson, 16 vols. (Edinburgh: Black, 1889), 8:291.

94. *PB*, 89.

95. *PB*, 67.

96. *PB*, 144.

97. *PB*, 57, 59.

98. *CH*, 651.

99. *PB*, 153.

100. *CP*, 167.

101. *PrW*, 2:491.

102. Walter Scott, *The Miscellaneous Prose Works of Sir Walter Scott Bart.*, 3 vols. (Edinburgh: Robert Cadell, 1847), 1:260.

103. Wordsworth, cited in *William Wordsworth: Interviews and Recollections*, ed. Harold Orel (Basingstoke: Palgrave Macmillan, 2005), 141.

104. Jonathan Wordsworth, "Wordsworthian Comedy," in *English Comedy*, ed. Michael Cordner, Peter Holland, and John Kerrigan (Cambridge: Cambridge University Press, 1994), 217.

105. *PB*, 137.

106. Walter Benjamin, "Toys and Play: Marginal Notes on a Monumental Work," in *1927–1930*, vol. 2, pt. 1 of *Selected Writings*, ed. Michael Jennings, Howard Eiland, and Gary Smith; trans. Rodney Livingstone et al. (Cambridge, MA: Belknap Press of Harvard University Press, 1999), 120.

107. *CH*, 679.

108. Laurence Sterne, *The Life and Opinions of Tristram Shandy, Gentleman*, ed. Melvyn and Joan New (London: Penguin, 2003), 530.

109. *PB*, 45.

110. *PB*, 60.

111. *PB*, 124.

112. *PB*, 125.

113. *PB*, 66.

114. *PB*, 152–53.

115. *PB*, 69.

116. Cited in *Wordsworth*, ed. Peter Swaab, Lives of the Great Romantics by Their Contemporaries 3 (London: Pickering and Chatto, 1996), 74.

117. *LY*, 2:439.

Playing—Idlers

1. *LB*, 173.

2. *EY*, 62.

3. Lionel Trilling, "Wordsworth and the Rabbis," in *The Opposing Self: Nine Essays in Criticism* (London: Secker and Warburg, 1955), 150, 127.

4. *LB*, line 22.

5. Johan Huizinga, *Homo ludens: A Study of the Play Element in Culture* (Boston: Beacon Press, 1950), 189. See also Mihai I. Spariosu, *Dionysus Reborn: Play and the Aesthetic Dimension in Modern Philosophical and Scientific Discourse* (Ithaca, NY: Cornell University Press, 1989).

6. Friedrich Schiller, *On the Aesthetic Education of Man*, ed. and trans. Elizabeth M. Wilkinson and L. A. Willoughby (Oxford: Clarendon, 1982), 211, 161.

7. A. R. Ammons, "A Poem Is a Walk," in *Set in Motion: Essays, Interviews, and Dialogues*, ed. Zofia Burr (Ann Arbor: University of Michigan Press, 1996), 19.

8. *1805*, I. 502–4.

9. For a wide-ranging treatment of idleness and play, see Willard Spiegelman, *Majestic Indolence: English Romantic Poetry and the Work of Art* (Oxford: Oxford University Press, 1995), esp. chap. 2, "Wordsworth at Work and Play," 21–57.

10. *1805*, III. 251.

11. *1805*, II. 168; X. 343.

12. *LB*, 298.

13. *EPF*, 512.

14. *LB*, 172.

15. *1805*, V. 429–31.

16. *P2V*, 68.

17. *LP*, 237.

18. *HG*, 87.

19. David Fairer, "The Pastoral-Georgic Tradition," in *William Wordsworth in Context*, ed. Andrew Bennett (Cambridge: Cambridge University Press, 2018), 115–16.

20. *PrW*, 3:36.

21. *PrW*, 2:85.

22. Samuel Beckett, *Company, Ill Seen Ill Said, Worstward Ho, Stirrings Still* (London: Faber and Faber, 2009), 89.

23. *LB*, 247–50.

24. *FN*, 75.

25. Simone Weil, "*The Iliad* or the Poem of Force," in *Simone Weil: An Anthology*, ed. Sian Miles (New York: Grove Press, 1986), 193.

26. *EY*, 365.

27. Hugh Kenner, *A Homemade World: The American Modernist Writers* (New York: Knopf, 1975), 117–18.

28. As Geoffrey Hill notes in a discussion of "The Female Vagrant," readers "glimpse the remoteness of words from suffering and yet are made to recognize that these words are totally committed to her existence"; "The Exemplary Failure of T. H. Green," in *Geoffrey Hill: Collected Critical Writings*, ed. Kenneth Haynes (Oxford: Oxford University Press, 2008), 123.

29. *LB*, lines 156–61.

30. *LB*, lines 155, 175–77.

31. *LL*, 1:265.

32. Samuel Taylor Coleridge, *Specimens of the Table Talk of the Late Samuel Taylor Coleridge*, 2 vols. (London: John Murray, 1835), 1:61–2.

33. *LB*, line 106.

34. *LB*, line 163.

35. As Nancy Yousef has observed in *Romantic Intimacy* (Stanford, CA: Stanford University Press, 2013), "the Wordsworthian encounter has itself become an object lesson or paradigmatic symptom of the ethical and political failings of romantic aesthetic practice" (81–82). Her chapter on "Sentimental Justice: Hume, Wordsworth, and the Ends of Sympathy" is a valuable corrective to such views (71–98).

36. David Simpson, *Wordsworth, Commodification and Social Concern* (Cambridge: Cambridge University Press, 2009), 26–28, 53.

37. Peter Robinson, "'Battles Long Ago': J. H. Prynne and 'The Solitary Reaper,'" *Literary Imagination* 17, no. 3 (November 2015): 302.

38. *JDW*, 1:47.

39. *JDW*, 1:77.

40. *P2V*, 113–15.

41. *P2V*, 407.

42. *Bord*, 1.1.56.

43. *LB*, line 126.

44. Peter Sloterdijk, *Stress and Freedom* (Cambridge: Polity, 2015), 22–23.

45. *EY*, 367.

46. John Bayley, *Selected Essays* (Cambridge: Cambridge University Press, 1984), 15.

47. *P2V*, 123–29.

48. William Empson, *Some Versions of Pastoral* (New York: New Directions, 1974), 263.

49. *P2V*, 323.

50. *EY*, 366.

51. T. S. Eliot, "Prose and Verse," *Chapbook*, April 1921, 9.

52. *BL*, 2:123.

53. Richard Mant, *The Simpliciad* (1808), ed. Jonathan Wordsworth (London: Woodstock, 1991), 47.

54. A. C. Bradley, "Wordsworth," in *Oxford Lectures on Poetry* (London: Macmillan, 1909), 136–37.

55. Elizabeth Bishop, *Words in Air: The Complete Correspondence between Elizabeth Bishop*

and Robert Lowell, ed. Thomas Travisano and Saskia Hamilton (London: Faber and Faber, 2008), 407.

56. *LB*, 242.

57. *P2V*, 319.

58. Lucy Newlyn, *Coleridge, Wordsworth, and the Language of Allusion* (1986; repr., Oxford: Oxford University Press, 2004), 137.

59. Lucy Newlyn, *Reading, Writing, and Romanticism: The Anxiety of Reception* (Oxford: Oxford University Press, 2000), 116.

60. George Oppen, *Selected Prose, Daybooks, and Papers*, ed. Stephen Cope (Berkeley: University of California Press, 2007), 99.

61. *LY*, 3:147.

62. Stanley Cavell, *The Senses of Walden: An Expanded Edition* (Chicago: University of Chicago Press, 1992), 109.

63. *CO*, 87.

64. *EY*, 366.

65. *P2V*, 323.

66. *EY*, 377.

67. *PrW*, 1:294.

68. John Worthen, *The Gang: Coleridge, the Hutchinsons, and the Wordsworths in 1802* (New Haven, CT: Yale University Press, 2001), 199–200.

69. Trilling, "Wordsworth and the Rabbis," 139. See also James Smith's claim that one of the vital new things about Wordsworth's poetry is "its preoccupation with *other things as other*" alongside his feeling that the poet "explored the significance, or examined the experience, of being for other things, and this modified the experience of being for himself" in "Wordsworth: A Preliminary Survey," *Scrutiny* 7 (1938), reprinted in *Wordsworth: A Critical Anthology*, ed. Graham McMaster (Harmondsworth: Penguin, 1972), 339, 344.

70. Donald Winnicott, *Playing and Reality* (1971; repr., London: Routledge, 2005), 65, 87.

71. Winnicott, *Playing and Reality*, 154.

72. *CO*, 93.

73. *Exc*, I. 462–33.

74. Stevie Smith, *Collected Poems and Drawings of Stevie Smith*, ed. Will May (London: Faber and Faber, 2015), 622.

75. See W. W. Robson's commentary on the poem in *Critical Essays* (London: Routledge and Kegan Paul, 1966): "Finally, when we go back to that opening having taken the poem as a whole, it seems a kind of proleptic clarification; Wordsworth, in 'laughing himself to scorn,' laughs himself back to a happiness which is felt to be still there" (126).

76. *WD*, line 479.

77. See *P2V*, 238, 86; *SP*, 249.

78. In *The Prelude*, a game is "a badge, glossy and fresh" that heralds "freedom" (*1805*, IV. 276–77).

79. Jean Piaget, *Play, Dreams and Imitation in Childhood* (London: Routledge and Kegan Paul, 1972), 108.

Fooling—Vices

1. *1805*, VIII. 642–43.

2. *MY*, 2:382.

3. *CH*, 918.

4. *LW*, 1:77.

5. *PrW*, 1:94.

6. *CH*, 687–88.

7. *CH*, 291.

8. William Jerdan, cited in *Wordsworth*, ed. Peter Swaab, Lives of the Great Romantics by Their Contemporaries 3 (London: Pickering and Chatto, 1996), 269.

9. *RCP*, lines 217–29.

10. Sianne Ngai, *Our Aesthetic Categories: Zany, Cute, Interesting* (Harvard, MA: Harvard University Press, 2015), 186.

11. *RCP*, line 239.

12. *BL*, 2:185.

13. *PrW*, 1:95. For Klopstock's very similar point, see Paul M. Haberland, *The Development of Comic Theory in Germany during the Eighteenth Century* (Goppingen: Alfred Kummerle, 1971), 101.

14. *LB*, 298–99.

15. *PrW*, 2:52.

16. William Shakespeare, *Hamlet*, ed. Ann Thompson and Neil Taylor (London: Arden, 2005), 5.1.179–82.

17. *PrW*, 2:52–53.

18. See Walter Kaiser, *Praisers of Folly: Erasmus, Rabelais, Shakespeare* (Harvard, MA: Harvard University Press, 1963), 24.

19. James Spedding, review of works by Thomas Love Peacock, *Edinburgh Review* 68 (January 1839): 433.

20. See Beatrice K. Otto, *Fools Are Everywhere: The Court Jester around the World* (Chicago: University of Chicago Press, 2007), 205. Wordsworth would have been familiar with the link between vices and jesters from many sources; see, for example, Thomas Percy, *Reliques of Ancient English Poetry*, 4th ed. (London: Nicols, 1794), 1:24. See also Sandra Billington, *A Social History of the Fool* (1984; repr., London: Faber and Faber, 2015), 25–26 and Henry Morley, *Memoirs of Bartholomew Fair* (London: Chatto and Windus, 1880), 115.

21. William Shakespeare, *Twelfth Night*, ed. Keir Elam (London: Arden, 2008), 4.2.123–25.

22. As David Bromwich notes, "The moral disturbance that Wordsworth found in himself would probably never have come to light without the courage he found in reading Shakespeare"; David Bromwich, *Disowned by Memory: Wordsworth's Poetry of the 1790s* (Chicago: University of Chicago Press, 2000), 44–45.

23. The world of *komos* and associated rites of misrule hover in the play's margins. Wordsworth's notebook of materials for *The Borderers* contains references to Bartholomew Fair along with a transcription from Burton's *Anatomy of Melancholy* that describes a scene of festivity, complete with maypole, Comus, Hymen, "masks and mum" (*Bord*, 365), "and all such merriments above measure . . . men to put on Women's apparel in some cases, and promiscuously to dance young and old, rich and poor, generous and base, of all sorts"(*Bord*, 305). On Wordsworth's use of May Day rituals, see Essaka Joshua, *The Romantics and the May Day Tradition* (London: Routledge, 2016), 27–53.

24. *Bord*, 813.

25. Francois Duc de La Rochefoucauld, *Reflections; or, Sentences and Moral Maxims*, ed. J. W. Willis Bund and J. Hain Friswell (London: Sampson Low, 1898), xxxiv, 27.

26. *1805*, I. 239–41.

27. *Bord*, 62–65.

28. *PrW*, 3:123.

29. *Bord*, 2.3.49–51. For most of this discussion, I will be quoting from the early version of the play and will cite by act, scene, and line number. When quoting from the later version, or from Wordsworth's note or preface, I will provide page number.

30. *Bord*, 2.1.5.

31. *Bord*, 1.3.256.

32. See *The London Stage: 1660–1800*, pt. 5, vol. 3, *1792–1800*, ed. Charles Beecher Hogan (Carbondale: Southern Illinois University Press, 1968), 1510.

33. *Thespian Magazine*, June 1793, 1 (cited in Hogan, *London Stage*, 1539).

34. *Bord*, 5.3.185–86.

35. *FN*, 77.

36. *EY*, 210.

37. *Morning Herald*, December 16, 1797.

38. *HW*, 17:118.

39. *CLC*, 1:379.

40. Matthew Gregory Lewis, *The Castle Spectre* (London: Davis, 1799), n.p.

41. Dennis Arundell, *The Story of Sadler's Wells* (London: Hamish Hamilton, 1965), 70.

42. *1805*, VII. 295–314; *1850*, VII. 289–90.

43. Samuel Taylor Coleridge, *Shakespearean Criticism*, ed. Thomas Middleton Raysor, 2 vols. (New York: Dutton, 1974), 2:167; 1:171–2.

44. Cited in Andrew McConnell Stott, *The Pantomime Life of Joseph Grimaldi: Laughter, Madness and The Story of Britain's Greatest Comedian* (London: Canongate, 2010), 66.

45. See John O'Brien, *Harlequin Britain: Pantomime and Entertainment, 1690–1760* (Baltimore: Johns Hopkins University Press, 2004), 139, 150ff; Jane Moody, *Illegitimate Theatre in London, 1770–1840* (Cambridge: Cambridge University Press, 2000), 214.

46. Cited in David Mayer, *Harlequin in His Element: The English Pantomime, 1806–1836* (Harvard, MA: Harvard University Press, 1969), 47.

47. Stott, *Pantomime Life*, 120.

48. Cited in Mayer, *Harlequin in His Element*, 185.

49. See Bart van Es, *Shakespeare in Company* (Oxford: Oxford University Press, 2013), 163–94.

50. William Shakespeare, *As You Like It*, ed. Juliet Dusinberre (London: Arden, 2004), 2.7.60–1

51. William Shakespeare, *Twelfth Night*, ed. Keir Elam (London: Arden, 2008), 1.5.4; 5.1.369–70.

52. William Shakespeare, *King Lear*, ed. R. A. Foakes (London: Arden, 2013), 3.4.77.

53. Shakespeare, *Twelfth Night*, 3.1.37.

54. Shakespeare, *As You Like It*, 3.3.72–75.

55. Shakespeare, *Twelfth Night*, 3.1.25–27.

56. *FN*, 77.

57. In one of the manuscripts, Wordsworth has Mortimer describe Herbert in terms that hint at his pantomimic model: "Foolish old man in the best of thy days most foolish"' (*Bord*, 411).

58. *Bord*, 3.3.14–17

59. *Bord*, 3.5.28–29.

60. Geoffrey Hartman, *Wordsworth's Poetry 1787–1814* (New Haven, CT: Yale University Press, 1964), 129.

61. Friedrich Nietzsche, *On The Genealogy of Morality*, ed. Keith Ansell-Pearson, trans. Carol Diethe (Cambridge: Cambridge University Press, 2010), 9.

62. *Bord*, 2.3.234–36.

63. *Bord*, 3.5.83–88.

64. William Shakespeare, *Othello*, ed. E. A. J. Honigmann, rev. ed. (London: Bloomsbury, 2016), 1.3.336–37; 5.2.16; 2.1.295.

65. *Bord*, 66.

66. Shakespeare, *Othello*, 2.1.293–95.

67. Shakespeare, 2.3.48.

68. Shakespeare, 4.2.148–49.

69. Shakespeare, 5.2.322.

70. Wordsworth pronounced *Othello* one of the three "most pathetic of human compositions" he had ever read (*CO*, 91).

71. Shakespeare, *Othello*, 2.1.136–37.

72. Shakespeare, 3.3.415; 5.2.130.

73. Shakespeare, 5.2.230–32.

74. When Thomas Rymer likened *Othello* to *commedia dell'arte* and to pantomime—"Such scenes as this have made all the World run after *Harlequin* and *Scaracmuccio* . . . the tragical part is, plainly none other, than a Bloody Farce"—he was picking up on something real in the play even as he dismissed it. See 'Short View of Tragedy," in *Critical Works of Thomas Rymer*, ed. Curt A. Zimansky (New Haven, CT: Yale University Press, 1956), 164.

75. Shakespeare, *Othello*, 1.3.382.

76. *Bord*, 2.1.1–8.

77. *Bord*, 4.2.24–25, 18–20.

78. *Bord*, 4.2.37, 46.

79. *Bord*, 4.2.108–10.

80. *Bord*, 4.2.171–72.

81. *Bord*, 59–61.

82. Shakespeare, *King Lear*, 2.2.236.

83. Barbara Everett, *Young Hamlet: Essays on Shakespeare's Tragedies* (Oxford: Clarendon, 1992), 67.

84. Shakespeare, *King Lear*, 1.4.221–22.

85. Shakespeare, *Othello*, 1.1.57.

86. Shakespeare, *King Lear*, 1.4.176–85.

87. *Bord*, 5.2.29–33.

88. W. H. Auden, "The Joker in the Pack," in *The Dyer's Hand* (New York: Vintage, 1968), 271–72.

89. Shakespeare, *Othello*, 5.2.300.

90. *Bord*, 5.2.23.

91. *Bord*, 67–68.

92. *Bord*, 213. (I quote here from the later text.)

93. *PrW*, 2:53.

94. *Bord*, 3.2.76.

95. *Bord*, 189.

96. *Bord*, 67.

97. *Bord*, 72.

98. Alexander Pope, *The Poems of Alexander Pope: A One-Volume Edition of the Twickenham Text with Selected Annotations*, ed. John Butt (London: Methuen, 1965), 554.

99. George Eliot, *The Mill on the Floss*, ed. and with an introduction and notes by A. S. Byatt (London: Penguin, 2003), 517.

100. *Bord*, 5.3.253–56. (I have followed the capitalization of *Fool* from the later version.)

101. *Bord*, 2.1.7–8.

102. William Empson, *The Structure of Complex Words* (1953; repr., London: Penguin 1995), 248.

103. Shakespeare, *Othello*, 5.2.284.

104. *Bord*, 65.

105. *Bord*, 5.3.265–66.

106. *Bord*, 3.5.67–69.

107. *Bord*, 1.1.18–19.

108. Carl Jung, *Four Archetypes: Mother, Rebirth, Spirit, Trickster*, trans. R. F. C. Hull (London: Routledge, 2003), 167–68; 178.

109. In the revised version of *The Borderers*, Wordsworth has Rivers observe that the world's contempt may well be "fear disguised in simulated scorn" (*Bord*, 241).

110. Jung, *Four Archetypes*, 171.

111. *Bord*, 3.4.6–11.

112. *Bord*, 66.

113. *Bord*, 67.

114. David Bromwich, *Disowned by Memory*, 67.

115. *CLC*, 1:216.

116. Robert Weimann, *Shakespeare and the Popular Tradition in the Theater: Studies in the Social Dimension of Dramatic Form and Function*, ed. Robert Schwartz (Baltimore: Johns Hopkins University Press, 1978), 153, 258.

117. *Bord*, 1.1.213–14.

118. Lewis Hyde, *Trickster Makes This World* (London: Canongate, 2008), 7–8.

119. *1805*, VII. 297, 301.

Fooling—Naturals

1. *LP*, 128.

2. *Bord*, 4.2.206–8.

3. See Ronald Paulson, *Satire and the Novel in Eighteenth-Century England* (New Haven, CT: Yale University Press, 1967), 14–15.

4. Laurence Sterne, *A Sentimental Journey through France and Italy*, ed. Katherine Turner (New York: Broadview, 2010), 87.

5. Robert Frost, *Collected Poems, Prose, and Plays*, ed. Richard Poirier and Mark Richardson (New York: Library of America, 1995), 756–57.

6. *PrW*, 1:116.

7. *BL*, 2:42–43.

8. *CH*, 211.

9. Richard Cumberland, cited in *Parodies: An Anthology from Chaucer to Beerbohm*, ed. Dwight MacDonald (London: Random House, 1960), 76.

10. *CH*, 155–56.

11. William Shakespeare, *Hamlet*, ed. Ann Thompson and Neil Taylor (London: Arden, 2005), 5.1.29–30.

12. William Shakespeare, *King Lear*, ed. R. A. Foakes (London: Arden, 2013), 4.6.187.

13. Shakespeare, *Hamlet*, 1.4.54.

14. *Shakespeare*, 5.1.138–39.

15. Samuel Taylor Coleridge, *Shakespearean Criticism*, ed. Thomas Middleton Raysor (New York: Dutton, 1974), 2:167.

16. Shakespeare, *Hamlet*, 3.2.118, 3.2.313, 5.2.191–93.

17. *LB*, line 255.

18. Shakespeare, *Hamlet*, 5.1.175–76.

19. *LB*, lines 99–109.

20. *LL*, 1:265.

21. *LB*, lines 350–51.

22. *LB*, lines 403–4.

23. *LB*, lines 421–22.

24. *LW*, 2:42–44.

25. Basil Bunting's comment comes to mind: "I think it is hardly too much to say that if the multiple ironies through which Wordsworth relates the story of 'The Brothers' had occurred to Henry James or to Conrad, we would have had a thirty page preface to explain them"; *Basil Bunting on Poetry*, ed. Peter Makin (Baltimore: Johns Hopkins University Press, 1999), 72.

26. See *The Prelude*, ed. Ernest de Selincourt (Oxford: Clarendon, 1959), 232.

27. *PrW*, 3:75.

28. Thomas Percy, *Reliques of Ancient English Poetry*, 4th ed. (London: Nicols, 1794), 1:17, 19, 28, 29, 30, 35–36, 28, 48–49, 287.

29. Maureen McLane, *Balladeering, Minstrelsy, and the Making of British Romantic Poetry* (Cambridge: Cambridge University Press, 2011), 149.

30. McLane, *Balladeering*, 164.

31. Andrew L. Griffin, "Wordsworth and the Problem of Imaginative Story: The Case of 'Simon Lee,'" *PMLA* 92, no. 3 (May 1977): 393–94.

32. See John Southworth, *Fools and Jesters at the English Court* (Stroud: Sutton, 1998), 5, 7–8, 13, 55, 61, 202, 264.

33. *LB*, 64–67.

34. *1805*, VII. 456–59.

35. Shakespeare, *King Lear*, 5.3.303–4.

36. John F. Danby, *The Simple Wordsworth: Studies in the Poems 1797–1807* (London: Routledge and Kegan Paul, 1960), 39–41.

37. *FN*, 37.

38. *LW*, 1:278.

39. *PrW*, 3:247.

40. Jean-Jacques Rousseau, *Emile; or, On Education* (London: Penguin, 1991), 196. For Wordsworth's reading of Rousseau, see Duncan Wu, *Wordsworth's Reading* (Cambridge: Cambridge University Press, 1993), 1:119.

41. *LY*, 1:602.

42. I am indebted here to David Dwan's discussions of "The Politics of Compassion" and "From Pity to Disgust," in *Liberty, Equality, and Humbug: Orwell's Political Ideals* (Oxford: Oxford University Press, 2018), 114–23.

43. Donald Davie, *Purity and Diction in English Verse* (1952; repr., Harmondsworth: Penguin, 1992), 51.

44. Danby, *Simple Wordsworth*, 44.

45. Given the allusions to folly elsewhere, one might be tempted to dig around in the roots of words: *clown* is linked to "clod, clot, lump . . . Danish dialect *klunds* = *klods* 'block, log, stump', also 'clown'" (for *clot*, the *OED* has "The stump of a tree or plant"). In "Simon Lee" a clot working a clot is, apparently, something that needs to be put out of its misery.

46. David Bromwich, *Disowned by Memory: Wordsworth's Poetry of the 1790s* (Chicago: University of Chicago Press, 2000), 99.

47. Sterne, *Sentimental Journey*, 90–91.

48. *LW*, 2:125.

49. *LL*, 1:135.

50. *LW*, 1:46.

51. Harold Laski, *Faith, Reason, and Civilisation: An Essay in Historical Analysis* (London: Gollancz, 1944), 113.

52. Elizabeth Bishop, *Poems, Prose, and Letters* (New York: Library of America, 2008), 340.

53. See, for example, Don Bialostosky's interpretation: "The poem coheres as an appropriately muddled response to a troubling encounter that in its wobbling description of Simon gives him back imaginatively some of the dignity and worth that the narrator's action took from him . . . telling can issue from troubling experiences, solicit help in making something of them, and even . . . compensate discursively for what cannot be made whole in the world"; *How to Play a Poem* (Pittsburgh: University of Pittsburgh Press, 2017), 176–78.

54. See Wordsworth's letter to Charles James Fox in 1801 (*EY*, 314–15) and also *PrW*, 3:245.

55. W. H. Auden, *Prose: 1939–1948*, ed. Edward Mendelson (Princeton, NJ: Princeton University Press, 2002), 347.

56. Kenneth Burke, "Comic Correctives," in *Attitudes toward History*, 3rd ed. (Berkeley: University of California Press, 1984), 41.

57. *1805*, I. 246–48.

58. Heather Glen, *Vision and Disenchantment: Blake's* Songs *and Wordsworth's* Lyrical Ballads (Cambridge: Cambridge University Press, 1983), 240.

59. James Williams, "Lear and the Fool," in *Edward Lear and the Play of Poetry*, ed. James Williams and Matthew Bevis (Oxford: Oxford University Press, 2016), 22.

60. *FN*, 37.

61. See John Worthen, *The Life of William Wordsworth: A Critical Biography* (London: Wiley-Blackwell, 2014), 4, 116, 127, 128.

62. David Simpson, *Wordsworth's Historical Imagination: The Poetry of Displacement* (London: Methuen, 1987), 153–55.

63. Mary Wordsworth's Memorandum, DCMS 167, Jerwood Centre, Grasmere.

64. Guy Davenport, "That Faire Field of Enna," in *The Geography of the Imagination* (London: Picador, 1984), 266.

Fooling—Idiots

1. *HG*, lines 918–20.

2. *EY*, 593.

3. *LY*, 2:691–92.

4. *CO*, 397.

5. *P2V*, 582.

6. *EY*, 357.

7. *PrW*, 3:65.

8. Desiderius Erasmus, *The Praise of Folly*, trans. Clarence H. Miller (New Haven, CT: Yale University Press, 2003), 128. Wordsworth owned a copy of the work; see Chester and Alice C. Shaver, *Wordsworth's Library: A Catalogue* (New York: Garland, 1979), 89

9. See Enid Welsford, *The Fool: His Social and Literary History* (New York: Anchor Books, 1961).

10. See *Book of Proverbs* [n. d], ref. 2003.82, 69, Jerwood Centre, Grasmere.

11. *LB*, line 96.

12. Erasmus, *Praise of Folly*, 22, 42, 118.

13. On this link, see Mary Jacobus, *Tradition and Experiment in Wordsworth's Lyrical Ballads 1798* (Oxford: Oxford University Press, 1979), 250–61.

14. *LB*, lines 117–21.

15. John Southworth, *Fools and Jesters at the English Court* (Stroud: Sutton, 1998), 6; *LB*, lines 59–61. The Fool figure in the Matthew poems ("the grey-haired Man of glee") has a "bough / Of wilding in his hand" as he sings his crazy, witty rhymes (*LB*, 214).

16. *LB*, lines 55–56.

17. *LB*, lines 9, 14.

18. *BL*, 2:48–49.

19. J.-B. Pontalis, *Windows*, trans. Anne Quinney (Lincoln: University of Nebraska Press, 2003), 11.

20. David B. Pirie, *William Wordsworth: The Poetry of Grandeur and of Tenderness* (London: Methuen, 1982), 128.

21. *LB*, line 99.

22. *LB*, lines 140–41.

23. *LB*, lines 153–55.

24. *LB*, lines 139, 142–46.

25. *LB*, lines 382–86.

26. Robert Southey's "The Idiot" (1798) tells of how "Old Sarah lov'd her helpless child, / Who helplessness made dear," but Southey insists on making the feelings of the couple tidily, comfortingly reciprocal as a way of defending the mother's love: "he was ev'rything to her, / And she to him was all"; Robert Southey, *Selected Shorter Poems*, vol. 5 of *Robert Southey: Poetical Works 1793–1810*, ed. Lynda Pratt (London: Pickering and Chatto, 2004), 216. This is a far remove from the spirit that animated Dorothy Wordsworth's lines: "Nor blush if o'er that heart be stealing / A love for things that have no feeling / Nor can repay, by loving you, / Aught that your care for them may do." Cited in *Dorothy Wordsworth and Romanticism*, ed. Susan M. Levin (New Brunswick, NJ: Rutgers University Press, 2009), 212.

27. Frank O'Hara, *Selected Poems*, ed. Donald Allen (Manchester: Carcanet, 2004), 94–95.

28. *LB*, lines 262, 269–71.

29. *LB*, lines 423–26.

30. See Sandra Billington, *A Social History of the Fool* (1984; repr., London: Faber and Faber, 2015), 52, 58–60.

31. *LB*, line 263.

32. See Billington, *Social History*, 81–2, 101.

33. See Sianne Ngai, *Our Aesthetic Categories: Zany, Cute, Interesting* (Harvard, MA: Harvard University Press, 2015), 195.

34. *P2V*, 137.

35. *LB*, lines 435–36.

36. *SSIP*, 614.

37. William Shakespeare, *A Midsummer Night's Dream*, ed. Peter Holland (Oxford: Oxford University Press, 2008), 3.1.21–25.

38. Shakespeare, 3.1.48–49; 2.2.6–7.

39. *LB*, lines 3, 444–45.

40. *LB*, lines 238, 332–33.

41. Erasmus, *Praise of Folly*, 137–38.

42. Shakespeare, *Midsummer Night's Dream*, 4.1.203–11.

43. *Midsummer Night's Dream*, 3.1.118; 5.1.266–77.

44. *LB*, lines 462–63.

45. *SSIP*, 774.

46. *LB*, lines 78–81.

47. *LB*, lines 395–96.

48. *LB*, lines 399–400.

49. Burns, "To R***** G***** of F*****, Esq," in *Poems and Songs*, ed. James Kinsley (Oxford: Oxford University Press, 1989), 464.

50. *LB*, line 136.

51. *LB*, lines 90–91.

52. *P2V*, 208–9.

53. *CH*, 177.

54. Wallace Stevens, "The Motive for Metaphor," in *Collected Poetry and Prose* (New York: Library of America, 1997), 257–58.

55. *EY*, 356–57.

56. *EY*, 355.

57. *FN*, 10.

58. *LB*, line 92.

59. Thomas Percy, *Reliques of Ancient English Poetry*, 3 vols., 4th ed. (London: Nicols, 1794), 1:36.

60. *LB*, lines 347–56.

61. Thomas De Quincey, *Recollections of the Lakes and the Lake Poets*, ed. David Wright (London: Penguin, 1978), 132.

62. *PrW*, 3:371–72.

63. *LB*, line 74.

64. *LB*, line 94.

65. *CH*, 289.

66. *LB*, line 360.

67. *1799*, I. 299–301.

68. *LB*, lines 236, 335, 342–43.

69. *1799*, I. 309–10.

70. *1799*, I. 322, 329–30.

71. *P2V*, lines 28–29.

72. *P2V*, lines 161–65.

73. *1799*, II. 273, 291. See Jonathan Wordsworth, *William Wordsworth: Borders of Vision* (Oxford: Clarendon, 1974), 79.

74. *LB*, lines 37–40.

75. *LB*, line 456.

76. *LB*, lines 347–48.

77. See Avital Ronell, *Stupidity* (Urbana: University of Illinois Press, 2002), 273.

78. See John Worthen, *The Life of William Wordsworth: A Critical Biography* (London: Wiley-Blackwell, 2014), 18–19.

79. *1799*, I. 352–53.

80. *1799*, I. 355, 357.

81. David Ellis, *Wordsworth, Freud, and the Spots of Time: Interpretation in* The Prelude (Cambridge: Cambridge University Press, 1985), 20, 23.

82. *1799*, I. 370–74.

83. Cited in Worthen, *Wordsworth*, 165, 171n20.

84. Robert Duncan, as reported by George Oppen, *Selected Prose, Daybooks, and Papers*, ed. Stephen Cope (Berkeley: University of California Press, 2007), 36.

85. *LB*, line 289.

86. *LB*, lines 113, 133.

87. *LB*, lines 387–89.

88. Sidney Keyes, "William Wordsworth," *The Collected Poems of Sidney Keyes*, ed. Michael Meyer (London: Routledge, 1988), 35.

89. *1850*, IV. 234–35.

90. *1805*, XI. 330–37.

91. *SPP*, 289.

92. Mark Strand, *Collected Poems* (New York: Knopf, 2016), 354.

93. Mark Strand, *The Weather of Words: Poetic Inventions* (New York: Knopf, 2001), 105–6.

94. *LB*, lines 82–86.

95. *1850*, III. 236.

96. *LB*, lines 357, 366.

Humoring—Oddities

1. *Bord*, 2.3.163.

2. *P2V*, 184–85.

3. Wordsworth, cited in Aubrey de Vere, *Essays, Chiefly on Poetry*, 2 vols. (London: Macmillan, 1887), 2:277–78.

4. *CH*, 706.

5. Thomas De Quincey, *Recollections of the Lakes and the Lake Poets*, ed. David Wright (London: Penguin, 1978), 190, 381.

6. *LP*, 275; *Exc*, III. 950.

7. *EY*, 324.

8. William Congreve, cited in *Critical Essays of the Seventeenth Century*, ed. J. E. Spingarn, 3 vols. (Bloomington: Indiana University Press, 1957), 3:248.

9. John Hughes, cited in Ronald Paulson, *Satire and the Novel in Eighteenth-Century England* (New Haven, CT: Yale University Press, 1967), 69.

10. Jonathan Swift, "To Mr Delany," in *Swift: Poetical Works*, ed. Herbert Davis (London: Oxford University Press, 1967), 159; Henry Fielding, *The History of Tom Jones, A Foundling*, ed. Thomas Keymer and Alice Wakely (London: Penguin, 2005), 365; Laurence Sterne, *The Life and Opinions of Tristram Shandy, Gentleman*, ed. Melvyn and Joan New (London: Penguin, 2003), 58.

11. "Wordsworth, Poet of Mere Sentiment," *Gentleman's Magazine*, May 1828, 399–400.

12. James Boswell, *Life of Johnson*, ed. R. W. Chapman (Oxford: Oxford University Press, 2008), 696.

13. *CH*, 189, 381.

14. Samuel Taylor Coleridge, *Literary Remains*, ed. Henry Nelson Coleridge, 4 vols. (London: Pickering, 1836–39), 1:137, 142.

15. *EY*, 588.

16. Hugh Sykes Davies, *Wordsworth and the Worth of Words*, ed. John Kerrigan and Jonathan Wordsworth (Cambridge: Cambridge University Press, 1986), 39.

17. *HG*, line 925.

18. *PrW*, 2:355–57.

19. *PrW*, 2:359.

20. *PrW*, 3:128.

21. Ralph Waldo Emerson, "The Comic," in *Theories of Comedy*, ed. Paul Lauter (New York: Doubleday, 1964), 379.

22. Immanuel Kant, *Critique of the Power of Judgment*, ed. Paul Guyer, trans. Paul Guyer and Eric Matthews (Cambridge: Cambridge University Press, 2000), 132, 134, 144.

23. Samuel Taylor Coleridge, *Specimens of the Table Talk of the Late Samuel Taylor Coleridge* (London: John Murray, 1835), 1:428.

24. *PrW*, 2:221, 319.

25. *1805*, VI. 90–100.

26. G. E. Bentley Jr., *Blake Records* (Oxford: Clarendon, 1969), 544.

27. Gaston Bachelard noted that "If you make a poetic image a little too specific, you will make it laughable too—a boundary line between enthusiasm and absurdity'; *Air and Dreams: An Essay on the Imagination of Movement*, trans. Edith R. Farrell and C. Frederick Farrell (Dallas: Dallas Institute: 1988), 67. As one of his contemporaries noted, Wordsworth doesn't appear to know "the precise boundary line between the sublime and the extravagant, between figure and nonsense" (*CH*, 774). See also F. W. Bateson, *Wordsworth: A Re-interpretation* (London: Longman, 1963), "There ought to be an inherent logical impossibility between the poetically sublime and the poetically ridiculous, but in Wordsworth's case curiously enough there isn't" (4).

28. *CH*, 706.

29. Jonathan Swift, *Gulliver's Travels*, ed. Claude Rawson (Oxford: Oxford University Press, 2008), 51, 77, 105, 136–37, 202.

30. *P2V*, 148.

31. *PrW*, 3:83.

32. Kant, *Critique of the Power of Judgment*, 141.

33. *1805*, VII. 574.

34. *1805*, VIII. 402; V. 457.

35. *LB*, lines 115–16.

36. *P2V*, 256.

37. *LB*, line 108.

38. *Exc*, VIII. 594–95.

39. *P2V*, 238.

40. *BL*, 1:39. For a discussion of the trope, see Susan Wolfson, "'Comparing Power': Coleridge and Simile," in *Rhetorical Traditions and British Romantic Literature*, ed. Don Bialostosky and Lawrence D. Needham (Bloomington: Indiana University Press, 1995), 28–47.

41. John Locke, *An Essay Concerning Human Understanding* (1690), ed. Peter H. Nidditch (Oxford: Clarendon, 1979), 156.

42. James Beattie, *Essays on Poetry and Music, as they Affect the Mind; On Laughter and Ludicrous Composition; On the Usefulness of Classical learning* (London: Dilly, 1779), 374.

43. *HW*, 6:11.

44. See Stuart Tave, *The Amiable Humorist: A Study of Comic Theory and Criticism of the Eighteenth and Early Nineteenth Centuries* (Chicago: University of Chicago Press, 1960), 64–67.

45. See Jonathan Lamb, "The Comic Sublime in Sterne's Fiction," *ELH* 48, no. 1 (Spring 1981), 130.

46. *DS*, 72.

47. *CH*, 19.

48. As Jonathan Lamb has noted, this disagreement lurked behind all theories of the sublime because it remained unresolved whether the sublime was "the coincidence of a loose circumstance with the rule that authorizes its appearance" or whether it was born of "the excessive accumulation of contingent particulars that evade all regulation"; "The Sublime," in *The Cambridge History of Literary Criticism*, vol. 4, *The Eighteenth Century*, ed. H. B. Nisbet and Claude Rawson (Cambridge: Cambridge University Press, 1997), 394–416; see also Leo Damrosch, "Generality and Particularity," 381–93, in the same volume.

49. Samuel Johnson, *Major Works*, ed. Donald Greene (Oxford: Oxford University Press, 2008), 352, 678.

50. Jean Paul Richter, *Horn of Oberon: Jean Paul Richter's School for Aesthetics*, trans. Margaret R. Hale (Detroit: Wayne State University Press, 1973), 100.

51. *PrW*, 3:36.

52. *PrW*, 3:125.

53. *LB*, 59.

54. *LB*, 80.

55. Longinus, "On Sublimity," in *Ancient Literary Criticism*, ed. and trans. D. A. Russell and M. Winterbottom (Oxford: Oxford University Press, 1972), 485–86. Wordsworth owned a copy of Longinus; see Chester and Alice C. Shaver, *Wordsworth's Library: A Catalogue* (New York: Garland, 1979), 162.

56. *PrW*, 3:31.

57. *P2V*, 207.

58. Dorothy *had* counted them: "William was writing a poem descriptive of the sights and sounds we saw and heard . . . a flat pasture with 42 cattle feeding' (*JDW*, 1:133).

59. *PrW*, 3:33.

60. *LB*, 74–75.

61. *PrW*, 2:222.

62. Swift, in *Swift: Poetical Works*, ed. Herbert Davis (London: Oxford University Press, 1967), 361–62. See Josephine MacDonagh for other ballad sources in *Child Murder and British Culture, 1720–1900* (Cambridge: Cambridge University Press, 2003), 221n41.

63. *LB*, lines 1–22.

64. *LB*, lines 52–53.

65. *LB*, lines 27–33.

66. Keston Sutherland, *Stupefaction: A Radical Anatomy of Phantoms* (London: Seagull, 2011), 141, 146–47.

67. *LB*, 351.

68. *BL*, 2:49.

69. *PrW*, 1:117.

70. *LB*, 351.

71. *LB*, 350.

72. See, for example, Robert Stagg's searching essay "Wordsworth, Pope, and Writing after Bathos," *Essays in Criticism*, 64, no. 1 (January 2014): 29–44.

73. Thomas De Quincey, "Schlosser's Literary History of the Eighteenth Century," in *De Quincey as Critic*, ed. John E. Jordan (London: Routledge and Kegan Paul, 1973), 314–15.

74. Swift, *Gulliver's Travels*, 22–23.

75. Sianne Ngai, *Ugly Feelings* (Harvard, MA: Harvard University Press, 2005), 280.

76. Ngai, 276, 256–57.

77. First spoken at *LB*, lines 65–66.

78. *LB*, lines 86–88.

79. *LB*, lines 210–11.

80. Cited in Sykes Davies, *Wordsworth*, 133.

81. *EY*, 367.

82. *FN*, 14.

83. For a range of responses, see MacDonagh, *Child Murder*, 220n29. See also Karen Swann, "'Martha's Name,' or the Scandal of 'The Thorn,'" in *Dwelling in Possibility: Women Poets and Critics on Poetry*, ed. Yopie Prins and Maeera Shreiber (Ithaca, NY: Cornell University Press, 1997), 60–79, and Frances Ferguson, "Writing and Orality around 1800: 'Speakers,' 'Readers,' and Wordsworth's 'The Thorn,'" in *Wordsworth's Poetic Theory*, ed. Stefan Hoesel-Uhlig and Alex Regier (London: Palgrave, 2010), 119–38.

84. *LB*, line 115.

85. *LB*, 80.

86. *LB*, line 133.

87. *LB*, line 64.

88. *LB*, lines 213–15.

89. *LB*, lines 223–24.

90. *EPF*, 446.

91. *LB*, lines 185–87.

92. *LB*, lines 188–91, 23–29.

93. *1799*, I. 341–63.

94. *1799*, lines 368–70.

95. *EPF*, 446–47.

96. Thomas Weiskel, *The Romantic Sublime: Studies in the Structure and Psychology of Transcendence* (Baltimore: Johns Hopkins University Press, 1976), 184.

97. Northrop Frye, *Anatomy of Criticism: Four Essays* (Princeton, NJ: Princeton University Press, 1973), 168.

98. *LB*, lines 91–92.

99. Swift, *A Tale of a Tub and Other Works*, ed. Angus Ross and David Woolley (Oxford: Oxford University Press, 2008), 20, 76.

100. *BL*, 2:52.

101. *LB*, line 23.

102. *LB*, lines 36–37.

103. *LB*, lines 197–98.

104. *LB*, 283.

105. *1805*, III. 186–88.

106. W. H. Auden, "Notes on the Comic," in *The Dyer's Hand* (New York: Vintage, 1968), 372.

Humoring—Medleys

1. *1805*, VII. 150–51.

2. *1805*, XIII. 400–3.

3. *1805*, XIII. 408.

4. *Bord*, 3.2.103–4.

5. *EPF*, 398.

6. *BL*, 2:137

7. *1805*, IV. 318–19.

8. *LB*, 219.

9. *1805*, III. 29.

10. *1805*, I. 224.

11. James Hogg, cited in *Parodies: An Anthology from Chaucer to Beerbohm*, ed. Dwight MacDonald (London: Random House, 1960), 85.

12. Hogg, cited in MacDonald, *Parodies*, 86.

13. *Exc*, II. 70.

14. *CP*, 340; *BL*, 1:302.

15. *1850*, V. 523–25.

16. *1805*, VIII. 743–44.

17. *1805*, VIII. 705–7.

18. *EY*, 434.

19. Samuel Johnson, *The Lives of the Poets*, ed. Roger Lonsdale (Oxford: Clarendon, 2006), 2:846. See also Ruth Abbott's excellent discussion "Wordsworth's Prosody," in *The Oxford Handbook of William Wordsworth*, ed. Richard Gravil and Daniel Robinson (Oxford: Oxford University Press, 2015), 516–32.

20. *PrW*, 3:28.

21. Wordsworth's edition of *The Seasons* (London: Strahan, 1778) is at the Jerwood Centre, Grasmere (ref. 1995.R.111); see the rook, who "ceaseless caws amusive" (30).

22. I. A. Richards, *Practical Criticism: A Study of Literary Judgment* (1929; repr., London: Routledge, 1991), 175–67.

23. Marshall Brown, *Preromanticism* (Stanford, CA: Stanford University Press, 1991), 62.

24. William Cowper, *The Task and Selected Other Poems*, ed. James Sambrook (London: Longman, 1994), 126.

25. Cowper, 61

26. *CLC*, 1:197.

27. *BL*, 1:195.

28. William Cowper, *The Letters and Prose Writings of William Cowper*, ed. James King and Charles Ryskamp, 5 vols. (Oxford: Clarendon, 1979–86), 1:367.

29. *CH*, 413, 731, 734.

30. Cowper, *Letters*, 1:506.

31. *CH*, 731–33.

32. Mark Storey has observed that "Someone who ends up taking himself as seriously as does Wordsworth finds that a sense of his own absurdity is an important part of that process"; *Poetry and Humour from Cowper to Clough* (London: Macmillan, 1979), 42.

33. *EY*, 586.

34. In the 1815 preface, Wordsworth included "the Mock-heroic" under "the first class of poetry," along with "the Epopœia, the Historic Poem, the Tale, the Romance and . . . the metrical Novel." *PrW*, 3:27

35. *LY*, 4:48

36. See Robert J. Griffin, *Wordsworth's Pope: A Study in Literary Historiography* (Cambridge: Cambridge University Press, 2008).

37. *PrW*, 1:150.

38. *PrW*, 2:18.

39. Alexander Pope, *The Dunciad in Four Books*, ed. Valerie Rumbold (Harlow: Pearson Longman, 2009), 116.

40. Pope, preface to *The Iliad*, in *The Iliad of Homer Translated by Alexander Pope*, ed. Steven Shankman (London: Penguin, 1996), 3, 11.

41. Pope, "Postscript," in *The Twickenham Edition of the Poems of Alexander Pope*, ed. John Butt, 11 vols. (London: Methuen, 1939–69), 10:387.

42. *MY*, 2:274.

43. Pope, "Postscript," 10:388.

44. Pope, "Postscript," 10:389.

45. In a note to his *Iliad of Homer*, 2.255, Pope observes that Milton is alone among the moderns for following Homer's willingness to include "ludicrous descriptions" in epic forms (see Pope, *Twickenham Edition*, 7:139–40). See also Pope, *Iliad of Homer*, 277–78: "That *Homer* was no enemy to mirth may appear from several places of his poem; which so serious as it is, is interspers'd with many gayeties, indeed more than he has been follow'd in by the succeeding Epic Poets. *Milton*, who was perhaps fonder of him than the rest, has given most into the ludicrous."

46. Pope, *Peri Bathous, or The Art of Sinking in Poetry* (1727; repr., London: One World, 2011), 81.

47. Pope, *Peri Bathous*, 49.

48. Pope, *Dunciad*, 271.

49. *1805*, VI. 647.

50. *1805*, VI. 645–46.

51. *1805*, VI. 654.

52. *1805*, VI. 637–38.

53. Pope, *Peri Bathous*, 68.

54. George Sewell, "Life of Philips," in John Philips, *Poems on Several Occasions* (London: Curll, 1720), 15.

55. Claude Rawson, "Mock-Heroic and English Poetry," in *The Cambridge Companion to the Epic*, ed. Catherine Bates (Cambridge: Cambridge University Press, 2010), 174–81.

56. Alexander Pope, *The Poems of Alexander Pope: A One-Volume Edition of the Twickenham Text with Selected Annotations*, ed. John Butt (London: Methuen, 1965), 218.

57. See Wordsworth's annotated copy of *Paradise Lost*, 2nd ed. (London: Simmons, 1674), 260. The volume is at the Jerwood Centre, Grasmere (ref. 1995.R62); Virgil, *Eclogues* 1.24, and *Georgics* 4.176.

58. See Rhona Brown, "The Long-Lost James Beattie: The Rediscovery of 'The Grotesquiad,'" *Review of English Studies* 65, no. 270 (June 2014): 456–73.

59. *EY*, 169.

60. John Wolcot [Peter Pindar, pseud.], *The Lousiad* (1794–96), in *The Works of Peter Pindar*, 4 vols. (London: Walker and Edwards, 1816), 1:132.

61. *1805*, XIII. 98–9; *LB*, 119.

62. *RCP*, 400.

63. "When we contemplate a finite in reference to the infinite, consciously or unconsciously, *humor*"; see "Wit and Humour," in *Coleridge's Miscellaneous Criticism*, ed. Thomas Middleton Raysor (London: Constable, 1936), 118–19.

64. Jean Paul Richter, *Horn of Oberon: Jean Paul Richter's School for Aesthetics*, trans. Margaret R. Hale (Detroit: Wayne State University Press, 1973), 88

65. John Limon, "Analytic of the Ridiculous: Mike Nichols and Elaine May," *Raritan* 16, no. 3 (Winter 1997): 102–22.

66. *CLC*, 2:988.

67. *1805*, VII. 263–83.

68. *1805*, VIII. 10.

69. *1805*, VIII. 46, 58.

70. *1805*, III. 591–92.

71. *1805*, III. 603–20.

72. *EPF*, 551. See also *LB*, 316, 560–65.

73. *LB*, 316.

74. *LW*, 2:69

75. *1799*, I. 1, 6–7.

76. See Jonathan Wordsworth, *William Wordsworth: Borders of Vision* (Oxford: Clarendon, 1974), 37; Daniel Robinson, *Myself and Some Other Being: Wordsworth and the Life of Writing* (Iowa City: University of Iowa Press, 2014), 37–38.

77. Christopher Ricks, *Allusion to the Poets* (Oxford: Oxford University Press, 2002), 93, 98, 104.

78. *1805*, I. 541–71.

79. Charles Cotton, *The Compleat Gamester* (London: Wilford, 1726), 53.

80. Thomas De Quincey, *De Quincey as Critic*, ed. John E. Jordan (London: Routledge and Kegan Paul, 1973), 299.

81. The sense that Wordsworth is mischievously playing with simile here is supported by one manuscript that has him continue from the "Bothnic main" to "And sometimes not unlike the sound that issues / From out the deep chest of a lonely Bull / By no apparent enmity provoked"; *The Prelude*, ed. Ernest de Selincourt (Oxford: Clarendon, 1959), 34.

82. *1805*, VI. 299–301.

83. *1805*, VII. 370–71.

84. *1805*, VII. 386–407.

85. Robert Lowell, "Ivana," in *Collected Poems of Robert Lowell*, ed. Frank Bidart and David Gewinter (New York: Farrar, Straus and Giroux, 2007), 694.

86. *PrW*, 1:339. On Wordsworth's "fascination with the spectacles of sexuality in London," see Kenneth R. Johnston, *The Hidden Wordsworth* (New York: W. W. Norton, 2001), 181, 185–87.

87. *LL*, 1:267.

88. *1805*, VII. 283–85.

89. *LW*, 1:50–52.

90. *JDW*, 1:277–78; 2:353.

91. *LY*, 2:227; Robert Anderson, *The Works of the British Poets*, 14 vols. (Edinburgh: Bradfute and Mundell, 1792–1807), 3:539.

92. Pope, *Peri Bathous*, 14; see also 42–43.

93. Pope, *Dunciad*, 107, 249–51.

94. Friedrich Schlegel, *Philosophical Fragments*, trans. Peter Firchow (Minneapolis: University of Minnesota Press, 1991), 26.

95. Anon., *Modern Poets: A Dialogue, in Verse* (London: White and Cochrane, 1813), 23.

96. Cited in John O'Brien, *Harlequin Britain: Pantomime and Entertainment, 1690–1760* (Baltimore: Johns Hopkins University Press, 2004), 229.

97. Pope, *Poems of Alexander Pope*, 232.

98. *1805*, VII. 287–89.

99. *1805*, VII. 463–46.

100. *HW*, 5:2.

101. *1805*, VII. 301–10.

102. Charles Dibdin, *Jack the Giant Killer, A Serio-comic Pantomime* (London, 1803), 9. See also David Francis Taylor, "Wordsworth at the Theatre: Illegitimate Spectacle in Book 7 of *The Prelude*," *European Romantic Review* 20, no. 1 (2009): 77–93.

103. See John O'Brien, "Pantomimic Politics," in *The Oxford Handbook of the Georgian Theatre, 1737–1832*, ed. Julia Swindells and David Francis Taylor (Oxford: Oxford University Press, 2014), 390–406.

104. Charles Dickens, "A Curious Dance Round a Curious Tree," *Household Words*, January 17, 1852, 386.

105. *1805*, V. 365.

106. *1805*, VII. 406–7.

107. Pope, *Peri Bathous*, 27; *Dunciad*, 97.

108. Henry Morley, *Memoirs of Bartholomew Fair* (London: Chatto and Windus, 1880), 370.

109. See Wordsworth's "Imitation of Juvenal" (1795), *EPF*, 806.

110. *1805*, VII. 656–95.

111. Peter Stallybrass and Allon White, *The Politics and Poetics of Transgression* (Ithaca, NY: Cornell University Press, 1986), 122. See also Timothy Webb, "Dangerous Plurals: Wordsworth's Bartholomew Fair and the Challenge of an Urban Poetics," in *London in Literature: Visionary Mappings of the Metropolis*, ed. Jaén Onega and John Stotesbury (Heidelberg: C. Winter, 2002), 53–82.

112. *1805*, VI. 31–32.

113. *MY*, 2:274. See Jenny Uglow, *Hogarth: A Life and a World* (London: Faber and Faber, 2010), 20–30.

114. *LP*, 271.

115. Donald Winnicott, cited in Adam Phillips, *Winnicott* (London: Penguin, 2007), 60.

116. *1805*, VII. 439–44, 475–76.

117. *CH*, 440.

118. *1805*, VIII. 651–52.

119. *1805*, VII. 347–51.

120. *1850*, VII. 320.

121. See, David Mayer, *Harlequin in His Element: The English Pantomime, 1806–1836* (Harvard, MA: Harvard University Press, 1969), 24.

122. *1805*, VII. 359, 409–11.

123. See *The Prelude*, ed. Ernest de Selincourt (Oxford: Clarendon, 1959), 240.

124. The *OED*'s first citation is 1847. *Literature Online* finds no use of the phrase before Wordsworth.

125. *1805*, VII. 711–12.

126. *1805*, VII. 736.

127. *1805*, 211.

128. *1805*, VII. 11–22. Needless to say, Wordsworth considerably simplifies the tangled history of composition; for details, see Mark Reed's meticulous account in *1805*, 39ff.

129. *New Writings of William Hazlitt*, ed. Duncan Wu, 2 vols. (Oxford: Oxford University Press, 2007), 2:191.

130. See *The Prelude*, ed. Ernest de Selincourt (Oxford: Clarendon, 1959), 247.

Humoring—Selves

1. See *The Prelude*, ed. Jonathan Wordsworth, M. H. Abrams, and Stephen Gill (New York: W. W. Norton, 1979), 503.

2. A. R. Ammons, *An Image for Longing: Selected Letters and Journals*, ed. Kevin McGuirk (Victoria, BC: ELS Editions, 2013), 268.

3. *MY*, 1:64.

4. *MY*, 1:77.

5. Laurence Sterne, "Evil-Speaking," in *The Sermons of Laurence Sterne*, ed. Melvyn New (Gainesville: University Press of Florida, 1996), 104.

6. *CN*, 3:4017.

7. *1805*, II. 28–33.

8. *1805*, IV. 346–47.

9. Hobbes, cited in *The Philosophy of Laughter and Humor*, ed. John Morreall (New York: State University of New York Press, 1987), 20, (my italics).

10. Immanuel Kant, *Critique of the Power of Judgment*, ed. Paul Guyer, trans. Paul Guyer and Eric Matthews (Cambridge: Cambridge University Press, 2000), 211.

11. Jean Paul Richter, *Horn of Oberon: Jean Paul Richter's School for Aesthetics*, trans. Margaret R. Hale (Detroit: Wayne State University Press, 1973), 79.

12. *P2V*, 579–80.

13. Richter, *Horn of Oberon*, 95

14. Freud, "Humour," reprinted in *The Penguin Freud Reader*, ed. Adam Phillips (London: Penguin, 2006), 564, 566.

15. *LY*, 1:474.

16. *LY*, 4:307.

17. James Thurber, *New York Post*, February 29, 1960.

18. *1805*, I. 55–59.

19. *PrW*, 1:148.

20. *1805*, I. 68–69.

21. *1805*, IV. 189.

22. Kant, cited in Frances Ferguson, *Solitude and the Sublime: Romanticism and the Aesthetics of Individuation* (London: Routledge, 1992), 38.

23. *1805*, I. 21–3.

24. *1805*, VII. 4–5.

25. *1805*, IV. 130–33.

26. *1805*, IV. 110–11.

27. *1805*, IV. 39–55.

28. R. P. Blackmur, *Language as Gesture: Essays in Poetry* (London: Allen and Unwin, 1961), 329.

29. This is Roland Barthes's question, in *Roland Barthes*, trans. Richard Howard (New York: Hill and Wang, 2012), 121. For a brief but highly suggestive discussion of "double perspective" and "the dialectic of loss and gain" in *The Prelude*, see Adam Piette's comments in *Black Box Manifold* 17 (Winter 2016), http://www.manifold.group.shef.ac.uk/issue17/AdamPietteBM17.html.

30. Lowell, letter to Elizabeth Bishop; cited in Brett C. Miller, *Elizabeth Bishop: Life and the Memory of It* (Berkeley: University of California Press, 1993), 489.

31. *1805*, V. 342.

32. *EY*, 56; Duncan Wu, *Wordsworth's Reading* (Cambridge: Cambridge University Press, 1993), 1:132–33; 2:205.

33. Wu, 1:58–9, 2:87

34. Thomas De Quincey, *Recollections of the Lakes and the Lake Poets*, ed. David Wright (London: Penguin, 1978), 383.

35. Henry Fielding, *The History of Tom Jones, A Foundling*, ed. Thomas Keymer and Alice Wakely (London: Penguin, 2005), 294.

36. Fielding, *Tom Jones*, 187; *Joseph Andrews and Shamela*, ed. Douglas Brooks-Davies and Martin C. Battestin (Oxford: Oxford University Press, 2008), 3.

37. See Ronald Paulson, *Satire and the Novel in Eighteenth-Century England* (New Haven, CT: Yale University Press, 1967), 265.

38. Friedrich Schlegel, cited in Richie Robertson, *Mock-Epic Poetry from Pope to Heine* (Oxford: Oxford University Press, 2009), 36.

39. See Robertson, 39.

40. *EY*, 628.

41. See *P2V*, 594; and *EPF*, 728. The only book Wordsworth took with him for his walking tour of the Alps in 1790 was his pocket copy of *Orlando Furioso*.

42. See Laura Bandiera, "Wordsworth's Ariosto: Translation as Metatext and Misreading," in *British Romanticism and Italian Literature: Translating, Reviewing, Rewriting*, ed. Laura Bandiera and Diego Saglia (New York: Rodopi, 2005), 129.

43. Wordsworth's copy of Ariosto, translated by John Harrington, 2nd ed. (1607), is at the Jerwood Centre, Grasmere (ref. 1995.R173).

44. *LB*, 305.

45. *1805*, VII. 538–39.

46. *1805*, IX. 446.

47. *1805*, IX. 450–55.

48. See *The Prelude*, ed. Jonathan Wordsworth, M. H. Abrams, and Stephen Gill (New York: W. W. Norton, 1979), 502.

49. *PB*, 55.

50. See, for example, *P2V*, 594.

51. *1805*, I. 150–55.

52. *1805*, I. 183.

53. *PrW*, 1:338–39.

54. *1805*, IX. 115–16.

55. *1805*, IX. 51–52.

56. Alenka Zupančič, *The Odd One In: On Comedy* (Cambridge, MA: MIT Press, 2008), 49, 53.

57. *1805*, V. 548, 250–51.

58. *1805*, V. 524, 556–57.

59. *1805*, V. 191–92.

60. *1805*, VIII. 571–72.

61. Henry Thoreau, "Walking," in *Collected Essays and Poems*, ed. Elizabeth Hall Witherell (New York: Library of America, 2001), 252.

62. Ralph Waldo Emerson, *Essays* (New York: Library of America, 1996), 553.

63. *1805*, IX. 453–44.

64. *EPF*, 728.

65. Heinrich Heine, *The Romantic School and Other Essays*, ed. and trans. Jost Hermand and Robert C. Holub (New York: Continuum, 2002), 65.

66. Heine, 67.

67. See T. R. Hart, *Cervantes and Ariosto: Renewing Fiction* (Princeton, NJ: Princeton University Press, 1989).

68. See Stuart Tave, *The Amiable Humorist: A Study of Comic Theory and Criticism of the Eighteenth and Early Nineteenth Centuries* (Chicago: University of Chicago Press, 1960), and Peter Conrad, *Shandyism: The Character of Romantic Irony* (Oxford: Basil Blackwell, 1978).

69. Miguel de Cervantes, *The History and Adventures of the Renowned Don Quixote*, trans. Tobias Smollett (New York: Random House, 2001), 31.

70. Cervantes, *Don Quixote*, trans. Edith Grossman (New York: Ecco, 2003), 23.

71. Cervantes, *Don Quixote*, trans. Grossman, 672.

72. *Bord*, 63.

73. I am grateful to Jonatan González for valuable assistance on Wordsworth's collection of Cervantes and for showing me his forthcoming article in typescript, "What *Don Quixote* Did Wordsworth Read?" Wu (*Wordsworth's Reading*, 2:44) ventures that the Wordsworths were rereading Cervantes in 1800; three years later, one entry in Dorothy's journal speaks of "a place which Don Quixote would have gloried in . . . it seemed to have made the first step from brute matter to life and purpose. . . . William made a remark to this effect, and Coleridge observed that it was like a giant with one idea" (*JDW*, 1:207–8).

74. See David Mayer, *Harlequin in His Element: The English Pantomime, 1806–1836* (Harvard, MA: Harvard University Press, 1969), 24.

75. *The London Stage: 1660–1800*, pt. 5, vol. 3, *1792–1800*, ed. Charles Beecher Hogan (Carbondale: Southern Illinois University Press, 1968), 2022.

76. Hogan, *London Stage*, 2032.

77. Ellen Ricketts, cited in *Wordsworth: A Life in Letters*, ed. Juliet Barker (London: Penguin, 2007), 247–48.

78. *CH*, 296, 677, 886; Thomas De Quincey, "On Wordsworth's Poetry," reprinted in *Romantic Critical Essays*, ed. David Bromwich (Cambridge: Cambridge University Press, 1978), 153.

79. *PrW*, 1:137.

80. *PrW*, 1:138.

81. Samuel Taylor Coleridge, *Coleridge's Miscellaneous Criticism*, ed. Thomas Middleton Raysor (London: Constable, 1936), 102–3.

82. *1805*, V. 49, 59–60.

83. *1805*, V. 115–17.

84. *1805*, V. 123–24.

85. *1805*, V. 140–64.

86. *CN*, 3:4409.

87. *1805*, V. 169–72.

88. Sándor Ferenczi, "Laughter" (1913), in *Final Contributions to the Problems and Methods of Psychoanalysis* (London: Karnac, 2002), 178, 180, 182.

89. See Douglas B. Wilson, *The Romantic Dream: Wordsworth and the Poetics of the Unconscious* (Lincoln: University of Nebraska Press, 1993), 177.

90. *1805*, I. 412.

91. *1805*, I. 420–21.

92. *1805*, I. 522, 615; III. 126; VIII. 565–66, 573–76.

93. *1805*, II. 369–71.

94. *1805*, III. 147; IV. 120.

95. Erich Auerbach, *Mimesis: The Representation of Reality in Western Thought* (1953; repr., Princeton, NJ: Princeton University Press, 2003), 350.

96. *1805*, V. 525–52.

97. *EY*, 37.

98. *LY*, 1:448.

99. Wordsworth, cited in David B. Pirie, *William Wordsworth: The Poetry of Grandeur and of Tenderness* (London: Methuen, 1982), 44.

100. *1805*, VI. 477–83.

101. *1805*, VI. 524–25.

102. Jonathan Wordsworth, *The Music of Humanity* (London: Nelson, 1969), 229–30.

103. Cervantes, *Don Quixote*, trans. Grossman, 931.

104. Cervantes, *Don Quixote*, trans. Grossman, 126ff.

105. *1805*, VIII. 245.

106. *1805*, VIII. 325–26.

107. *1805*, VIII. 346–47.

108. *1805*, VIII. 391.

109. *1805*, VIII. 431.

110. *1805*, VIII. 397–428.

111. Cervantes, *Don Quixote*, trans. Grossman, 937.

112. W. H. Auden, *The Dyer's Hand* (New York: Vintage, 1968), 137.

113. *The Prelude*, ed. Ernest de Selincourt (Oxford: Clarendon, 1959), 580.

114. *DS*, 46.

115. *1805*, III. 546–49.

116. *1805*, IV. 181–202.

117. Gillian Rose, *Love's Work* (New York: New York Review of Books, 1995), 134–35.

118. *EY*, 236.

Index

Note: Where locators are followed by "quoted" and a note number in parentheses, the note number refers to the position of the quotation on that page, not to the endnotes.